UNCTAD/DITE/2(Vol. V)

United Nations Conference on Trade and Development
Division on Investment, Technology and Enterprise Development

International Investment Instruments: A Compendium

Volume V
Regional Integration, Bilateral and Non-governmental Instruments

United Nations
New York and Geneva, 2000

Note

UNCTAD serves as the focal point within the United Nations Secretariat for all matters related to foreign direct investment and transnational corporations. In the past, the Programme on Transnational Corporations was carried out by the United Nations Centre on Transnational Corporations (1975-1992) and the Transnational Corporations and Management Division of the United Nations Department of Economic and Social Development (1992-1993). In 1993, the Programme was transferred to the United Nations Conference on Trade and Development. UNCTAD seeks to further the understanding of the nature of transnational corporations and their contribution to development and to create an enabling environment for international investment and enterprise development. UNCTAD's work is carried on through intergovernmental deliberations, technical assistance activities, seminars, workshops and conferences.

The term "country", as used in the boxes added by the UNCTAD secretariat at the beginning of the instruments reproduced in this volume, also refers, as appropriate, to territories or areas; the designations employed and the presentation of the material do not imply the expression of any opinion whatsoever on the part of the Secretariat of the United Nations concerning the legal status of any country, territory, city or area or of its authorities, or concerning the delimitation of its frontiers or boundaries. Moreover, the country or geographical terminology used in the boxes may occasionally depart from standard United Nations practice when this is made necessary by the nomenclature used at the time of negotiation, signature, ratification or accession of a given international instrument.

To preserve the integrity of the texts of the instruments reproduced in this volume, references to the sources of the istruments that are not contained in their original text are identified as "note added by the editor".

The texts of the instruments included in this volume are reproduced as they were written in one of their original languages or as an official translation thereof. When an obvious linguistic mistake has been found, the word "sic" has been added in brackets.

The materials contained in this volume have been reprinted with special permission of the relevant institutions. For those materials under copyright protection, all rights are reserved by the copyright holders.

It should be further noted that this collection of instruments has been prepared for documentation purposes only, and its contents do not engage the responsibility of UNCTAD.

UNCTAD/DITE/2 Vol. V

UNITED NATIONS PUBLICATION

Sales No. E.00.II.D.14

ISBN 92-1-112483-2

PREFACE

International Investment Instruments: A Compendium contains a collection of international instruments relating to foreign direct investment (FDI) and transnational corporations (TNCs). The collection is presented in five volumes. The first three volumes were published in 1996. *Volumes IV* and *V* are published four years later, in 2000, in order to bring the collection up to date. The last two volumes also expand the collection further by including a number of instruments adopted in earlier years which were not included in the previous volumes.

The collection has been prepared to make the texts of international investment instruments conveniently available to interested policy-makers, scholars and business executives. The need for such a collection has increased in recent years as bilateral, regional and multilateral instruments dealing with various aspects of FDI have proliferated, and as new investment instruments are being negotiated at all levels.

While by necessity selective, the present collection seeks to provide a faithful record of the evolution and present status of intergovernmental cooperation concerning FDI and TNCs. Although the emphasis of the collection is on relatively recent documents (more than half of the instruments reproduced date from after 1990), it was deemed useful to include important older instruments as well, with a view towards providing some indications of the historical development of international concerns over FDI in the decades since the end of the Second World War.

The core of this collection consists of legally binding international instruments, mainly multilateral conventions and regional agreements that have entered into force. In addition, a number of "soft law" documents, such as guidelines, declarations and resolutions adopted by intergovernmental bodies, have been included since these instruments also play a role in the elaboration of an international framework for foreign direct investment. In an effort to enhance the understanding of the efforts behind the elaboration of this framework, certain draft instruments that never entered into force, or texts of instruments on which the negotiations were not concluded, are also included; and, in annexes, several prototypes of bilateral investment treaties are reproduced. Included also are a number of influential documents prepared by business, consumer and labour organizations. It is clear from the foregoing that no implications concerning the legal status or the legal effect of an instrument can be drawn from its inclusion in this collection.

In view of the great diversity of the instruments in this *Compendium* -- in terms of subject matter, approach, legal form and extent of participation of States -- the simplest possible method of presentation was deemed the most appropriate. Thus, the relevant instruments are distributed among the *five volumes of the Compendium* as follows:

- *Volume I* is devoted to multilateral instruments, that is to say, multilateral conventions as well as resolutions and other documents issued by multilateral organizations.

- *Volume II* covers interregional and regional instruments, including agreements, resolutions and other texts from regional organizations with an inclusive geographical context.

- *Volume III* is divided into three annexes covering three types of instruments that differ in their context or their origin from those included in the first two volumes:

• Annex A reproduces investment-related provisions in free trade and regional integration agreements. The specific function and, therefore, the effect of such provisions is largely determined by the economic integration process which they are intended to promote and in the context of which they operate.

• Annex B (the only section that departs from the chronological pattern) offers the texts of prototype bilateral treaties for the promotion and protection of foreign investments (BITs) of several developed and developing countries, as well as a list of these treaties concluded up to July 1995. The bilateral character of these treaties differentiates them from the bulk of the instruments included in this *Compendium*. Over 900 such treaties had been adopted by July 1995.

• Annex C supplies the texts of documents prepared by non-governmental organizations; these give an indication of the broader environment in which the instruments collected here are prepared.

• *Volume IV*, divided into two parts, covers additional multilateral (Part One) and regional instruments (Part Two) not covered in *Volumes I* and *II*, including, but not limited to, those adopted between 1996 and the end of 1999.

• *Volume V* is divided into four parts, as follows:

• Part One reproduces investment-related provisions in a number of additional free trade and economic integration agreements not covered in *Volume III*.
• Part Two includes for the first time investment-related provisions in association agreements as well as bilateral and interregional cooperation agreements. These are divided into three annexes. Annex A is devoted to agreements signed between the countries members of the European Free Trade Association (EFTA) and third countries. Annex B covers investment-related provisions in agreements signed between the countries members of the European Community (EC) and third countries as well as other regional groups. Annex C includes types of bilateral agreements related to investment that differ from those covered in other parts.

• Part Three contains the texts of a number of additional prototype BITs of several developed and developing countries, as well as a list of these treaties concluded between July 1995 and the end of 1998, when the total number of BITs concluded since 1959 reached over 1,730.

• Part Four reproduces additional texts of recent documents prepared by non-governmental organizations.

Within each of these subdivisions, instruments are reproduced in chronological order, except for the sections dedicated to BIT prototypes.

The multilateral and regional instruments covered are widely differing in scope and coverage. Some are designed to provide an overall, general framework for FDI and cover many, although rarely all, aspects of investment operations. Most instruments deal with particular aspects and issues concerning FDI. A significant number address core FDI issues, such as the promotion and protection of investment, investment liberalization, dispute settlement and insurance and guarantees. Others cover specific issues, of direct but not exclusive relevance to FDI and TNCs, such as transfer of technology, intellectual property, avoidance of double taxation, competition and the protection of consumers and the environment. A relatively small number of instruments of this last category has been reproduced, since each of these specific issues often constitutes an entire system of legal regulation of its own, whose proper coverage would require an extended exposition of many kinds of instruments and arrangements.

The *Compendium* is meant to be a collection of instruments, not an anthology of relevant provisions. Indeed, to understand a particular instrument, it is normally necessary to take its entire text into consideration. An effort has been made, therefore, to reproduce complete instruments, even though, in a number of cases, reasons of space and relevance have dictated the inclusion of excerpts.

The UNCTAD secretariat has deliberately refrained from adding its own commentary to the texts reproduced in the *Compendium*. The only exception to this rule is the boxes added to each instrument. They provide some basic facts, such as its date of adoption, date of entry into force, status as of 1995 and 1999 respectively, and, where appropriate, signatory countries. Also in the case of agreements signed between the EFTA countries or the EC countries with third countries or regional groups -- where only a few samples of the types of agreements with investment-related provisions are included -- a list of similar agreements signed by these two groups of countries has been included to give an indication of the range of countries involved in these types of agreements. Moreover, to facilitate the identification of each instrument in the table of contents, additional information has been added, in brackets, next to each title, on the year of its signature and the name of the relevant institution involved.

Rubens Ricupero
Secretary-General of UNCTAD

Geneva, January 2000

ACKNOWLEDGEMENTS

Volumes IV and *V* of the *Compendium* were prepared by Boubacar Hassane, with major inputs from Abraham Negash, under the guidance of Victoria Aranda and the overall direction of Karl P. Sauvant. Arghyrios A. Fatouros and Peter Muchlinski provided overall advice. Comments on the table of contents were given by Patrick Juillard, Mark Koulen, Maryse Robert, Patrick Robinson and Thomas Waelde. The volumes were typeset by Florence Hudry. The cooperation of the relevant organizations from which the relevant instruments originate is acknowledged with gratitude.

CONTENTS

VOLUME I
MULTILATERAL INSTRUMENTS

VOLUME II
REGIONAL INSTRUMENTS

REGIONAL INSTRUMENTS

VOLUME III

REGIONAL INTEGRATION, BILATERAL AND NON-GOVERNMENTAL INSTRUMENTS

ANNEX C. NON-GOVERNMENTAL INSTRUMENTS

VOLUME IV

MULTILATERAL AND REGIONAL INSTRUMENTS

PART ONE

MULTILATERAL INSTRUMENTS

PART TWO

REGIONAL INSTRUMENTS

VOLUME V

REGIONAL INTEGRATION, BILATERAL AND NON-GOVERNMENTAL INSTRUMENTS

PART ONE

INVESTMENT-RELATED PROVISIONS IN FREE TRADE AND ECONOMIC INTEGRATION AGREEMENTS

PART TWO

INVESTMENT-RELATED PROVISIONS IN ASSOCIATION AGREEMENTS, BILATERAL AND INTERREGIONAL COOPERATION AGREEMENTS

ANNEX A. INVESTMENT-RELATED PROVISIONS IN FREE TRADE AGREEMENTS SIGNED BETWEEN THE COUNTRIES MEMBERS OF THE EUROPEAN FREE TRADE ASSOCIATION AND THIRD COUNTRIES AND LIST OF AGREEMENTS SIGNED (END-1999)

ANNEX B. INVESTMENT-RELATED PROVISIONS IN ASSOCIATION, PARTNERSHIP AND COOPERATION AGREEMENTS SIGNED BETWEEN THE COUNTRIES MEMBERS OF THE EUROPEAN COMMUNITY AND THIRD COUNTRIES AND LIST OF AGREEMENTS SIGNED (END-1999)

ANNEX C.   OTHER BILATERAL INVESTMENT-RELATED AGREEMENTS

PART THREE

PROTOTYPE BILATERAL INVESTMENT TREATIES AND LIST OF BILATERAL INVESTMENT TREATIES (MID-1995 — END-1998)

PART FOUR

NON-GOVERNMENTAL INSTRUMENTS

*   *   *

PART ONE

INVESTMENT-RELATED PROVISIONS IN FREE TRADE AND ECONOMIC INTEGRATION AGREEMENTS

FREE TRADE AGREEMENT BETWEEN CANADA AND THE UNITED STATES OF AMERICA[*]
[excerpts]

> The Free Trade Agreement between Canada and the United States of America was signed in Ottawa on 22 December 1987 and 2 January 1988, and in Washington, D.C. and Palm Springs, on 23 December 1987 and 2 January 1988. This Agreement was the precursor of the North American Free Trade Agreement (NAFTA) between Canada, Mexico, and the United States of America signed on 17 September 1992 (see *volume III* of this *Compendium*), and was superseded by the latter, which entered into force on 1 January 1994.

PART FOUR. SERVICES, INVESTMENT AND TEMPORARY ENTRY

Chapter Sixteen. Investment

Article 1601. Scope and Coverage

1.   Subject to paragraphs 2 and 3, this Chapter shall apply to any measure of a Party affecting investment within or into its territory by an investor of the other Party.

2.   This Chapter shall not apply to any measure affecting investments related to:

    a)   the provision of financial services unless such measure relates to the provision of insurance services and is not dealt with under paragraph 1 of Article 1703;

    b)   government procurement; or

    c)   the provision of transportation services.

3.   The provisions of subparagraph 1 (c) of Article 1602 shall not apply to any measure affecting investments related to the provision of services other than covered services.

Article 1602. National Treatment

1.   Except as otherwise provided in this Chapter, each Party shall accord to investors of the other Party treatment no less favourable than that accorded in like circumstances to its investors with respect to its measures affecting:

    a)   the establishment of new business enterprises located in its territory;

---

[*]   *Source*: The Government of Canada and the Government of the United States of America (1988). "Canada-United States: Free Trade Agreement", *International Legal Materials*, vol. 27, pp. 281-400. [Note added by the editor.]

b)   the acquisition of business enterprises located in its territory;

c)   the conduct and operation of business enterprises located in its territory; and

d)   the sale of business enterprises located in its territory.

2.   Neither Party shall impose on an investor of the other Party requirement that a minimum level of equity (other than nominal qualifying shares for directors or incorporators of corporations) be held by its nationals in a business enterprise located in its territory controlled by such investor.

3.   Neither Party shall require an investor of the other Party by reason of its nationality to sell or otherwise dispose of an investment (or any part thereof) made in its territory.

4.   The treatment accorded by a Party under paragraph 1 shall mean, with respect to a province or a state, treatment no less favourable than the most favourable treatment accorded by such province or state in like circumstances to investors of the Party of which it forms a part.

5.   Canada may introduce any new measure in respect of any business enterprise that is carried on at the date of entry into force of this Agreement by or on behalf of Canada or a province or a Crown corporation that:

a)   is inconsistent with the provisions of paragraphs 1 or 2 and relates to the acquisition or sale of such business enterprise; or

b)   relates to the direct or indirect ownership at any time of such business enterprise.

6.   Once Canada has introduced a new measure pursuant to paragraph 5, it shall not:

a)   in the case of a new measure introduced pursuant to subparagraph 5(a), amend such new measure or introduce any subsequent measure that, as the case may be, renders such new measure more inconsistent with, or is more inconsistent with, the provisions of paragraphs 1 or 2; or

b)   in the case of a new measure introduced pursuant to subparagraph 5(b), increase any ownership restrictions contained in such new measure.

7.   If, subsequent to the date of entry into force of this Agreement, a business enterprise is established or acquired by or on behalf of Canada or a province or a Crown corporation, the provisions of paragraphs 1 and 2 shall not apply to the subsequent acquisition of such business enterprise as a result of its disposition by or on behalf of Canada or a province or a Crown corporation. Once such subsequent acquisition has been completed, the provisions of paragraphs 1 and 2 shall apply.

8.   Notwithstanding paragraph 1, the treatment a Party accords to investors of the other Party may be different from the treatment the Party accords its investors provided that:

a)   the difference in treatment is no greater than that necessary for prudential, fiduciary, health and safety, or consumer protection reasons;

b) such different treatment is equivalent in effect to the treatment accorded by the Party to its investors for such reasons; and

c) prior notification of the proposed treatment has been given in accordance with Article 1803.

9. The Party proposing or according different treatment under paragraph 8 shall have the burden of establishing that such treatment is consistent with that paragraph.

Article 1603. Performance Requirements

1. Neither Party shall impose on an investor of the other Party, as a term or condition of permitting an investment in its territory, or in connection with the regulation of the conduct or operation of a business enterprise located in its territory, a requirement to:

a) export a given level or percentage of goods or services;

b) substitute goods or services from the territory of such Party for imported goods or services;

c) purchase goods or services used by the investor in the territory of such Party or from suppliers located in such territory or accord a preference to goods or services produced in such territory; or

d) achieve a given level or percentage of domestic content.

2. Neither Party shall impose on an investor of a third country, as a term or condition of permitting an investment in its territory, or in connection with the regulation of the conduct or operation of a business enterprise located in its territory, a commitment to meet any of the requirements described in paragraph 1 where meeting such a requirement could have a significant impact on trade between the two Parties.

3. For purposes of paragraphs 1 and 2 and paragraph 2 of Article 1602, a Party "imposes" a requirement or commitment on an investor when it requires particular action of an investor or when, after the date of entry into force of this Agreement, it enforces any undertaking or commitment of the type described in paragraphs 1 and 2 or in paragraph 2 of Article 1602 given to that Party after that date.

Article 1604. Monitoring

1. Each Party may require an investor of the other Party who makes or has made an investment in its territory to submit to it routine information respecting such investment solely for informational and statistical purposes. The Party shall protect such business information that is confidential from disclosure that would prejudice the investor's competitive position.

2. Nothing in paragraph 1 shall preclude a Party from otherwise obtaining or disclosing information in connection with the non-discriminatory and good faith application of its laws.

Article 1605. Expropriation

Neither Party shall directly or indirectly nationalize or expropriate an investment in its territory by an investor of the other Party or take any measure or series of measures tantamount to an expropriation of such an investment, except:

    a)   for a public purpose;

    b)   in accordance with due process of law;

    c)   on a non-discriminatory basis; and

    d)   upon payment of prompt, adequate and effective compensation at fair market value.

Article 1606. Transfers

1.   Subject to paragraph 2, neither Party shall prevent an investor of the other Party from transferring:

    a)   any profits from an investment, including dividends;

    b)   any royalties, fees, interest and other earnings from an investment; or

    c)   any proceeds from the sale of all or any part of an investment or from the partial or complete liquidation of such investment.

2.   A Party may, through the equitable, non-discriminatory and good faith application of its laws, prevent any transfer referred to in paragraph 1 if such transfer is inconsistent with any measure of general application relating to:

    a)   bankruptcy, insolvency or the protection of the rights of creditors;

    b)   issuing, trading or dealing in securities;

    c)   criminal or penal offences;

    d)   reports of currency transfers;

    e)   withholding taxes; or

    f)   ensuring the satisfaction of judgments in adjudicatory proceedings.

Article 1607. Existing Legislation

1.   The provisions of Articles 1602, 1603, 1604, 1605 and 1606 of this Chapter shall not apply to:

    a)   a non-conforming provision of any existing measure;

b) the continuation or prompt renewal of a non-conforming provision of any existing measure; or

c) an amendment to a non-conforming provision of any existing measure to the extent that the amendment does not decrease its conformity with any of the provisions of Articles 1602, 1603, 1604, 1605 or 1606.

2. The Party asserting that paragraph 1 applies shall have the burden of establishing the validity of such assertion.

3. The *Investment Canada Act,* its regulations and guidelines shall be amended as provided for in Annex 1607.3.

4. In the event that Canada requires the divestiture of a business enterprise located in Canada in a cultural industry pursuant to its review of an indirect acquisition of such business enterprise by an investor of the United States of America, Canada shall offer to purchase the business enterprise from the investor of the United States of America at fair open market value, as determined by an independent, impartial assessment.

Article 1608. Disputes

1. A decision by Canada following a review under the *Investment Canada* Act, with respect to whether or not to permit an acquisition that is subject to review, shall not be subject to the dispute settlement provisions of this Agreement.

2. Each Party and investors of each Party retain their respective rights and obligations under customary international law with respect to portfolio and direct investment not covered under this Chapter or to which the provisions of this Chapter do not apply.

3. Nothing in this Chapter shall affect the rights and obligations of either Party under the *General Agreement on Tariffs and Trade* or under any other international agreement to which both are party.

4. In view of the special nature of investment disputes and the expertise required to resolve them, where the procedures of Chapter Eighteen (Institutional Provisions) are invoked, the Parties and the Commission shall give the fullest consideration, in any particular case, to settling any dispute regarding the interpretation or application of this Chapter by arbitration or panel procedures pursuant to Articles 1806 or 1807, and shall make every attempt to ensure that the panelists are individuals experienced and competent in the field of international investment. When deciding a dispute pursuant to Articles 1806 or 1807, the panel shall take into consideration how such disputes before it are normally dealt with by internationally recognized rules for commercial arbitration.

Article 1609. Taxation and Subsidies

1. Subject to Article 2011, this Chapter shall not apply to any new taxation measure, provided that such measure does not constitute a means of arbitrary or unjustifiable discrimination between investors of the Parties or a disguised restriction on the benefits accorded to investors of the Parties under this Chapter.

2.   Subject to Article 2011, this Chapter shall not apply to any subsidy, provided that such subsidy does not constitute a means of arbitrary or unjustifiable discrimination between investors of the Parties or a disguised restriction on the benefits accorded to investors of the Parties under this Chapter.

Article 1610. International Agreements

The Parties shall endeavour, in the Uruguay Round and in other international forums, to improve multilateral arrangements and agreements with respect to investment.

Article 1611. Definitions

For purposes of this Chapter, not including Annex 1607.3

acquisition with respect to:

a)   a business enterprise carried on by an entity, means an acquisition, as a result of one or more transactions, of the ultimate direct or indirect control of the entity through the acquisition of the ownership of voting interests; or

b)   any business enterprise, means an acquisition, as a result of one or more transactions, of the ownership of all or substantially all of the assets of the business enterprise used in carrying on the business.

business enterprise means a business that has, or in the case of an establishment thereof will have:

a)   a place of business;

b)   an individual or individuals employed or self-employed in connection with the business; and

c)   assets used in carrying on the business.

NOTE: A part of a business enterprise that is capable of being carried on as a separate business enterprise is itself a business enterprise.

control or controlled, with respect to:

a)   a business enterprise carried on by an entity, means

   i)   the ownership of all or substantially all of the assets used in carrying on the business enterprise, and
   ii)   includes, with respect to an entity that controls a business enterprise in the manner described in subparagraph (i), the ultimate direct or indirect control of such entity through the ownership of voting interests; and

b)   a business enterprise other than a business enterprise carried on by an entity, means the ownership of all or substantially all of the assets used in carrying on the business enterprise.

Crown corporation means a Crown corporation within the meaning of the *Financial Administration Act (Canada)* or a Crown corporation within the meaning of any comparable provincial legislation or that is incorporated under other applicable provincial legislation or that is incorporated under the other applicable provincial legislation.

cultural industry has the same meaning as in Article 2012.

entity means a corporation, partnership, trust or joint venture.

establishment means a start-up of a new business enterprise and the activities related thereto.

indirect acquisition has the same meaning as in Annex 1607. 3.

Investment means:

a)   the establishment of a new business enterprise, or

b)   the acquisition of a business enterprise;

and includes:

c)   as carried on, the new business enterprise so established or the business enterprise so acquired, and controlled by the investor who has made the investment; and

d)   the share or other investment interest in such business enterprise owned by the investor provided that such business enterprise continues to be controlled by such investor.

Investor of a Party means:

a)   such Party or agency thereof;

b)   a province or state of such Party or agency thereof;

c)   a national of such Party;

d)   an entity ultimately controlled directly or indirectly through the ownership of voting interests by:

     i)   such Party or one or more agencies thereof,

     ii)   one or more provinces or states of such Party or one or more agencies thereof,

     iii)   one or more nationals of such Party,

       iv)   one or more entities described in paragraph (e), or

       v)   any combination of persons or entities described in (i), (ii) (iii) and (iv); or

e)   an entity that is not ultimately controlled directly or indirectly through the ownership of voting interests where a majority of the voting interests of such entity are owned by:

       i)   persons described in subparagraphs (d) (i), (ii) and (iii),

       ii)   entities incorporated or otherwise duly constituted in the territory of such Party and, in the case of entities that carry on business, carrying on a business enterprise located in the territory of such Party, other than any such entity in respect of which it is established that nationals of a third country control such entity or own a majority of the voting interests of such entity, or

       iii)   any combination of persons or entities described in (i) and (ii);

that makes or has made an investment.

NOTE: For purposes of paragraph (e), in respect of individuals each of whom holds not more than one percent of the total number of the voting interests of an entity the voting interests of which are publicly traded, it shall be presumed, in the absence of evidence to the contrary, that those voting interests are owned by nationals of such Party on the basis of a statement by a duly authorized officer of the entity that, according to the records of the entity, those individuals have addresses in the territory of such Party and that the signatory to the statement has no knowledge or reason to believe that those voting interests are owned by individuals who are not nationals of such Party.

investor of a third country means an investor other than an investor of a Party, that makes or has made an investment.

investor of the United States of America for purposes of paragraph 4 of Article 1607 shall have the same meaning as in Annex 1607.3.

joint venture means an association of two or more persons or entities where the relationship among those associated persons or entities does not, under the laws in force in the territory of the Party in which the investment is made, constitute a corporation, a partnership or a trust and where all those associated persons or entities own or will own assets of a business enterprise, or directly or indirectly own or will own voting interests in an entity that carries on a business enterprise.

located in the territory of a Party means, with respect to a business enterprise, a business enterprise that is, or in the case of an establishment will be, carried on in the territory of such Party and has, or in the case of an establishment will have therein:

a)   a place of business;

b)   an individual or individuals employed or self-employed in connection with the business; and

c)   assets used in carrying on the business.

measure shall have the same meaning as in Article 201, except that it shall also include any published policy.

ownership means beneficial ownership and with respect to assets also includes the beneficial ownership of a leasehold interest in such assets.

person means a Party or agency thereof, a province or state of a Party or agency thereof, or a national of a Party.

voting interest with respect to

a)   a corporation with share capital, means a voting share;

b)   a corporation without share capital, means an ownership interest in the assets thereof that entitles the owner to rights similar to those enjoyed by the owner of a voting share; and

c)   a partnership, trust, joint venture or other organization means an ownership interest in the assets thereof that entitles the owner to receive a share of the profits and to share in the assets on dissolution.

voting share means a share in the capital of a corporation to which is attached a voting right ordinarily exercisable at meetings of shareholders of the corporation and to which is ordinarily attached a right to receive a share of the profits, or to share in the assets of the corporation on dissolution, or both.

Annex 1607.3

1.   Unless otherwise expressly provided in this Annex, words and phrases used herein shall be interpreted and construed in accordance with the provisions of the *Investment Canada Act* and its regulations.

2.   The *Investment Canada Act* and its regulations shall be amended as of the date of entry into force of this Agreement in accordance with the provisions that follow:

a)   Canada may continue to review the acquisition of control of a Canadian business by an investor of the United States of America, in order to determine whether or not to permit the acquisition, provided that the value of the gross assets of the Canadian business is not less than the following applicable threshold.

i)   The threshold for the review of a direct acquisition of control of a Canadian business shall be:

A)   for the twelve-month period commencing on the date of entry into force of this Agreement, current Canadian $25 million;

B)   for the twelve-month period commencing on the first anniversary of the date of entry into force of this Agreement, current Canadian $50 million;

C)   for the twelve-month period commencing on the second anniversary of the date of entry into force of this Agreement, current Canadian $100 million;

D)   for the twelve-month period commencing on the third anniversary of the date of entry into force of this Agreement, current Canadian $150 million; and

E)   commencing on the fourth anniversary of the date of entry into force of this Agreement, Canadian $150 million in constant third-anniversary-year dollars.

ii)   The threshold for the review of an indirect acquisition of control of a Canadian business shall be:

A)   for the twelve-month period commencing on the date of entry into force of this Agreement, current Canadian $100 million;

B)   for the twelve-month period commencing on the first anniversary of the date of entry into force of this Agreement, current Canadian $250 million;

C)   for the twelve-month period commencing on the second anniversary of the date of entry into force of this Agreement, current Canadian $500 million; and

D)   commencing on the third anniversary of the date of entry into force of this Agreement, there shall be no review of indirect acquisitions implemented on or after that date.

b)   In the event that a Canadian business controlled by an investor of the United States of America is being acquired by an investor of a third country, Canada may continue to review such acquisition to determine whether or not to permit it, provided that the value of the gross assets of the business is not less than the applicable threshold referred to in this paragraph.

c)   i)   The Canadian $150 million in constant third-anniversary-year dollars referred to in subparagraph (a)(i)(E) shall be determined in January of each year after 1992 by use of the following formula:

$$\frac{\text{Current GDP Price Index}}{\text{Effective Date GDP Price Index}} \quad \text{times} \quad \$150 \text{ million}$$

where:

GDP Price Index means the seasonally adjusted implicit quarterly price index for Gross Domestic Product at market prices as most recently published by Statistics Canada, or any successor index thereto.

Current GDP Price Index means the arithmetic average of the GDP Price Indices for the four most recent consecutive quarters available on the date on which a calculation takes place.

Effective Date GDP Price Index means the arithmetic average of the GDP Price Indices for the four most recent consecutive quarters available as of January 1, 1992.

ii)   The amounts obtained by applying the formula set out in (i) shall be rounded to the nearest million dollars.

3.   The guidelines or regulations pursuant to the *Investment Canada Act* shall be amended to provide that Canada shall comply with the provisions of paragraphs 2 and 3 of Article 1602 and the provisions of Article 1603.

4.   The amendments described in paragraphs 2 and 3 and the provisions of paragraph 2 of Article 1602 and of Article 1603 shall not apply in respect of the oil and gas and uranium-mining industries. These industries are subject to published policies that are implemented through the review process set out in the *Investment Canada Act*. The Parties shall by exchange of letters, prior to introduction of legislation to implement this Agreement by either Party in its respective legislature, set out the aforementioned policies, which policies shall be no more restrictive than those in effect on October 4, 1987.

5.   For purposes of this Annex:

American shall have the same meaning as investor of the United States of America.

controlled by an Investor of the United States of America, with respect to a Canadian business, means:

a)   the ultimate direct or indirect control by such investor through the ownership of voting interests; or

b)   the ownership by such investor of all or substantially all of the assets used in carrying on the Canadian business.

direct acquisition of control means an acquisition of control pursuant to the provisions of the *Investment Canada Act* other than an indirect acquisition of control.

indirect acquisition of control means an acquisition of control pursuant to the provisions of the *Investment Canada Act* through the acquisition of voting interests of an entity that controls, directly or indirectly, an entity in Canada carrying on the Canadian business where:

a)   there is an acquisition of control described in subparagraph 28(1)(d)(ii) of the *Investment Canada Act;* and

b)   the value, calculated in the manner prescribed, of the assets of the entity carrying on the Canadian business, and of all other entities in Canada, the control of which is acquired, directly or indirectly, amounts to not more than fifty percent of the value, calculated in the manner prescribed, of the assets of all entities the control of which is acquired, directly or indirectly, in the transaction of which the acquisition of control of the Canadian business forms a part.

investor of a third country means an individual, a government or an agency thereof or an entity that is not a Canadian within the meaning of the *Investment Canada Act* and is not an investor of the United States of America.

investor of the United States of America means:

a)   an individual who is a "national of the United States" or an individual who is "lawfully admitted for permanent residence" as those terms are defined in the existing provisions of the United States *Immigration and Nationality Act,* other than an individual who is a Canadian within the meaning of the *Investment Canada Act;*

b)   a government of the United States of America, whether federal or state, or an agency thereof; or

c)   an entity that is not Canadian-controlled as determined pursuant to subsections 26(1) and (2) of the *Investment Canada Act* and is American-controlled.

NOTE: For purposes only of determining whether an entity is "American-controlled" under paragraph (c), the rules in subsections 26 (1) and (2) of the *Investment Canada Act* shall be applied as though the references therein to "Canadian", "Canadians", "non-Canadian", "non-Canadians" and "Canadian-controlled", were references to "American", "Americans", "non-American", "non-Americans" and "American-controlled".

non-American means an individual, a government or an agency thereof or an entity that is not an American and is not a Canadian within the meaning of the *Investment Canada Act.*

*   *   *

TREATY ESTABLISHING THE AFRICAN ECONOMIC COMMUNITY[*]
[excerpts]

The Treaty Establishing the African Economic Community was signed in Abuja on 3 June 1991 and entered into force on 12 May 1994. As of October 1999, the following countries, member States of the Organization of African Unity (OAU), had signed or acceded to the Treaty: Algeria, Angola, Benin, Botswana, Burkina Faso, Burundi, Cameroon, Cape Verde, Central African Republic, Chad, Comoros, Congo, Côte d'Ivoire, Democratic Republic of Congo, Djibouti, Egypt, Equatorial Guinea, Eritrea, Ethiopia, Gabon, Gambia, Ghana, Guinea, Guinea-Bissau, Kenya, Lesotho, Liberia, Libya, Madagascar, Malawi, Mali, Mauritania, Mauritius, Mozambique, Namibia, Niger, Nigeria, Rwanda, Sahrawi Arab Democratic Republic, Sao Tome and Principe, Senegal, Seychelles, Sierra Leone, Somalia, South Africa, Sudan, Swaziland, United Republic of Tanzania, Togo, Tunisia, Uganda, Zambia and Zimbabwe. As of October 1999, the following countries had ratified the Treaty: Algeria, Angola, Benin, Botswana, Burkina Faso, Burundi, Cameroon, Cape Verde, Central African Republic, Chad, Comoros, Congo, Côte d'Ivoire, Democratic Republic of Congo, Egypt, Ethiopia, Gambia, Ghana, Guinea, Guinea-Bissau, Kenya, Lesotho, Liberia, Libya, Malawi, Mali, Mauritius, Mozambique, Namibia, Niger, Nigeria, Rwanda, Sahrawi Arab Democratic Republic, Sao Tome and Principe, Senegal, Seychelles, Sierra Leone, Sudan, United Republic of Tanzania, Togo, Tunisia, Uganda, Zambia and Zimbabwe.

CHAPTER II

ESTABLISHMENT, PRINCIPLES, OBJECTIVES, GENERAL UNDERTAKING AND MODALITIES

Article 4
Objectives

1.   The objectives of the Community shall be:

 (a)   to promote economic, social and cultural development and the integration of African economies in order to increase economic self-reliance and promote an endogenous and self-sustained development;

 (b)   to establish, on a continental scale, a framework for the development, mobilization and utilization of the human and material resources of Africa in order to achieve a self-reliant development;

---

[*]   *Source*: Organization of African Unity-African Economic Community (1991). "Treaty Establishing the African Economic Community", *International Legal Materials*, vol. 30 (1991), pp. 1245-1282; available also on the Internet (http://www.infocomafrica.com/treaties/aec/index.html). [Note added by the editor.]

(c)   to promote cooperation in all fields of human endeavour in order to raise the standard of living of African peoples, and maintain and enhance economic stability, foster close and peaceful relations among Member States and contribute to the progress, development and the economic integration of the Continent; and

(d)   to coordinate and harmonize policies among existing and future economic communities in order to foster the gradual establishment of the Community.

2.   In order to promote the attainment of the objectives of the Community as set out in paragraph I of this Article, and in accordance with the relevant provisions of this Treaty, the Community shall, by stages, ensure:

(a)   the strengthening of existing regional economic communities and the establishment of other communities where they do not exist;

(b)   the conclusion of agreements aimed at harmonizing and coordinating policies among existing and future sub-regional and regional economic communities;

(c)   the promotion and strengthening of joint investment programmes in the production and trade of major products and inputs within the framework of collective self-reliance;

(d)   the liberalization of trade through the abolition, among Member States, of Customs Duties levied on imports and exports and the abolition, among Member States of Non-Tariff Barriers in order to establish a free trade area at the level of each regional economic community;

(e)   the harmonization of national policies in order to promote Community activities, particularly in the fields of agriculture, industry, transport and communications, energy, natural resources, trade, money and finance, human resources, education, culture, science and technology;

(f)   the adoption of a common trade policy vis-a-vis third States;

(g)   the establishment and maintenance of a common external tariff;

(h)   the establishment of a common market;

(i)   the gradual removal, among Member States, of obstacles to the free movement of persons, goods, services and capital and the right of residence and establishment;

(j)   the establishment of a Community Solidarity, Development and Compensation Fund;

(k)   the granting of special treatment to Member States classified as least developed countries and the adoption of special measures in favour of land-locked, semi-land-locked and island countries;

(l)   the harmonization and rationalization of the activities of existing African multi-national institutions and the establishment of such institutions, as and when necessary, with a view to their possible transformation into organs of the Community;

(m)   the establishment of appropriate organs for trade in agricultural and cultural products, minerals, metals, and manufactured and semi-manufactured goods within the Community;

(n)   the establishment of contacts and the promotion of information flow among trading organizations such as State commercial enterprises, export promotion and marketing bodies, chambers of commerce, associations of businessmen, and business and advertising agencies;

(o)   the harmonization and coordination of environmental protection policies; and

(p)   any other activity that Member States may decide to undertake jointly with a view to attaining the objectives of the Community

CHAPTER VI

FREE MOVEMENT OF PERSONS, RIGHTS OF RESIDENCE AND ESTABLISHMENT

Article 43
General Provisions

1.   Member States agree to adopt, individually, at bilateral or regional levels, the necessary measures, in order to achieve progressively the free movement of persons, and to ensure the enjoyment of the right of residence and the right of establishment by their nationals within the Community.

2.   For this purpose, Member States agree to conclude a Protocol on the Free Movement of Persons, Right of Residence and Right of Establishment.

CHAPTER VII

MONEY, FINANCE AND PAYMENTS

Article 45
Movement of Capital

1.   Member States shall ensure the free movement of capital within the Community through the elimination of restrictions on the transfer of capital funds between Member States in accordance with a time-table to be determined by the Council.

2.   The capital referred to in paragraph 1 of this Article is that of Member States or persons of Member States.

3.   The Assembly, having regard to the development objectives of national, regional and continental plans, and upon the recommendation of the Commission and after the approval of the Council acting on the recommendation of the Commission, shall prescribe the conditions for the movement within the Community of the capital funds other than those referred to in paragraph (2) of this Article.

4.   For the purpose of regulating the movement of capital between Member States and Third States, the Assembly, upon the approval of the Council, acting on the recommendation of the Commission, shall take steps aimed at coordinating progressively the national and regional exchange control policies.

CHAPTER IX

INDUSTRY, SCIENCE, TECHNOLOGY, ENERGY, NATURAL RESSOURCES AND ENVIRONMENT

Article 48
Industry

1.   For the purpose of promoting industrial development of Member States and integrating their economies, Member States shall within the Community harmonize their industrialisation policies.

2.   In this connection, Member States shall:

   (a)   strengthen the industrial base of the Community, in order to modernize the priority sectors and foster self-sustained and self-reliant development;

   (b)   promote joint industrial development projects at regional and Community levels, as well as the creation of African multinational enterprises in priority industrial sub-sectors likely to contribute to the development of agriculture, transport and communications, natural resources and energy.

Article 49
Industrial Development

In order to create a solid basis for industrialization and promote collective self-reliance, Member States shall:

   (a)   ensure the development of the following basic industries essential for collective self-reliance and the modernization of priority sectors of the economy:

      (i)   food and agro-based industries;

      (ii)   building and construction industries;

      (iii)   metallurgical industries;

(iv)   mechanical industries;

(v)   electrical and electronics industries;

(vi)   chemical and petro-chemical industries;

(vii)   forestry industries;

(viii)   energy industries;

(ix)   textile and leather industries;

(x)   transport and communications industries; and

(xi)   bio-technology industries;

(b)   ensure the promotion of small-scale industries with a view to enhancing the generation of employment opportunities in Member States;

(c)   promote intermediate industries that have strong linkages to the economy in order to increase the local component of industrial output within the Community;

(d)   prepare master plans at regional and Community levels for the establishment of African multinational industries particularly those whose construction cost and volume of production exceed national financial and absorptive capacities;

(e)   strengthen and establish, where they do not exist, specialized institutions for the financing of African multinational industrial projects;

(f)   facilitate the establishment of African multinational enterprises and encourage and give financial and technical support to African entrepreneurs;

(g)   promote the sale and consumption of strategic industrial products manufactured in Member States;

(h)   promote technical cooperation and the exchange of experience in the field of industrial technology and implement technical training programmes among Member States;

(i)   strengthen the existing multinational institutions, particularly, the African Regional Centre for Technology, the African Regional Centre for Design and Manufacture and the African Industrial Development Fund;

(j)   establish a data and statistical information base to serve industrial development at the regional and continental levels;

(k)   promote South-South and North-South cooperation for the attainment of industrialization objectives in Africa;

(l)   promote industrial specialization in order to enhance the complementarity of African economies and expand the intra-Community trade base, due account being taken of national and regional resource endowments; and

(m)   adopt common standards and appropriate quality control systems which are crucial to industrial cooperation and integration.

Article 50
Protocol on Industry

For the purposes of Articles 48 and 49 of this Treaty, Member States agree to cooperate in accordance with the provisions of the Protocol on Industry.

*   *   *

AGREEMENT ON THE EUROPEAN ECONOMIC AREA*
[excerpts]

The Agreement on the European Economic Area was signed in Oporto on 2 May 1992 between the European Community and its member States, namely, Belgium, Denmark, France, Germany, Greece, Ireland, Italy, Luxembourg, Netherlands, Portugal, Spain, and the United Kingdom, on the one part, and the European Free Trade Area (EFTA) and its Member States, namely, Austria, Finland, Iceland, Norway, Sweden and Switzerland, on the other part. Switzerland did not ratify the Agreement. As a result, it was amended by the Protocol Adjusting the Agreement on the European Economic Area ("Adjusting Protocol") of 17 March 1993. Austria, Finland, and Sweden acceded to the European Community on 1 January 1995. Liechtenstein acceded to the Agreement on 1 May 1995 according to the Council Decision 1/1995 of 10 March 1995. The Agreement is updated on a regular basis by decisions of the EEA Joint Committee. The decisions incorporate new European Community legislation into the Annexes and some Protocols of the Agreement. They do not change the corpus of the Treaty.

PART I. OBJECTIVES AND PRINCIPLES

Article 1

1.   The aim of this Agreement of association is to promote a continuous and balanced strengthening of trade and economic relations between the Contracting Parties with equal conditions of competition, and the respect of the same rules, with a view to creating a homogeneous European Economic Area, hereinafter referred to as the EEA.

2.   In order to attain the objectives set out in paragraph 1, the association shall entail, in accordance with the provisions of this Agreement:

   (a)   the free movement of goods;

   (b)   the free movement of persons;

   (c)   the free movement of services;

   (d)   the free movement of capital;

---

* *Source*: European Communities (1994). "The Agreement on the European Economic Area", *Official Journal of the European Communities*, L 1, 3 January 1994, pp. 3-606, as amended by the Protocol Adjusting the Agreement on the European Economic Area ("Adjusting Protocol") of 17 March 1993, *Official Journal of the European Communities*, L 1, 3 January 1994, p. 574; and "The Council Decision 1/1995 Concerning the Accession of Liechtenstein to the Agreeement on the European Economic Area", *Official Journal of the European Communities*, L 68, 20 April 1995, p. 58; for updates on the Agreement on the European economic Area, see the EFTA Internet homepage (http://www.efta.int/structure/EFTA/efta-sec.cfm). [Note added by the editor.]

(e)   the setting up of a system ensuring that competition is not distorted and that the rules thereon are equally respected; as well as

(f)   closer cooperation in other fields, such as research and development, the environment, education and social policy.

Article 4

Within the scope of application of this Agreement, and without prejudice to any special provisions contained therein, any discrimination on grounds of nationality shall be prohibited.

PART III. FREE MOVEMENT OF PERSONS, SERVICES AND CAPITAL

CHAPTER 1. WORKERS AND SELF-EMPLOYED PERSONS

Article 28

1.   Freedom of movement for workers shall be secured among EC Member States and EFTA States.

2.   Such freedom of movement shall entail the abolition of any discrimination based on nationality between workers of EC Member States and EFTA States as regards employment, remuneration and other conditions of work and employment.

3.   It shall entail the right, subject to limitations justified on grounds of public policy, public security or public health:

(a)   to accept offers of employment actually made;

(b)   to move freely within the territory of EC Member States and EFTA States for this purpose;

(c)   to stay in the territory of an EC Member State or an EFTA State for the purpose of employment in accordance with the provisions governing the employment of nationals of that State laid down by law, regulation or administrative action;

(d)   to remain in the territory of an EC Member State or an EFTA State after having been employed there.

4.   The provisions of this Article shall not apply to employment in the public service.

5.   Annex V contains specific provisions on the free movement of workers.

Article 30

In order to make it easier for persons to take up and pursue activities as workers and self-employed persons, the Contracting Parties shall take the necessary measures, as contained in Annex VII, concerning the mutual recognition of diplomas, certificates and other evidence of formal qualifications, and the coordination of the provisions laid down by law, regulation or administrative action in the Contracting Parties concerning the taking up and pursuit of activities by workers and self-employed persons.

CHAPTER 2. RIGHT OF ESTABLISHMENT

Article 31

1.   Within the framework of the provisions of this Agreement, there shall be no restrictions on the freedom of establishment of nationals of an EC Member State or an EFTA State in the territory of any other of these States. This shall also apply to the setting up of agencies, branches or subsidiaries by nationals of any EC Member State or EFTA State established in the territory of any of these States.

Freedom of establishment shall include the right to take up and pursue activities as self-employed persons and to set up and manage undertakings, in particular companies or firms within the meaning of Article 34, second paragraph, under the conditions laid down for its own nationals by the law of the country where such establishment is effected, subject to the provisions of Chapter 4.

2.   Annexes VIII to XI contain specific provisions on the right of establishment.

Article 32

The provisions of this Chapter shall not apply, so far as any given Contracting Party is concerned, to activities which in that Contracting Party are connected, even occasionally, with the exercise of official authority.

Article 33

The provisions of this Chapter and measures taken in pursuance thereof shall not prejudice the applicability of provisions laid down by law, regulation or administrative action providing for special treatment for foreign nationals on grounds of public policy, public security or public health.

Article 34

Companies or firms formed in accordance with the law of an EC Member State or an EFTA State and having their registered office, central administration or principal place of business within the territory of the Contracting Parties shall, for the purposes of this Chapter, be treated in the same way as natural persons who are nationals of EC Member States or EFTA States.

'Companies or firms' means companies or firms constituted under civil or commercial law, including cooperative societies, and other legal persons governed by public or private law, save for those which are non-profit-making.

Article 35

The provisions of Article 30 shall apply to the matters covered by this Chapter.

CHAPTER 3. SERVICES

Article 36

1.   Within the framework of the provisions of this Agreement, there shall be no restrictions on freedom to provide services within the territory of the Contracting Parties in respect of nationals of EC Member States and EFTA States who are established in an EC Member State or an EFTA State other than that of the person for whom the services are intended.

2.   Annexes IX to XI contain specific provisions on the freedom to provide services.

Article 37

Services shall be considered to be 'services' within the meaning of this Agreement where they are normally provided for remuneration, in so far as they are not governed by the provisions relating to freedom of movement for goods, capital and persons.

Services shall in particular include:

   (a)   activities of an industrial character;

   (b)   activities of a commercial character;

   (c)   activities of craftsmen;

   (d)   activities of the professions.

Without prejudice to the provisions of Chapter 2, the person providing a service may, in order to do so, temporarily pursue his activity in the State where the service is provided, under the same conditions as are imposed by that State on its own nationals.

Article 38

Freedom to provide services in the field of transport shall be governed by the provisions of Chapter 6.

Article 39

The provisions of Articles 30 and 32 to 34 shall apply to the matters covered by this Chapter.

CHAPTER 4. CAPITAL

Article 40

Within the framework of the provisions of this Agreement, there shall be no restrictions between the Contracting Parties on the movement of capital belonging to persons resident in EC Member States or EFTA States and no discrimination based on the nationality or on the place of residence of the parties or on the place where such capital is invested. Annex XII contains the provisions necessary to implement this Article.

Article 41

Current payments connected with the movement of goods, persons, services or capital between Contracting Parties within the framework of the provisions of this Agreement shall be free of all restrictions.

Article 42

1.   Where domestic rules governing the capital market and the credit system are applied to the movements of capital liberalized in accordance with the provisions of this Agreement, this shall be done in a non-discriminatory manner.

2.   Loans for the direct or indirect financing of an EC Member State or an EFTA State or its regional or local authorities shall not be issued or placed in other EC Member States or EFTA States unless the States concerned have reached agreement thereon.

Article 43

1.   Where differences between the exchange rules of EC Member States and EFTA States could lead persons resident in one of these States to use the freer transfer facilities within the territory of the Contracting Parties which are provided for in Article 40 in order to evade the rules of one of these States concerning the movement of capital to or from third countries, the Contracting Party concerned may take appropriate measures to overcome these difficulties.

2.   If movements of capital lead to disturbances in the functioning of the capital market in any EC Member State or EFTA State, the Contracting Party concerned may take protective measures in the field of capital movements.

3.   If the competent authorities of a Contracting Party make an alteration in the rate of exchange which seriously distorts conditions of competition, the other Contracting Parties may take, for a strictly limited period, the necessary measures in order to counter the consequences of such alteration.

4.   Where an EC Member State or an EFTA State is in difficulties, or is seriously threatened with difficulties, as regards its balance of payments either as a result of an overall disequilibrium in its balance of payments, or as a result of the type of currency at its disposal, and where such difficulties are liable in particular to jeopardize the functioning of this Agreement, the Contracting Party concerned may take protective measures.

Article 44

The Community, on the one hand, and the EFTA States, on the other, shall apply their internal procedures, as provided for in Protocol 18, to implement the provisions of Article 43.

Article 45

1.   Decisions, opinions and recommendations related to the measures laid down in Article 43 shall be notified to the EEA Joint Committee.

2.   All measures shall be the subject of prior consultations and exchange of information within the EEA Joint Committee.

3.   In the situation referred to in Article 43(2), the Contracting Party concerned may, however, on the grounds of secrecy and urgency take the measures, where this proves necessary, without prior consultations and exchange of information.

4.   In the situation referred to in Article 43(4), where a sudden crisis in the balance of payments occurs and the procedures set out in paragraph 2 cannot be followed, the Contracting Party concerned may, as a precaution, take the necessary protective measures. Such measures must cause the least possible disturbance in the functioning of this Agreement and must not be wider in scope than is strictly necessary to remedy the sudden difficulties which have arisen.

5.   When measures are taken in accordance with paragraphs 3 and 4, notice thereof shall be given at the latest by the date of their entry into force, and the exchange of information and consultations as well as the notifications referred to in paragraph 1 shall take place as soon as possible thereafter.

PART IV.   COMPETITION AND OTHER COMMON RULES

CHAPTER 1.   RULES APPLICABLE TO UNDERTAKINGS

Article 53

1.   The following shall be prohibited as incompatible with the functioning of this Agreement: all agreements between undertakings, decisions by associations of undertakings and concerted practices which may affect trade between Contracting Parties and which have as their object or effect the prevention, restriction or distortion of competition within the territory covered by this Agreement, and in particular those which:

(a)   directly or indirectly fix purchase or selling prices or any other trading conditions;

(b)   limit or control production, markets, technical development, or investment;

(c)   share markets or sources of supply;

(d)   apply dissimilar conditions to equivalent transactions with other trading parties, thereby placing them at a competitive disadvantage;

(e)   make the conclusion of contracts subject to acceptance by the other parties of supplementary obligations which, by their nature or according to commercial usage, have no connection with the subject of such contracts.

2.   Any agreements or decisions prohibited pursuant to this Article shall be automatically void.

3.   The provisions of paragraph 1 may, however, be declared inapplicable in the case of:

-      any agreement or category of agreements between undertakings;

-      any decision or category of decisions by associations of undertakings;

-        any concerted practice or category of concerted practices;

which contributes to improving the production or distribution of goods or to promoting technical or economic progress, while allowing consumers a fair share of the resulting benefit, and which does not:

(a)   impose on the undertakings concerned restrictions which are not indispensable to the attainment of these objectives;

(b)   afford such undertakings the possibility of eliminating competition in respect of a substantial part of the products in question.

Article 54

Any abuse by one or more undertakings of a dominant position within the territory covered by this Agreement or in a substantial part of it shall be prohibited as incompatible with the functioning of this Agreement in so far as it may affect trade between Contracting Parties.

Such abuse may, in particular, consist in:

(a)   directly or indirectly imposing unfair purchase or selling prices or other unfair trading conditions;

(b)   limiting production, markets or technical development to the prejudice of consumers;

(c)   applying dissimilar conditions to equivalent transactions with other trading parties, thereby placing them at a competitive disadvantage;

(d)   making the conclusion of contracts subject to acceptance by the other parties of supplementary obligations which, by their nature or according to commercial usage, have no connection with the subject of such contracts.

Article 55

1.   Without prejudice to the provisions giving effect to Articles 53 and 54 as contained in Protocol 21 and Annex XIV of this Agreement, the EC Commission and the EFTA Surveillance Authority provided for in Article 108(1) shall ensure the application of the principles laid down in Articles 53 and 54.

The competent surveillance authority, as provided for in Article 56, shall investigate cases of suspected infringement of these principles, on its own initiative, or on application by a State within the respective territory or by the other surveillance authority. The competent surveillance authority shall carry out these investigations in cooperation with the competent national authorities in the respective territory and in cooperation with the other surveillance authority, which shall give it its assistance in accordance with its internal rules.

If it finds that there has been an infringement, it shall propose appropriate measures to bring it to an end.

2.   If the infringement is not brought to an end, the competent surveillance authority shall record such infringement of the principles in a reasoned decision.

The competent surveillance authority may publish its decision and authorize States within the respective territory to take the measures, the conditions and details of which it shall determine, needed to remedy the situation. It may also request the other surveillance authority to authorize States within the respective territory to take such measures.

Article 56

1   Individual cases falling under Article 53 shall be decided upon by the surveillance authorities in accordance with the following provisions:

(a)   individual cases where only trade between EFTA States is affected shall be decided upon by the EFTA Surveillance Authority;

(b)   without prejudice to subparagraph (c), the EFTA Surveillance Authority decides, as provided for in the provisions set out in Article 58, Protocol 21 and the rules adopted for its implementation, Protocol 23 and Annex XIV, on cases where the turnover of the undertakings concerned in the territory of the EFTA States equals 33 per cent or more of their turnover in the territory covered by this Agreement;

(c)   the EC Commission decides on the other cases as well as on cases under (b) where trade between EC Member States is affected, taking into account the provisions set out in Article 58, Protocol 21, Protocol 23 and Annex XIV.

2.   Individual cases falling under Article 54 shall be decided upon by the surveillance authority in the territory of which a dominant position is found to exist. The rules set out in paragraph 1(b) and (c) shall apply only if dominance exists within the territories of both surveillance authorities.

3.   Individual cases falling under subparagraph (c) of paragraph 1, whose effects on trade between EC Member States or on competition within the Community are not appreciable, shall be decided upon by the EFTA Surveillance Authority.

4.   The terms 'undertaking' and 'turnover' are, for the purposes of this Article, defined in Protocol 22.

Article 57

1.   Concentrations the control of which is provided for in paragraph 2 and which create or strengthen a dominant position as a result of which effective competition would be significantly impeded within the territory covered by this Agreement or a substantial part of it, shall be declared incompatible with this Agreement.

2.   The control of concentrations falling under paragraph 1 shall be carried out by:

(a)   the EC Commission in cases falling under Regulation (EEC) No 4064/89 in accordance with that Regulation and in accordance with Protocols 21 and 24 and

Annex XIV to this Agreement. The EC Commission shall, subject to the review of the EC Court of Justice, have sole competence to take decisions on these cases;

(b)   the EFTA Surveillance Authority in cases not falling under subparagraph (a) where the relevant thresholds set out in Annex XIV are fulfilled in the territory of the EFTA States in accordance with Protocols 21 and 24 and Annex XIV. This is without prejudice to the competence of EC Member States.

Article 58

With a view to developing and maintaining a uniform surveillance throughout the European Economic Area in the field of competition and to promoting a homogeneous implementation, application and interpretation of the provisions of this Agreement to this end, the competent authorities shall cooperate in accordance with the provisions set out in Protocols 23 and 24.

Article 59

1.   In the case of public undertakings and undertakings to which EC Member States or EFTA States grant special or exclusive rights, the Contracting Parties shall ensure that there is neither enacted nor maintained in force any measure contrary to the rules contained in this Agreement, in particular to those rules provided for in Articles 4 and 53 to 63.

2.   Undertakings entrusted with the operation of services of general economic interest or having the character of a revenue-producing monopoly shall be subject to the rules contained in this Agreement, in particular to the rules on competition, in so far as the application of such rules does not obstruct the performance, in law or in fact, of the particular tasks assigned to them. The development of trade must not be affected to such an extent as would be contrary to the interests of the Contracting Parties.

3.   The EC Commission as well as the EFTA Surveillance Authority shall ensure within their respective competence the application of the provisions of this Article and shall, where necessary, address appropriate measures to the States falling within their respective territory.

Article 60

Annex XIV contains specific provisions giving effect to the principles set out in Articles 53, 54, 57 and 59.

CHAPTER 2. STATE AID

Article 61

1.   Save as otherwise provided in this Agreement, any aid granted by EC Member States, EFTA States or through State resources in any form whatsoever which distorts or threatens to distort competition by favouring certain undertakings or the production of certain goods shall, in so far as it affects trade between Contracting Parties, be incompatible with the functioning of this Agreement.

2.   The following shall be compatible with the functioning of this Agreement:

(a)   aid having a social character, granted to individual consumers, provided that such aid is granted without discrimination related to the origin of the products concerned;

(b)   aid to make good the damage caused by natural disasters or exceptional occurrences;

(c)   aid granted to the economy of certain areas of the Federal Republic of Germany affected by the division of Germany, in so far as such aid is required in order to compensate for the economic disadvantages caused by that division.

3.   The following may be considered to be compatible with the functioning of this Agreement:

(a)   aid to promote the economic development of areas where the standard of living is abnormally low or where there is serious underemployment;

(b)   aid to promote the execution of an important project of common European interest or to remedy a serious disturbance in the economy of an EC Member State or an EFTA State;

(c)   aid to facilitate the development of certain economic activities or of certain economic areas, where such aid does not adversely affect trading conditions to an extent contrary to the common interest;

(d)   such other categories of aid as may be specified by the EEA Joint Committee in accordance with Part VII.

Article 62

1.   All existing systems of State aid in the territory of the Contracting Parties, as well as any plans to grant or alter State aid, shall be subject to constant review as to their compatibility with Article 61. This review shall be carried out:

(a)   as regards the EC Member States, by the EC Commission according to the rules laid down in Article 93 of the Treaty establishing the European Economic Community;

(b)   as regards the EFTA States, by the EFTA Surveillance Authority according to the rules set out in an agreement between the EFTA States establishing the EFTA Surveillance Authority which is entrusted with the powers and functions laid down in Protocol 26.

2.   With a view to ensuring a uniform surveillance in the field of State aid throughout the territory covered by this Agreement, the EC Commission and the EFTA Surveillance Authority shall cooperate in accordance with the provisions set out in Protocol 27.

Article 63

Annex XV contains specific provisions on State aid.

Article 64

1.   If one of the surveillance authorities considers that the implementation by the other surveillance authority of Articles 61 and 62 of this Agreement and Article 5 of Protocol 14 is not in conformity with the maintenance of equal conditions of competition within the territory covered by this Agreement, exchange of views shall be held within two weeks according to the procedure of Protocol 27, paragraph (f).

If a commonly agreed solution has not been found by the end of this two-week period, the competent authority of the affected Contracting Party may immediately adopt appropriate interim measures in order to remedy the resulting distortion of competition. Consultations shall then be held in the EEA Joint Committee with a view to finding a commonly acceptable solution.

If within three months the EEA Joint Committee has not been able to find such a solution, and if the practice in question causes, or threatens to cause, distortion of competition affecting trade between the Contracting Parties, the interim measures may be replaced by definitive measures, strictly necessary to offset the effect of such distortion. Priority shall be given to such measures that will least disturb the functioning of the EEA.

2.   The provisions of this Article will also apply to State monopolies, which are established after the date of signature of the Agreement.

PART V.   HORIZONTAL PROVISIONS RELEVANT TO THE FOUR FREEDOMS

CHAPTER 1. SOCIAL POLICY

Article 66

The Contracting Parties agree upon the need to promote improved working conditions and an improved standard of living for workers.

Article 67

1.   The Contracting Parties shall pay particular attention to encouraging improvements, especially in the working environment, as regards the health and safety of workers. In order to help achieve this objective, minimum requirements shall be applied for gradual implementation, having regard to the conditions and technical rules obtaining in each of the Contracting Parties. Such minimum requirements shall not prevent any Contracting Party from maintaining or introducing more stringent measures for the protection of working conditions compatible with this Agreement.

2.   Annex XVIII specifies the provisions to be implemented as the minimum requirements referred to in paragraph 1.

Article 68

In the field of labour law, the Contracting Parties shall introduce the measures necessary to ensure the good functioning of this Agreement. These measures are specified in Annex XVIII.

Article 69

1.   Each Contracting Party shall ensure and maintain the application of the principle that men and women should receive equal pay for equal work.

For the purposes of this Article, 'pay' means the ordinary basic or minimum wage or salary and any other consideration, whether in cash or in kind, which the worker receives, directly or indirectly, in respect of his employment from his employer.

Equal pay without discrimination based on sex means:

   (a)   that pay for the same work at piece rates shall be calculated on the basis of the same unit of measurement;

   (b)   that pay for work at time rates shall be the same for the same job.

2.   Annex XVIII contains specific provisions for the implementation of paragraph 1.

Article 70

The Contracting Parties shall promote the principle of equal treatment for men and women by implementing the provisions specified in Annex XVIII.

Article 71

The Contracting Parties shall endeavour to promote the dialogue between management and labour at European level.

CHAPTER 2. CONSUMER PROTECTION

Article 72

Annex XIX contains provisions on consumer protection.

CHAPTER 3. ENVIRONMENT

Article 73

1.   Action by the Contracting Parties relating to the environment shall have the following objectives:

   (a)   to preserve, protect and improve the quality of the environment;

(b)   to contribute towards protecting human health;

(c)   to ensure a prudent and rational utilization of natural resources.

2.   Action by the Contracting Parties relating to the environment shall be based on the principles that preventive action should be taken, that environmental damage should as a priority be rectified at source, and that the polluter should pay. Environmental protection requirements shall be a component of the Contracting Parties' other policies.

Article 74

Annex XX contains the specific provisions on protective measures which shall apply pursuant to Article 73.

Article 75

The protective measures referred to in Article 74 shall not prevent any Contracting Party from maintaining or introducing more stringent protective measures compatible with this Agreement.

CHAPTER 5.   COMPANY LAW

Article 77

Annex XXII contains specific provisions on company law.

PART VI.   COOPERATION OUTSIDE THE FOUR FREEDOMS

Article 78

The Contracting Parties shall strengthen and broaden cooperation in the framework of the Community's activities in the fields of:

...

-    small and medium-sized enterprises,

...

in so far as these matters are not regulated under the provisions of other Parts of this Agreement.

Article 80

The cooperation provided for in Article 78 shall normally take one of the following forms:

-    participation by EFTA States in EC framework programmes, specific programmes, projects or other actions;

- establishment of joint activities in specific areas, which may include concertation or coordination of activities, fusion of existing activities and establishment of ad hoe joint activities;

- the formal and informal exchange or provision of information;

- common efforts to encourage certain activities throughout the territory of the Contracting Parties;

- parallel legislation, where appropriate, of identical or similar content;

- coordination, where this is of mutual interest, of efforts and activities via, or in the context of, international organizations, and of cooperation with third countries.

Article 83

Where cooperation takes the form of an exchange of information between public authorities, the EFTA States shall have the same rights to receive, and obligations to provide, information as EC Member States, subject to the requirements of confidentiality, which shall be fixed by the EEA Joint Committee.

Article 84

Provisions governing cooperation in specific fields are set out in Protocol 3 1.

Article 85

Unless otherwise provided for in Protocol 31, cooperation already established between the Community and individual EFTA States in the fields referred to in Article 78 on the date of entry into force of this Agreement shall thereafter be governed by the relevant provisions of this Part and of Protocol 3 1.

Article 86

The EEA Joint Committee shall, in accordance with Part VII, take all decisions necessary for the implementation of Articles 78 to 85 and measures derived therefrom, which may include, inter alia, supplementing and amending the provisions of Protocol 31, as well as adopting any transitional arrangements required by way of implementation of Article 85.

Article 87

The Contracting Parties shall take the necessary steps to develop, strengthen or broaden cooperation in the framework of the Community's activities in fields not listed in Article 78, where such cooperation is considered likely to contribute to the attainment of the objectives of this Agreement, or is otherwise deemed by the Contracting Parties to be of mutual interest. Such steps may include the amendment of Article 78 by the addition of new fields to those listed therein.

Article 88

Without prejudice to provisions of other Parts of this Agreement, the provisions of this Part shall not preclude the possibility for any Contracting Party to prepare, adopt and implement measures independently.

PART VII. INSTITUTIONAL PROVISIONS

CHAPTER 4. SAFEGUARD MEASURES

Article 112

1.   If serious economic, societal or environmental difficulties of a sectorial or regional nature liable to persist are arising, a Contracting Party may unilaterally take appropriate measures under the conditions and procedures laid down in Article 113.

2.   Such safeguard measures shall be restricted with regard to their scope and duration to what is strictly necessary in order to remedy the situation. Priority shall be given to such measures as will least disturb the functioning of this Agreement.

3.   The safeguard measures shall apply with regard to all Contracting Parties.

Article 113

1   A Contracting Party which is considering taking safeguard measures under Article 112 shall, without delay, notify the other Contracting Parties through the EEA Joint Committee and shall provide all relevant information.

2.   The Contracting Parties shall immediately enter into consultations in the EEA Joint Committee with a view to finding a commonly acceptable solution.

3.   The Contracting Party concerned may not take safeguard measures until one month has elapsed after the date of notification under paragraph 1, unless the consultation procedure under paragraph 2 has been concluded before the expiration of the stated time limit. When exceptional circumstances requiring immediate action exclude prior examination, the Contracting Party concerned may apply forthwith the protective measures strictly necessary to remedy the situation.

For the Community, the safeguard measures shall be taken by the EC Commission.

4.   The Contracting Party concerned shall, without delay, notify the measures taken to the EEA Joint Committee and shall provide all relevant information.

5.   The safeguard measures taken shall be the subject of consultations in the EEA Joint Committee every three months from the date of their adoption with a view to their abolition before the date of expiry envisaged, or to the limitation of their scope of application. Each Contracting Party may at any time request the EEA Joint Committee to review such measures.

Article 114

1   If a safeguard measure taken by a Contracting Party creates an imbalance between the rights and obligations under this Agreement, any other Contracting Party may towards that Contracting Party take such proportionate rebalancing measures as are strictly necessary to remedy the imbalance. Priority shall be given to such measures as will least disturb the functioning of the EEA.

2.   The procedure under Article 113 shall apply.

*   *   *

REVISED TREATY OF THE ECONOMIC COMMUNITY OF WEST AFRICAN STATES (ECOWAS)*
[excerpts]

The Revised Treaty of the Economic Community of West African States (ECOWAS) was signed in Cotonou, Benin, on 24 July 1993. The States signatories were Benin, Burkina Faso, Cape Verde, Côte d'Ivoire, Gambia, Ghana, Guinea, Guinea Bissau, Liberia, Mali, Mauritania, Niger, Nigeria, Senegal, Sierra Leone and Togo. It entered into force on 23 August 1995. As of 10 August 1999, thirteen member States had ratified the Revised Treaty, namely Benin, Burkina Faso, Côte d'Ivoire, Gambia, Ghana, Guinea, Liberia, Mali, Niger, Nigeria, Senegal, Sierra Leone and Togo. Mauritania did not ratified the Revised Treaty.

CHAPTER II

ESTABLISHMENT, COMPOSITION, AIMS AND OBJECTIVES AND FUNDAMENTAL PRINCIPLES OF THE COMMUNITY

ARTICLE 3

AIMS AND OBJECTIVES

1.   The aims of the Community are to promote co-operation and integration, leading to the establishment of an economic union in West Africa in order to raise the living standards of its peoples, and to maintain and enhance economic stability, foster relations among Member States and contribute to the progress and development of the African Continent.

2.   In order to achieve the aims set out in the paragraph above, and in accordance with the relevant provisions of this Treaty, the Community shall, by stages, ensure;

...

c)   the promotion of the establishment of joint production enterprises;

d)   the establishment of a common market through:

...

---

*   *Source*: Economic Community of West African States (ECOWAS) (1993). "Revised Treaty of the Economic Community of West African States", *Economic Community of West African States (ECOWAS) - Revised Treaty* (Abuja, Nigeria: ECOWAS Executive Secretariat); also available in *International Legal Materials*, vol. 35 (1996), pp. 660-697. [Note added by the editor.]

iii)   the removal, between Member States, of obstacles to the free movement of persons, goods, services and capital, and to the right of residence and establishment;

...

f)   the promotion of joint ventures by private sector enterprises and other economic operators, in particular through the adoption of a regional agreement on cross-border investments;

g)   the adoption of measures for the integration of the private sectors, particularly the creation of an enabling environment to promote small and medium scale enterprises,

h)   the establishment of an enabling legal environment;

i)   the harmonisation of national investment codes leading to the adoption of a single Community investment code;

...

k)   the promotion of balanced development of the region, paying attention to the special problems of each Member State particularly those of landlocked and small island Member States;

CHAPTER V

CO-OPERATION IN INDUSTRY, SCIENCE AND TECHNOLOGY AND ENERGY

ARTICLE 26

INDUSTRY

1.   For the purpose of promoting industrial development of Member States and integrating their economies, Member States shall, harmonise their industrialisation policies.

2.   In this connection, Member States shall:

a)   strengthen the industrial base of the Community, modernise the priority sectors and foster self-sustained and self-reliant development;

b)   promote joint industrial development projects as well as the creation of multinational enterprises in priority industrial sub-sectors likely to contribute to the development of agriculture, transport and communications, natural resources and energy.

3.   In order to create a solid basic for industrialisation and promote collective self-reliance, Member States shall:

a)   ensure, on the one hand, the development of industries essential for collective self-reliance and, on the other, the modernisation of priority sectors of the economy especially:

   i)   food and agro-based industries;

   ii)   building and construction industries;

   iii)   metallurgical industries;

   iv)   mechanical industries;

   v)   electrical, electronics and computer industries;

   vi)   pharmaceutical, chemical and petro-chemical industries;.

   vii)   forestry industries;

   viii) energy industries;

   ix)   textile and leather industries;

   x)   transport and communications industries;

   xi)   bio-technology industries;

   xi)   tourist and cultural industries.

b)   give priority and encouragement to the establishment and strengthening of private and public multinational industrial projects likely to promote integration;

c)   ensure the promotion of medium and small-scale industries;

d)   promote intermediate industries that have strong linkages to the economy in order to increase the local component of industrial output within the Community;

e)   prepare a regional master plan for the establishment of industries particularly those whose construction cost and volume of production exceed national, financial and absorptive capacities;

f)   encourage the establishment of specialised institutions for the financing of West African multinational industrial projects;

g)   facilitate the establishment of West African multinational enterprises and encourage the participation of West African entrepreneurs in the regional industrialisation process.

h) promote the sale and consumption of strategic industrial products manufactured in Member States;

i) promote technical co-operation and the exchange of experience in the field of industrial technology and implement technical training programmes among Member States;

j) establish a regional data and statistical information base to support industrial development at the regional and continental levels;

k) promote, on the basis of natural resource endowments, industrial specialisation in order to enhance complementarity and expand the intra-Community trade base; and

l) adopt common standards and appropriate quality control systems.

CHAPTER VIII

CO-OPERATION IN TRADE, CUSTOMS, TAXATION, STATISTICS, MONEY AND PAYMENTS

ARTICLE 53

MOVEMENT OF CAPITAL AND CAPITAL ISSUES COMMITTEE

1. For the purpose of ensuring the free movement of capital between Member States in accordance with the objectives of this Treaty, there is hereby established a Capital Issues Committee which shall comprise one representative of each of the Member States and which shall, subject to the provisions of this Treaty, prepare its own rules of procedure.

2. Member States shall, in appointing their representatives referred to in paragraph 1 of this Article, designate persons with financial, commercial or banking experience and qualifications.

3. The Capital Issues Committee, in the performance of the duties assigned to it under paragraph 1 of this Article, shall:

a) ensure the unimpeded flow of capital within the Community through:

   i) the removal of controls on the transfer of capital among the Member States in accordance with a time-table determined by Council;

   ii) the encouragement of the establishment of national and regional stock exchanges; and

   iii) the interlocking of capital markets and stock exchanges.

b)   ensure that nationals of a Member State are given the opportunity of acquiring stocks, shares and other securities or otherwise of investing in enterprises in the territories of other Member States;

c)   establish a machinery for the wide dissemination in the Member States of stock exchange quotations of each Member State;

d)   establish appropriate machinery for the regulation of the capital issues market to ensure its proper functioning and the protection of the investors therein.

CHAPTER IX

ESTABLISHMENT AND COMPLETION OF AN ECONOMIC AND MONETARY UNION

ARTICLE 54

ESTABLISHMENT OF AN ECONOMIC UNION

1.   Member States undertake to achieve the status of an economic union within a maximum period of fifteen (15) years following the commencement of the regional trade liberalisation scheme, adopted by the Authority through its Decision A/DEC.1/9/83 of 20 May, 1983 and launched on 1 January, 1990.

2.   Member States shall give priority to the role of the private sector and joint regional multinational enterprises in the regional economic integration process.

CHAPTER XIII

ARTICLE 68

LAND-LOCKED AND ISLAND MEMBER STATES

Member States, taking into consideration the economic and social difficulties that may arise in certain Member States, particularly island and land-locked States, agree to grant them where appropriate, special treatment in respect of the application of certain provisions of this Treaty and to accord them any other assistance that they may need.

*   *   *

TRATADO DE LIBRE COMERCIO ENTRE MÉXICO Y COSTA RICA[*]
[excerpts]

The Free Trade Agreement between Mexico and Costa Rica was signed on 5 April 1994. It entered into force on 1 January 1995.

Capítulo XIII. Inversión

Sección A - Inversión

Artículo 13-01. Definiciones

Para efectos de este capítulo, se entenderá por:

CIADI: Centro Internacional de Arreglo de Diferencias Relativas a Inversiones;

Convención de Nueva York: Convención de Naciones Unidas sobre el Reconocimiento y Ejecución de Laudos Arbitrales Extranjeros, celebrada en Nueva York, el 10 de junio de 1958;

Convención Interamericana: Convención Interamericana sobre Arbitraje Comercial Internacional, celebrada en Panamá el 30 de enero de 1975;

Convenio de CIADI: el Convenio sobre Arreglo de Diferencias Relativas a Inversiones entre Estados y Nacionales de otros Estados, celebrado en Washington el 18 de marzo de 1965;

demanda: la reclamación hecha por el inversionista contendiente contra una Parte en los términos de la sección B de este capítulo;

empresa: cualquier persona jurídica, constituida u organizada conforme a la legislación de una Parte, tenga o no fines de lucro y sea de propiedad privada o gubernamental, así como otras organizaciones o unidades económicas que se encuentren constituidas o, en cualquier caso, debidamente organizadas según esa legislación, tales como sucursales, fideicomisos, participaciones, empresas de propietario único, coinversiones u otras asociaciones;

empresa de una Parte: una empresa constituida u organizada de conformidad con la legislación de una Parte y que tenga su domicilio en el territorio de esa Parte; y una sucursal ubicada en territorio de una Parte que desempeñe actividades comerciales en el mismo;

inversión: todo tipo de bienes y derechos de cualquier naturaleza, adquiridos con recursos transferidos al territorio de una Parte, o reinvertidos en ésta, por parte de los inversionistas de otra Parte, tales como:

---

[*] *Source*: The Government of Mexico and the Government of Costa Rica (1995). "Tratado de Libre Comercio entre México y Costa Rica"; available on the Internet (http://www.sice.oas.org/trade/Mexcr_s/mcrind.stm). [Note added by the editor.]

- acciones y cualquier otra forma de participación en el capital social de las sociedades constituidas u organizadas de conformidad con la legislación de la otra Parte;

- derechos derivados de todo tipo de aportaciones realizadas con el propósito de crear valor económico (u obligaciones, créditos y derechos a cualquier prestación que tengan valor económico);

- bienes muebles e inmuebles, así como otros derechos reales tales como hipotecas, derechos de prenda, usufructo y derechos similares;

- derechos en el ámbito de la propiedad intelectual; y

- derechos para realizar actividades económicas y comerciales otorgados por la legislación o en virtud de un contrato.

pero no incluye:

- una obligación de pago de, ni el otorgamiento de un crédito a, el Estado o una empresa del Estado; ni

- reclamaciones pecuniarias derivadas exclusivamente de:

   a)   contratos comerciales para la venta de bienes o servicios por un nacional o empresa en territorio de una Parte a un nacional o a una empresa en territorio de otra Parte; o

   b)   el otorgamiento de crédito en relación con una transacción comercial, cuya fecha de vencimiento sea menor a tres años, como el financiamiento al comercio;

inversionista contendiente: un inversionista que someta a arbitraje una demanda en los términos de la sección B de este capítulo;

inversión de un inversionista de una Parte: la inversión propiedad o bajo control de un inversionista de una Parte efectuada en el territorio de otra Parte. En caso de una empresa, una inversión es propiedad de un inversionista de una Parte si ese inversionista tiene la titularidad de más del 49% de su capital social. Una inversión está bajo el control de un inversionista de una Parte si ese inversionista tiene la facultad de designar a la mayoría de sus directores o de dirigir de cualquier otro modo sus operaciones;

inversionista de una Parte: una Parte o una empresa de la misma, o un nacional o empresa de esa Parte, que lleve a cabo los actos jurídicos tendientes a materializar la inversión, estando en vías de comprometer un monto importante de capital o, en su caso, realice o haya realizado una inversión en territorio de la otra Parte;

nacional de una Parte: una persona natural que sea nacional de una Parte de conformidad con su legislación;

Parte contendiente: la Parte contra la cual se formula una demanda en arbitraje en los términos de la sección B de este capítulo;

parte contendiente: el inversionista contendiente o la Parte contendiente;

partes contendientes: el inversionista contendiente y la Parte contendiente;

Reglas de Arbitraje de CNUDMI: Reglas de Arbitraje de la Comisión de Naciones Unidas sobre Derecho Mercantil Internacional (CNUDMI), aprobadas por la Asamblea General de las Naciones Unidas el 15 de diciembre de 1976;

Secretario General: Secretario General de CIADI;

transferencias: las remisiones y pagos internacionales;

tribunal: un tribunal establecido conforme al artículo 13-25;

tribunal de acumulación: un tribunal arbitral establecido conforme al artículo 13-28.

Artículo 13-02. Ambito de aplicación y extensión de las obligaciones

1.   Este capítulo se aplica a las medidas que adopte o mantenga una Parte relativas a:

   a)   los inversionistas de otra Parte, en todo lo relacionado con su inversión;

   b)   las inversiones de inversionistas de otra Parte realizadas en el territorio de la Parte a partir de la entrada en vigor de este Tratado. No obstante, también se aplicará a las inversiones realizadas con anterioridad a su vigencia y que tuvieren la calidad de inversión extranjera. No se aplicará, sin embargo, a las controversias o reclamaciones surgidas o resueltas con anterioridad a su entrada en vigor, o relacionadas con hechos acaecidos con anterioridad a su vigencia incluso si sus efectos permanecen aún después de ésta; y

   c)   todas las inversiones de los inversionistas de una Parte en el territorio de otra Parte, en lo relativo al artículo 13-06.

2.   Este capítulo no se aplica a:

   a)   las actividades económicas reservadas a cada Parte, de conformidad con su legislación vigente a la fecha de la firma de este Tratado, las cuales se listarán en un plazo no mayor de un año a partir de la entrada en vigor de este Tratado;

   b)   las medidas que adopte o mantenga una Parte en materia de servicios financieros;

   c)   las medidas que adopte una Parte para restringir la participación de las inversiones de inversionistas de otra Parte en su territorio por razones de orden público o de seguridad nacional.

3.   Este capítulo se aplica en todo el territorio de las Partes y en cualquier nivel u orden de gobierno a pesar de las medidas incompatibles que pudieran existir en las legislaciones de esos niveles u órdenes de gobierno.

Artículo 13-03. Trato nacional

Cada Parte brindará a los inversionistas de otra Parte y a las inversiones de inversionistas de otra Parte, un trato no menos favorable que el que otorgue, en circunstancias similares, a sus propios inversionistas y a las inversiones de esos inversionistas.

Artículo 13-04. Trato de nación más favorecida

1.   Cada Parte brindará a los inversionistas de otra Parte y a las inversiones de inversionistas de otra Parte, un trato no menos favorable que el que otorgue en circunstancias similares, a los inversionistas y a las inversiones de los inversionistas de otra Parte o de un país que no sea parte, salvo lo dispuesto en el párrafo 2.

2.   Si una Parte hubiere otorgado un tratamiento especial a los inversionistas o a las inversiones de éstos, provenientes de un país que no sea parte, en virtud de tratados bilaterales de inversión o convenios que establezcan zonas de libre comercio, uniones aduaneras, mercados comunes, uniones económicas o monetarias u otras instituciones de integración económica similares, esa Parte no estará obligada a otorgar el tratamiento de que se trate a los inversionistas o a las inversiones de los inversionistas de otra Parte.

Artículo 13-05. Trato en caso de pérdidas

Cada Parte otorgará a los inversionistas de otra Parte, respecto de las inversiones que sufran pérdidas en su territorio debidas a conflictos armados o contiendas civiles, a caso fortuito o fuerza mayor (desastres naturales), trato no discriminatorio respecto de cualquier medida que adopte o mantenga en relación con esas pérdidas.

Artículo 13-06. Requisitos de desempeño

1.   Ninguna Parte podrá imponer ni obligar al cumplimiento de los siguientes requisitos o compromisos, en relación con cualquier inversión de un inversionista de otra Parte en su territorio:

a)   exportar un determinado nivel o porcentaje de bienes;

b)   alcanzar un determinado grado o porcentaje de contenido nacional;

c)   adquirir o utilizar u otorgar preferencia a bienes producidos en su territorio o adquirir bienes de productores en su territorio; o

d)   relacionar en cualquier forma el volumen o valor de las importaciones con el volumen o valor de las exportaciones, o con el monto de las entradas de divisas asociadas con esa inversión.

2.   Ninguna Parte podrá condicionar la recepción de un incentivo o que se continúe recibiendo el mismo, al cumplimiento de los siguientes requisitos, en relación con cualquier inversión de un inversionista de otra Parte en su territorio:

   a)   adquirir o utilizar u otorgar preferencia a bienes producidos en su territorio o a comprar bienes de productores en su territorio;

   b)   alcanzar un determinado grado o porcentaje de contenido nacional; o

   c)   relacionar en cualquier forma el volumen o valor de las importaciones con el volumen o valor de las exportaciones, o con el monto de las entradas de divisas asociadas con esa inversión.

3.   Los párrafos 1 y 2 no se aplican a requisito alguno distinto a los señalados en los mismos.

4.   Las disposiciones contenidas en:

   a)   los literales a), b) y c) del párrafo 1 y los literales a) y b) del párrafo 2 no se aplican en lo relativo a los requisitos para calificación de los bienes con respecto a programas de promoción a las exportaciones y de ayuda externa;

   b)   los literales b) y c) del párrafo 1 y los literales a) y b) del párrafo 2 no se aplican a las compras realizadas por una Parte o por una empresa del Estado;

   c)   los literales a) y b) del párrafo 2 no se aplican a los requisitos impuestos por una Parte importadora relacionados con el contenido necesario de los bienes para calificar respecto de aranceles o cuotas preferenciales.

5.   Nada de lo dispuesto en este artículo se interpretará como impedimento para que una Parte imponga, en relación con cualquier inversión en su territorio, requisitos de localización geográfica de unidades productivas, de generación de empleo o capacitación de mano de obra, o de realización de actividades en materia de investigación y desarrollo.

6.   En caso de que, a juicio de una Parte, la imposición por otra Parte de alguno de los requisitos señalados a continuación afecte negativamente el flujo comercial o constituya una barrera significativa a la inversión de un inversionista de otra Parte, el asunto será considerado por la Comisión:

   a)   restringir las ventas en su territorio de los bienes que esa inversión produzca, relacionando de cualquier manera esas ventas al volumen o valor de sus exportaciones o a ganancias en divisas que generen;

   b)   transferir a una persona en su territorio, tecnología, proceso productivo u otro conocimiento reservado, salvo cuando el requisito se imponga por un tribunal judicial o administrativo o autoridad competente para reparar una supuesta violación a la legislación en materia de competencia o para actuar de una manera que no sea incompatible con otras disposiciones de este Tratado; o

   c)   actuar como el proveedor exclusivo de los bienes que produzca para un mercado específico, regional o mundial.

7.   Si la Comisión encontrare que, en efecto, el requisito en cuestión afecta negativamente el flujo comercial o constituye una barrera significativa a la inversión de un inversionista de otra Parte, adoptará las disposiciones necesarias para suprimir la práctica de que se trate. Las Partes considerarán estas disposiciones como incorporadas a este Tratado.

Artículo 13-07. Alta dirección empresarial

1.   Ninguna Parte podrá exigir que una empresa de una Parte, designe a individuos de alguna nacionalidad en particular para ocupar puestos de alta dirección en esa empresa.

2.   Una Parte podrá exigir que la mayoría de los miembros de los órganos de administración de una empresa, sean de una nacionalidad en particular, siempre que el resultado no menoscabe materialmente la capacidad del inversionista para ejercer el control de su inversión.

Artículo 13-08. Reservas y excepciones

1.   Los artículos 13-03, 13-04, 13-06 y 13-07 no se aplican a cualquier medida incompatible que mantenga o adopte una Parte, sea cual fuere el nivel u orden de gobierno, las cuales se listarán en un plazo no mayor a un año a partir de la entrada en vigor de este Tratado. La medida incompatible que adopte una Parte no podrá ser más restrictiva que aquellas existentes al momento en que se dicte esa medida.

2.   El trato otorgado por una Parte de conformidad con el artículo 13-04, no se aplica a los tratados o sectores listados en un plazo no mayor a un año a partir de la entrada en vigor de este Tratado.

3.   Los artículos 13-03, 13-04 y 13-07 no se aplican a:

    a)   las adquisiciones realizadas por una Parte o por una empresa del Estado; o

    b)   subsidios o aportaciones, incluyendo los préstamos, garantías y seguros gubernamentales otorgados por una Parte o por una empresa del Estado, salvo por lo dispuesto en el párrafo 2 del artículo 13-05.

Artículo 13-09. Transferencias

1.   Cada Parte permitirá que todas las transferencias relacionadas con la inversión de un inversionista de una Parte en territorio de otra Parte, se hagan libremente y sin demora. Esas transferencias incluyen:

    a)   ganancias, dividendos, intereses, ganancias de capital, pagos por regalías, gastos por administración, asistencia técnica, ganancias en especie y otros montos derivados de la inversión;

    b)   bienes derivados de la venta o liquidación, total o parcial, de la inversión;

    c)   pagos realizados conforme a un contrato del que sea parte un inversionista o su inversión, incluidos pagos efectuados conforme a un convenio de préstamo;

d)   pagos derivados de compensaciones por concepto de expropiación; y

e)   pagos que provengan de la aplicación de las disposiciones relativas al mecanismo de solución de controversias contenido en la sección B de este capítulo.

2.   Cada Parte permitirá que las transferencias se realicen en divisas de libre convertibilidad al tipo de cambio vigente de mercado en la fecha de la transferencia.

3.   No obstante lo dispuesto en los párrafos 1 y 2, las Partes podrán impedir la realización de transferencias, mediante la aplicación equitativa y no discriminatoria de su legislación en los siguientes casos:

a)   quiebra, insolvencia o protección de los derechos de los acreedores;

b)   emisión, comercio y operaciones de valores;

c)   infracciones penales o administrativas;

d)   reportes de transferencias de divisas u otros instrumentos monetarios;

e)   garantía del cumplimiento de sentencias o laudos dictados en un proceso contencioso; o

f)   establecimiento de los instrumentos o mecanismos necesarios para asegurar el pago de impuestos sobre la renta por medios tales como la retención del monto relativo a dividendos u otros conceptos.

4.   No obstante lo dispuesto en este artículo, cada Parte tendrá derecho en circunstancias de dificultades excepcionales o graves de balanza de pagos, a limitar temporalmente las transferencias, en forma equitativa y no discriminatoria, de conformidad con los criterios internacionalmente aceptados. Las limitaciones adoptadas o mantenidas por una Parte de conformidad con este párrafo, así como su eliminación, se notificarán con prontitud a la otra Parte.

Artículo 13-10. Expropiación y compensación

1.   Ninguna Parte podrá nacionalizar ni expropiar, directa o indirectamente, una inversión de un inversionista de otra Parte en su territorio, ni adoptar medida alguna equivalente a la expropiación o nacionalización de esa inversión ("expropiación"), salvo que sea:

a)   por causa de utilidad pública;

b)   sobre bases no discriminatorias;

c)   con apego al principio de legalidad; y

d)   mediante indemnización conforme a los párrafos 2 a 4.

2.   La indemnización será equivalente al valor justo de mercado que tenga la inversión expropiada inmediatamente antes de que la medida expropiatoria se haya llevado a cabo ("fecha

de expropiación"), y no reflejará cambio alguno en el valor debido a que la intención de expropiar se haya conocido con antelación a la fecha de expropiación. Los criterios de valuación incluirán el valor fiscal declarado de bienes tangibles, así como otros criterios que resulten apropiados para determinar el valor justo de mercado.

3. El pago de la indemnización se hará sin demora y será completamente liquidable.

4. La cantidad pagada no será inferior a la cantidad equivalente que por indemnización se hubiere pagado en una divisa de libre convertibilidad en el mercado financiero internacional, en la fecha de expropiación, y esta divisa se hubiese convertido a la cotización de mercado vigente en la fecha de valuación, más los intereses que hubiese generado a una tasa comercial razonable para esa divisa, seleccionada por la Parte de acuerdo con los parámetros internacionales, hasta la fecha del día del pago.

Artículo 13-11. Formalidades especiales y requisitos de información

1. Nada de lo dispuesto en el artículo 13-03 se interpretará en el sentido de impedir a una Parte adoptar o mantener una medida que prescriba formalidades especiales conexas al establecimiento de inversiones por inversionistas de otra Parte, tales como que las inversiones se constituyan conforme a la legislación de la Parte, siempre que esas formalidades no menoscaben de manera importante la protección otorgada por una Parte conforme a este capítulo.

2. No obstante lo dispuesto en los artículos 13-03 y 13-04, las Partes podrán exigir de un inversionista de otra Parte o de su inversión en su territorio, que proporcione información rutinaria, referente a esa inversión exclusivamente con fines de información o estadística. La Parte protegerá la información que sea confidencial, de cualquier divulgación que pudiera afectar negativamente la situación competitiva de la inversión o del inversionista.

Artículo 13-12. Relación con otros capítulos

En caso de incompatibilidad entre una disposición de este capítulo y la disposición de otro, prevalecerá la de este último en la medida de la incompatibilidad.

Artículo 13-13. Denegación de beneficios

Una Parte, previa notificación y consulta con otra Parte, podrá negar los beneficios de este capítulo a un inversionista de otra Parte que sea una empresa de esa Parte y a las inversiones de ese inversionista, si inversionistas de un país no Parte son propietarios o controlan la empresa, en los términos indicados en la definición de " inversión de un inversionista de una Parte" del artículo 13-01, y la empresa no tiene actividades empresariales substanciales en el territorio de la Parte conforme a cuya legislación está constituida u organizada.

Artículo 13-14. Aplicación extraterritorial de la legislación de una Parte

1. Cada Parte, en relación con las inversiones de sus inversionistas constituidas u organizadas conforme a la legislación de otra Parte, no podrá ejercer jurisdicción ni adoptar medida alguna que tenga por efecto la aplicación extraterritorial de su legislación o la obstaculización del comercio entre las Partes, o entre una Parte y un país que no sea Parte.

2.   Si una Parte incumpliere lo dispuesto en el párrafo 1, la Parte en donde la inversión se hubiere constituido podrá, a su discreción, adoptar las medidas y ejercitar las acciones que considere necesarias, a fin de dejar sin efectos la legislación o la medida de que se trate y los obstáculos al comercio consecuencia de las mismas.

Artículo 13-15. Medidas relativas a medio ambiente

1.   Nada de lo dispuesto en este capítulo se interpretará como impedimento para que una Parte adopte, mantenga o ponga en ejecución cualquier medida consistente con este capítulo que considere apropiada para asegurar que las inversiones en su territorio observen la legislación ecológica o ambiental en esa Parte.

2.   Las Partes reconocen que es inadecuado alentar la inversión por medio de la atenuación de las medidas internas aplicables a la salud, seguridad o relativas a la ecología o el medio ambiente. En consecuencia, ninguna Parte eliminará o se comprometerá a eximir de la aplicación de esas medidas a la inversión de un inversionista, como medio para inducir el establecimiento, la adquisición, la expansión o conservación de la inversión en su territorio. Si una Parte estima que otra Parte ha alentado una inversión de esa forma, podrá solicitar consultas con esa Parte.

Artículo 13-16. Promoción de inversiones e intercambio de información

1.   Con la intención de incrementar significativamente la participación recíproca de la inversión, cada Parte elaborará documentos de promoción de oportunidades de inversión y diseñará mecanismos para su difusión; asimismo, cada Parte mantendrá y perfeccionará mecanismos financieros que hagan viables las inversiones de una Parte en el territorio de otra Parte.

2.   Cada Parte dará a conocer información detallada sobre oportunidades de:

   a)   inversión en su territorio, que puedan ser desarrolladas por inversionistas de otra Parte;

   b)   alianzas estratégicas entre inversionistas de cada Parte, mediante la investigación y recopilación de intereses y oportunidades de asociación;

   c)   inversión en sectores económicos específicos que interesen a cada Parte y a sus inversionistas, de acuerdo a la solicitud expresa que haga una Parte.

3.   Las Partes acuerdan mantenerse informadas y actualizadas respecto de:

   a)   las oportunidades de inversión de que trata el párrafo 2, incluyendo la difusión de los instrumentos financieros disponibles que coadyuven al incremento de la inversión en el territorio de las Partes;

   b)   legislación que, directa o indirectamente, afecte a la inversión extranjera incluyendo, entre otros, regímenes cambiarios y de carácter fiscal;

   c)   el comportamiento de la inversión extranjera en sus respectivos territorios.

4.   Nada de lo dispuesto en los párrafos 1 al 3 impondrá obligación adicional alguna a cada Parte en relación con los sistemas de registro, control, verificación o investigación de las oportunidades de inversión o de la inversión existentes en su territorio.

Artículo 13-17. Doble tributación

Las Partes, con el ánimo de promover las inversiones dentro de sus respectivos territorios mediante la eliminación de obstáculos de índole fiscal y la vigilancia en el cumplimiento de las obligaciones fiscales a través del intercambio de información tributaria, convienen en iniciar negociaciones tendientes a la celebración de convenios para evitar la doble tributación, de acuerdo al calendario que se establezca entre las autoridades competentes de las Partes.

Sección B - Solución de controversias entre una Parte y un inversionista de otra Parte

Artículo 13-18. Objetivo

Esta sección establece un mecanismo para la solución de controversias de naturaleza jurídica en materia de inversión que se susciten como consecuencia de la violación de una obligación establecida en la sección A de este capítulo, y que surjan entre una Parte y un inversionista de otra Parte a partir de la entrada en vigor de este Tratado, y que asegura, tanto el trato igual entre inversionistas de las Partes de acuerdo con el principio de reciprocidad internacional, como el debido ejercicio de la garantía de audiencia y defensa dentro de un proceso legal ante un tribunal arbitral imparcial.

Artículo 13-19. Demanda del inversionista de una Parte por cuenta propia o en representación de una empresa

1.   Salvo lo dispuesto en el anexo a este artículo y de conformidad con esta sección, el inversionista de una Parte podrá, por cuenta propia o en representación de una empresa de otra Parte que sea una persona moral de su propiedad o bajo su control directo o indirecto, someter a arbitraje una demanda cuyo fundamento sea que otra Parte o una empresa controlada directa o indirectamente por esa Parte, ha violado una obligación de las establecidas en este capítulo, siempre y cuando el inversionista o su inversión haya sufrido pérdidas o daños en virtud de la violación o a consecuencia de ésta.

2.   El inversionista no podrá presentar una demanda conforme a esta sección, si han transcurrido más de tres años a partir de la fecha en la cual tuvo conocimiento o debió haber tenido conocimiento de la presunta violación cometida y de las pérdidas o daños sufridos.

3.   Cuando un inversionista presente una demanda en representación de una empresa que sea una persona moral de su propiedad o bajo su control directo o indirecto, y de manera paralela un inversionista que no tenga el control de una empresa presente una demanda por cuenta propia como consecuencia de los mismos actos, o dos o más demandas se sometan a arbitraje en virtud de la misma medida adoptada por una Parte, el tribunal de acumulación establecido de conformidad con el artículo 13-28 examinará conjuntamente esas demandas, salvo que ese tribunal determine que los intereses jurídicos de una parte contendiente se verían perjudicados.

4.   Una inversión no podrá someter una demanda a arbitraje conforme a esta sección.

Artículo 13-20. Solución de controversias mediante consulta y negociación

Las partes contendientes intentarán primero dirimir la controversia por vía de consulta o negociación.

Artículo 13-21. Notificación de la intención de someter la reclamación a arbitraje

El inversionista contendiente notificará por escrito a la Parte contendiente su intención de someter una reclamación a arbitraje, cuando menos 90 días antes de que se presente formalmente la demanda. La notificación señalará lo siguiente:

a)   el nombre y domicilio del inversionista contendiente y, cuando la demanda se haya realizado en representación de una empresa, la denominación o razón social y el domicilio de la misma;

b)   las disposiciones de este capítulo presuntamente incumplidas y cualquier otra disposición aplicable;

c)   los hechos en que se motive la demanda; y

d)   la reparación que se solicite y el monto aproximado de los daños reclamados, en la moneda en que se haya realizado la inversión.

Artículo 13-22. Condiciones previas al sometimiento de una reclamación al procedimiento arbitral

1.   El consentimiento de las partes contendientes al procedimiento de arbitraje conforme a este capítulo se considerará como consentimiento a ese arbitraje con exclusión de cualquier otro mecanismo.

2.   Cada Parte podrá exigir el agotamiento previo de sus recursos administrativos como condición a su consentimiento al arbitraje conforme a este capítulo. Sin embargo, si transcurridos seis meses a partir del momento en que se interpusieron los recursos administrativos correspondientes, las autoridades administrativas no han emitido su resolución final, el inversionista podrá recurrir directamente al arbitraje, de conformidad con lo establecido en esta sección.

3.   Un inversionista contendiente por cuenta propia y un inversionista en representación de una empresa, podrán someter una reclamación al procedimiento arbitral de conformidad con esta sección, sólo si:

a)   en el caso del inversionista por cuenta propia, éste consiente en someterse al arbitraje en los términos de los procedimientos establecidos en esta sección;

b)   en el caso del inversionista en representación de una empresa, tanto el inversionista como la empresa consienten en someterse al arbitraje en los términos de los procedimientos establecidos en esta sección; y

c)   tanto el inversionista como una empresa de otra Parte, renuncian a su derecho de iniciar procedimientos ante cualquier tribunal judicial de cualquier Parte con respecto a la medida presuntamente violatoria de las disposiciones de este capítulo, salvo el desahogo de los recursos administrativos ante las propias autoridades ejecutoras de la medida presuntamente violatoria, previstos en la legislación de la Parte contendiente.

4.   El consentimiento y la renuncia requeridos por este artículo se manifestarán por escrito, se entregarán a la Parte contendiente y se incluirán en el sometimiento de la reclamación a arbitraje.

Artículo 13-23. Sometimiento de la reclamación al arbitraje

1.   Salvo lo dispuesto en el anexo a este artículo y siempre que hayan transcurrido seis meses desde que tuvieron lugar las medidas que motivan la reclamación, un inversionista contendiente podrá someter la demanda a arbitraje de acuerdo con:

a)   el convenio de CIADI, siempre que la Parte contendiente y la Parte del inversionista sean parte del mismo;

b)   las Reglas del Mecanismo Complementario de CIADI, cuando la Parte contendiente o la Parte del inversionista, pero no ambas, sean parte del convenio de CIADI;

c)   las Reglas de Arbitraje de CNUDMI, cuando la Parte contendiente y la Parte del inversionista no sean parte del convenio de CIADI.

2.   Las reglas propias de cada uno de los procedimientos arbitrales establecidos en este capítulo serán aplicables salvo en la medida de lo modificado por esta sección.

Artículo 13-24. Consentimiento al arbitraje

1.   Cada Parte consiente en someter reclamaciones a arbitraje con apego a los procedimientos y requisitos señalados en esta sección.

2.   El sometimiento de una reclamación a arbitraje por parte de un inversionista contendiente implicará haber cumplido con los requisitos señalados en:

a)   el capítulo II del convenio de CIADI y las Reglas del Mecanismo Complementario que exigen el consentimiento por escrito de las Partes;

b)   el artículo II de la Convención de Nueva York, que exige un acuerdo por escrito; y

c)   el artículo I de la Convención Interamericana, que requiere un acuerdo.

Artículo 13-25. Número de árbitros y método de nombramiento

Con excepción de lo dispuesto por el artículo 13-28, y sin perjuicio de que las Partes contendientes acuerden algo distinto, el tribunal estará integrado por tres árbitros. Cada Parte contendiente nombrará a un árbitro; el tercer árbitro, quien será el presidente del tribunal arbitral, será designado por las Partes contendientes de común acuerdo, pero no será nacional de una de las partes contendientes.

Artículo 13-26. Integración del tribunal en caso de que una Parte contendiente no designe árbitro o no se logre un acuerdo en la designación del presidente del tribunal arbitral

1. El Secretario General nombrará a los árbitros en los procedimientos de arbitraje, de conformidad con esta sección.

2. Cuando un tribunal que no sea el establecido de conformidad con el artículo 13-28, no se integre en un plazo de 90 días contado a partir de la fecha en que la reclamación se someta al arbitraje, el Secretario General, a petición de cualquiera de las partes contendientes y, en lo posible, previa consulta a las mismas nombrará al árbitro o árbitros no designados todavía, pero no al presidente del tribunal, quién será designado conforme a lo dispuesto en el párrafo 3. En todo caso, la mayoría de los árbitros no podrán ser nacionales de una de las partes contendientes.

3. El Secretario General designará al presidente del tribunal de entre los árbitros de la lista a la que se refiere el párrafo 4, asegurándose que el presidente del tribunal no sea nacional de la Parte contendiente o nacional de la Parte del inversionista contendiente. En caso de que no se encuentre en la lista un árbitro disponible para presidir el tribunal, el Secretario General designará, del Panel de árbitros de CIADI, al presidente del tribunal, siempre que no sea nacional de la Parte contendiente o de la Parte del inversionista contendiente.

4. A la fecha de entrada en vigor de este Tratado, las Partes establecerán y mantendrán una lista de 15 árbitros como posibles presidentes del tribunal arbitral, que reúnan las cualidades establecidas en el convenio de CIADI, que cuenten con experiencia en derecho internacional y en asuntos en materia de inversión. Los miembros de la lista serán designados por consenso sin importar su nacionalidad por un plazo de dos años, renovables si por consenso las Partes así lo acuerdan. En caso de muerte o renuncia de un miembro de la lista, las Partes de mutuo acuerdo designarán a otra persona que le reemplace en sus funciones para el resto del período para el que aquél fue nombrado.

Artículo 13-27. Consentimiento para la designación de árbitros

Para los propósitos del artículo 39 del convenio de CIADI y del artículo 7 de la parte C de las Reglas del Mecanismo Complementario, y sin perjuicio de objetar a un árbitro con fundamento en el párrafo 3 del artículo 13-26, o sobre base distinta a la nacionalidad:

a) la Parte contendiente acepta la designación de cada uno de los miembros de un tribunal establecido de conformidad con el convenio de CIADI o con las Reglas del Mecanismo Complementario;

b) un inversionista contendiente, sea por cuenta propia o en representación de una empresa, podrá someter una reclamación a arbitraje o continuar el procedimiento conforme al convenio de CIADI o las Reglas del Mecanismo Complementario, únicamente a condición de que el inversionista contendiente y, en su caso, la empresa que representa, manifiesten su consentimiento por escrito sobre la designación de cada uno de los miembros del tribunal.

Artículo 13-28. Acumulación de procedimientos

1.   Un tribunal de acumulación establecido conforme a este artículo se instalará con apego a las Reglas de Arbitraje de CNUDMI y procederá de conformidad con lo contemplado en esas Reglas, salvo lo que disponga esta sección.

2.   Cuando un tribunal de acumulación determine que las reclamaciones sometidas a arbitraje de acuerdo con el artículo 13-22 plantean cuestiones en común de hecho y de derecho, el tribunal de acumulación, en interés de su resolución justa y eficiente, y habiendo escuchado a las partes contendientes, podrá asumir jurisdicción, dar trámite y resolver:

   a)   todas o parte de las reclamaciones, de manera conjunta; o

   b)   una o más de las reclamaciones sobre la base de que ello contribuirá a la resolución de las otras.

3.   Una parte contendiente que pretenda se determine la acumulación en los términos del párrafo 2, solicitará al Secretario General que instale un tribunal de acumulación y especificará en su solicitud:

   a)   el nombre y el domicilio de las partes contendientes contra las cuales se pretenda obtener el acuerdo de acumulación;

   b)   la naturaleza del acuerdo de acumulación solicitado; y

   c)   el fundamento en que se apoya la petición solicitada.

4.   En un plazo de 60 días contado a partir de la fecha de la petición, el Secretario General instalará un tribunal de acumulación integrado por tres árbitros. El Secretario General nombrará de la lista de árbitros a que se refiere el párrafo 4 del artículo 13-26, al presidente del tribunal de acumulación, quien no será nacional de la Parte contendiente o nacional de la Parte del inversionista contendiente. En caso de que no se encuentre en la lista un árbitro disponible para presidir el tribunal de acumulación, el Secretario General designará, del Panel de Arbitros de CIADI, al presidente de ese tribunal, quien no será nacional de la Parte contendiente o nacional de la Parte del inversionista contendiente. El Secretario General designará a los otros dos integrantes del tribunal de acumulación de la lista a que se refiere el párrafo 4 del artículo 13-26 y, cuando no estén disponibles en esa lista, los seleccionará de la lista de árbitros de CIADI. De no haber disponibilidad de árbitros en esa lista, el Secretario General hará discrecionalmente los nombramientos faltantes, siendo uno de los miembros nacional de la Parte contendiente y el otro miembro nacional de una Parte de los inversionistas contendientes.

5.   Cuando se haya establecido un tribunal de acumulación, el inversionista contendiente que haya sometido una reclamación a arbitraje, y no haya sido mencionado en la petición de acumulación hecha de acuerdo con el párrafo 3, podrá solicitar por escrito al tribunal de

acumulación que se le incluya en la petición de acumulación formulada de acuerdo con el párrafo 2, y especificará en esa solicitud:

a) el nombre y domicilio del inversionista contendiente y, en su caso, la denominación o razón social y el domicilio de la empresa;

b) la naturaleza del acuerdo de acumulación solicitado; y

c) los fundamentos en que se apoya la petición solicitada.

6. El tribunal de acumulación proporcionará, a costa del inversionista interesado, copia de la petición de acumulación a los inversionistas contendientes contra quienes se pretende obtener el acuerdo de acumulación.

7. Un tribunal establecido conforme al artículo 13-22 no tendrá jurisdicción para resolver una demanda, o parte de ella, respecto de la cual haya asumido competencia un tribunal de acumulación.

8. A solicitud de una parte contendiente, un tribunal de acumulación podrá disponer, en espera de su decisión conforme al párrafo 2, que los procedimientos de un tribunal establecido de acuerdo al artículo 13-22 se suspendan, hasta en tanto se resuelva sobre la procedencia de la acumulación.

9. Una Parte contendiente entregará al Secretariado, en un plazo de 15 días contado a partir de la fecha en que se reciba por la Parte contendiente:

a) una solicitud de arbitraje hecha conforme al párrafo 1 del artículo 36 del convenio de CIADI;

b) una notificación de arbitraje en los términos del artículo 2 de la parte C de las Reglas del Mecanismo Complementario de CIADI; o

c) una notificación de arbitraje en los términos previstos por las Reglas de Arbitraje de CNUDMI.

10. Una Parte contendiente entregará al Secretariado copia de la solicitud formulada en los términos del párrafo 3:

a) en un plazo de 15 días contado a partir de la recepción de la solicitud, en el caso de una petición hecha por el inversionista contendiente; o

b) en un plazo de 15 días contado a partir de la fecha de la solicitud, en el caso de una petición hecha por la Parte contendiente.

11. Una Parte contendiente entregará al Secretariado copia de una solicitud formulada en los términos del párrafo 6 en un plazo de 15 días contado a partir de la fecha de recepción de la solicitud.

12. El Secretariado conservará un registro público de los documentos a los que se refieren los párrafos del 9 al 11.

Artículo 13-29. Notificación

La Parte contendiente entregará a otra Parte no contendiente:

a)   notificación escrita de una reclamación que se haya sometido a arbitraje a más tardar 30 días después de la fecha de sometimiento de la reclamación a arbitraje; y

b)   copia de todas las comunicaciones presentadas en el procedimiento arbitral.

Artículo 13-30. Participación de una Parte

Una Parte podrá presentar comunicaciones a cualquier tribunal establecido conforme a esta sección sobre una cuestión de interpretación de este Tratado, notificando al mismo tiempo y por escrito el contenido de esa comunicación a las partes contendientes.

Artículo 13-31. Documentación

1.   Una Parte tendrá, cubriendo los gastos que en su caso se generen, derecho a recibir de la Parte contendiente una copia de:

a)   las pruebas ofrecidas a cualquier tribunal establecido conforme a esta sección; y

b)   las comunicaciones escritas presentadas por las partes contendientes.

2.   Una Parte que reciba información conforme a lo dispuesto en el párrafo 1, dará tratamiento confidencial a la información como si fuera una Parte contendiente.

Artículo 13-32. Sede del procedimiento arbitral

La sede del procedimiento arbitral estará ubicada en el territorio de la Parte contendiente, salvo que las partes contendientes acuerden algo distinto, en cuyo caso cualquier tribunal establecido conforme a esta sección llevará a cabo el procedimiento arbitral en el territorio de una Parte que sea parte de la Convención de Nueva York, el cual será elegido de conformidad con:

a)   las Reglas del Mecanismo Complementario de CIADI, si el arbitraje se rige por esas reglas o por el convenio de CIADI; o

b)   las Reglas de Arbitraje de CNUDMI, si el arbitraje se rige por esas reglas.

Artículo 13-33. Derecho aplicable

1.   Cualquier tribunal establecido conforme a esta sección decidirá las controversias que se sometan a su consideración de conformidad con este Tratado, las reglas aplicables del derecho internacional y, supletoriamente, la legislación de la Parte contendiente.

2   La interpretación que formule la Comisión sobre una disposición de este Tratado, será obligatoria para cualquier tribunal establecido de conformidad con esta sección.

Artículo 13-34. Interpretación de los anexos

1.   Cuando una Parte alegue como defensa que una medida presuntamente violatoria cae en el ámbito de una reserva o excepción consignada en cualquiera de los anexos, a petición de la Parte contendiente, cualquier tribunal establecido de conformidad con esta sección solicitará a la Comisión una interpretación sobre ese asunto. La Comisión, en un plazo de 60 días contado a partir de la entrega de la solicitud, presentará por escrito a ese tribunal su interpretación.

2.   La interpretación de la Comisión a que se refiere el párrafo 1, será obligatoria para cualquier tribunal establecido de conformidad con esta sección. Si la Comisión no somete una interpretación dentro de un plazo de 60 días, ese tribunal decidirá sobre el asunto.

Artículo 13-35. Medidas provisionales o precautorias

Un tribunal establecido conforme a esta sección podrá solicitar a los tribunales nacionales, o dictar a las partes contendientes, medidas provisionales de protección para preservar los derechos de la parte contendiente o para asegurar que la competencia o jurisdicción del tribunal surta plenos efectos. Ese tribunal no podrá ordenar el acatamiento a o la suspensión de la aplicación de la medida presuntamente violatoria a la que se refiere el artículo 13-19.

Artículo 13-36. Laudo definitivo

1.   Cuando un tribunal establecido conforme a esta sección dicte un laudo desfavorable a una Parte, ese tribunal sólo podrá otorgar:

   a)   daños pecuniarios y los intereses correspondientes; o

   b)   la restitución de la propiedad, en cuyo caso el laudo dispondrá que la Parte contendiente pueda pagar daños pecuniarios, más los intereses que procedan, en lugar de la restitución.

2.   Cuando la reclamación la haga un inversionista en representación de una empresa con base en el artículo 13-19:

   a)   el laudo que prevea la restitución de la propiedad dispondrá que la restitución se otorgue a la empresa;

   b)   el laudo que conceda daños pecuniarios e intereses correspondientes dispondrá que la suma de dinero se pague a la empresa.

3.   Para efectos de los párrafos 1 y 2 los daños se determinarán en la moneda en que se haya realizado la inversión.

4.   El laudo se dictará sin perjuicio de los derechos que un tercero con interés jurídico tenga sobre la reparación de los daños que haya sufrido, conforme a la legislación aplicable.

Artículo 13-37. Ejecución del laudo

1.   El laudo dictado por cualquier tribunal establecido conforme a esta sección será obligatorio sólo para las partes contendientes y únicamente respecto del caso concreto.

2.   Conforme a lo dispuesto en el párrafo 3 y sin perjuicio de que los procedimientos de aclaración, revisión o anulación del laudo previstos bajo el mecanismo aplicable sean procedentes a juicio del Secretario General, una parte contendiente acatará y cumplirá con el laudo sin demora.

3.   Una parte contendiente podrá solicitar la ejecución de un laudo definitivo siempre que:

   a)   en el caso de un laudo definitivo dictado conforme al convenio de CIADI:

      i)   hayan transcurrido 120 días desde la fecha en que se dictó el laudo sin que una parte contendiente haya solicitado la aclaración, revisión o anulación del mismo; o

      ii)   hayan concluido los procedimientos de aclaración, revisión o anulación referidos en el numeral i); y

   b)   en el caso de un laudo definitivo conforme a las Reglas del Mecanismo Complementario de CIADI o las Reglas de Arbitraje de CNUDMI:

      i)   hayan transcurrido tres meses desde la fecha en que se dictó el laudo sin que una parte contendiente haya iniciado un procedimiento para revisarlo o anularlo; o

      ii)   un tribunal de la Parte contendiente haya denegado (desechado) o admitido una solicitud de reconsideración o anulación del laudo que una de las partes contendientes haya presentado a los tribunales nacionales conforme a su legislación y esta resolución no pueda recurrirse.

4.   Cada Parte dispondrá la debida ejecución de un laudo en su territorio. El laudo se ejecutará de acuerdo con las normas que sobre ejecución de sentencias o laudos estuvieren en vigor en los territorios en que esa ejecución se pretenda.

5.   Cuando una Parte contendiente incumpla un laudo, la Comisión, a la recepción de una solicitud de una Parte cuyo inversionista fue parte en el procedimiento de arbitraje, integrará un panel conforme al capítulo XVII (Solución de controversias). La Parte solicitante podrá invocar esos procedimientos para obtener:

   a)   una determinación en el sentido de que el incumplimiento de los términos del laudo es contrario a las obligaciones de este Tratado; y

   b)   una recomendación en el sentido de que la Parte se ajuste y observe el laudo en cuestión.

6.   El inversionista contendiente podrá recurrir a la ejecución de un laudo arbitral conforme al convenio de CIADI, la Convención de Nueva York o la Convención Interamericana, independientemente de que se hayan iniciado o no los procedimientos contemplados en el párrafo 5.

7.   Para efectos del artículo I de la Convención de Nueva York y del artículo I de la Convención Interamericana, se considerará que la reclamación que se somete a arbitraje conforme a esta sección, surge de una relación u operación comercial.

Artículo 13-38. Disposiciones generales

1.   Momento en que la reclamación se considera sometida al procedimiento arbitral.

Una reclamación se considera sometida a arbitraje en los términos de esta sección cuando:

   a)   la solicitud para un arbitraje conforme al artículo 36 de CIADI ha sido recibida por el Secretario General;

   b)   la notificación de arbitraje, de conformidad con la parte C de las Reglas del Mecanismo Complementario de CIADI, ha sido recibida por el Secretario General; o

   c)   la notificación de arbitraje contemplada en las Reglas de Arbitraje de CNUDMI, ha sido recibida por la Parte contendiente.

2.   Entrega de documentos.

La entrega de la notificación y otros documentos a una Parte, se hará en el lugar que ésta designe a más tardar a la fecha de entrada en vigor de este Tratado.

3.   Pagos conforme a Contratos de Seguro o Garantía.

En un procedimiento arbitral conforme a lo previsto en esta sección, una Parte no aducirá como defensa, contrademanda, derecho de compensación, u otros, que el inversionista contendiente recibió o recibirá, de acuerdo a un contrato de seguro o garantía, indemnización u otra compensación por todos o parte de los presuntos daños cuya restitución solicita.

4.   Publicación de laudos.

Los laudos se publicarán únicamente en el caso de que exista acuerdo por escrito entre las partes contendientes.

Artículo 13-39. Exclusiones

Las disposiciones de solución de controversias de esta sección y las del capítulo XVII (Solución de controversias) no se aplicarán a los supuestos contenidos en el anexo a este artículo.

Anexo al artículo 13-19

Demanda del inversionista de una Parte, por cuenta propia o en representación de una empresa

1.   Sin perjuicio de lo dispuesto en el artículo 13-28, para el caso de que un inversionista haya instaurado un proceso por cuenta propia y, paralelamente, otro inversionista de la misma

inversión haya instaurado un proceso en representación de esa inversión por la misma causa, el primero de esos procesos se acumulará a este último.

2.	Para el caso en que un inversionista haya instaurado un proceso por cuenta propia ante un tribunal arbitral y, paralelamente, otro inversionista de la misma inversión haya instaurado por cuenta propia un proceso ante un tribunal nacional, procederá la atracción por parte de este último.

Anexo al artículo 13-23

Sometimiento de la reclamación al arbitraje

Cuando una empresa de una Parte que sea una persona jurídica propiedad de un inversionista de otra Parte o que éste bajo su control directo o indirecto, alegue en procedimientos ante un tribunal judicial o administrativo, que otra Parte ha violado presuntamente una obligación a las que se refiere la sección A de este capítulo, el o los inversionistas no podrán alegar la presunta violación en un procedimiento arbitral conforme a la sección B de este capítulo.

Anexo al artículo 13-39

Exclusiones

No estarán sujetas a los mecanismos de solución de controversias previstos en la sección B de este capítulo o del capítulo XVII (Solución de controversias), las resoluciones que adopte una Parte en virtud del párrafo 2 del artículo 13-02, ni la resolución que prohiba o restrinja la adquisición de una inversión en su territorio que sea propiedad o esté controlada por nacionales de esa Parte, por parte de un inversionista de otra Parte, de conformidad con la legislación de cada Parte.

*	*	*

TREATY ON FREE TRADE BETWEEN THE REPUBLIC OF COLOMBIA, THE REPUBLIC OF VENEZUELA AND THE UNITED MEXICAN STATES*
[excerpts]

The Treaty on Free Trade between Colombia, Venezuela and Mexico, also called "the Group of Three Economic Treaty", was signed on 13 June 1994. It entered into force on 1 January 1995.

CHAPTER XVII. Investment

Section A - Investment

Article 17-01. Definitions

For the purposes of this Chapter, the following definitions shall apply:

Enterprise: any entity constituted, organized, or protected according to applicable law, whether or not for profit and whether it is privately or governmentally owned. The term includes corporations, foundations, companies, branches, trusts, partnerships, sole proprietorships, joint ventures, or other associations.

Investment: resources transferred to the national territory of one Party or reinvested therein by investors of the other Party, including:

(a)   any type of asset or right the purpose of which is to produce economic benefits;

(b)   equity interest, in any proportion, by the investors of one Party in companies constituted or organized under the laws of another Party;

(c)   enterprises owned or effectively controlled by a investor of that Party that have been constituted or organized in the territory of the other Party; and

(d)   any other resources considered an investment under the laws of that Party.

Investment shall not include credit or debt transactions, such as:

(a)   a debt security of the State or a State enterprise, or a loan to the State or to a State enterprise;

(b)   claims to money that arise solely from:

---

* *Source*: The Government of Colombia, the Government of Mexico and the Government of Venezuela (1995). "Treaty on Free Trade Between the Republic of Colombia, the Republic of Venezuela and the United Mexican States"; available on the Internet (http://www.sice.oas.org/Trade/G3_E/G3E_TOC.stm). [Note added by the editor.]

    i.   commercial contracts for the sale of goods or services by a national or enterprise in the territory of a Party to an enterprise in the territory of another Party; or

    ii.   the extension of credit in connection with a commercial transaction, such as trade financing.

Investor of a Party: any of the following persons owing an investment in the territory of the other Party:

(a)   the Party itself or any of its public entities or State enterprises;

(b)   a natural person who is a national of that Party in accordance with its laws;

(c)   an enterprise constituted, organized, or protected in accordance with the laws of that Party;

(d)   a branch located in the territory of that Party that engages in commercial activities therein.

Article 17-02. Scope

1.   This Chapter applies to measures adopted or maintained by a Party relating to:

(a)   investments of investors of another Party in the territory of the Party;

(b)   investors of another Party in all matters relating to their investment; and

(c)   with respect to Article 17-04, all investments in the territory of the Party.

2.   This Chapter does not apply to measures adopted or maintained by the Parties with respect to financial services under Chapter XII, except as expressly provided therein.

3.   This Chapter applies throughout the territory of the Parties, at any level or for any type of government.

4.   Nothing in this Chapter shall be construed to prevent a Party from adopting or maintaining measures for preserving its national security or public order, or implementing the Provisions of its criminal laws.

Article 17-03. National and Most-Favored Nation Treatment

1.   Each Party shall accord to investors of another Party, and to their investments, treatment no less favorable than that it accords, in like circumstances, to its own investors and investments.

2.   Each Party shall grant investors of another Party, and to their investments, treatment no less favorable than that it accords, in like circumstances, to investors, and their investments, of another Party or of a non-Party. Most-favored-nation treatment shall not apply with respect to the provisions of Article 17-01.

3.   The provisions of paragraphs 1 and 2 shall extend to any measure adopted or maintained by a Party in relation to losses owing to armed conflict, civil strife, disturbances of the public order, acts of God or force majeure.

4.   No Party shall be required to accord the investors or investments of another Party the advantages it has accorded or may accord to investors or investments of another Party or of a non-Party, by virtue of a treaty for the avoidance of double taxation.

Article 17-04. Performance Requirements

1.   No Party shall impose performance requirements by adopting investment-related measures that are mandatory or required for the establishment or operation of an investment, or for which compliance is necessary in order to obtain or maintain an advantage or incentive, or which prohibit:

(a)   the purchase or use by an enterprise of goods of national origin of that Party, or from its national sources, whether specified in terms of specific goods, in terms of volume or value of the goods, or as a proportion of the volume or value of its local production;

(b)   the purchase or use of imported goods by an enterprise from being limited to an amount related to the volume or value of the local goods exported by the enterprise;

(c)   restrictions on imports of goods used by an enterprise in its local production or related thereto, limiting access by the enterprise to foreign exchange to an amount related to the entry of foreign exchange imputable to said enterprise;

(d)   restrictions on the exportation or the sale for exportation of goods by an enterprise, whether specified in terms of the volume or value of the goods, or as a proportion of the volume or value of its local production.

2.   The provisions of:

(a)   Paragraph 1(a) and (d) shall not apply with respect to requirements for the qualification of goods for export promotion programs;

(b)   Paragraph 1(a) shall not apply with respect to purchase or use by a Party or by a State enterprise;

(c)   Paragraph 1(a) shall not apply with respect to the requirements imposed by an importing Party with respect to the content required for goods in order to quality for preferential tariffs or duties.

3.   Nothing in the provisions of this article shall be construed as preventing a Party from imposing, with regard to any investment in its territory, requirements to locate production, generate jobs, train workers, or carry out research and development.

4.   If, in the judgment of a Party, another Party imposes a requirement not stipulated in paragraph 1 that adversely affects the flow of trade or that constitutes a significant barrier to investment, the matter shall be considered by the Commission.

5.   If the Commission finds that the requirement in question adversely affects the flow of trade or   constitutes a significant barrier to investment, it shall recommend to the Party in question that it suspend the requirement.

Article 17-05. Employment and Enterprise Management

Limits on the number or proportion of foreigners that may work in an enterprise or perform managerial or administrative duties under the laws of each Party may in no case prevent or hinder an investor from exercising control over its investment.

Article 17-06. Reservations

1.   Within eight months of the signature of the Treaty, the Parties shall establish a Protocol containing four lists of the sectors and subsectors for which each Party may maintain measures not conforming with Articles 17-03, 17-04, and 17-05, based on the following criteria:

> (a)   with respect to the measures contained in list 1, no Party shall increase the level of non-conformity with those articles as of the date of signature of this Treaty. No amendment to any of those measures shall decrease the level of conformity of the measure, as it existed immediately before the amendment;

> (b)   with respect to the measures contained in list 2, each Party may adopt or maintain new non-conforming measures or make such measures more restrictive;

> (c)   list 3 shall contain the list of economic activities reserved for the State;

> (d)   list 4 shall contain exceptions to Article 17-4, paragraph 2, with regard to the bilateral or multilateral international treaties concluded or to be concluded by the Parties.

2.   In the negotiations to which list 2 in paragraph 1 refers, the Parties shall endeavor to reach agreements on the basis of reciprocity with a view to obtaining a comprehensive balance in the concessions granted.

Article 17-07. Transfers

1.   Each Party shall permit all transfers relating to an investment of an investor of another Party in the territory of the Party to be made freely and without delay.

Such transfers include:

> (a)   profits, dividends, interest, capital gains, royalty payments, management fees, technical assistance, returns in kind, and other amounts derived from the investment;

(c)   proceeds from the sale or liquidation of the investment, in whole or in part;

(c)   payments made under a contract entered into by an investor or its investment;

(d)   payments derived from compensation for expropriation; and

(e)   payments derived from implementation of the provisions relating to the system for settling disputes.

2.   Each Party shall permit transfers to be made in a freely convertible currency at the market rate of exchange prevailing on the date of transfer with respect to spot transactions in the currency to be transferred, without prejudice to the provisions of paragraph 6.

3.   Notwithstanding paragraphs 1 and 2, each Party may, to the extent and for such time as may be necessary, prevent transfers through the equitable and non-discriminatory application of its laws with respect to:

(a)   bankruptcy, insolvency, or the protection of the rights of creditors;

(b)   issuing, trading, and dealing in securities;

(c)   criminal or administrative offenses; or

(d)   ensuring the satisfaction of judgments in adjudicatory proceedings;

4.   Moreover, each Party may, through the equitable and non-discriminatory application of its laws, request information and impose requirements concerning reports of transfers of currency or other monetary instruments.

5.   Each Party may maintain laws and regulations that impose income and additional taxes by such means as the withholding of taxes on dividends and other transfers, provided such measures are not discriminatory.

6.   The provisions of this article notwithstanding, each Party shall be entitled, under circumstances of exceptional or serious balance-of-payments difficulties, to limit transfers temporarily in an equitable and non-discriminatory manner, in accordance with internationally accepted criteria.

Article 17-08. Expropriation and Compensation

1.   No Party, except as provided in the Annex to this Article, shall directly or indirectly expropriate or nationalize an investment of an investor of another Party in its territory, or take any measure tantamount to expropriation or nationalization of such an investment ("expropriation"), except:

(a)   for a public purpose;

(b)   on a non-discriminatory basis;

(c)   in accordance with due process of law; and

(d)   on payment of compensation in accordance with paragraphs 2 through 4.

2.   Compensation shall be equivalent to the fair market value of the investment at the time of expropriation, and shall not reflect any change in value owing to the fact that the intent to expropriate became known prior to the date of expropriation. Valuation criteria shall include declared tax value of tangible property and other criteria, as appropriate, to determine fair market value.

3.   Compensation shall be fully realizable and freely transferable under the terms of Article 17-07.

4.   Payment shall be made without delay. The time elapsing between the time the compensation is determined and the time payment is made shall not adversely affect the investor. As a result, the amount of compensation shall be sufficient to ensure that should the investor decide to transfer his payment, he can obtain, at the time of payment, an equal amount of the international currency normally used as a reference by the Party making the expropriation. Payment shall also include interest at the current market rate for the reference currency.

Article 17-09. Special Formalities and Information Requirements

1.   Nothing in Article 17-03 shall be construed to prevent a Party from adopting or maintaining a measure that prescribes special formalities in connection with the establishment of investments by investors of another Party, such as a requirement that investments be constituted under the laws and regulations of the Party, provided that such formalities do not materially impair the protections afforded by a Party in accordance with the provisions of this Chapter.

2.   Notwithstanding Articles 17-03 and 17-04, each Party may require an investor of another Party or its investment in its territory to provide information concerning that investment in accordance with the laws of that Party. Each Party shall protect information that is confidential from any disclosure that might prejudice the competitive position of the investment or the investor.

Article 17-10. Relation to Other Chapters

In the event of any inconsistency between any provision of this Chapter and any other provision of this Treaty, the latter shall prevail to the extent of the inconsistency.

Article 17-11. Denial of Benefits

Subject to prior notification and consultation with the other Party, a Party may deny the benefits of this Chapter to an investor of another Party that is an enterprise of such Party and to the investments of such investor, if investors of a non-Party are majority shareholders in or control the enterprise, and the enterprise has no substantial business activities in the territory of the Party under whose law it is constituted or organized.

Article 17-12. Extraterritorial Application of the Laws of a Party

No Party may, with respect to the investments of its investors constituted and organized according to the laws and regulations of another Party, exercise jurisdiction or adopt any measure which results in the extraterritorial application of its laws or constitutes a hindrance to trade between the Parties or between a Party and a non-Party.

Article 17-13. Environmental Measures

No Party shall eliminate domestic health, safety, or environmental measures, or shall undertake to waive the application thereof, as an encouragement for the establishment, acquisition, expansion, or retention in its territory, of an investment of an investor. If a Party considers that another Party has encouraged an investment in this way, it may request consultations with that other Party.

Article 17-14. Promotion of Investment and Exchange of Information

1.   With a view to increasing reciprocal investments, the Parties shall design and implement mechanisms for the dissemination, promotion, and exchange of information relating to investment opportunities.

2.   The Parties undertake to establish mechanisms relating to the exchange of financial and tax information.

Article 17-15. Double Taxation

The Parties agree to initiate, between themselves, bilateral negotiations for the conclusion of agreements on the avoidance of double taxation, within a time frame to be established by their respective appropriate authorities.

Section B - Settlement of Disputes Between a Party and an Investor of Another Party

Article 17-16. Purpose and Scope

1.   The purpose of this Section and the Annex to this Chapter is to ensure equal treatment of the investors of each Party on the basis of reciprocity and observance of the rules and principles of international law, and that the guarantees of a hearing and defense can be duly exercised on the basis of due process before an impartial tribunal.

2.   The mechanism established in this Section shall apply to the investment claims made by an investor of a Party (disputing investor) against a Party (disputing Party) with respect to the breach of an obligation set forth in this Chapter, from the date of entry into force of this Treaty, without prejudice to the fact that the disputing investor and the disputing Party (disputing parties) intend to settle the dispute through consultation or negotiation.

Article 17-17. Conditions for Submission of a Claim

1.   An investor of a Party may, on his own account or on behalf of an enterprise that it owns or effectively controls, submit to arbitration a claim that the other Party has breached an obligation under this Chapter, provided the investor has incurred loss or damage by reason of, or arising out of, such breach.

2.   An enterprise that is an investment may not submit a claim to arbitration under this Section.

3.   An investor may not make a claim under this Section if more than three years have elapsed from the date on which it acquired, or should have acquired, knowledge of the alleged breach and of the loss or damage incurred.

4.   An investor that initiates proceedings before any judicial tribunal with respect to the alleged breach of the provisions of this Chapter may not make a claim under this Section, nor may it make a claim under this Section on behalf of an enterprise it owns or controls that has initiated a procedure before any judicial tribunal with respect to the same breach. This provision shall not apply to the exercise of administrative appeals, provided under the laws of the disputing Party, before the same authorities that implemented the measure allegedly in breach of said provisions.

5.   An investor that makes a claim under this Section or an enterprise on whose behalf the claim is made may not initiate proceedings before any judicial tribunal with respect to the alleged breach.

Article 17-18. Communication and Submission of the Claim to Arbitration

1.   A disputing investor that intends to submit a claim to arbitration under the terms of this Section shall communicate that fact to the disputing Party.

2.   Provided that 90 days have elapsed since the communication referred to in the above paragraph and six months from the measures giving rise to the claim, a disputing investor may submit the claim to arbitration under:

(a)   the rules of the International Convention on the Settlement of Investment Disputes between States and Nationals of Other States (ICSID Convention), signed at Washington on March 18, 1965, provided the disputing Party and the Party of the investor are parties to the Convention;

(b)   the Additional Facility Rules of the ICSID, provided that either the disputing Party or the Party of the investor, but not both, is a party to the ICSID Convention; or

(c)   the Arbitration Rules of the United Nations Commission on International Trade Law (UNCITRAL Arbitration Rules), approved by the United Nations General Assembly on December 15, 1976, provided the disputing Party and the Party of the investor are not parties to the ICSID Convention, or the latter cannot be availed of.

3.   The rules of each of the arbitral procedures mentioned in the above paragraph shall be applicable except to the extent provided by this Section.

4.   Each Party shall consent to submit claims to arbitration in accordance with the provisions of this Section.

Article 17-19. Consolidation of Procedures

1.   If any of the disputing parties requests that the procedures be consolidated, a consolidation tribunal shall be established on the basis of the UNCITRAL Arbitration Rules and shall function in accordance with the provisions thereof, except as provided in this Section.

2.   The procedures shall be consolidated in the following cases:

(a)   when an investor submits a claim on behalf of an enterprise that is under its effective control and at the same time another investor or other investors that are shareholders in the same enterprise but do not control it submit claims on their own behalf as a result of the same breaches; or

(b)   when two or more claims are submitted which, with respect to the same breach by a Party, have questions of law and of fact in common.

3.   The consolidation tribunal shall review the claims together, except when it has determined that the interests of one of the disputing parties would be harmed.

Article 17-20. Applicable Law

1.   Any tribunal constituted under this Section shall decide the disputes submitted for its review in accordance with this Treaty and with the applicable rules of international law.

2.   An interpretation by the Commission of a provision of this Treaty shall be binding on any tribunal constituted under this Section.

Article 17-21. Final Award

1.   When a tribunal established under this Section makes an award against a Party, the tribunal may award only:

(a)   monetary damages and any applicable interest; or

(b)   restitution of property, in which case the award shall provide that the disputing Party may pay monetary damages and any applicable interest in lieu of restitution, said amount being indicated.

2.   When the claim is made by an investor on behalf of an enterprise:

(a)   an award of restitution of property shall provide that the restitution or, as appropriate, the compensation in lieu thereof, shall be made to the enterprise;

(b)   an award of monetary damages and any applicable interest shall provide that the money be paid to the enterprise.

3.   The award shall be made without prejudice to the rights that any person with a legal interest may have to compensation under applicable law.

Article 17-22. Payments Under Insurance or Guarantee Contracts

The disputing Party shall not allege as a defense, counterclaim, right of set off or otherwise, that the disputing investor has received or will receive, under an insurance or guarantee contract, indemnification or other compensation for all or part of the damages whose restitution it is seeking.

Article 17-23. Finality and Enforcement of an Award

1.   An award made by a tribunal constituted under this Section shall be binding only for the disputing parties and solely in respect of the particular case.

2.   The disputing Party shall abide by and comply with the award without delay and shall ensure that it is duly implemented.

3.   If a Party whose investor was a party to the arbitration proceeding considers that the disputing Party has failed to comply with or to abide by the final award, it may avail itself of the dispute-settlement procedure established in Chapter XIX to obtain, where appropriate, a decision by which the disputing Party will observe the final award and comply therewith.

4.   A disputing investor may seek enforcement of an arbitration award under the ICSID Convention, the United Nations Convention on the Recognition and Enforcement of Foreign Arbitral Awards, done at New York on June 10, 1958 (the New York Convention), or the Inter-American Convention on International Commercial Arbitration, done at Panama City on January 30, 1975 (the Inter-American Convention), regardless of whether proceedings have been taken under paragraph 3.

Article 17-24. Exclusions

Such measures as a Party adopts pursuant to Article 17-02, paragraph 4, or a decision to prohibit or restrict the acquisition of an investment in its territory by an investor of another Party, shall not be subject to the dispute-settlement mechanism provided in this Section.

Annex to Article 17-08

1.   Colombia reserves in full its right to apply Article 17-08 of this Chapter. Colombia shall not establish measures with respect to nationalization, expropriation, and compensation that are more restrictive than those in effect at the time this Treaty enters into force.

2.   Mexico and Venezuela shall apply said article with respect to Colombia only as of the time Colombia has informed them that it has withdrawn its reservation.

Annex to Article 17-16

Rules of Procedure

Rule 1. Notice of Intent to Submit a Claim to Arbitration

In notifying the disputing Party of its intent to submit a claim to arbitration, the disputing investor shall specify the following:

(a) the name, corporate name, and address of the disputing investor, and the name or firm name and address of the enterprise when the claim is made in its behalf, with evidence of its ownership or effective control thereof;

(b) the provisions alleged to have been breached and any other relevant provisions;

(c) the factual basis for the claim; and

(d) the relief sought and the approximate amount of damages claimed.

Rule 2. Conditions Precedent to Submission of a Claim to Arbitration

1. A disputing investor may submit a claim to arbitration on his own behalf, and a investor representing an enterprise may submit a claim to arbitration in accordance with Section B of this Chapter and this Annex only if:

(a) an investor acting on his own behalf consents to arbitration under the terms of the procedures set out in Section B of this Chapter and this Annex;

(b) in cases concerning an investor representing an enterprise, both the investor and the enterprise consent to arbitration under the terms of the procedures set out in Section B of this Chapter and this Annex; and

(c) the investor or the enterprise, or both, as appropriate, undertake in writing not to initiate proceedings before any judicial tribunal with respect to the alleged breach of this Chapter, except with respect to administrative appeals before the same authorities that adopted the measure alleged to be a breach, under the law of the disputing Party.

2. The consent required by this Rule shall be expressed in writing, shall be delivered to the disputing Party, and shall be included in the submission of the claim to arbitration.

3. The consent of the investor to submit the claim to arbitration shall be considered sufficient to satisfy the requirements of:

(a) Chapter II of the ICSID Convention and the Additional Facility Rules for written consent of the parties;

(b) Article II of the New York Convention for an agreement in writing; and

(c) Article I of the Inter-American Convention for an agreement.

Rule 3. Number of Arbitrators and Method of Appointment

Except in respect of a consolidation tribunal under Article 17-19 of this Chapter and unless the disputing parties agree otherwise, the tribunal shall comprise three arbitrators. Each of the disputing parties shall appoint an arbitrator. The third arbitrator, who shall be the presiding arbitrator, shall be appointed by agreement of the disputing parties.

Rule 4. Constitution of a Tribunal When a Party Fails to Appoint an Arbitrator or the Disputing Parties Are Unable to Agree on a Presiding Arbitrator

1.   The Secretary-General of the ICSID shall appoint the arbitrators in the arbitration proceedings in accordance with the provisions of this Annex.

2.   If a tribunal, other than a consolidation tribunal, has not been constituted within 90 days of the date that a claim is submitted to arbitration, the Secretary-General, on the request of either disputing party, shall appoint, at his discretion, the arbitrator or arbitrators not yet appointed, except that the presiding arbitrator shall be appointed in accordance with paragraph 3 of this Rule.

3.   The Secretary-General shall appoint the presiding arbitrator of the tribunal from the roster of arbitrators referred to in paragraph 4, and shall ensure that the presiding arbitrator is not a national of the disputing Party or a national of the Party of the disputing investor. In the event there is no one on the roster available to serve as presiding arbitrator, the Secretary-General shall appoint, from the ICSID Panel of Arbitrators, a presiding arbitrator who is not a national of the disputing Party or of the Party of the disputing investor.

4.   Beginning on the date of entry into force of this Agreement, the Parties shall establish and maintain a roster of 15 possible presiding arbitrators of the arbitral tribunal, meeting the qualifications of the ICSID Convention. The roster members shall be appointed by consensus and without regard to nationality.

Rule 5. Agreement to the Appointment of Arbitrators

For purposes of Article 39 of the ICSID Convention and Article 7 of Schedule C of the Additional Facility Rules, and without prejudice to the objection of an arbitrator on a ground other than nationality:

(a)   the disputing Party agrees to the appointment of each individual member of a tribunal established under the ICSID Convention or the Additional Facility Rules;

(b)   a disputing investor may, either on his own behalf or on behalf of an enterprise, submit a claim to arbitration or continue a claim under the ICSID Convention or the Additional Facility Rules, only on condition that the disputing investor and, where appropriate, the enterprise it represents, agree in writing to the appointment of each individual member of the tribunal.

Rule 6. **Consolidation of Proceedings**

1.   When a consolidation tribunal determines that claims submitted to arbitration under Article 17-17 of this Chapter have questions or law or fact in common, the consolidation tribunal may, in the interests of fair and expeditious resolution of the claims, and after hearing the disputing parties, agree to:

    (a)   assume jurisdiction over, and hear and determine together, some or all of the claims; or

    (b)   assume jurisdiction over, and hear and determine one or more of the claims, the determination of which would assist in the resolution of the others.

2.   A disputing party that seeks a consolidation of claims under the terms of paragraph 1, shall request the ICSID Secretary-General to establish a consolidation tribunal and shall specify in its request:

    (a)   the name of the disputing Party or disputing investors with regard to which the order for consolidation is sought;

    (b)   the nature of the consolidation order sought; and

    (c)   the grounds on which the request is made.

3.   Within 60 days of the date of the request, the ICSID Secretary-General shall appoint from the roster to which Rule 5, paragraph 4 of this Annex refers, three members of the consolidation tribunal and shall designate the presiding arbitrator. In the event that the roster contains no one who can be appointed, the Secretary-General shall make the appointments from the ICSID Panel of Arbitrators, and to the extent not available from that Panel, the Secretary-General shall make the remaining appointments at his discretion. One member of the tribunal shall be a national of the disputing Party and the other shall be a national of the Party of the disputing investors. In no case shall the presiding arbitrator of the consolidation tribunal be a national of the Party or Parties of the disputing investor or investors.

4.   When a consolidation tribunal has been constituted, a disputing investor that submitted a claim to arbitration and has not been mentioned in the consolidation request made under paragraph 2, may request in writing from the tribunal that it be included in the request for consolidation established in accordance with paragraph 1, and shall specify in that request:

    (a)   the name and address of the disputing investor and, where appropriate, the name or corporate name and domicile of the enterprise;

    (b)   the type of consolidation order sought; and

    (c)   the grounds on which the request is made.

The consolidation tribunal shall provide, at the cost of the interested investor, a copy of the consolidation request to the disputing investors against which the consolidation order is sought.

5.   Once the consolidation tribunal has assumed jurisdiction over a claim, the jurisdiction of the tribunal constituted to hear the claim shall cease. At the request of a disputing party, the consolidation tribunal may, pending its decision on its jurisdiction with respect to a claim, instruct the arbitral tribunal constituted to settle the claim to stay the proceedings.

6.   Within 15 days of the date of receipt, the disputing Party shall transmit to the Commission a copy of:

   (a)   the request for arbitration made under paragraph (1) of Article 36 of the ICSID Convention;

   (b)   a notice of arbitration made under Article 2 of Schedule C of the ICSID Additional Facility Rules;

   (c)   a notice of arbitration made under the terms of the UNCITRAL Arbitration Rules;

   (d)   a request for consolidation made by a disputing investor;

   (e)   a request for consolidation made by a disputing Party; or

   (f)   a request for inclusion in a consolidation request made by a disputing investor.

The Commission shall maintain a register of the documents referred to in this paragraph.

Rule 7. Notice

The disputing Party shall deliver to the other Parties:

   (a)   notice of a claim that has been submitted to arbitration within 30 days of the date of submission of the claim; and

   (b)   if requested, and at their cost, copies of all submissions made in the arbitral proceeding.

Rule 8. Participation by a Party

Upon notice to the disputing parties, a Party may transmit to any tribunal constituted under Section B of this Chapter its opinion regarding a question of interpretation of this Treaty.

Rule 9. Documents

1.   Each Party shall be entitled to receive from the disputing Party, at the request and cost of the requesting Party, a copy of:

   (a)   the evidence that has been tendered to any tribunal constituted under Section B of this Chapter; and

   (b)   the written submissions of the disputing parties.

2.   A Party receiving information pursuant to paragraph 1 shall treat the information as confidential.

Rule 10. Place of Arbitration

Except as otherwise agreed by the disputing parties, any tribunal constituted under Section B of this Chapter shall conduct the arbitral proceeding in the territory of one of the Parties.

Rule 11. Interpretation of Annexes With Respect to Reservations and Exceptions

1.   The interpretation of the Commission with respect to any provision of this Treaty shall be binding for any tribunal constituted under Section B of this Chapter.

2.   At the request of a Party, the arbitral tribunal shall request the interpretation of the Commission when that Party asserts as a defense that the measure alleged to be a breach of this Treaty is within the scope of a reservation or exception set out in any of its annexes. If the Commission does not submit its interpretation in writing within 60 days of the delivery of the request, the arbitral tribunal shall rule on the matter.

Rule 12. Interim or Precautionary Measures

A tribunal constituted under Section B of this Chapter may adopt interim measures to establish its jurisdiction or to preserve the rights of the disputing parties. The tribunal may not order precautionary measures of enforcement or suspension of the application of the measure alleged to be a breach of this Treaty.

Rule 13. Finality and Enforcement of the Award

1.   The disputing party may seek enforcement of a final award provided that:

   (a)   in the case of a final award made under the ICSID Convention

      i.   120 days have elapsed from the date the award was rendered and no disputing party has requested revision or annulment of the award, or

      ii.   revision or annulment proceedings have been completed; and

   (b)   in the case of a final award under the ICSID Additional Facility Rules or the UNCITRAL Arbitration Rules

      i.   three months have elapsed from the date the award was rendered and no disputing party has commenced a proceeding to revise or annul the award; or

      ii.   a court of the disputing Party has dismissed or allowed an application to revise or annual the award and there is no further appeal.

2.   For the purposes of Article I of the New York Convention and Article I of the Inter-American Convention, a claim that is submitted to arbitration under Section B of this Chapter shall be considered to arise out of a commercial relationship or transaction.

Rule 14. **General Provisions**

1.   A claim is considered to have been submitted to arbitration under the terms of Section B of this Chapter when:

> (a)   the request for arbitration under paragraph (1) of Article 36 of the ICSID Convention has been received by the Secretary-General;

> (b)   the notice of arbitration under Article 2 of Schedule C of the ICSID Additional Facility Rules has been received by the Secretary-General; or

> (c)   the notice of arbitration given in the UNCITRAL Arbitration Rules has been received by the disputing Party.

2.   Delivery of notices and other documents to a Party shall be made to the national section of that Party at the address referred to in Article 20-20, paragraph 1.

3.   Final awards shall be published only if the disputing parties have so agreed in writing.

*   *   *

CANADA-CHILE FREE TRADE AGREEMENT[*]
[excerpts]

The Canada-Chile Free Trade Agreement was signed in Santiago on 5 December 1996. It entered into force on 5 July 1997.

PART THREE. INVESTMENT, SERVICES AND RELATED MATTERS

Chapter G. Investment

Section I - Investment

Article G-01. Scope and Coverage[1]

1.   This Chapter applies to measures adopted or maintained by a Party relating to:

(a)   investors of the other Party;

(b)   investments of investors of the other Party in the territory of the Party; and

(c)   with respect to Articles G-06 and G-14, all investments in the territory of the Party.

2.   This Chapter does not apply to measures adopted or maintained by a Party relating to investors of the other Party, and investments of such investors, in financial institutions in the Party's territory.

3.   (a)   Notwithstanding paragraph 2, Articles G-09, G-10 and Section II for breaches by a Party of Articles G-09 and G-10 shall apply to investors of the other Party, and investments of such investors, in financial institutions in the Party's territory, which have obtained the appropriate authorization.

(b)   The Parties agree to seek further liberalization as set out in Annex G-01.3(b).

4.   Nothing in this Chapter shall be construed to prevent a Party from providing a service or performing a function such as law enforcement, correctional services, income security or

---

[*]   *Source*: The Government of Canada and the Government of Chile (1997). "Canada-Chile Free Trade Agreement", *International Legal Materials*, vol. 36, pp. 1067-1192; also available on the Internet (http://www.sice.oas.org/trade/chican_e/chcatoc.stm). [Note added by the editor.]

1.   This Chapter covers investments existing on the date of entry into force of this Agreement as well as investments made or acquired thereafter.

insurance, social security or insurance, social welfare, public education, public training, health, and child care, in a manner that is not inconsistent with this Chapter.

Article G-02. National Treatment

1. Each Party shall accord to investors of the other Party treatment no less favourable than that it accords, in like circumstances, to its own investors with respect to the establishment, acquisition, expansion, management, conduct, operation, and sale or other disposition of investments.

2. Each Party shall accord to investments of investors of the other Party treatment no less favourable than that it accords, in like circumstances, to investments of its own investors with respect to the establishment, acquisition, expansion, management, conduct, operation, and sale or other disposition of investments.

3. The treatment accorded by a Party under paragraphs 1 and 2 means, with respect to a province, treatment no less favourable than the most favourable treatment accorded, in like circumstances, by that province to investors, and to investments of investors, of the Party of which it forms a part.

4. For greater certainty, no Party may:

    (a)   impose on an investor of the other Party a requirement that a minimum level of equity in an enterprise in the territory of the Party be held by its nationals, other than nominal qualifying shares for directors or incorporators of corporations; or

    (b)   require an investor of the other Party, by reason of its nationality, to sell or otherwise dispose of an investment in the territory of the Party.

Article G-03. Most-Favoured-Nation Treatment

1. Each Party shall accord to investors of the other Party treatment no less favourable than that it accords, in like circumstances, to investors of any non-Party with respect to the establishment, acquisition, expansion, management, conduct, operation, and sale or other disposition of investments.

2. Each Party shall accord to investments of investors of the other Party treatment no less favourable than that it accords, in like circumstances, to investments of investors of any nonParty with respect to the establishment, acquisition, expansion, management, conduct, operation, and sale or other disposition of investments.

Article G-04. Standard of Treatment

1. Each Party shall accord to investors of the other Party and to investments of investors of the other Party the better of the treatment required by Articles G-02 and G-03.

2. Annex G-04.2 sets out certain specific obligations by the Party specified in that Annex.

Article G-05. Minimum Standard of Treatment

1.   Each Party shall accord to investments of investors of the other Party treatment in accordance with international law, including fair and equitable treatment and full protection and security.

2.   Without prejudice to paragraph 1 and notwithstanding Article G-08(7)(b), each Party shall accord to investors of the other Party, and to investments of investors of the other Party, nondiscriminatory treatment with respect to measures it adopts or maintains relating to losses suffered by investments in its territory owing to armed conflict or civil strife.

3.   Paragraph 2 does not apply to existing measures relating to subsidies or grants that would be inconsistent with Article G-02 but for Article G-08(7)(b).

Article G-06. Performance Requirements[2]

1.   Neither Party may impose or enforce any of the following requirements, or enforce any commitment or undertaking, in connection with the establishment, acquisition, expansion, management, conduct or operation of an investment of an investor of a Party or of a nonParty in its territory:

   (a)   to export a given level or percentage of goods or services;

   (b)   to achieve a given level or percentage of domestic content;

   (c)   to purchase, use or accord a preference to goods produced or services provided in its territory, or to purchase goods or services from persons in its territory;

   (d)   to relate in any way the volume or value of imports to the volume or value of exports or to the amount of foreign exchange inflows associated with such investment;

   (e)   to restrict sales of goods or services in its territory that such investment produces or provides by relating such sales in any way to the volume or value of its exports or foreign exchange earnings;

   (f)   to transfer technology, a production process or other proprietary knowledge to a person in its territory, except when the requirement is imposed or the commitment or undertaking is enforced by a court, administrative tribunal or competition authority to remedy an alleged violation of competition laws or to act in a manner not inconsistent with other provisions of this Agreement; or

   (g)   to act as the exclusive supplier of the goods it produces or services it provides to a specific region or world market.

---

2. Article G-06 does not preclude enforcement of any commitment, undertaking or requirement between private parties.

2.   A measure that requires an investment to use a technology to meet generally applicable health, safety or environmental requirements shall not be construed to be inconsistent with paragraph 1(f). For greater certainty, Articles G-02 and G-03 apply to the measure.

3.   Neither Party may condition the receipt or continued receipt of an advantage, in connection with an investment in its territory of an investor of a Party or of a non-Party, on compliance with any of the following requirements:

(a)   to achieve a given level or percentage of domestic content;

(b)   to purchase, use or accord a preference to goods produced in its territory, or to purchase goods from producers in its territory;

(c)   to relate in any way the volume or value of imports to the volume or value of exports or to the amount of foreign exchange inflows associated with such investment; or

(d)   to restrict sales of goods or services in its territory that such investment produces or provides by relating such sales in any way to the volume or value of its exports or foreign exchange earnings.

4.   Nothing in paragraph 3 shall be construed to prevent a Party from conditioning the receipt or continued receipt of an advantage, in connection with an investment in its territory of an investor of a Party or of a nonParty, on compliance with a requirement to locate production, provide a service, train or employ workers, construct or expand particular facilities, or carry out research and development, in its territory.

5.   Paragraphs 1 and 3 do not apply to any requirement other than the requirements set out in those paragraphs.

6.   Provided that such measures are not applied in an arbitrary or unjustifiable manner, or do not constitute a disguised restriction on international trade or investment, nothing in paragraph 1(b) or (c) or 3(a) or (b) shall be construed to prevent a Party from adopting or maintaining measures, including environmental measures:

(a)   necessary to secure compliance with laws and regulations that are not inconsistent with the provisions of this Agreement;

(b)   necessary to protect human, animal or plant life or health; or

(c)   necessary for the conservation of living or non-living exhaustible natural resources.

Article G-07. Senior Management and Boards of Directors

1.   Neither Party may require that an enterprise of that Party that is an investment of an investor of the other Party appoint to senior management positions individuals of any particular nationality.

2.   A Party may require that a majority of the board of directors, or any committee thereof, of an enterprise of that Party that is an investment of an investor of the other Party, be of a particular nationality, or resident in the territory of the Party, provided that the requirement does not materially impair the ability of the investor to exercise control over its investment.

Article G-08. Reservations and Exceptions

1.   Articles G-02, G-03, G-06 and G-07 do not apply to:

(a)   any existing nonconforming measure that is maintained by

(i)   a Party at the national or provincial level, as set out in its Schedule to Annex I, or

(ii)   a local government;

(b)   the continuation or prompt renewal of any nonconforming measure referred to in subparagraph (a); or

(c)   an amendment to any nonconforming measure referred to in subparagraph (a) to the extent that the amendment does not decrease the conformity of the measure, as it existed immediately before the amendment, with Articles G-02, G-03, G-06 and G-07.

2.   Articles G-02, G-03, G-06 and G-07 do not apply to any measure that a Party adopts or maintains with respect to sectors, subsectors or activities, as set out in its Schedule to Annex II.

3.   Neither Party may, under any measure adopted after the date of entry into force of this Agreement and covered by its Schedule to Annex II, require an investor of the other Party, by reason of its nationality, to sell or otherwise dispose of an investment existing at the time the measure becomes effective.

4.   Articles G-02 and G-03 do not apply to any measure that is an exception to, or derogation from, a Party's obligations under the TRIPS Agreement, as specifically provided for in that agreement.

5.   Article G-03 does not apply to treatment accorded by a Party pursuant to agreements, or with respect to sectors, set out in its Schedule to Annex III.

6.   Articles G-02, G-03 and G-07 do not apply to:

(a)   procurement by a Party or a state enterprise; or

(b)   subsidies or grants provided by a Party or a state enterprise, including government-supported loans, guarantees and insurance.

7.   The provisions of:

(a)   Article G-06(1)(a), (b) and (c), and (3)(a) and (b) do not apply to qualification requirements for goods or services with respect to export promotion and foreign aid programs;

(b)   Article G-06(1)(b), (c), (f) and (g), and (3)(a) and (b) do not apply to procurement by a Party or a state enterprise; and

(c)   Article G-06(3)(a) and (b) do not apply to requirements imposed by an importing Party relating to the content of goods necessary to qualify for preferential tariffs or preferential quotas.

Article G-09. Transfers

1.   Except as provided in Annex G-09.1, each Party shall permit all transfers relating to an investment of an investor of the other Party in the territory of the Party to be made freely and without delay. Such transfers include:

(a)   profits, dividends, interest, capital gains, royalty payments, management fees, technical assistance and other fees, returns in kind and other amounts derived from the investment;

(b)   proceeds from the sale of all or any part of the investment or from the partial or complete liquidation of the investment;

(c)   payments made under a contract entered into by the investor, or its investment, including payments made pursuant to a loan agreement;

(d)   payments made pursuant to Article G-10; and

(e)   payments arising under Section II.

2.   Each Party shall permit transfers to be made in a freely usable currency at the market rate of exchange prevailing on the date of transfer with respect to spot transactions in the currency to be transferred.

3.   Neither Party may require its investors to transfer, or penalize its investors that fail to transfer, the income, earnings, profits or other amounts derived from, or attributable to, investments in the territory of the other Party.

4.   Notwithstanding paragraphs 1 and 2, a Party may prevent a transfer through the equitable, nondiscriminatory and good faith application of its laws relating to:

(a)   bankruptcy, insolvency or the protection of the rights of creditors;

(b)   issuing, trading or dealing in securities;

(c)   criminal or penal offenses;

(d)   reports of transfers of currency or other monetary instruments; or

(e)   ensuring the satisfaction of judgments in adjudicatory proceedings.

5.   Paragraph 3 shall not be construed to prevent a Party from imposing any measure through the equitable, nondiscriminatory and good faith application of its laws relating to the matters set out in subparagraphs (a) through (e) of paragraph 4.

6.   Notwithstanding paragraph 1, a Party may restrict transfers of returns in kind in circumstances where it could otherwise restrict such transfers under this Agreement, including as set out in paragraph 4.

Article G-10. Expropriation and Compensation

1.   Neither Party may directly or indirectly nationalize or expropriate an investment of an investor of the other Party in its territory or take a measure tantamount to nationalization or expropriation of such an investment ("expropriation"), except:

(a)   for a public purpose;

(b)   on a nondiscriminatory basis;

(c)   in accordance with due process of law and Article G-05(1); and

(d)   on payment of compensation in accordance with paragraphs 2 through 6.

2.   Compensation shall be equivalent to the fair market value of the expropriated investment immediately before the expropriation took place ("date of expropriation"), and shall not reflect any change in value occurring because the intended expropriation had become known earlier. Valuation criteria shall include going concern value, asset value including declared tax value of tangible property, and other criteria, as appropriate, to determine fair market value.

3.   Compensation shall be paid without delay and be fully realizable.

4.   If payment is made in a G7 currency, compensation shall include interest at a commercially reasonable rate for that currency from the date of expropriation until the date of actual payment.

5.   If a Party elects to pay in a currency other than a G7 currency, the amount paid on the date of payment, if converted into a G7 currency at the market rate of exchange prevailing on that date, shall be no less than if the amount of compensation owed on the date of expropriation had been converted into that G7 currency at the market rate of exchange prevailing on that date, and interest had accrued at a commercially reasonable rate for that G7 currency from the date of expropriation until the date of payment.

6.   On payment, compensation shall be freely transferable as provided in Article G-09.

7.   This Article does not apply to the issuance of compulsory licences granted in relation to intellectual property rights, or to the revocation, limitation or creation of intellectual property rights, to the extent that such issuance, revocation, limitation or creation is consistent with the TRIPS Agreement.

8.   For purposes of this Article and for greater certainty, a non-discriminatory measure of general application shall not be considered a measure tantamount to an expropriation of a debt security or loan covered by this Chapter solely on the ground that the measure imposes costs on the debtor that cause it to default on the debt.

Article G-11. Special Formalities and Information Requirements

1.   Nothing in Article G-02 shall be construed to prevent a Party from adopting or maintaining a measure that prescribes special formalities in connection with the establishment of investments by investors of the other Party, such as a requirement that investors be residents of the Party or that investments be legally constituted under the laws or regulations of the Party, provided that such formalities do not materially impair the protections afforded by a Party to investors of the other Party and investments of investors of the other Party pursuant to this Chapter.

2.   Notwithstanding Articles G-02 or G-03, a Party may require an investor of the other Party, or its investment in its territory, to provide routine information concerning that investment solely for informational or statistical purposes. The Party shall protect such business information that is confidential from any disclosure that would prejudice the competitive position of the investor or the investment. Nothing in this paragraph shall be construed to prevent a Party from otherwise obtaining or disclosing information in connection with the equitable and good faith application of its law.

Article G-12. Relation to Other Chapters

1.   In the event of any inconsistency between this Chapter and another Chapter, the other Chapter shall prevail to the extent of the inconsistency.

2.   A requirement by a Party that a service provider of the other Party post a bond or other form of financial security as a condition of providing a service into its territory does not of itself make this Chapter applicable to the provision of that crossborder service. This Chapter applies to that Party's treatment of the posted bond or financial security.

Article G-13. Denial of Benefits

1.   A Party may deny the benefits of this Chapter to an investor of the other Party that is an enterprise of such Party and to investments of such investor if investors of a nonParty own or control the enterprise and the denying Party:

   (a)   does not maintain diplomatic relations with the non-Party; or

   (b)   adopts or maintains measures with respect to the nonParty that prohibit transactions with the enterprise or that would be violated or circumvented if the benefits of this Chapter were accorded to the enterprise or to its investments.

2.   Subject to prior notification and consultation in accordance with Articles L-03 (Notification and Provision of Information) and N-06 (Consultations), a Party may deny the benefits of this Chapter to an investor of the other Party that is an enterprise of such Party and to investments of such investors if investors of a non-Party own or control the enterprise and the

enterprise has no substantial business activities in the territory of the Party under whose law it is constituted or organized.

Article G-14. Environmental Measures

1.   Nothing in this Chapter shall be construed to prevent a Party from adopting, maintaining or enforcing any measure otherwise consistent with this Chapter that it considers appropriate to ensure that investment activity in its territory is undertaken in a manner sensitive to environmental concerns.

2.   The Parties recognize that it is inappropriate to encourage investment by relaxing domestic health, safety or environmental measures. Accordingly, a Party should not waive or otherwise derogate from, or offer to waive or otherwise derogate from, such measures as an encouragement for the establishment, acquisition, expansion or retention in its territory of an investment of an investor. If a Party considers that the other Party has offered such an encouragement, it may request consultations with the other Party and the two Parties shall consult with a view to avoiding any such encouragement.

Article G-15. Energy Regulatory Measures

Each Party shall seek to ensure that in the application of any energy regulatory measure, energy regulatory bodies within its territory avoid disruption of contractual relationships to the maximum extent practicable, and provide for orderly and equitable implementation appropriate to such measures.

Section II. Settlement of Disputes between a Party and an Investor of the Other Party

Article G-16. Purpose

Without prejudice to the rights and obligations of the Parties under Chapter N (Institutional Arrangements and Dispute Settlement Procedures), this Section establishes a mechanism for the settlement of investment disputes that assures both equal treatment among investors of the Parties in accordance with the principle of international reciprocity and due process before an impartial tribunal.

Article G-17. Claim by an Investor of a Party on Its Own Behalf

1.   An investor of a Party may submit to arbitration under this Section a claim that the other Party has breached an obligation under:

(a)   Section I or Article J-03(2) (State Enterprises), or

(b)   Article J-02(3)(a) (Monopolies and State Enterprises) where the monopoly has acted in a manner inconsistent with the Party's obligations under Section I,

and that the investor has incurred loss or damage by reason of, or arising out of, that breach.

2.   An investor may not make a claim if more than three years have elapsed from the date on which the investor first acquired, or should have first acquired, knowledge of the alleged breach and knowledge that the investor has incurred loss or damage.

Article G-18. Claim by an Investor of a Party on Behalf of an Enterprise

1.   An investor of a Party, on behalf of an enterprise of the other Party that is a juridical person that the investor owns or controls directly or indirectly, may submit to arbitration under this Section a claim that the other Party has breached an obligation under:

(a)   Section I or Article J-03(2) (State Enterprises), or

(b)   Article J-02(3)(a) (Monopolies and State Enterprises) where the monopoly has acted in a manner inconsistent with the Party's obligations under Section I,

and that the enterprise has incurred loss or damage by reason of, or arising out of, that breach.

2.   An investor may not make a claim on behalf of an enterprise described in paragraph 1 if more than three years have elapsed from the date on which the enterprise first acquired, or should have first acquired, knowledge of the alleged breach and knowledge that the enterprise has incurred loss or damage.

3.   Where an investor makes a claim under this Article and the investor or a non-controlling investor in the enterprise makes a claim under Article G-17 arising out of the same events that gave rise to the claim under this Article, and two or more of the claims are submitted to arbitration under Article G-21, the claims should be heard together by a Tribunal established under Article G-27, unless the Tribunal finds that the interests of a disputing party would be prejudiced thereby.

4.   An investment may not make a claim under this Section.

Article G-19. Settlement of a Claim through Consultation and Negotiation

The disputing parties should first attempt to settle a claim through consultation or negotiation.

Article G-20. Notice of Intent to Submit a Claim to Arbitration

The disputing investor shall deliver to the disputing Party written notice of its intention to submit a claim to arbitration at least 90 days before the claim is submitted, which notice shall specify:

(a)   the name and address of the disputing investor and, where a claim is made under Article G-18, the name and address of the enterprise;

(b)   the provisions of this Agreement alleged to have been breached and any other relevant provisions;

(c)   the issues and the factual basis for the claim; and

(d)   the relief sought and the approximate amount of damages claimed.

Article G-21. Submission of a Claim to Arbitration

1.   Except as provided in Annex G-21.1, and provided that six months have elapsed since the events giving rise to a claim, a disputing investor may submit the claim to arbitration under:

(a)   the ICSID Convention, provided that both the disputing Party and the Party of the investor are parties to the Convention;

(b)   the Additional Facility Rules of ICSID, provided that either the disputing Party or the Party of the investor, but not both, is a party to the ICSID Convention; or

(c)   the UNCITRAL Arbitration Rules.

2.   The applicable arbitration rules shall govern the arbitration except to the extent modified by this Section.

Article G-22. Conditions Precedent to Submission of a Claim to Arbitration

1.   A disputing investor may submit a claim under Article G-17 to arbitration only if:

(a)   the investor consents to arbitration in accordance with the procedures set out in this Agreement; and

(b)   the investor and, where the claim is for loss or damage to an interest in an enterprise of the other Party that is a juridical person that the investor owns or controls directly or indirectly, the enterprise, waive their right to initiate or continue before any administrative tribunal or court under the law of a Party, or other dispute settlement procedures, any proceedings with respect to the measure of the disputing Party that is alleged to be a breach referred to in Article G-17, except for proceedings for injunctive, declaratory or other extraordinary relief, not involving the payment of damages, before an administrative tribunal or court under the law of the disputing Party.

2.   A disputing investor may submit a claim under Article G-18 to arbitration only if both the investor and the enterprise:

(a)   consent to arbitration in accordance with the procedures set out in this Agreement; and

(b)   waive their right to initiate or continue before any administrative tribunal or court under the law of a Party, or other dispute settlement procedures, any proceedings with respect to the measure of the disputing Party that is alleged to be a breach referred to in Article G-18, except for proceedings for injunctive, declaratory or other extraordinary relief, not involving the payment of damages, before an administrative tribunal or court under the law of the disputing Party.

3.   A consent and waiver required by this Article shall be in writing, shall be delivered to the disputing Party and shall be included in the submission of a claim to arbitration.

4.   Only where a disputing Party has deprived a disputing investor of control of an enterprise:

   (a)   a waiver from the enterprise under paragraph 1(b) or 2(b) shall not be required; and

   (b)   Annex G-21.1(b) shall not apply.

Article G-23. Consent to Arbitration

1.   Each Party consents to the submission of a claim to arbitration in accordance with the procedures set out in this Agreement.

2.   The consent given by paragraph 1 and the submission by a disputing investor of a claim to arbitration shall satisfy the requirement of:

   (a)   Chapter II of the ICSID Convention (Jurisdiction of the Centre) and the Additional Facility Rules for written consent of the parties;

   (b)   Article II of the New York Convention for an agreement in writing; and

   (c)   Article I of the Inter-American Convention for an agreement.

Article G-24. Number of Arbitrators and Method of Appointment

   Except in respect of a Tribunal established under Article G-27, and unless the disputing parties otherwise agree, the Tribunal shall comprise three arbitrators, one arbitrator appointed by each of the disputing parties and the third, who shall be the presiding arbitrator, appointed by agreement of the disputing parties.

Article G-25. Constitution of a Tribunal When a Party Fails to Appoint an Arbitrator or the Disputing Parties Are Unable to Agree on a Presiding Arbitrator

1.   The Secretary-General shall serve as appointing authority for an arbitration under this Section.

2.   If a Tribunal, other than a Tribunal established under Article G-27, has not been constituted within 90 days from the date that a claim is submitted to arbitration, the Secretary-General, on the request of either disputing party, shall appoint, in his discretion, the arbitrator or arbitrators not yet appointed, except that the presiding arbitrator shall be appointed in accordance with paragraph 3.

3.   The Secretary-General shall appoint the presiding arbitrator from the roster of presiding arbitrators referred to in paragraph 4, provided that the presiding arbitrator shall not be a national of the disputing Party or a national of the Party of the disputing investor. In the event that no

such presiding arbitrator is available to serve, the Secretary-General shall appoint, from the ICSID Panel of Arbitrators, a presiding arbitrator who is not a national of either of the Parties.

4.   On the date of entry into force of this Agreement, the Parties shall establish, and thereafter maintain, a roster of 30 presiding arbitrators, none of whom may be a national of a Party, meeting the qualifications of the Convention and rules referred to in Article G-21 and experienced in international law and investment matters. The roster members shall be appointed by mutual agreement.

Article G-26. Agreement to Appointment of Arbitrators

For purposes of Article 39 of the ICSID Convention and Article 7 of Schedule C to the ICSID Additional Facility Rules, and without prejudice to an objection to an arbitrator based on Article G-25(3) or on a ground other than nationality:

(a)   the disputing Party agrees to the appointment of each individual member of a Tribunal established under the ICSID Convention or the ICSID Additional Facility Rules;

(b)   a disputing investor referred to in Article G-17 may submit a claim to arbitration, or continue a claim, under the ICSID Convention or the ICSID Additional Facility Rules, only on condition that the disputing investor agrees in writing to the appointment of each individual member of the Tribunal; and

(c)   a disputing investor referred to in Article G-18(1) may submit a claim to arbitration, or continue a claim, under the ICSID Convention or the ICSID Additional Facility Rules, only on condition that the disputing investor and the enterprise agree in writing to the appointment of each individual member of the Tribunal.

Article G-27. Consolidation

1.   A Tribunal established under this Article shall be established under the UNCITRAL Arbitration Rules and shall conduct its proceedings in accordance with those Rules, except as modified by this Section.

2.   Where a Tribunal established under this Article is satisfied that claims have been submitted to arbitration under Article G-21 that have a question of law or fact in common, the Tribunal may, in the interests of fair and efficient resolution of the claims, and after hearing the disputing parties, by order:

(a)   assume jurisdiction over, and hear and determine together, all or part of the claims; or

(b)   assume jurisdiction over, and hear and determine one or more of the claims, the determination of which it believes would assist in the resolution of the others.

3.   A disputing party that seeks an order under paragraph 2 shall request the Secretary-General to establish a Tribunal and shall specify in the request:

(a)   the name of the disputing Party or disputing investors against which the order is sought;

(b)   the nature of the order sought; and

(c)   the grounds on which the order is sought.

4.   The disputing party shall deliver to the disputing Party or disputing investors against which the order is sought a copy of the request.

5.   Within 60 days of receipt of the request, the Secretary-General shall establish a Tribunal comprising three arbitrators. The Secretary-General shall appoint the presiding arbitrator from the roster referred to in Article G-25(4). In the event that no such presiding arbitrator is available to serve, the Secretary-General shall appoint, from the ICSID Panel of Arbitrators, a presiding arbitrator who is not a national of either Party. The Secretary-General shall appoint the two other members from the roster referred to in Article G-25(4), and to the extent not available from that roster, from the ICSID Panel of Arbitrators, and to the extent not available from that Panel, in the discretion of the Secretary-General. One member shall be a national of the disputing Party and one member shall be a national of the Party of the disputing investors.

6.   Where a Tribunal has been established under this Article, a disputing investor that has submitted a claim to arbitration under Article G-17 or G-18 and that has not been named in a request made under paragraph 3 may make a written request to the Tribunal that it be included in an order made under paragraph 2, and shall specify in the request:

(a)   the name and address of the disputing investor;

(b)   the nature of the order sought; and

(c)   the grounds on which the order is sought.

7.   A disputing investor referred to in paragraph 6 shall deliver a copy of its request to the disputing parties named in a request made under paragraph 3.

8.   A Tribunal established under Article G-21 shall not have jurisdiction to decide a claim, or a part of a claim, over which a Tribunal established under this Article has assumed jurisdiction.

9.   On application of a disputing party, a Tribunal established under this Article, pending its decision under paragraph 2, may order that the proceedings of a Tribunal established under Article G-21 be stayed, unless the latter Tribunal has already adjourned its proceedings.

10.   A disputing Party shall deliver to the Secretariat, within 15 days of receipt by the disputing Party, a copy of:

(a)   a request for arbitration made under paragraph (1) of Article 36 of the ICSID Convention;

(b)   a notice of arbitration made under Article 2 of Schedule C of the ICSID Additional Facility Rules; or

(c)   a notice of arbitration given under the UNCITRAL Arbitration Rules.

11.   A disputing Party shall deliver to the Secretariat a copy of a request made under paragraph 3:

(a)   within 15 days of receipt of the request, in the case of a request made by a disputing investor;

(b)   within 15 days of making the request, in the case of a request made by the disputing Party.

12.   A disputing Party shall deliver to the Secretariat a copy of a request made under paragraph 6 within 15 days of receipt of the request.

13.   The Secretariat shall maintain a public register of the documents referred to in paragraphs 10, 11 and 12.

Article G-28. Notice

A disputing Party shall deliver to the other Party:

(a)   written notice of a claim that has been submitted to arbitration no later than 30 days after the date that the claim is submitted; and

(b)   copies of all pleadings filed in the arbitration.

Article G-29. Participation by a Party

On written notice to the disputing parties, a Party may make submissions to a Tribunal on a question of interpretation of this Agreement.

Article G-30. Documents

1.   A Party shall be entitled to receive from the disputing Party, at the cost of the requesting Party a copy of:

(a)   the evidence that has been tendered to the Tribunal; and

(b)   the written argument of the disputing parties.

2.   A Party receiving information pursuant to paragraph 1 shall treat the information as if it were a disputing Party.

Article G-31. Place of Arbitration

Unless the disputing parties agree otherwise, a Tribunal shall hold an arbitration in the territory of a Party that is a party to the New York Convention, selected in accordance with:

(a)   the ICSID Additional Facility Rules if the arbitration is under those Rules or the ICSID Convention; or

(b)   the UNCITRAL Arbitration Rules if the arbitration is under those Rules.

Article G-32. Governing Law

1.   A Tribunal established under this Section shall decide the issues in dispute in accordance with this Agreement and applicable rules of international law.

2.   An interpretation by the Commission of a provision of this Agreement shall be binding on a Tribunal established under this Section.

Article G-33. Interpretation of Annexes

1.   Where a disputing Party asserts as a defense that the measure alleged to be a breach is within the scope of a reservation or exception set out in Annex I, Annex II or Annex III, on request of the disputing Party, the Tribunal shall request the interpretation of the Commission on the issue. The Commission, within 60 days of delivery of the request, shall submit in writing its interpretation to the Tribunal.

2.   Further to Article G-32(2), a Commission interpretation submitted under paragraph 1 shall be binding on the Tribunal. If the Commission fails to submit an interpretation within 60 days, the Tribunal shall decide the issue.

Article G-34. Expert Reports

Without prejudice to the appointment of other kinds of experts where authorized by the applicable arbitration rules, a Tribunal, at the request of a disputing party or, unless the disputing parties disapprove, on its own initiative, may appoint one or more experts to report to it in writing on any factual issue concerning environmental, health, safety or other scientific matters raised by a disputing party in a proceeding, subject to such terms and conditions as the disputing parties may agree.

Article G-35. Interim Measures of Protection

A Tribunal may order an interim measure of protection to preserve the rights of a disputing party, or to ensure that the Tribunal's jurisdiction is made fully effective, including an order to preserve evidence in the possession or control of a disputing party or to protect the Tribunal's jurisdiction. A Tribunal may not order attachment or enjoin the application of the measure alleged to constitute a breach referred to in Article G-17 or G-18. For purposes of this paragraph, an order includes a recommendation.

Article G-36. Final Award

1.   Where a Tribunal makes a final award against a Party, the Tribunal may award, separately or in combination, only:

(a)   monetary damages and any applicable interest;

(b)   restitution of property, in which case the award shall provide that the disputing Party may pay monetary damages and any applicable interest in lieu of restitution.

A Tribunal may also award costs in accordance with the applicable arbitration rules.

2.   Subject to paragraph 1, where a claim is made under Article G-18(1):

  (a)   an award of restitution of property shall provide that restitution be made to the enterprise;

  (b)   an award of monetary damages and any applicable interest shall provide that the sum be paid to the enterprise; and

  (c)   the award shall provide that it is made without prejudice to any right that any person may have in the relief under applicable domestic law.

3.   A Tribunal may not order a Party to pay punitive damages.

Article G-37. Finality and Enforcement of an Award

1.   An award made by a Tribunal shall have no binding force except between the disputing parties and in respect of the particular case.

2.   Subject to paragraph 3 and the applicable review procedure for an interim award, a disputing party shall abide by and comply with an award without delay.

3.   A disputing party may not seek enforcement of a final award until:

  (a)   in the case of a final award made under the ICSID Convention

      (i)   120 days have elapsed from the date the award was rendered and no disputing party has requested revision or annulment of the award, or

      (ii)   revision or annulment proceedings have been completed; and

  (b)   in the case of a final award under the ICSID Additional Facility Rules or the UNCITRAL Arbitration Rules

      (i)   three months have elapsed from the date the award was rendered and no disputing party has commenced a proceeding to revise, set aside or annul the award, or

      (ii)   a court has dismissed or allowed an application to revise, set aside or annul the award and there is no further appeal.

4.   Each Party shall provide for the enforcement of an award in its territory.

5.   If a disputing Party fails to abide by or comply with a final award, the Commission, on delivery of a request by a Party whose investor was a party to thearbitration, shall establish a panel under Article N-08 (Request for an Arbitral Panel). The requesting Party may seek in such proceedings:

(a)   a determination that the failure to abide by or comply with the final award is inconsistent with the obligations of this Agreement; and

(b)   a recommendation that the Party abide by or comply with the final award.

6.   A disputing investor may seek enforcement of an arbitration award under the ICSID Convention, the New York Convention or the Inter-American Convention regardless of whether proceedings have been taken under paragraph 5.

7.   A claim that is submitted to arbitration under this Section shall be considered to arise out of a commercial relationship or transaction for purposes of Article I of the New York Convention and Article I of the Inter-American Convention.

Article G-38. General

Time when a Claim is Submitted to Arbitration

1.   A claim is submitted to arbitration under this Section when:

(a)   the request for arbitration under paragraph (1) of Article 36 of the ICSID Convention has been received by the Secretary-General;

(b)   the notice of arbitration under Article 2 of Schedule C of the ICSID Additional Facility Rules has been received by the Secretary-General; or

(c)   the notice of arbitration given under the UNCITRAL Arbitration Rules is received by the disputing Party.

Service of Documents

2.   Delivery of notice and other documents on a Party shall be made to the place named for that Party in Annex G-38.2.

Receipts under Insurance or Guarantee Contracts

3.   In an arbitration under this Section, a Party shall not assert, as a defense, counterclaim, right of setoff or otherwise, that the disputing investor has received or will receive, pursuant to an insurance or guarantee contract, indemnification or other compensation for all or part of its alleged damages.

Publication of an Award

4.   Annex G-38.4 applies to the Parties specified in that Annex with respect to publication of an award.

Article G-39. Exclusions

1.   Without prejudice to the applicability or non-applicability of the dispute settlement provisions of this Section or of Chapter N (Institutional Arrangements and Dispute Settlement

Procedures) to other actions taken by a Party pursuant to Article O-02 (National Security), a decision by a Party to prohibit or restrict the acquisition of an investment in its territory by an investor of the other Party, or its investment, pursuant to that Article shall not be subject to such provisions.

2.   The dispute settlement provisions of this Section and of Chapter N shall not apply to the matters referred to in Annex G-39.2.

Section III - Definitions

Article G-40. Definitions

For purposes of this Chapter:

disputing investor means an investor that makes a claim under Section II;

disputing parties means the disputing investor and the disputing Party;

disputing Party means a Party against which a claim is made under Section II;

disputing party means the disputing investor or the disputing Party;

energy and basic petrochemical goods refer to those goods classified under the Harmonized System as:

(a)   subheading 2612.10;

(b)   headings 27.01 through 27.06;

(c)   subheading 2707.50;

(d)   subheading 2707.99 (only with respect to solvent naphtha, rubber extender oils and carbon black feedstocks);

(e)   headings 27.08 and 27.09;

(f)   heading 27.10 (except for normal paraffin mixtures in the range of C9 to C15);

(g)   heading 27.11 (except for ethylene, propylene, butylene and butadiene in purities over 50 percent);

(h)   headings 27.12 through 27.16;

(i)   subheadings 2844.10 through 2844.50 (only with respect to uranium compounds classified under those subheadings);

(j)   subheadings 2845.10; and

(k)   subheading 2901.10 (only with respect to ethane, butanes, pentanes, hexanes, and heptanes);

energy regulatory measure means any measure by governmental entities that directly affects the transportation, transmission or distribution, purchase or sale, of an energy or basic petrochemical good;

enterprise means an "enterprise" as defined in Article B-01 (Definitions of General Application), and a branch of an enterprise;

enterprise of a Party means an enterprise constituted or organized under the law of a Party, and a branch located in the territory of a Party and carrying out business activities there.

equity or debt securities includes voting and non-voting shares, bonds, convertible debentures, stock options and warrants;

existing means in effect on January 1, 1994 for Canada and December 29, 1995 for Chile;

financial institution means any financial intermediary or other enterprise that is authorized to do business and regulated or supervised as a financial institution under the law of the Party in whose territory it is located;

G7 currency means the currency of Canada, France, Germany, Italy, Japan, the United Kingdom of Great Britain and Northern Ireland or the United States of America;

ICSID means the International Centre for Settlement of Investment Disputes;

ICSID Convention means the *Convention on the Settlement of Investment Disputes between States and Nationals of other States*, done at Washington, March 18, 1965;

Inter-American Convention means the *Inter-American Convention on International Commercial Arbitration*, done at Panama, January 30, 1975;

investment means:

    (a)   an enterprise;

    (b)   an equity security of an enterprise;

    (c)   a debt security of an enterprise

        (i)   where the enterprise is an affiliate of the investor, or

        (ii)   where the original maturity of the debt security is at least three years,

but does not include a debt security, regardless of original maturity, of a state enterprise;

    (d)   a loan to an enterprise

        (i)   where the enterprise is an affiliate of the investor, or

        (ii)   where the original maturity of the loan is at least three years, but does not include a loan, regardless of original maturity, to a state enterprise;

(e)   an interest in an enterprise that entitles the owner to share in income or profits of the enterprise;

(f)   an interest in an enterprise that entitles the owner to share in the assets of that enterprise on dissolution, other than a debt security or a loan excluded from subparagraph (c) or (d);

(g)   real estate or other property, tangible or intangible, acquired in the expectation or used for the purpose of economic benefit or other business purposes; and

(h)   interests arising from the commitment of capital or other resources in the territory of a Party to economic activity in such territory, such as under:

    (i)   contracts involving the presence of an investor's property in the territory of the Party, including turnkey or construction contracts, or concessions, or

    (ii)   contracts where remuneration depends substantially on the production, revenues or profits of an enterprise;

but investment does not mean,

(i)   claims to money that arise solely from

    (i)   commercial contracts for the sale of goods or services by a national or enterprise in the territory of a Party to an enterprise in the territory of the other Party, or

    (ii)   the extension of credit in connection with a commercial transaction, such as trade financing, other than a loan covered by subparagraph (d); or

(j)   any other claims to money,

that do not involve the kinds of interests set out in subparagraphs (a) through (h); or

(k)   with respect to "loans" and "debt securities" referred to in subparagraphs (c) and (d) as it applies to investors of the other Party, and investments of such investors, in financial institution in the Party's territory

    (i)   a loan or debt security issued by a financial institution that is not treated as regulatory capital by the Party in whose territory the financial institution is located,

    (ii)   a loan granted by or debt security owned by a financial institution, other than a loan to or debt security of a financial institution referred to in subparagraph (i), and

    (iii)   a loan to, or debt security issued by, a Party or a state enterprise thereof;

investment of an investor of a Party means an investment owned or controlled directly or indirectly by an investor of such Party;

investor of a Party means a Party or state enterprise thereof, or a national or an enterprise of such Party, that seeks to make, is making or has made an investment;

investor of a non-Party means an investor other than an investor of a Party, that seeks to make, is making or has made an investment;

New York Convention means the *United Nations Convention on the Recognition and Enforcement of Foreign Arbitral Awards*, done at New York, June 10, 1958;

person of a Party means "person of a Party" as defined in Chapter B (General Definitions) except that with respect to Article G-01(2) and (3), "persons of a Party" does not include a branch of an enterprise of a non-Party;

Secretary-General means the Secretary-General of ICSID;

transfers means transfers and international payments;

Tribunal means an arbitration tribunal established under Article G-21 or G-27; and

UNCITRAL Arbitration Rules means the arbitration rules of the United Nations Commission on International Trade Law, approved by the United Nations General Assembly on December 15, 1976.

Annex G-01.3(b)

Further Liberalization

If the negotiations for Chile's accession to NAFTA have not been engaged within 15 months of the entry into force of this Agreement, the Parties shall commence negotiations with a view to entering into an agreement, based on Chapter 14 on Financial Services of the NAFTA, by no later than April 30, 1999.

Annex G-04.2

Standard of Treatment

1.   Chile shall accord to an investor of Canada or an investment of such investor that is party to an investment contract pursuant to Decree Law 600 of 1974 ("Decreto Ley 600 de 1974"), the better of the treatment required under this Agreement or granted under the contract pursuant to the said Decree Law.

---

2.   Chile shall permit an investor of Canada or an investment or such investor, referred to in paragraph 1, to amend the investment contract in order to reflect the rights and obligations of this Agreement.

Annex G-09.1

1.   For the purpose of preserving the stability of its currency, Chile reserves the right:

(a)   to maintain existing requirements that transfers from Chile of proceeds from the sale of all or any part of an investment of an investor of Canada or from the partial or complete liquidation of the investment may not take place until a period not to exceed:

(i)   in the case of an investment made pursuant to Law 18.657 *Foreign Capital Investment Fund Law* ("Ley 18.657, Ley Sobre Fondo de Inversiones de Capitales Extranjeros"), five years has elapsed from the date of transfer to Chile, or

(ii)   subject to subparagraph (c);

(iii)   in all other cases, one year has elapsed from the date of transfer to Chile;

(b)   to apply a reserve requirement pursuant to Article 49 No. 2 of Law 18.840, *Organic Law of the Central Bank of Chile*, ("Ley 18.840, Ley Orgánica del Banco Central de Chile") on an investment of an investor of Canada, other than foreign direct investment, and on foreign credits relating to an investment, provided that such a reserve requirement shall not exceed 30 per cent of the amount of the investment, or the credit, as the case may be;

(c)   to adopt

(i)   measures imposing a reserve requirement referred to in (b) for a period which shall not exceed two years from the date of transfer to Chile,

(ii)   any reasonable measure consistent with paragraph 3 necessary to implement or to avoid circumvention of the measures under (a) or (b), and

(iii)   measures, consistent with Article G-09 and this Annex, establishing future special voluntary investment programs in addition to the general regime for foreign investment in Chile, except that any such measures may restrict transfers from Chile of proceeds from the sale of all or any part of an investment of an investor of Canada or from the partial or complete liquidation of the investment for a period not to exceed 5 years from the date of transfer to Chile; and

(d)   to apply, pursuant to the Law 18.840, measures with respect to transfers relating to an investment of an investor of Canada that

(i)   require that foreign exchange transactions for such transfers take place in the Formal Exchange Market,

(ii)   require authorization for access to the Formal Exchange Market to purchase foreign currency, at the rate agreed upon by the parties to the transaction, which access shall be granted without delay when such transfers are:

    (A)   payments for current international transactions,

    (B)   proceeds from the sale of all or any part, and from the partial or complete liquidation of an investment of an investor of Canada, or

    (C)   payments pursuant to a loan provided they are made in accordance with the maturity dates originally agreed upon in the loan agreement, and

(iii)   require that foreign currency be converted into Chilean pesos, at the rate agreed upon by the parties to the transaction, except for transfers referred to in (ii) (A) through (C) which are exempt from this requirement.

2.   Where Chile proposes to adopt a measure referred to in paragraph 1(c), Chile shall, to the extent practicable:

(a)   provide in advance to Canada the reasons for the proposed adoption of the measure as well as any relevant information in relation to the measure; and

(b)   provide Canada with a reasonable opportunity to comment on the proposed measure.

3.   A measure that is consistent with this Annex but inconsistent with Article G-02, shall be deemed not to contravene Article G-02 provided that, as required under existing Chilean law, it does not discriminate among investors that enter into transactions of the same nature.

4.   This Annex applies to Law 18.840, to the *Decree Law 600 of 1974* ("Decreto Ley 600 de 1974") to Law 18.657 and any other law establishing a future special voluntary investment program consistent with sub-paragraph 1(c)(iii) and to the continuation or prompt renewal of such laws, and to amendments to those laws, to the extent that any such amendment does not decrease the conformity of the amended law with Article G-09(1) as it existed immediately before the amendment.

5.   For the purposes of this Annex:

Chilean juridical person means an enterprise that is constituted or organized in Chile for profit in a form which under Chilean law is recognized as being a juridical person;

date of transfer means the settlement date when the funds that constitute the investment were converted into Chilean pesos, or the date of the importation of the equipment and technology;

existing means in effect on October 24, 1996;

foreign credit means any type of debt financing originating in foreign markets whatever its nature, form or maturity period;

foreign direct investment means an investment of an investor of Canada, other than a foreign credit, made in order:

(a)   to establish a Chilean juridical person or to increase the capital of an existing Chilean juridical person with the purpose of producing an additional flow of goods or services, excluding purely financial flows; or

(b)   to acquire equity of an existing Chilean juridical person and to participate in its management, but excludes such an investment that is of a purely financial character and that is designed only to gain indirect access to the financial market of Chile;

Formal Exchange Market means the market constituted by the banking entities and other institutions authorized by the competent authority; and

payments for current international transactions means "payments for current international transactions" as defined under the *Articles of Agreement of the International Monetary Fund*, and for greater certainty, does not include payments of principal pursuant to a loan which are not made in accordance with the maturity dates originally agreed upon in the loan agreement.

Annex G-21.1

Submission of a Claim to Arbitration

Chile

1.   With respect to the submission of a claim to arbitration:

(a)   an investor of Canada may not allege that Chile has breached an obligation under

i.   Section I or Article J-03(2) (State Enterprises), or

ii.   Article J-02(3)(a) (Monopolies and State Enterprises) where the monopoly has acted in a manner inconsistent with Chile's obligations under Section I,

both in an arbitration under this Section and in proceedings before a Chilean court or administrative tribunal; and

(b)   where an enterprise of Chile that is a juridical person that an investor of Canada owns or controls directly or indirectly alleges in proceedings before a Chilean court or administrative tribunal that Chile has breached an obligation under

    i.   Section I or Article J-03(2) (State Enterprises), or

    ii.   Article J-02(3)(a) (Monopolies and State Enterprises) where the monopoly has acted in a manner inconsistent with Chile's obligations under Section I,

the investor may not allege the breach in an arbitration under this Section.

2.   For greater certainty, where an investor of Canada or an enterprise of Chile that is a juridical person that an investor of Canada owns or controls directly or indirectly makes an allegation referred to in paragraph 1(a) or (b) before a Chilean court or administrative tribunal, the selection of the Chilean court or administrative tribunal shall be final and such investor or enterprise may not thereafter allege the breach in an arbitration under this Section.

Annex G-38.2

Service of Documents on a Party Under Section II

Canada

The place for delivery of notice and other documents under this Section for Canada is:

Office of the Deputy Attorney General of Canada
Justice Building
239 Wellington Street
Ottawa, Ontario
K1A 0H8

This information shall be published in the *Canada Gazette*.

Chile

The place for delivery of notice and other documents under this Section for Chile is:

Dirección de Asuntos Jurídicos del Ministerio de Relaciones
Exteriores de la República de Chile
Morandé 441
Santiago, Chile

Annex G-38.4

Publication of an Award

Canada

Where Canada is the disputing Party, either Canada or a disputing investor that is a party to the arbitration may make an award public.

Chile

Where Chile is the disputing Party, either Chile or a disputing investor that is a party to arbitration may make an award public.

Annex G-39.2

Exclusions from Dispute Settlement

Canada

A decision by Canada following a review under the *Investment Canada Act*, with respect to whether or not to permit an acquisition that is subject to review, shall not be subject to the dispute settlement provisions of Section II or of Chapter N (Institutional Arrangements and Dispute Settlement Procedures).

*   *   *

TRATADO DE LIBRE COMERCIO ENTRE MÉXICO Y NICARAGUA[*]
[excerpts]

The Free Trade Agreement between Mexico and Nicaragua was signed on 18 December 1997. It entered into force on 1 July 1998.

SEXTA PARTE. INVERSION

Capítulo XVI. Inversión

Sección A - Inversión

Artículo 16-01. Definiciones

Para efectos de este capítulo, se entenderá por:

CIADI: el Centro Internacional de Arreglo de Diferencias Relativas a Inversiones;

Convenio del CIADI: el Convenio sobre Arreglo de Diferencias Relativas a Inversiones entre Estados y Nacionales de otros Estados, celebrado en Washington el 18 de marzo de 1965;

Convención Interamericana: la Convención Interamericana sobre Arbitraje Comercial Internacional, celebrada en Panamá el 30 de enero de 1975;

Convención de Nueva York: la Convención de Naciones Unidas sobre el Reconocimiento y Ejecución de Laudos Arbitrales Extranjeros, celebrada en Nueva York el 10 de junio de 1958;

demanda: la reclamación hecha por el inversionista contendiente contra una Parte, cuyo fundamento sea una presunta violación a las disposiciones contenidas en este capítulo;

empresa de una Parte: una empresa de una Parte y una sucursal ubicada en territorio de esa Parte que desempeñe actividades comerciales en el mismo;

inversión, entre otros:

    a)   una empresa;

    b)   acciones de una empresa;

    c)   instrumentos de deuda de una empresa:

---

[*] *Source*: The Government of Mexico and the Government of Nicaragua (1998). "Tratado de Libre Comercio entre México y Nicaragua"; available on the Internet (http://www.sice.oas.trade/menifta/indice.stm). [Note added by the editor.]

    i.   cuando la empresa es una filial del inversionista; o

    ii.   cuando la fecha de vencimiento original del instrumento de deuda sea por lo menos de tres años, pero no incluye un instrumento de deuda de una empresa del Estado, independientemente de la fecha original de vencimiento;

d)   un préstamo a una empresa:

    i.   cuando la empresa es una filial del inversionista; o

    ii.   cuando la fecha de vencimiento original del préstamo sea por lo menos de tres años, pero no incluye un préstamo a una empresa del Estado, independientemente de la fecha original del vencimiento;

e)   una participación en una empresa, que le permita al propietario participar en los ingresos o en las utilidades de la empresa;

f)   una participación en una empresa, que otorgue derecho al propietario para participar del haber social de esa empresa en una liquidación, siempre que ésta no derive de una obligación o de un préstamo excluidos conforme a los literales c) y d);

g)   bienes inmuebles;

h)   otra propiedad, tangible o intangible, adquirida o utilizada con el propósito de obtener un beneficio económico o para otros fines empresariales;

i)   beneficios provenientes de destinar capital u otros recursos para el desarrollo de una actividad económica en territorio de la otra Parte, entre otros, conforme a:

    i.   contratos que involucran la presencia de la propiedad de un inversionista en territorio de la otra Parte, incluidos las concesiones, licencias, permisos, los contratos de construcción y de llave en mano; o

    ii.   contratos donde la remuneración dependa substancialmente de la producción, ingresos o ganancias de una empresa; e

j)   un préstamo otorgado a una institución financiera o un valor de deuda emitido por una institución financiera que sea tratado como capital para los efectos regulatorios por la Parte en cuyo territorio está ubicada la institución financiera;

no se entenderá por inversión:

k)   reclamaciones pecuniarias que no conlleven los tipos de derechos dispuestos en los literales de la definición de inversión derivadas exclusivamente de:

       i.   contratos comerciales para la venta de bienes o servicios por un nacional o empresa en territorio de una Parte a una empresa en territorio de la otra Parte; o

       ii.   el otorgamiento de crédito en relación con una transacción comercial, como el financiamiento al comercio, salvo un préstamo cubierto por las disposiciones del literal d);

    l)   cualquier otra reclamación pecuniaria que no conlleve los tipos de derechos dispuestos en los literales de la definición de inversión;

inversión de un inversionista de una Parte: la inversión propiedad de un inversionista de una Parte o bajo el control directo o indirecto de éste;

inversionista de una Parte: una Parte o una empresa de la misma, o un nacional o empresa de esa Parte, que pretenda realizar, realice o ha realizado una inversión;

inversionista contendiente: un inversionista que formula una reclamación en los términos de la sección B;

Parte contendiente: la Parte contra la cual se formula una demanda en arbitraje en los términos de la sección B;

parte contendiente: el inversionista contendiente o la Parte contendiente;

partes contendientes: el inversionista contendiente y la Parte contendiente;

Reglas de Arbitraje de la CNUDMI: las Reglas de Arbitraje de la Comisión de Naciones Unidas sobre Derecho Mercantil Internacional (CNUDMI), aprobadas por la Asamblea General de las Naciones Unidas, el 15 de diciembre de 1976;

Secretario General: el Secretario General del CIADI;

transferencias: las remisiones y pagos internacionales;

tribunal: un tribunal arbitral establecido conforme al artículo 16-21; y

tribunal de acumulación: un tribunal arbitral establecido conforme al artículo 16-27.

Artículo 16-02. Ambito de aplicación

1.   Este capítulo se aplica a las medidas que adopte o mantenga una Parte relativas a:

    a)   los inversionistas de la otra Parte, en todo lo relacionado con su inversión;

    b)   las inversiones de inversionistas de la otra Parte realizadas en el territorio de la Parte; y

    c)   en lo relativo al artículo 16-05, todas las inversiones en el territorio de la Parte.

2.   Este capítulo no se aplica a:

   a)   las actividades económicas reservadas a cada Parte, de conformidad con su legislación vigente a la fecha de la firma de este Tratado, las cuales se listarán en el anexo a este artículo en un plazo no mayor de un año a partir de la entrada en vigor de este Tratado;

   b)   las medidas que adopte o mantenga una Parte en materia de servicios financieros de conformidad con el capítulo XII (Servicios Financieros), en la medida que estén sujetas a ese capítulo; ni

   c)   las medidas que adopte una Parte para restringir la participación de las inversiones de inversionistas de la otra Parte en su territorio, por razones de orden público o de seguridad nacional.

Artículo 16-03. Trato nacional

1.   Cada Parte brindará a los inversionistas de la otra Parte y a las inversiones de los inversionistas de la otra Parte, un trato no menos favorable que el que otorgue, en circunstancias similares, a sus propios inversionistas y a las inversiones de dichos inversionistas.

2.   Cada Parte otorgará a los inversionistas de la otra Parte, respecto de las inversiones que sufran pérdidas en su territorio debidas a conflictos armados o contiendas civiles, a caso fortuito o fuerza mayor, trato no discriminatorio respecto de cualquier medida que adopte o mantenga en relación con esas pérdidas.

Artículo 16-04. Trato de nación más favorecida

1.   Cada Parte brindará a los inversionistas de la otra Parte y a las inversiones de inversionistas de la otra Parte, un trato no menos favorable que el que otorgue, en circunstancias similares, a los inversionistas y a las inversiones de inversionistas de la otra Parte o de un país que no sea Parte, salvo en lo dispuesto por el párrafo 2.

2.   Si una Parte hubiere otorgado un trato especial a los inversionistas o a las inversiones de éstos, provenientes de un país que no sea Parte, en virtud de convenios que establezcan zonas de libre comercio, uniones aduaneras, mercados comunes, uniones económicas o monetarias e instituciones similares y disposiciones para evitar la doble tributación, dicha Parte no estará obligada a otorgar el trato especial a los inversionistas ni a las inversiones de inversionistas de la otra Parte.

Artículo 16-05. Requisitos de desempeño

1.   Ninguna Parte podrá imponer ni obligar al cumplimiento de los siguientes requisitos o compromisos, en relación con cualquier inversión en su territorio:

   a)   exportar un determinado nivel o porcentaje de bienes o servicios;

   b)   alcanzar un determinado grado o porcentaje de contenido nacional;

c)   adquirir o utilizar u otorgar preferencia a bienes producidos o a servicios prestados en su territorio, o adquirir bienes de productores o servicios de prestadores de servicios en su territorio;

d)   relacionar en cualquier forma el volumen o valor de las importaciones con el volumen o valor de las exportaciones, o con el monto de las entradas de divisas asociadas con dicha inversión;

e)   restringir las ventas en su territorio de los bienes o servicios que tal inversión produzca o preste, relacionando de cualquier manera dichas ventas al volumen o valor de sus exportaciones o a ganancias en divisas que generen;

f)   transferir a una persona en su territorio, tecnología, proceso productivo u otro conocimiento reservado, salvo cuando el requisito se imponga por un tribunal judicial o administrativo o autoridad competente para reparar una supuesta violación a las leyes en materia de competencia o para actuar de una manera que no sea incompatible con otras disposiciones de este Tratado; ni

g)   actuar como el proveedor exclusivo de los bienes que produzca o servicios que preste para un mercado específico, regional o mundial.

Este párrafo no se aplica a ningún otro requisito distinto a los señalados en el mismo.

2.   Ninguna Parte podrá condicionar la recepción de un incentivo o que se continúe recibiendo el mismo, al cumplimiento de los siguientes requisitos, en relación con cualquier inversión en su territorio:

a)   adquirir o utilizar u otorgar preferencia a bienes producidos en su territorio o a comprar bienes de productores en su territorio;

b)   alcanzar un determinado grado o porcentaje de contenido nacional;

c)   relacionar en cualquier forma el volumen o valor de las importaciones con el volumen o valor de las exportaciones, o con el monto de las entradas de divisas asociadas con dicha inversión; ni

d)   restringir las ventas en su territorio de los bienes o servicios que tal inversión produzca o preste, relacionando de cualquier manera dichas ventas al volumen o valor de sus exportaciones o a ganancias en divisas que generen.

Este párrafo no se aplica a ningún otro requisito distinto a los señalados en el mismo.

3.   Nada de lo dispuesto en este artículo se interpretará como impedimento para que una Parte imponga, en relación con cualquier inversión en su territorio, requisitos de localización geográfica de unidades productivas, de generación de empleo o capacitación de mano de obra o de realización de actividades en materia de investigación y desarrollo.

Artículo 16-06. Empleo y dirección empresarial

Las limitaciones respecto del número o la proporción de extranjeros que puedan trabajar en una empresa o desempeñar funciones directivas o de administración conforme lo disponga la legislación de cada Parte, no podrán impedir u obstaculizar el ejercicio por un inversionista del control de su inversión.

Artículo 16-07. Reservas y excepciones

1.   Los artículos 16-03 al 16-06 no se aplican a cualquier medida incompatible que mantenga o adopte una Parte, sea cual fuere el nivel de gobierno. En un plazo no mayor a un año a partir de la entrada en vigor de este Tratado las Partes inscribirán esas medidas en sus listas del anexo a este artículo. Cualquier medida incompatible que adopte una Parte después de la entrada en vigor de este Tratado no podrá ser más restrictiva que aquéllas vigentes al momento en que se dicte esa medida.

2.   Los artículos, 16-03, 16-04 y 16-06 no se aplican a:

   a)   las compras realizadas por una Parte o por una empresa del Estado; ni

   b)   los subsidios o aportaciones, incluyendo los préstamos, garantías y seguros gubernamentales otorgados por una Parte o por una empresa del Estado, salvo por lo dispuesto en el párrafo 2 del artículo 16-03.

3.   Las disposiciones contenidas en:

   a)   los literales a), b) y c) del párrafo 1 y a) y b) del párrafo 2, del artículo 16-05 no aplican en lo relativo a los requisitos para calificación de los bienes y servicios con respecto a programas de promoción a las exportaciones;

   b)   los literales b), c), f) y g) del párrafo 1 y a) y b) del párrafo 2, del artículo 16-05 no se aplican a las compras realizadas por una Parte o por una empresa del Estado; y

   c)   los literales a) y b) del párrafo 2, del artículo 16-05 no aplican a los requisitos de contenido impuestos por una Parte importadora a los bienes para calificar para aranceles o cuotas preferenciales.

Artículo 16-08. Transferencias

1.   Cada Parte permitirá que todas las transferencias relacionadas con la inversión de un inversionista de la otra Parte en territorio de la Parte, se hagan libremente y sin demora. Esas transferencias incluyen:

   a)   ganancias, dividendos, intereses, ganancias de capital, pagos por regalías, gastos por administración, asistencia técnica y otros gastos, ganancias en especie y otros montos derivados de la inversión;

   b)   productos derivados de la venta o liquidación, total o parcial, de la inversión;

c) pagos realizados conforme a un contrato del que sea parte un inversionista o su inversión;

d) pagos derivados de compensaciones por concepto de expropiación, de conformidad con el artículo 16-09; o

e) pagos que resulten de un procedimiento de solución de controversias conforme a la sección B.

2. Cada Parte permitirá que las transferencias se realicen en divisa de libre convertibilidad al tipo de cambio vigente de mercado en la fecha de la transferencia para transacciones al contado de la divisa que vaya a transferirse, sin perjuicio de lo dispuesto en el artículo 13-18.

3. Ninguna Parte podrá exigir a sus inversionistas que efectúen transferencias de sus ingresos, ganancias o utilidades u otros montos derivados de inversiones llevadas a cabo en territorio de otra Parte, o atribuibles a ellas.

4. No obstante lo dispuesto en los párrafos 1 y 2, las Partes podrán impedir la realización de transferencias, mediante la aplicación equitativa y no discriminatoria de sus leyes en los siguientes casos:

a) quiebra, insolvencia o protección de los derechos de los acreedores;

b) emisión, comercio y operaciones de valores;

c) infracciones penales o administrativas;

d) reportes de transferencias de divisas u otros instrumentos monetarios;

e) garantía del cumplimiento de las sentencias o laudos en un procedimiento contencioso; o

f) establecimiento de los instrumentos o mecanismos necesarios para asegurar el pago de impuestos sobre la renta por medios tales como la retención del monto relativo a dividendos u otros conceptos.

Artículo 16-09. Expropiación e indemnización

1. Ninguna Parte podrá nacionalizar ni expropiar, directa o indirectamente, una inversión de un inversionista de la otra Parte en su territorio, ni adoptar medida alguna equivalente a la expropiación o nacionalización de esa inversión ("expropiación"), salvo que sea:

a) por causa de utilidad pública;

b) sobre bases no discriminatorias;

c) con apego al principio de legalidad; y

d) mediante indemnización conforme a los párrafos 2 al 4.

2.   La indemnización será equivalente al valor justo de mercado que tenga la inversión expropiada inmediatamente antes de que la medida expropiatoria se haya llevado a cabo (fecha de expropiación), y no reflejará ningún cambio en el valor debido a que la intención de expropiar se haya conocido con antelación a la fecha de expropiación. Los criterios de valuación incluirán el valor fiscal declarado de bienes tangibles, así como otros criterios que resulten apropiados para determinar el valor justo de mercado.

3.   El pago de la indemnización se hará sin demora y será completamente liquidable.

4.   La cantidad pagada no será inferior a la cantidad equivalente que por indemnización se hubiera pagado en una divisa de libre convertibilidad en el mercado financiero internacional, en la fecha de expropiación, y esta divisa se hubiese convertido a la cotización de mercado vigente en la fecha de valuación, más los intereses que hubiese generado a una tasa comercial razonable para dicha divisa seleccionada por la Parte de acuerdo con los parámetros internacionales hasta la fecha del día del pago.

Artículo 16-10. Formalidades especiales y requisitos de información

1.   Nada de lo dispuesto en el artículo 16-03 se interpretará en el sentido de impedir a una Parte adoptar o mantener una medida que prescriba formalidades especiales conexas al establecimiento de inversiones por inversionistas de la otra Parte, tales como que las inversiones se constituyan conforme a las leyes y reglamentos de la Parte, siempre que dichas formalidades no menoscaben sustancialmente la protección otorgada por una Parte conforme a este capítulo.

2.   No obstante lo dispuesto en los artículos 16-03 y 16-04, las Partes podrán exigir de un inversionista de la otra Parte o de su inversión, en su territorio, que proporcione información rutinaria, referente a esa inversión exclusivamente con fines de información o estadística. La Parte protegerá la información que sea confidencial, de cualquier divulgación que pudiera afectar negativamente la situación competitiva de la inversión o del inversionista.

Artículo 16-11. Relación con otros capítulos

En caso de incompatibilidad entre una disposición de este capítulo y una disposición de otro, prevalecerá la de este último en la medida de la incompatibilidad.

Artículo 16-12. Denegación de beneficios

Una Parte, previa notificación y consulta con la otra Parte, podrá denegar parcial o totalmente los beneficios derivados de este capítulo a un inversionista de la otra Parte que sea una empresa de dicha Parte y a las inversiones de tal inversionista, cuando la Parte determine que inversionistas de un país no Parte son propietarios o controlan la empresa y ésta no tiene actividades de negocios importantes en el territorio de la Parte conforme a cuya legislación está constituida u organizada.

Artículo 16-13. Aplicación extraterritorial de la legislación de una Parte

1.   Las Partes, en relación con las inversiones de sus inversionistas constituidas y organizadas conforme a las leyes y reglamentos de la otra Parte, no podrán ejercer jurisdicción ni

adoptar medida alguna que tenga por efecto la aplicación extraterritorial de su legislación o la obstaculización del comercio entre las Partes, o entre una Parte y un país no Parte.

2.   Si alguna de las Partes incumpliere lo dispuesto por el párrafo 1, la Parte en donde la inversión se hubiere constituido podrá, a su discreción, adoptar las medidas y ejercitar las acciones que considere necesarias, a fin de dejar sin efectos la legislación o la medida de que se trate y los obstáculos al comercio consecuencia de las mismas.

Artículo 16-14. Medidas relativas al ambiente

1.   Nada de lo dispuesto en este capítulo se interpretará como impedimento para que una Parte adopte, mantenga o ponga en ejecución cualquier medida, compatible con este capítulo, que considere apropiada para asegurar que las inversiones en su territorio observen la legislación ecológica.

2.   Las Partes reconocen que es inadecuado alentar la inversión por medio de un relajamiento de las medidas internas aplicables a la salud, seguridad o relativas al ambiente. En consecuencia, ninguna Parte deberá eliminar o comprometerse a eximir de la aplicación de esas medidas a la inversión de un inversionista, como medio para inducir el establecimiento, la adquisición, la expansión o conservación de la inversión en su territorio. Si una Parte estima que la otra Parte ha alentado una inversión de tal manera, podrá solicitar consultas con esa otra Parte.

Artículo 16-15. Promoción de inversiones e intercambio de información

1.   Con la intención de incrementar significativamente la participación recíproca de la inversión, las Partes elaborarán documentos de promoción de oportunidades de inversión y diseñarán mecanismos para su difusión; así mismo, las Partes mantendrán y perfeccionarán mecanismos financieros que hagan viable las inversiones de una Parte en el territorio de la otra Parte.

2.   Las Partes darán a conocer información detallada sobre:

a)   oportunidades de inversión en su territorio, que puedan ser desarrolladas por inversionistas de la otra Parte;

b)   oportunidades de alianzas estratégicas entre inversionistas de las Partes, mediante la investigación y recopilación de intereses y oportunidades de asociación; y

c)   oportunidades de inversión en sectores económicos específicos que interesen a las Partes y a sus inversionistas, de acuerdo a la solicitud expresa que haga cualquiera de las Partes.

3.   Las Partes se mantendrán informadas y actualizadas respecto de:

a)   las oportunidades de inversión de que trata el párrafo 2, incluyendo la difusión de los instrumentos financieros disponibles que coadyuven al incremento de la inversión en el territorio de las Partes;

b)   las leyes, reglamentos o disposiciones que, directa o indirectamente, afecten a la inversión extranjera incluyendo regímenes cambiarios y de carácter fiscal; y

c)   el comportamiento de la inversión extranjera en sus respectivos territorios.

Artículo 16-16. Doble tributación

Las Partes, con el ánimo de promover las inversiones dentro de sus respectivos territorios, mediante la eliminación de obstáculos de índole fiscal y la vigilancia en el cumplimiento de las obligaciones fiscales a través del intercambio de información tributaria, iniciarán negociaciones tendientes a la celebración de convenios para evitar la doble tributación, de acuerdo al calendario que se establezca entre las autoridades competentes de las Partes.

Sección B - Solución de controversias entre una Parte y un inversionista de la otra Parte

Artículo 16-17. Objetivo

Esta sección establece un mecanismo para la solución de controversias de naturaleza jurídica en materia de inversión, que se susciten como consecuencia de la violación de una obligación establecida en la sección A que surjan entre una Parte y un inversionista de la otra Parte a partir de la entrada en vigor de este Tratado relacionadas con hechos ocurridos a partir de ese momento, y que asegura, tanto el trato igual entre inversionistas de las Partes de acuerdo con el principio de reciprocidad internacional, como el debido ejercicio de la garantía de audiencia y defensa dentro de un proceso legal ante un tribunal imparcial.

Artículo 16-18. Demanda del inversionista de una Parte, por cuenta propia o en representación de una empresa

1.   De conformidad con esta sección, el inversionista de una Parte podrá, por cuenta propia o en representación de una empresa de la otra Parte que sea una persona moral de su propiedad o que esté bajo su control directo o indirecto, someter a arbitraje una demanda cuyo fundamento sea el que la otra Parte o una empresa del Estado de esa Parte, ha violado una obligación establecida en la sección A, siempre y cuando el inversionista o su inversión hayan sufrido pérdidas o daños en virtud de la violación o a consecuencia de ella.

2.   El inversionista no podrá presentar una demanda conforme a esta sección, si han transcurrido más de tres años a partir de la fecha en la cual tuvo conocimiento o debió haber tenido conocimiento de la presunta violación, así como de las pérdidas o daños sufridos.

3.   Cuando un inversionista presente una demanda en representación de una empresa que sea una persona moral de su propiedad o que esté bajo su control directo o indirecto, y de manera paralela un inversionista que no tenga el control de una empresa presente una emanda por cuenta propia como consecuencia de los mismos actos, o dos o más demandas se sometan a arbitraje en virtud de la misma medida adoptada por una Parte, un tribunal de acumulación examinará conjuntamente dichas demandas, salvo que dicho tribunal determine que los intereses de una parte contendiente se verían perjudicados.

4.   Una inversión no podrá someter una demanda a arbitraje conforme a esta sección.

Artículo 16-19. Solución de controversias mediante consulta y negociación

Las partes contendientes primero intentarán dirimir la controversia por vía de consulta y negociación.

Artículo 16-20. Notificación de la intención de someter la reclamación a arbitraje

El inversionista contendiente notificará por escrito a la Parte contendiente su intención de someter una reclamación a arbitraje, cuando menos 90 días antes de que se presente formalmente la demanda. La notificación señalará lo siguiente:

a) el nombre y domicilio del inversionista contendiente y, cuando la demanda se haya realizado en representación de una empresa, la denominación o razón social y el domicilio de la misma;

b) las disposiciones de este Tratado presuntamente incumplidas y cualquier otra disposición aplicable;

c) los hechos en que se funde la demanda; y

d) la reparación que se solicite y el monto aproximado de los daños reclamados.

Artículo 16-21. Sometimiento de la reclamación a arbitraje

1. Siempre que hayan transcurrido seis meses desde que tuvieron lugar las medidas que motivan la reclamación, un inversionista contendiente podrá someter la demanda a arbitraje de acuerdo con:

a) el Convenio del CIADI, siempre que tanto la Parte contendiente como la Parte del inversionista, sean Estados parte del mismo;

b) las Reglas del Mecanismo Complementario del CIADI, cuando la Parte contendiente o la Parte del inversionista, pero no ambas, sean Estados parte del Convenio del CIADI; o

c) las Reglas de Arbitraje de la CNUDMI.

2. Cuando una empresa de una Parte que sea una persona moral propiedad de un inversionista de la otra Parte o que esté bajo su control directo o indirecto alegue, en procedimientos ante un tribunal judicial o administrativo, que la otra Parte ha violado presuntamente una obligación de la sección A, el o los inversionistas de esa empresa no podrán alegar la presunta violación en un arbitraje conforme a la sección B.

3. Salvo lo dispuesto por el artículo 16-27, y siempre que tanto la Parte contendiente como la Parte del inversionista contendiente sean Estados parte del Convenio del CIADI, toda controversia entre las mismas será sometida conforme al literal a) del párrafo 1.

4. Las reglas que se elijan para un arbitraje establecido conforme a este capítulo serán aplicables al mismo, salvo en la medida de lo modificado por esta sección.

Artículo 16-22. Condiciones previas al sometimiento de una reclamación a arbitraje

1.   Un inversionista contendiente por cuenta propia y un inversionista en representación de una empresa, podrán someter una reclamación a arbitraje de conformidad con esta sección, sólo si:

   a)   en el caso del inversionista por cuenta propia, éste consiente en someterse a arbitraje en los términos de los procedimientos establecidos en esta sección;

   b)   en el caso del inversionista en representación de una empresa, tanto el inversionista como la empresa consienten en someterse a arbitraje en los términos de los procedimientos establecidos en esta sección; y

   c)   tanto el inversionista como una empresa de la otra Parte, renuncian a su derecho de iniciar procedimientos ante cualquier tribunal judicial o administrativo de cualquiera de las Partes, con respecto a la medida presuntamente violatoria de las disposiciones de este capítulo, salvo que se agoten los recursos administrativos ante las propias autoridades ejecutoras de la medida presuntamente violatoria previstos en la legislación de la Parte contendiente.

2.   El consentimiento y la renuncia requeridos por este artículo se manifestarán por escrito, se entregarán a la Parte contendiente y se incluirán en el sometimiento de la reclamación a arbitraje.

Artículo 16-23. Consentimiento a arbitraje

1.   Cada Parte consiente en someter reclamaciones a arbitraje con apego a los procedimientos y requisitos señalados en esta sección.

2.   El sometimiento de una reclamación a arbitraje por parte de un inversionista contendiente cumplirá con los requisitos señalados en:

   a)   el capítulo II del Convenio del CIADI (Jurisdicción del Centro) y las Reglas del Mecanismo Complementario del CIADI que exigen el consentimiento por escrito de las Partes;

   b)   el artículo II de la Convención de Nueva York, que exige un acuerdo por escrito; y

   c)   el artículo I de la Convención Interamericana, que requiere un acuerdo.

Artículo 16-24. Número de árbitros y método de nombramiento

Con excepción de lo dispuesto por el artículo 16-27, y sin perjuicio de que las partes contendientes acuerden algo distinto, el tribunal estará integrado por tres árbitros. Cada parte contendiente nombrará a un árbitro; el tercer árbitro, quien será el presidente del tribunal arbitral, será designado por las partes contendientes de común acuerdo, pero no será nacional de ninguna de ellas.

Artículo 16-25. Integración del tribunal en caso de que una parte contendiente no designe árbitro o no se logre un acuerdo en la designación del presidente del tribunal

1. El Secretario General nombrará a los árbitros en los procedimientos de arbitraje, de conformidad con esta sección.

2. Cuando un tribunal, que no sea el establecido de conformidad con el artículo 16-27, no se integre en un plazo de 90 días a partir de la fecha en que la reclamación se someta a arbitraje, el Secretario General, a petición de cualquiera de las partes contendientes, nombrará, a su discreción, al árbitro o árbitros no designados todavía, pero no al presidente del tribunal, quién será designado conforme a lo dispuesto en el párrafo 3.

3. El Secretario General designará al presidente del tribunal de entre los árbitros de la lista a la que se refiere el párrafo 4, asegurándose que el presidente del tribunal no sea nacional de la Parte contendiente o nacional de la Parte del inversionista contendiente. En caso de que no se encuentre en la lista un árbitro disponible para presidir el tribunal, el Secretario General designará, del panel de árbitros del CIADI, al presidente del tribunal, siempre que sea de nacionalidad distinta a la de la Parte contendiente o a la de la Parte del inversionista contendiente. 4. A la fecha de entrada en vigor de este Tratado, las Partes establecerán y mantendrán una lista de cinco árbitros como posibles presidentes del tribunal, que reúnan las cualidades establecidas en el Convenio del CIADI y en las reglas contempladas en el artículo 16-21 y que cuenten con experiencia en derecho internacional y en asuntos en materia de inversiones. Los miembros de la lista serán designados por consenso sin importar su nacionalidad.

Artículo 16-26. Consentimiento para la designación de árbitros

Para efectos del artículo 39 del Convenio del CIADI y del artículo 7 de la parte C de las Reglas del Mecanismo Complementario del CIADI, y sin perjuicio de objetar a un árbitro con fundamento en el párrafo 3 del artículo 16-25 o sobre base distinta a la de nacionalidad:

a) la Parte contendiente acepta la designación de cada uno de los miembros de un tribunal establecido de conformidad con el Convenio del CIADI o con las Reglas del Mecanismo Complementario del CIADI; y

b) un inversionista contendiente, sea por cuenta propia o en representación de una empresa, podrá someter una reclamación a arbitraje o continuar el procedimiento conforme al Convenio del CIADI o las Reglas del Mecanismo Complementario del CIADI, únicamente a condición de que el inversionista contendiente y, en su caso, la empresa que representa, manifiesten su consentimiento por escrito sobre la designación de cada uno de los miembros del tribunal.

Artículo 16-27. Acumulación de procedimientos

1. Un tribunal de acumulación establecido conforme a este artículo se instalará con apego a las Reglas de Arbitraje de la CNUDMI y procederá de conformidad con lo contemplado en dichas reglas, salvo lo que disponga esta sección.

2. Cuando un tribunal de acumulación determine que las reclamaciones sometidas a arbitraje de acuerdo con el artículo 16-22 plantean cuestiones de hecho y de derecho en común,

el tribunal de acumulación, en interés de una resolución justa y eficiente, y habiendo escuchado a las partes contendientes, podrá asumir jurisdicción, dar trámite y resolver:

a) todas o parte de las reclamaciones, de manera conjunta; o

b) una o más de las reclamaciones sobre la base de que ello contribuirá a la resolución de las otras.

3. Una parte contendiente que pretenda se determine la acumulación en los términos del párrafo 2, solicitará al Secretario General que instale un tribunal de acumulación y especificará en su solicitud:

a) el nombre y el domicilio de las partes contendientes contra las cuales se pretenda obtener el acuerdo de acumulación;

b) la naturaleza del acuerdo de acumulación solicitado; y

c) el fundamento en que se apoya la petición solicitada.

4. En un plazo de 60 días a partir de la fecha de la petición, el Secretario General instalará un tribunal de acumulación integrado por tres árbitros. El Secretario General nombrará de la lista de árbitros a que se refiere el párrafo 4 del artículo 16-25, al presidente del tribunal de acumulación, quien no será nacional de la Parte contendiente ni nacional de la Parte del inversionista contendiente. En caso de que no se encuentre en la lista un árbitro disponible para presidir el tribunal de acumulación, el Secretario General designará, del panel de árbitros del CIADI, al presidente de dicho tribunal, quien no será nacional de la Parte contendiente ni nacional de la Parte del inversionista contendiente. El Secretario General designará a los otros dos integrantes del tribunal de acumulación de la lista a la que se refiere el párrafo 4 del artículo 16-25 y, cuando no estén disponibles en dicha lista, los seleccionará del panel de árbitros del CIADI; de no haber disponibilidad de árbitros en ese panel, el Secretario General hará discrecionalmente los nombramientos faltantes. Uno de los miembros será nacional de la Parte contendiente y el otro miembro del tribunal de acumulación será nacional de una Parte de los inversionistas contendientes.

5. Cuando se haya establecido un tribunal de acumulación, el inversionista contendiente que haya sometido una reclamación a arbitraje, y no haya sido mencionado en la petición de acumulación hecha de acuerdo con el párrafo 3, podrá solicitar por escrito al tribunal de acumulación que se le incluya en la petición de acumulación formulada de acuerdo con el párrafo 2, y especificará en dicha solicitud:

a) el nombre y domicilio del inversionista contendiente y, en su caso, la denominación o razón social y el domicilio de la empresa;

b) la naturaleza del acuerdo de acumulación solicitado; y

c) los fundamentos en que se apoya la petición.

6. El tribunal de acumulación proporcionará, a costa del inversionista interesado, copia de la petición de acumulación a los inversionistas contendientes contra quienes se pretende obtener el acuerdo de acumulación.

7. Un tribunal establecido conforme al artículo 16-21 no tendrá jurisdicción para resolver una demanda, o parte de ella, respecto de la cual haya asumido jurisdicción un tribunal de acumulación.

8. A solicitud de una parte contendiente, un tribunal de acumulación podrá, en espera de su decisión conforme al párrafo 2, disponer que los procedimientos de un tribunal establecido de acuerdo el artículo 16-21 se suspendan, hasta en tanto se resuelva sobre la procedencia de la acumulación.

Artículo 16-28. Notificación al Secretariado

1. Una Parte contendiente entregará al Secretariado, en un plazo de 15 días a partir de la fecha en que se reciba por la Parte contendiente:

   a)   una solicitud de arbitraje hecha conforme al párrafo 1 del artículo 36 del Convenio del CIADI;

   b)   una notificación de arbitraje en los términos del artículo 2 de la Parte C de las Reglas del Mecanismo Complementario del CIADI; o

   c)   una notificación de arbitraje en los términos previstos por las Reglas de Arbitraje de la CNUDMI.

2. Una Parte contendiente entregará al Secretariado copia de la solicitud formulada en los términos del párrafo 3 del artículo 16-27:

   a)   en un plazo de 15 días a partir de la recepción de la solicitud, en el caso de una petición hecha por el inversionista contendiente; o

   b)   en un plazo de 15 días a partir de la fecha de la solicitud, en el caso de una petición hecha por la Parte contendiente.

3. Una Parte contendiente entregará al Secretariado copia de una solicitud formulada en los términos del párrafo 6 del artículo 16-27 en un plazo de 15 días a partir de la fecha de recepción de la solicitud.

4. El Secretariado conservará un registro público de los documentos a los que se refiere este artículo.

Artículo 16-29. Notificación a la otra Parte

La Parte contendiente entregará a la otra Parte:

1. notificación escrita de una reclamación que se haya sometido a arbitraje a más tardar 30 días después de la fecha de sometimiento de la reclamación a arbitraje; y

2.   copias de todas las comunicaciones presentadas en el arbitraje.

Artículo 16-30. Participación de una Parte

Previa notificación escrita a las partes contendientes, una Parte podrá presentar comunicaciones a cualquier tribunal establecido conforme a esta sección sobre una cuestión de interpretación de este Tratado.

Artículo 16-31. Documentación

1.   Una Parte tendrá, a su costa, derecho a recibir de la Parte contendiente una copia de:

   a)   las pruebas ofrecidas a cualquier tribunal establecido conforme a esta sección; y

   b)   las comunicaciones escritas presentadas por las partes contendientes.

2.   Una Parte que reciba información conforme a lo dispuesto en el párrafo 1, dará tratamiento a la información como si fuera una Parte contendiente.

Artículo 16-32. Sede del arbitraje

La sede del arbitraje estará ubicada en el territorio de la Parte contendiente, salvo que las partes contendientes acuerden algo distinto, en cuyo caso cualquier tribunal establecido conforme a esta sección llevará a cabo el procedimiento arbitral en el territorio de una Parte que sea Estado parte de la Convención de Nueva York, el cual será elegido de conformidad con:

   a)   las Reglas del Mecanismo Complementario del CIADI, si el arbitraje se rige por esas Reglas o por el Convenio del CIADI; o

   b)   las Reglas de Arbitraje de la CNUDMI, si el arbitraje se rige por esas Reglas.

Artículo 16-33. Derecho aplicable

1.   Cualquier tribunal establecido conforme a esta sección decidirá las controversias que se sometan a su consideración de conformidad con este Tratado y las reglas aplicables del derecho internacional.

2.   La interpretación que formule la Comisión sobre una disposición de este Tratado, será obligatoria para cualquier tribunal establecido de conformidad con esta sección.

Artículo 16-34. Interpretación de los anexos

1.   Cuando una Parte alegue como defensa que una medida presuntamente violatoria cae en el ámbito de una reserva o excepción inscrita en el anexo al artículo 16-07, a petición de a Parte contendiente, cualquier tribunal establecido de conformidad con esta sección solicitará a la Comisión una interpretación sobre ese asunto. La Comisión, en un plazo de 60 días a partir de la entrega de la solicitud, presentará por escrito a dicho tribunal su interpretación.

2.   La interpretación de la Comisión sometida conforme al párrafo 1 será obligatoria para cualquier tribunal establecido de conformidad con esta sección. Si la Comisión no somete una interpretación dentro de un plazo de 60 días, dicho tribunal decidirá sobre el asunto.

Artículo 16-35. Medidas provisionales o precautorias

Un tribunal establecido conforme a esta sección podrá solicitar a los tribunales nacionales, o dictar a las partes contendientes, medidas provisionales de protección para preservar los derechos de la parte contendiente o para asegurar que la jurisdicción del tribunal surta plenos efectos. Ese tribunal no podrá ordenar el acatamiento a o la suspensión de la aplicación de la medida presuntamente violatoria a que se refiere el artículo 16-18.

Artículo 16-36. Laudo definitivo

1.   Cuando un tribunal establecido conforme a esta sección dicte un laudo desfavorable a una Parte, dicho tribunal sólo podrá disponer:

a)   el pago de daños pecuniarios y de los intereses correspondientes; o

b)   la restitución de la propiedad, en cuyo caso el laudo dispondrá que la Parte contendiente pueda pagar daños pecuniarios, más los intereses que procedan, en lugar de la restitución.

2.   Cuando la reclamación la haga un inversionista en representación de una empresa:

a)   el laudo que prevea la restitución de la propiedad dispondrá que la restitución se otorgue a la empresa; y

b)   el laudo que conceda daños pecuniarios e intereses correspondientes dispondrá que la suma de dinero se pague a la empresa.

3.   El laudo se dictará sin perjuicio de los derechos que un tercero con interés jurídico tenga sobre la reparación de los daños que haya sufrido, conforme a la legislación aplicable.

Artículo 16-37. Definitividad y ejecución del laudo

1.   El laudo dictado por cualquier tribunal establecido conforme a esta sección será obligatorio sólo para las partes contendientes y únicamente respecto del caso concreto.

2.   Conforme a lo dispuesto en el párrafo 3 y al procedimiento de revisión aplicable a un laudo provisional, una parte contendiente acatará y cumplirá el laudo sin demora.

3.   Una parte contendiente podrá solicitar la ejecución de un laudo definitivo siempre que:

a)   en el caso de un laudo definitivo dictado conforme al Convenio del CIADI:

i.   hayan transcurrido 120 días desde la fecha en que se dictó el laudo sin que alguna parte contendiente haya solicitado la revisión o anulación del mismo;o

ii.   hayan concluido los procedimientos de revisión o anulación; y

b)   en el caso de un laudo definitivo conforme a las Reglas del Mecanismo Complementario del CIADI o las Reglas de Arbitraje de la CNUDMI:

i.   hayan transcurrido tres meses desde la fecha en que se dictó el laudo sin que alguna parte contendiente haya iniciado un procedimiento para revisarlo, desecharlo o anularlo; o

ii.   un tribunal de la Parte contendiente haya desechado o admitido una solicitud de reconsideración o anulación del laudo que haya presentado una de las partes contendientes a los tribunales nacionales conforme a su legislación, y esta resolución no pueda recurrirse.

4.   Cada Parte dispondrá la debida ejecución de un laudo en su territorio.

5.   Cuando una Parte contendiente incumpla o no acate un laudo definitivo, la Comisión, a la recepción de una solicitud de una Parte cuyo inversionista fue parte en el arbitraje, integrará un tribunal conforme al capítulo XX (Solución de Controversias). La Parte solicitante podrá invocar dichos procedimientos para obtener:

a)   una determinación en el sentido de que el incumplimiento o desacato de los términos del laudo definitivo es contrario a las obligaciones de este Tratado; y

b)   una recomendación en el sentido de que la Parte se ajuste y observe el laudo definitivo.

6.   El inversionista contendiente podrá recurrir a la ejecución de un laudo arbitral conforme al Convenio del CIADI, la Convención de Nueva York o la Convención Interamericana, independientemente de que se hayan iniciado o no los procedimientos contemplados en el párrafo 5.

7.   Para efectos del artículo I de la Convención de Nueva York y del artículo I de la Convención Interamericana, se considerará que la reclamación que se somete a arbitraje conforme a esta sección, surge de una relación u operación comercial.

Artículo 16-38. Disposiciones generales

Momento en que la reclamación se considera sometida a arbitraje

1.   Una reclamación se considera sometida a arbitraje en los términos de esta sección cuando:

a)   la solicitud para un arbitraje conforme al párrafo 1 del artículo 36 del Convenio del CIADI ha sido recibida por el Secretario General;

b)   la notificación de arbitraje, de conformidad con el artículo 2 de la Parte C de las Reglas del Mecanismo Complementario del CIADI, ha sido recibida por el Secretario General; o

c)   la notificación de arbitraje contemplada en las Reglas de Arbitraje de la CNUDMI, se ha recibido por la Parte contendiente.

Entrega de Documentos

2.   La entrega de la notificación y de otros documentos, se hará en el lugar designado por cada Parte, conforme al anexo a este artículo.

Pagos conforme a contratos de seguro o garantía

3.   En un arbitraje conforme a esta sección, una Parte no aducirá como defensa, contrademanda, derecho de compensación, u otros, que el inversionista contendiente recibió o recibirá, de acuerdo con un contrato de seguro o garantía, indemnización u otra compensación por todos o parte de los presuntos daños cuya restitución solicita.

Publicación de laudos

4.   Los laudos definitivos se publicarán únicamente en el caso de que exista acuerdo por escrito entre las Partes.

Artículo 16-39. Exclusiones

Las disposiciones de solución de controversias de esta sección y las del capítulo XX (Solución de Controversias) no se aplicarán a los supuestos contenidos en el anexo a este artículo.

Anexo al Artículo 16-38. Entrega de Documentos

La entrega de la notificación y de otros documentos se hará:

a)   en el caso de México, a la Dirección General de Inversión Extranjera de la Secretaría de Comercio y Fomento Industrial, o cualquier otro lugar que la propia Secretaría designe, mediante notificación a la otra Parte, y

b)   en el caso de Nicaragua, a su Secretariado.

Anexo al Artículo 16-39. Exclusiones de México

No estarán sujetas a los mecanismos de solución de controversias previstos en la sección B de este capítulo ni a las del capítulo XX (Solución de Controversias), las resoluciones que adopte una Parte en virtud del párrafo 2 del artículo 16-02, ni la resolución que prohíba o restrinja la adquisición de una inversión en su territorio que sea propiedad o esté controlada por nacionales de esa Parte, por parte de un inversionista de otra Parte, de conformidad con la legislación de cada Parte.

*   *   *

TRATADO DE LIBRE COMERCIO ENTRE CENTROAMÉRICA Y REPÚBLICA DOMINICANA[*]
[excerpts]

The Free Trade Agreement between Central America and the Dominican Republic was signed in Santo Domingo on 16 April 1998. It has not yet entered into force.

Capítulo IX. Inversión

Artículo 9.01. Definiciones

Para efectos de este capítulo, se entenderá por:

CIADI: Centro Internacional de Arreglo de Diferencias Relativas a Inversiones, creado por el Convenio Sobre Arreglo de Diferencias Relativas a Inversiones entre Estados y Nacionales de Otros Estados, abierto para la firma en Washington el 18 de marzo de 1965;

Empresa de una Parte: cualquier persona jurídica o cualquier otra entidad constituida u organizada conforme a la legislación vigente de alguna de las Partes, que tenga su domicilio en el territorio de esa Parte, tenga o no fines de lucro y sea de propiedad privada o gubernamental, incluidas las compañías, y sus sucursales que desempeñen actividades económicas en el territorio de una Parte, fideicomisos, participaciones accionarias, empresas de propietario único o coinversiones;

Inversión: toda clase de bienes o derechos de cualquier naturaleza definidos de acuerdo con el ordenamiento jurídico del país receptor, adquiridos o utilizados con el propósito de obtener un beneficio económico o para otros fines empresariales, adquiridos con recursos transferidos al territorio de una Parte, o reinvertidos en éste, por parte de inversionistas de otra Parte, siempre que la inversión se haya efectuado de conformidad con las leyes de la Parte en cuyo territorio se realizó y comprenderá en particular aunque no exclusivamente:

    a)   acciones y cuotas societarias y cualquier otra forma de participación económica, en cualquier proporción, en sociedades constituidas u organizadas de conformidad con la legislación de la otra Parte;

    b)   derechos de crédito o cualquier otra prestación que tenga valor económico directamente vinculada con una inversión;

    c)   bienes muebles e inmuebles, así como todos los demás derechos reales tales como hipotecas, prendas, servidumbres y usufructos;

---

[*] *Source*: The Government of Costa Rica, the Government of El Salvador, the Government of Guatemala, the Government of Honduras, the Government of Nicaragua and the Government of the Dominican Republic (1998). "Tratado de Libre Comercio entre Centroamérica y República Dominica"; available on the Internet (http://www.sice.oas.org/trade/camdrep/indice.stm). [Note added by the editor.]

d) derechos en el ámbito de la propiedad intelectual de acuerdo con la legislación interna de las respectivas Partes;

e) derechos derivados de concesiones o derechos similares otorgados por ley o en virtud de un contrato o de otro acto de acuerdo a la legislación interna de cada país, para realizar actividades económicas o comerciales.

La definición de inversión no incluye:

1. una obligación de pago ni el otorgamiento de un crédito al Estado o a una empresa del Estado;

2. reclamaciones pecuniarias derivadas exclusivamente de:

    a) contratos comerciales para la venta de bienes o servicios por un inversionista de una Parte en territorio de esa Parte a un inversionista en territorio de otra Parte; o

    b) el otorgamiento de crédito en relación con una transacción comercial, cuya fecha de vencimiento sea menor a un año, como el financiamiento al comercio;

Inversionista de una Parte: una Parte, o empresa propiedad de la misma, un nacional de acuerdo a la legislación de cada una de las Partes, o una empresa constituida en una de las Partes, que lleve a cabo los actos jurídicos tendientes a materializar una inversión y esté en vías de comprometer capital, o en su caso, realice o haya realizado una inversión en el territorio de otra Parte;

Transferencias las remisiones y pagos internacionales tal y como se especifica en el artículo 9.10.

Artículo 9.02. Ambito de aplicación y extensión de las obligaciones

1. Este capítulo se aplica a las medidas que adopte o mantenga una Parte relativas a:

    a) los inversionistas de otra Parte en todo lo directamente relacionado con su inversión; y

    b) las inversiones de inversionistas de una Parte realizadas en el territorio de otra Parte a partir de la entrada en vigor de este Tratado. No obstante, también se aplicará a las inversiones realizadas con anterioridad a su vigencia y que tuvieren la calidad de inversión extranjera, de acuerdo a lo establecido en el párrafo 2, inciso c) de este artículo;

2. Este capítulo no se aplicará a:

    a) las actividades económicas reservadas por cada Parte de acuerdo a su legislación interna vigente a la fecha de suscripción del presente Tratado;

    b) las medidas que adopte una Parte para restringir la participación de las inversiones de inversionistas de otra Parte en su territorio, por razones de seguridad nacional u orden público, protección del patrimonio cultural y ambiental, y conservación del medio ambiente; y

c)   las controversias o reclamaciones surgidas con anterioridad a su entrada en vigor, o relacionadas con hechos acaecidos con anterioridad a su vigencia, incluso si sus efectos permanecen aún después de ésta.

Artículo 9.03. Nivel mínimo de trato

1.   Cada Parte deberá garantizar un tratamiento acorde al Derecho Internacional, incluyendo el trato justo y equitativo, y el goce de plena protección y seguridad dentro de su territorio a las inversiones de inversionistas de la otra Parte.

2.   Cada Parte cumplirá los compromisos que hubiere contraído con respecto a las inversiones y en modo alguno menoscabará, mediante la adopción de medidas arbitrarias y discriminatorias, la dirección, la explotación, el mantenimiento, la utilización, el usufructo, la adquisición, la expansión o la enajenación de las inversiones.

Artículo 9.04. Trato Nacional

Cada Parte otorgará a los inversionistas de otra Parte en relación directa con su inversión y a las inversiones de los inversionistas de otra Parte, un trato no menos favorable que el que otorgue a sus propios inversionistas y a las inversiones de dichos inversionistas.

Artículo 9.05. Trato de Nación más Favorecida

1.   Cada Parte otorgará a los inversionistas de otra Parte en relación directa con su inversión y a las inversiones de inversionistas de otra Parte, un trato no menos favorable que el que otorgue a los inversionistas y a las inversiones de inversionistas de otra Parte o de país que no sea Parte, salvo en lo dispuesto en el párrafo 2 de este artículo.

2.   Si una Parte hubiere otorgado un tratamiento especial a los inversionistas o a las inversiones de éstos, provenientes de un país que no sea Parte, en virtud de convenios que establezcan disposiciones para evitar la doble tributación, zonas de libre comercio, uniones aduaneras, mercados comunes, uniones económicas o monetarias, dicha Parte no estará obligada a otorgar el tratamiento de que se trate a los inversionistas o a las inversiones de la otra Parte.

Artículo 9.06. Trato en caso de pérdidas

Cada Parte otorgará a los inversionistas de otra Parte, respecto de las inversiones de éstos que sufran pérdidas en el territorio de la Parte donde están establecidas, debidas a guerras, conflictos armados o contiendas civiles, un estado de emergencia nacional u otros acontecimientos similares, un trato no discriminatorio respecto al que otorgue a sus inversionistas nacionales o inversionistas de cualquier tercer Estado, con relación a cualquier medida que adopte o mantenga en vinculación con esas pérdidas.

Artículo 9.07. Requisitos de desempeño

Las Partes no podrán imponer, en relación con permitir el establecimiento o la adquisición de una inversión, o hacer cumplir, en relación con la regulación subsiguiente de esa inversión, ninguno de los requisitos de desempeño estipulados en el Acuerdo sobre las Medidas en Materia de Inversiones Relacionadas con el Comercio del Acuerdo sobre la OMC.

Artículo 9.08. Situación migratoria de inversionistas

1.   Con sujeción a su legislación interna relativa a la entrada y permanencia de extranjeros, cada Parte permitirá la entrada y permanencia en su territorio a los inversionistas de la otra Parte y a las personas por ellos contratadas, en virtud de ocupar puestos de alta gerencia o en virtud de sus conocimientos especializados, con el propósito de establecer, desarrollar, administrar o asesorar el funcionamiento de la inversión, en la cual tales inversionistas hayan comprometido capital u otros recursos.

2.   A fin de dar cumplimiento al presente artículo, las Partes aplicarán lo estipulado en el capítulo XI (Entrada Temporal de Personas de Negocios) del presente Tratado.

Artículo 9.09. Alta dirección empresarial y consejos de administración

Ninguna de las Partes podrá exigir que una empresa de una Parte, designe a individuos de alguna nacionalidad en particular para ocupar puestos de alta dirección, salvo lo establecido en la legislación de cada Parte.

Artículo 9.10. Transferencias

1.   Cada Parte permitirá que todas las transferencias relacionadas con la inversión de un inversionista de una Parte en el territorio de otra de las Partes, se hagan libremente y sin demora, de acuerdo a su legislación interna.

Dichas transferencias incluyen:

a)   ganancias, dividendos, intereses, ganancias de capital, pagos por regalías y otros montos derivados de la inversión;

b)   gastos por administración;

c)   montos derivados de la venta o liquidación, total o parcial, de la inversión;

d)   los aportes adicionales al capital hechos para el mantenimiento o el desarrollo de una inversión;

e)   pagos realizados conforme a un contrato del que sea parte un inversionista en relación con su inversión, incluidos pagos efectuados conforme a un convenio de préstamos;

f)   pagos derivados de indemnizaciones por concepto de expropiación; y

g) pagos que provengan de la aplicación de las disposiciones relativas al mecanismo de solución de controversias en este Tratado.

2. Cada una de las Partes permitirá que las transferencias se realicen en divisas de libre convertibilidad al tipo de cambio vigente de mercado en la fecha de la transferencia, de acuerdo con la legislación interna de cada Parte.

3. Asimismo, cada Parte podrá, mediante la aplicación equitativa y no discriminatoria de su legislación, solicitar información y establecer requisitos relativos a reportes de transferencias de divisas u otros instrumentos monetarios.

4. No obstante lo dispuesto en este artículo, las Partes podrán establecer controles temporales a las operaciones cambiarias, siempre y cuando la balanza de pagos de la Parte de que se trate presente un serio desequilibrio e instrumente un programa de acuerdo a los estándares internacionalmente aceptados. Las limitaciones adoptadas o mantenidas por una Parte de conformidad con este párrafo, así como su eliminación se notificarán con prontitud a la otra Parte.

Artículo 9.11. Expropiación e indemnización

1. Las inversiones de los inversionistas de un país de una Parte en el territorio de otra Parte, no serán sometidas a nacionalización, expropiación o cualquier otra medida que tenga efectos equivalentes (en adelante "expropiación"), a menos que se cumplan las siguientes condiciones de acuerdo a su legislación nacional:

a) las medidas sean adoptadas por razones de utilidad pública conforme a lo dispuesto en el anexo a este artículo;

b) las medidas no sean discriminatorias; y

c) las medidas vayan acompañadas de una indemnización pronta, adecuada y efectiva.

2. La indemnización será equivalente al justo precio que la inversión expropiada tenía inmediatamente antes de que la medida de expropiación se adoptara o antes de que la inminencia de la medida fuera de conocimiento público, lo que suceda primero. La indemnización incluirá el pago de intereses calculados desde el día de la desposesión del bien expropiado hasta el día del pago. Estos intereses serán calculados sobre la base de una tasa pasiva promedio del sistema bancario nacional de la Parte donde se efectúa la expropiación. La indemnización se abonará sin demora en moneda convertible y será efectivamente realizable y libremente transferible. El monto de la indemnización se determinará de la siguiente manera:

a) un dictamen pericial de acuerdo a la legislación interna de cada una de las Partes, que deberá incluir todos los datos necesarios para individualizar el bien que se valora;

b) cuando se trate de inmuebles, el dictamen contendrá la valoración independientemente del terreno, los cultivos, las construcciones, los inquilinatos, los arrendamientos, los derechos comerciales, los yacimientos y cualesquiera otros bienes o derechos susceptibles de indemnización;

c)   cuando se trate de bienes muebles, cada uno se valorará separadamente y se indicarán las características que influyen en su valoración;

d)   los avalúos tomarán en cuenta sólo los daños reales permanentes. No se incluirán ni se tomarán en cuenta los hechos futuros ni las expectativas de derecho que afecten el bien. Tampoco podrán reconocerse plusvalías derivadas del proyecto que origina la expropiación;

e)   todo dictamen pericial deberá indicar, en forma amplia y detallada, los elementos de juicio en que se fundamenta el valor asignado al bien y la metodología empleada.

3.   El inversionista afectado tendrá derecho, de conformidad con la legislación interna de la Parte que realiza la expropiación, a la pronta revisión, por parte de la autoridad judicial u otra autoridad competente e independiente de dicha Parte, de su caso para determinar si la expropiación y la valoración de su inversión se han adoptado de acuerdo con los principios establecidos en este artículo.

4.   Nada de lo dispuesto en este artículo afectará la potestad del Gobierno de una Parte de decidir negociar o no con la otra Parte, o con terceros Estados, restricciones cuantitativas de sus exportaciones, ni su potestad de definir la asignación de las cuotas eventualmente negociadas a través de los mecanismos y criterios que estime pertinentes, de conformidad con las disciplinas multilaterales.

Artículo 9.12. Formalidades especiales y requisitos de información

1.   Nada de lo dispuesto en el artículo 9.03 se interpretará en el sentido de impedir a una Parte adoptar o mantener una medida que determine formalidades especiales conexas al establecimiento de inversiones por inversionistas de otra Parte, tales como que las inversiones se constituyan conforme a la legislación de la Parte, siempre que dichas formalidades no menoscaben sustancialmente la protección otorgada por una Parte conforme a este capítulo.

2.   No obstante lo dispuesto en los artículos 9.03 y 9.04, las Partes podrán solicitar de un inversionista de otra Parte en relación con la inversión realizada en su territorio, que proporcione información rutinaria, referente a esa inversión exclusivamente con fines de información o estadísticas. La Parte protegerá la información que sea confidencial, de cualquier divulgación que pudiera afectar negativamente la situación competitiva de la inversión o del inversionista.

3.   Cada Parte publicará todo tipo de leyes, decretos y reglamentos administrativos relativos a las inversiones.

Artículo 9.13. Relación con otros capítulos

Para efectos de la aplicación de este capítulo, en caso de incompatibilidad entre una de sus disposiciones y las de otro capítulo, prevalecerá la de este último, en la medida de la incompatibilidad.

Artículo 9.14. Denegación de beneficios

Una Parte, previa notificación y consulta con la otra Parte, podrá denegar los beneficios de este capítulo a un inversionista de otra Parte que sea una empresa de dicha Parte y a las inversiones de tal inversionista, si inversionistas de un país no Parte son propietarios de la empresa y esta no tiene actividades empresariales substanciales en el territorio de la Parte conforme a cuya ley está constituida u organizada.

Artículo 9.15. Medidas relativas al medio ambiente

Cada Parte podrá adoptar, mantener, o poner en ejecución cualquier medida consistente con este capítulo que considere apropiada para asegurar que las inversiones en su territorio observen la legislación en materia de medio ambiente en esa Parte.

Artículo 9.16. Promoción de inversiones e intercambio de información

1.   Cada Parte, con sujeción a su política general en el campo de las inversiones extranjeras, incentivará y creará condiciones favorables en su territorio para la realización de inversiones por inversionistas de la otra Parte y las admitirá de conformidad con su legislación.

2.   Con la finalidad de incrementar los flujos de inversión entre las Partes, éstas elaborarán documentos sobre oportunidades de inversión y diseñarán mecanismos para su difusión. En particular, cada Parte se esforzará, a petición de alguna Parte, en informar a ésta última sobre:

   a)   oportunidades de inversión en su territorio que puedan ser desarrolladas por inversionistas de la otra Parte;

   b)   oportunidades de alianzas estratégicas entre inversionistas de las Partes; y

   c)   oportunidades basadas en sus respectivos procesos de privatización o capitalización de empresas del sector público, que interese a un inversionista de otra Parte.

3.   Cada Parte notificará la entidad o autoridad nacional competente para los efectos del párrafo 2 del presente artículo.

Artículo 9.17. Subrogación

1.   Cuando una Parte o un organismo autorizado hubiere otorgado un contrato de seguro o alguna otra garantía financiera contra riesgos no comerciales, con respecto a alguna inversión de uno de los inversionistas en el territorio de la otra Parte, esta última deberá reconocer los derechos de la primera Parte de subrogarse en los derechos del inversionista, cuando hubiere efectuado un pago en virtud de dicho contrato o garantía.

2.   Cuando una Parte haya pagado a su inversionista y en tal virtud haya asumido sus derechos y prestaciones, dicho inversionista no podrá reclamar tales derechos y prestaciones a la otra Parte, salvo autorización expresa de la primera Parte.

Artículo 9.18. Doble tributación

Las Partes, con el animo de promover las inversiones dentro de sus respectivos territorios mediante la eliminación de obstáculos de índole fiscal y la vigilancia en el cumplimiento de las obligaciones fiscales a través del intercambio de información tributaria, convienen en iniciar las negociaciones tendientes a la celebración de convenios para evitar la doble tributación, de acuerdo al que se establezca entre las autoridades competentes de las Partes.

Artículo 9.19. Compromiso específico

Las inversiones que hubiesen sido objeto de un compromiso particular de una de las Partes hacia inversionistas de la otra Parte serán administradas, sin perjuicio de las disposiciones del presenteTratado, por los términos de ese compromiso caso que éste incluya disposiciones más favorables que las previstas por el presente Tratado.

Artículo 9.20. Solución de controversias entre una Parte y un inversionista de otra Parte

1.   Las controversias que surjan en el ámbito de este Tratado, entre una de las Partes y un inversionista de la otra Parte que haya realizado inversiones en el territorio de la primera, serán, en la medida de lo posible, solucionadas por medio de consultas amistosas.

2.   Si mediante dichas consultas no se llegare a una solución dentro de cinco (5) meses a partir de la fecha de solicitud de arreglo, el inversionista podrá remitir la controversia:

    a)   a los tribunales competentes de la Parte en cuyo territorio se efectuó la inversión; o

    b)   al arbitraje nacional de la Parte en cuyo territorio se haya realizado la inversión; o

    c)   al arbitraje internacional:

        i)   al CIADI, cuando ambas Partes sean miembros del mismo; o

        ii)   a las Reglas del Mecanismo Complementario para administración de procedimientos de conciliación, arbitraje y comprobación de hechos por la Secretaría del CIADI, cuando una de las Partes no sea miembro del CIADI; o

        iii)   al arbitraje de conformidad con las Reglas de la Comisión de las Naciones Unidas para el Derecho Mercantil Internacional (CNUDMI), en el caso de que ninguna de las Partes sea miembro del CIADI.

Con este fin, cada Parte da su consentimiento anticipado e irrevocable para que toda diferencia pueda ser sometida a este arbitraje.

3.   Una vez que el inversionista haya remitido la controversia al tribunal nacional competente de la Parte en cuyo territorio se hubiera efectuado la inversión o un tribunal arbitral, la elección de uno u otro procedimiento será definitiva.

4.   El tribunal arbitral decidirá sobre la base de:

a)   las disposiciones del presente Tratado y de otros Acuerdos relacionados concluidos entre las Partes;

b)   el Derecho nacional de la Parte en cuyo territorio se ha realizado la inversión, incluidos los términos de eventuales acuerdos particulares concluidos con relación a la inversión; y

c)   las reglas y los principios universalmente reconocidos del Derecho Internacional.

5.   Los laudos arbitrales serán definitivos y obligatorios para las Partes en litigio y serán ejecutados en conformidad con la ley interna de la Parte en cuyo territorio se hubiere efectuado la inversión.

6.   Las Partes se abstendrán de tratar, por medio de canales diplomáticos, asuntos relacionados con controversias sometidas a proceso judicial o a arbitraje, de conformidad a lo dispuesto en este artículo, hasta que los procesos correspondientes estén concluidos, salvo en el caso en que la otra Parte en la controversia no haya dado cumplimiento al fallo judicial o a la decisión del tribunal arbitral, en los términos establecidos en la respectiva sentencia o decisión y de conformidad con la legislación interna.

Anexo al Artículo 9.11

Para efectos del inciso a) del artículo 9.11 se entenderán comprendidos en el término de utilidad pública para:

Costa Rica: interés público legalmente comprobado;

El Salvador: utilidad pública e interés social;

Guatemala: utilidad colectiva, beneficio social o interés público;

Honduras: necesidad o interés público;

Nicaragua: utilidad pública e interés social; y

República Dominicana: utilidad pública e interés social.

*   *   *

TRATADO DE LIBRE COMERCIO ENTRE CHILE Y MÉXICO[*]
[excerpts]

> The Free Trade Agreement between Chile and Mexico was signed in Santiago de Chile, Chile, on 17 April 1998. It entered into force on 1 August 1999.

CUARTA PARTE - INVERSION, SERVICIOS Y ASUNTOS RELACIONADOS

Capítulo 9. Inversión

Sección A - Definiciones

Artículo 9-01. Definiciones Para efectos de este capítulo, se entenderá por

acciones de capital o instrumentos de deuda: incluyen acciones con o sin derecho a voto, bonos o instrumentos de deuda convertibles, opciones sobre acciones y certificados de opción de acciones (warrants);

CIADI: el Centro Internacional de Arreglo de Diferencias Relativas a Inversiones;

Convención de Nueva York: la Convención de Naciones Unidas sobre el Reconocimiento y Ejecución de las Sentencias Arbitrales Extranjeras, celebrada en Nueva York, el 10 de junio de 1958;

Convención Interamericana: la Convención Interamericana sobre Arbitraje Comercial Internacional, celebrada en Panamá, el 30 de enero de 1975;

Convenio del CIADI: el Convenio sobre Arreglo de Diferencias Relativas a Inversiones entre Estados y Nacionales de otros Estados, celebrado en Washington, el 18 de marzo de 1965;

empresa: una "empresa", tal como se define en el artículo 2-01 (Definiciones de aplicación general), y la sucursal de una empresa;

empresa de una Parte: una empresa constituida u organizada de conformidad con la legislación de una Parte; y una sucursal ubicada en territorio de una Parte y que desempeñe actividades comerciales en el mismo;

existente: en vigor al 14 de enero de 1997;

---

[*] *Source*: The Government of Chile and the Government of Mexico (1998). "Tratado de Libre Comercio entre Chile y México"; available on the Internet (http://www.sice.oas.org/trade/chmefta/indice.stm). [Note added by the editor.]

institución financiera: cualquier intermediario financiero u otra empresa que esté autorizada para hacer negocios y esté regulada o supervisada como una institución financiera conforme a la legislación de la Parte en cuyo territorio se encuentre ubicada;

inversión:

a) una empresa;

b) acciones de capital de una empresa;

c) instrumentos de deuda de una empresa:

    i. cuando la empresa es una filial del inversionista, o

    ii. cuando la fecha de vencimiento original del instrumento de deuda sea por lo menos de tres años, pero no incluye un instrumento de deuda del Estado o de una empresa del Estado, independientemente de la fecha original del vencimiento;

d) un préstamo a una empresa:

    i. cuando la empresa es una filial del inversionista, o

    ii. cuando la fecha de vencimiento original del préstamo sea por lo menos de tres años, pero no incluye un préstamo a una empresa estatal, independientemente de la fecha original del vencimiento;

e) una participación en una empresa, que le permita al propietario participar en los ingresos o en las utilidades de la empresa;

f) una participación en una empresa que otorgue derecho al propietario para participar del haber social de esa empresa en una liquidación, siempre que éste no derive de un instrumento de deuda o un préstamo excluidos conforme los literales c) o d);

g) bienes raíces u otra propiedad, tangibles o intangibles, adquiridos con la expectativa de, o utilizados con el propósito de obtener un beneficio económico o para otros fines empresariales; y

h) la participación que resulte del capital u otros recursos comprometidos para el desarrollo de una actividad económica en territorio de la otra Parte, entre otros, conforme a:

    i. contratos que involucran la presencia de la propiedad de un inversionista en territorio de la otra Parte, incluidos, las concesiones, los contratos de construcción y de llave en mano, o

    ii. contratos donde la remuneración depende sustancialmente de la producción, ingresos o ganancias de una empresa;

pero no se entenderá por inversión:

    i)   reclamaciones pecuniarias derivadas exclusivamente de:

          i.   contratos comerciales para la venta de bienes o servicios por un nacional o empresa en territorio de una Parte a una empresa en territorio de la otra Parte, o

          ii.   el otorgamiento de crédito en relación con una transacción comercial, como el financiamiento al comercio, salvo un préstamo cubierto por las disposiciones del literal d); o

    j)   cualquier otra reclamación pecuniaria; que no conlleve los tipos de interés dispuestos en los literales a) a h); y

    k)   con respecto a "instrumentos de deuda" y "préstamo", a que hacen referencia los literales c) y d) como se aplica a los inversionistas de la otra Parte, y a las inversiones de tales inversionistas, en instituciones financieras en el territorio de la Parte:

          i.   un préstamo otorgado a una institución financiera o un instrumento de deuda emitido por una institución financiera cuando no sea tratado como capital para efectos regulatorios por la Parte en cuyo territorio está ubicada la institución financiera,

          ii.   un préstamo otorgado por una institución financiera o un instrumento de deuda propiedad de una institución financiera, salvo por un préstamo a una institución financiera o un instrumento de deuda de una institución financiera a que se hace referencia en el inciso i), y

          iii.   un préstamo a o un instrumento de deuda emitido por una Parte o una empresa del Estado de la misma;

inversión de un inversionista de una Parte: la inversión propiedad o bajo control directo o indirecto de un inversionista de dicha Parte;

inversionista contendiente: un inversionista que formula una reclamación en los términos de la sección C;

inversionista de una Parte: una Parte o una empresa de la misma, o un nacional o empresa de dicha Parte, que pretende realizar, realiza o ha realizado una inversión;

inversionista de un país que no es Parte: un inversionista que no es inversionista de una Parte, que pretende realizar, realiza, o ha realizado una inversión;

moneda del Grupo de los Siete: la moneda de Alemania, Canadá, Estados Unidos de América, Francia, Italia, Japón, o el Reino Unido de Gran Bretaña e Irlanda del Norte;

Parte contendiente: la Parte contra la cual se hace una reclamación en los términos de la sección C;

parte contendiente: el inversionista contendiente o la Parte contendiente;

partes contendientes: el inversionista contendiente y la Parte contendiente;

persona de una Parte: "persona de una Parte", tal como se define en el capítulo 2 (Definiciones de aplicación general), excepto que con respecto al artículo 9-02(3) y (4), "persona de una Parte", no incluye una sucursal de una empresa de un país no Parte;

Reglas de Arbitraje de la CNUDMI: las Reglas de Arbitraje de la Comisión de Naciones Unidas sobre Derecho Mercantil Internacional (CNUDMI), aprobadas por la Asamblea General de las Naciones Unidas, el 15 de diciembre de 1976;

Secretario General: el Secretario General del CIADI;

transferencias: transferencias y pagos internacionales; y

Tribunal: un tribunal arbitral establecido conforme al artículo 9-21 ó 9-27.

Sección B - Inversión

Artículo 9-02. Ámbito de aplicación

1.   Este capítulo se aplica a las medidas que adopte o mantenga una Parte relativas a:

    a)   los inversionistas de la otra Parte;

    b)   las inversiones de inversionistas de la otra Parte realizadas en territorio de la Parte; y

    c)   todas las inversiones en el territorio de la Parte, conforme a lo establecido en los artículos 9-07 y 9-15.

2.   Este capítulo se aplica tanto a las inversiones existentes a la fecha de entrada en vigor de este Tratado, como a las inversiones hechas o adquiridas con posterioridad.

3.   Este capítulo no se aplica a las medidas que adopte o mantenga una Parte en relación a inversionistas de la otra Parte e inversiones de tales inversionistas en instituciones financieras en el territorio de la Parte.

4.   Las Partes acuerdan que:

    a)   sin perjuicio del párrafo 3, los artículos 9-10 y 9-11 y la sección C por violación de una Parte a los artículos 9-10 y 9-11, se aplicarán a los inversionistas de la otra Parte e inversiones de tales inversionistas en instituciones financieras en el territorio de la Parte, que hayan obtenido la correspondiente autorización; y

b)   buscarán una mayor liberalización de acuerdo a lo establecido en el artículo 20-08(a) (Negociaciones futuras).

5.   Una Parte tiene el derecho de desempeñar exclusivamente las actividades económicas señaladas en el Anexo III, y de negarse a autorizar el establecimiento de inversiones en tales actividades. En la medida en que una Parte permita realizar una inversión en una actividad establecida en el Anexo III, tal inversión estará cubierta por la protección de este capítulo.

6.   Ninguna disposición de este capítulo se interpretará en el sentido de impedir a una Parte prestar servicios o llevar a cabo funciones tales como la ejecución de las leyes, servicios de readaptación social, pensión o seguro de desempleo o servicios de seguridad social, bienestar social, educación pública, capacitación pública, salud y protección de la niñez cuando se desempeñen de manera que no sea incompatible con este capítulo.

Artículo 9-03. Trato nacional

1.   Cada Parte otorgará a los inversionistas de la otra Parte un trato no menos favorable que el que otorgue, en circunstancias similares, a sus propios inversionistas en lo referente al establecimiento, adquisición, expansión, administración, conducción, operación, venta u otra disposición de las inversiones.

2.   Cada Parte otorgará a las inversiones de inversionistas de la otra Parte un trato no menos favorable que el que otorga, en circunstancias similares, a las inversiones de sus propios inversionistas en el establecimiento, adquisición, expansión, administración, conducción, operación, venta u otra disposición de las inversiones.

3.   El trato otorgado por una Parte, de conformidad con los párrafos 1 y 2, significa, respecto a un estado, un trato no menos favorable que el trato más favorable que ese estado otorgue, en circunstancias similares, a los inversionistas e inversiones de inversionistas de la Parte de la que forman parte integrante.

4.   Para mayor certeza, ninguna Parte podrá:

a)   imponer a un inversionista de la otra Parte el requisito de que un nivel mínimo de participación accionaria en una empresa establecida en territorio de la Parte, esté en manos de sus nacionales, salvo que se trate de un cierto número de acciones exigidas para directivos o miembros fundadores de sociedades; ni

b)   requerir que un inversionista de la otra Parte, por razón de su nacionalidad, venda o disponga de cualquier otra manera de una inversión en el territorio de una Parte.

Artículo 9-04. Trato de nación más favorecida

1.   Cada Parte otorgará a los inversionistas de la otra Parte un trato no menos favorable que el que otorgue, en circunstancias similares, a los inversionistas de un país no Parte, en lo referente al establecimiento, adquisición, expansión, administración, conducción, operación, venta u otra disposición de inversiones.

2.   Cada Parte otorgará a las inversiones de inversionistas de la otra Parte un trato no menos favorable que el que otorgue, en circunstancias similares, a las inversiones de inversionistas de

un país no Parte, en lo referente al establecimiento, adquisición, expansión, administración, conducción, operación, venta u otra disposición de inversiones.

Artículo 9-05. Nivel de trato

Cada Parte otorgará a los inversionistas de la otra Parte y a las inversiones de los inversionistas de la otra Parte, el mejor de los tratos requeridos por los artículos 9-03 y 9-04.

Artículo 9-06. Nivel mínimo de trato

1.   Cada Parte otorgará a las inversiones de los inversionistas de la otra Parte, trato acorde con el derecho internacional, incluido trato justo y equitativo, así como protección y seguridad plenas.

2.   Sin perjuicio de lo dispuesto por el párrafo 1 y no obstante lo dispuesto en el artículo 9-09(6)(b), cada Parte otorgará a los inversionistas de la otra Parte y a las inversiones de inversionistas de la otra Parte, cuyas inversiones sufran pérdidas en su territorio debidas a conflictos armados o contiendas civiles, trato no discriminatorio respecto de cualquier medida que adopte o mantenga en relación con esas pérdidas.

3.   El párrafo 2 no se aplica a las medidas existentes relacionadas con subsidios o donaciones que pudieran ser incompatibles con el artículo 9-03, salvo por lo dispuesto por el artículo 9-09(6)(b).

Artículo 9-07. Requisitos de desempeño

1.   Ninguna Parte podrá imponer ni hacer cumplir cualquiera de los siguientes requisitos o hacer cumplir ningún compromiso u obligación, en relación con el establecimiento, adquisición, expansión, administración, conducción u operación de una inversión de un inversionista de una Parte o de un país no Parte en su territorio para:

      a)   un determinado niveexportarl o porcentaje de bienes o servicios;

      b)   alcanzar un determinado grado o porcentaje de contenido nacional;

      c)   adquirir o utilizar u otorgar preferencia a bienes producidos o a servicios prestados en su territorio, o adquirir bienes o servicios de personas en su territorio;

      d)   relacionar en cualquier forma el volumen o valor de las importaciones con el volumen o valor de las exportaciones, o con el monto de las entradas de divisas sociadas con dicha inversión;

      e)   restringir las ventas en su territorio de los bienes o servicios que tal inversión produce o presta, relacionando de cualquier manera dichas ventas al volumen o valor de sus exportaciones o a las ganancias que generen en divisas;

      f)   transferir a una persona en su territorio tecnología, un proceso productivo u otro conocimiento de su propiedad, salvo cuando el requisito se imponga o el compromiso u obligación se hagan cumplir por un tribunal judicial o administrativo o una autoridad de competencia para reparar una supuesta violación a las leyes en materia de competencia o para actuar de una manera que no sea incompatible con otras disposiciones de este Tratado; o

g) actuar como el proveedor exclusivo de los bienes que produce o servicios que presta para un mercado específico, regional o mundial.

2. La medida que exija que una inversión emplee una tecnología para cumplir con requisitos de salud, seguridad o ambiente de aplicación general, no se considerará incompatible con el párrafo 1(f). Para brindar mayor certeza, los artículos 9-03 y 9-04 se aplican a la citada medida.

3. Ninguna Parte podrá condicionar la recepción de una ventaja o que se continúe recibiendo la misma, en relación con una inversión en su territorio por parte de un inversionista de un país Parte o no Parte, al cumplimiento de cualquiera de los siguientes requisitos:

a) alcanzar un determinado grado o porcentaje de contenido nacional;

b) adquirir, utilizar u otorgar preferencia a bienes producidos en su territorio, o a adquirir bienes de productores en su territorio;

c) relacionar, en cualquier forma, el volumen o valor de las importaciones con el volumen o valor de las exportaciones, o con el monto de las entradas de divisas asociadas con dicha inversión; o

d) restringir las ventas en su territorio de los bienes o servicios que tal inversión produce o presta, relacionando de cualquier manera dichas ventas al volumen o valor de sus exportaciones o a las ganancias que generen en divisas.

4. Nada de lo dispuesto en el párrafo 3 se interpretará como impedimento para que una Parte condicione la recepción de una ventaja o la continuación de su recepción, en relación con una inversión en su territorio por parte de un inversionista de un país Parte o no Parte, al cumplimiento de un requisito de que ubique la producción, preste servicios, capacite o emplee trabajadores, construya o amplíe instalaciones particulares, o lleve a cabo investigación y desarrollo, en su territorio.

5. Los párrafos 1 y 3 no se aplican a requisito alguno distinto a los señalados en esos párrafos.

6. Siempre que dichas medidas no se apliquen de manera arbitraria o injustificada, o no constituyan una restricción encubierta al comercio o inversión internacional, nada de lo dispuesto en el párrafo 1(b), 1(c), 3(a) o 3(b) se interpretará en el sentido de impedir a una Parte adoptar o mantener medidas, incluidas las de naturaleza ambiental necesarias para:

a) asegurar el cumplimiento de leyes y reglamentaciones que no sean incompatibles con las disposiciones de este Tratado;

b) proteger la vida o salud humana, animal o vegetal; o

c) la preservación de recursos naturales no renovables, vivos o no.

7.   Este artículo no excluye la aplicación de cualquier compromiso, obligación o requisito entre partes privadas.

Artículo 9-08. Altos ejecutivos y directorios o consejos de administración

1.   Ninguna Parte podrá exigir que una empresa de esa Parte, que sea una inversión de un inversionista de la otra Parte, designe a individuos de alguna nacionalidad en particular para ocupar puestos de alta dirección.

2.   Una Parte podrá exigir que la mayoría de los miembros de un directorio o consejo de administración, o de cualquier comité de tal directorio o consejo de administración, de una empresa de esa Parte que sea una inversión de un inversionista de la otra Parte, sea de una nacionalidad en particular o sea residente en territorio de la Parte, siempre que el requisito no menoscabe significativamente la capacidad del inversionista para ejercer el control de su inversión.

Artículo 9-09. Reservas y excepciones

1.   Los artículos 9-03, 9-04, 9-07 y 9-08 no se aplican a:

   a)   cualquier medida disconforme existente que sea mantenida por:

   i.   una Parte a nivel nacional o federal, o estatal, según corresponda, como se establece en su Lista del Anexo I o III, o

   ii.   un gobierno municipal;

   b)   la continuación o pronta renovación de cualquier medida disconforme a que se refiere el literal a); ni

   c)   la modificación de cualquier medida disconforme a que se refiere el literal a) siempre que dicha modificación no disminuya el grado de conformidad de la medida, tal y como estaba en vigor antes de la modificación, con los artículos 9-03, 9-04, 9-07 y 9-08.

2.   Los artículos 9-03, 9-04, 9-07 y 9-08 no se aplican a cualquier medida que una Parte adopte o mantenga, en relación con los sectores, subsectores o actividades, tal como se indica en su Lista del Anexo II.

3.   Ninguna Parte podrá exigir, de conformidad con cualquier medida adoptada después de la fecha de entrada en vigor de este Tratado y comprendida en su Lista del Anexo II, a un inversionista de la otra Parte, por razón de su nacionalidad, que venda o disponga de alguna otra manera de una inversión existente al momento en que la medida cobre vigencia.

4.   Los artículos 9-03 y 9-04 no se aplican a cualquier medida que constituya una excepción o derogación a las obligaciones de una Parte conforme al Acuerdo ADPIC, según lo disponga específicamente ese Acuerdo.

5.   El artículo 9-04 no es aplicable al trato otorgado por una Parte de conformidad con los tratados, o con respecto a los sectores, establecidos en su Lista del Anexo IV.

6.   Los artículos 9-03, 9-04 y 9-08 no se aplican a:

a)   las compras realizadas por una Parte o por una empresa del Estado; ni

b)   subsidios o donaciones, incluyendo los préstamos, garantías y seguros respaldados por el gobierno, otorgados por una Parte o por una empresa del Estado.

7.   Las disposiciones contenidas en:

a)   los párrafos 1(a), 1(b), 1(c), 3(a) y 3(b) del artículo 9-07 no se aplican a los requisitos para calificación de los bienes y servicios con respecto a programas de promoción a las exportaciones y de ayuda externa;

b)   los párrafos 1(b), 1(c), 1(f), 1(g), 3(a) y 3(b) del artículo 9-07 no se aplican a las compras realizadas por una Parte o por una empresa del Estado; y

c)   los párrafos 3(a) y 3(b) del artículo 9-07 no se aplican a los requisitos impuestos por una Parte importadora a los bienes que, en virtud de su contenido, califiquen para aranceles o cuotas preferenciales.

Artículo 9-10. Transferencias

1.   Salvo lo previsto en el anexo 9-10, cada Parte permitirá que todas las transferencias relacionadas con una inversión de un inversionista de la otra Parte en el territorio de la Parte, se hagan libremente y sin demora. Dichas transferencias incluyen:

a)   ganancias, dividendos, intereses, ganancias de capital, pagos por regalías, gastos por administración, asistencia técnica y otros cargos, ganancias en especie y otros montos derivados de la inversión;

b)   productos derivados de la venta o liquidación, total o parcial, de la inversión;

c)   pagos realizados conforme a un contrato del que sea parte un inversionista o su inversión, incluidos pagos efectuados conforme a un convenio de préstamo;

d)   pagos efectuados de conformidad con el artículo 9-11; y

e)   pagos que provengan de la aplicación de la sección C.

2.   En lo referente a las transacciones al contado (spot) de la divisa que vaya a transferirse, cada Parte permitirá que las transferencias se realicen en divisa de libre uso al tipo de cambio vigente en el mercado en la fecha de la transferencia.

3.   Ninguna Parte podrá exigir a sus inversionistas que efectúen transferencias de sus ingresos, ganancias, o utilidades u otros montos derivados de, o atribuibles a, inversiones

llevadas a cabo en territorio de la otra Parte, ni los sancionará en caso de que no realicen la transferencia.

4.   No obstante lo dispuesto en los párrafos 1 y 2, una Parte podrá impedir la realización de una transferencia, por medio de la aplicación equitativa, no discriminatoria y de buena fe de sus leyes en los siguientes casos:

a)   quiebra, insolvencia o protección de los derechos de los acreedores;

b)   emisión, comercio y operaciones de valores;

c)   infracciones penales;

d)   informes de transferencias de divisas u otros instrumentos monetarios; o

e)   garantía del cumplimiento de fallos en procedimientos contenciosos.

5.   El párrafo 3 no se interpretará como un impedimento para que una Parte, a través de la aplicación de sus leyes de manera equitativa, no discriminatoria y de buena fe, imponga cualquier medida relacionada con el párrafo 4(a) al (e).

6.   No obstante lo dispuesto en el párrafo 1, una Parte podrá restringir las transferencias de ganancias en especie, en circunstancias en donde pudiera, de otra manera, restringir dichas transferencias conforme a lo dispuesto en este Tratado, incluyendo lo señalado en el párrafo 4.

Artículo 9-11. Expropiación e indemnización

1.   Ninguna Parte podrá nacionalizar ni expropiar, directa o indirectamente, una inversión de un inversionista de la otra Parte en su territorio, ni adoptar ninguna medida equivalente a la expropiación o nacionalización de esa inversión (expropiación), salvo que sea:

a)   por causa de utilidad pública;

b)   sobre bases no discriminatorias;

c)   con apego al principio de legalidad y al artículo 9-06(1); y d) mediante indemnización conforme a los párrafos 2 a 6.

d)   mediante indemnización conforme a los párrafos 2 a 6.

2.   La indemnización será equivalente al valor justo de mercado que tenga la inversión expropiada inmediatamente antes de que la medida expropiatoria se haya llevado a cabo (fecha de expropiación), y no reflejará cambio alguno en el valor debido a que la intención de expropiar se conoció con antelación a la fecha de expropiación. Los criterios de valuación incluirán el valor de negocio en marcha o valor corriente, el valor del activo incluyendo el valor fiscal declarado de bienes tangibles, así como otros criterios que resulten apropiados para determinar el valor justo de mercado.

3.   El pago de la indemnización se hará sin demora y será completamente liquidable.

4.   En caso de que la indemnización sea pagada en una moneda del Grupo de los Siete, la indemnización incluirá intereses a una tasa comercial razonable para la moneda, a partir de la fecha de la expropiación hasta la fecha efectiva de pago.

5.   Si una Parte elige pagar en una moneda distinta a la del Grupo de los Siete, la cantidad pagada no será inferior a la equivalente que por indemnización se hubiera pagado en la divisa de alguno de los países miembros del Grupo de los Siete en la fecha de expropiación y esta divisa se hubiese convertido al tipo de cambio de mercado vigente en la fecha de expropiación, más los intereses que hubiese generado a una tasa comercial razonable para dicha divisa hasta la fecha del pago.

6.   Una vez pagada, la indemnización podrá transferirse libremente de conformidad con el artículo 9-10.

7.   Este artículo no se aplica a la expedición de licencias obligatorias otorgadas en relación a derechos de propiedad intelectual, o a la revocación, limitación o creación de dichos derechos en la medida que dicha expedición, revocación, limitación o creación sea conforme con el Acuerdo ADPIC.

8.   Para los efectos de este artículo y para mayor certeza, no se considerará que una medida no discriminatoria de aplicación general es una medida equivalente a la expropiación de un instrumento de deuda o un préstamo cubiertos por este capítulo, sólo porque dicha medida imponga costos a un deudor cuyo resultado sea la falta de pago de la deuda.

Artículo 9-12. Formalidades especiales y requisitos de información

1.   Nada de lo dispuesto en el artículo 9-03 se interpretará en el sentido de impedir a una Parte adoptar o mantener una medida que prescriba formalidades especiales conexas al establecimiento de inversiones por inversionistas de la otra Parte, tales como que las inversiones se constituyan conforme a sus leyes y reglamentaciones, siempre que esas formalidades no menoscaben sustancialmente la protección otorgada por dicha Parte conforme a este capítulo.

2.   No obstante lo dispuesto en los artículos 9-03 y 9-04, una Parte podrá exigir de un inversionista de la otra Parte o de su inversión en su territorio, que proporcione información rutinaria referente a esa inversión, exclusivamente con fines de información o estadística. La Parte protegerá de cualquier divulgación la información de negocios que sea confidencial, que pudiera afectar negativamente la situación competitiva de la inversión o del inversionista. Nada de lo dispuesto en este párrafo se interpretará como un impedimento para que una Parte obtenga o divulgue información referente a la aplicación equitativa y de buena fe de su legislación.

Artículo 9-13. Relación con otros capítulos

1.   En caso de incompatibilidad entre una disposición de este capítulo y una disposición de otro capítulo, prevalecerá la de este último en la medida de la incompatibilidad.

2.   El hecho de que una Parte requiera a un prestador de servicios de la otra Parte que deposite una fianza u otra forma de garantía financiera como condición para prestar un servicio en su territorio no hace, por sí mismo, aplicable este capítulo a la prestación transfronteriza de ese servicio. Este capítulo se aplica al trato que otorgue esa Parte a la fianza depositada o garantía financiera.

Artículo 9-14. Denegación de beneficios

1.   Una Parte podrá denegar los beneficios de este capítulo a un inversionista de la otra Parte que sea una empresa de esa Parte y a las inversiones de dicho inversionista, si dicha empresa es propiedad de o está controlada por inversionistas de un país no Parte y:

   a)   la Parte que deniegue los beneficios no mantiene relaciones diplomáticas con el país no Parte; o

   b)   la Parte que deniegue los beneficios adopta o mantiene medidas en relación con el país no Parte, que prohiben transacciones con esa empresa o que serían violadas o eludidas si los beneficios de este capítulo se otorgan a esa empresa o a sus inversiones.

2.   Previa notificación y consulta, de conformidad con los artículos 16-04 (Notificación y suministro de información) y 18-04 (Consultas), una Parte podrá denegar los beneficios de este capítulo a un inversionista de la otra Parte que sea una empresa de dicha Parte y a las inversiones de tal inversionista, si inversionistas de un país no Parte son propietarios o controlan la empresa y ésta no tiene actividades comerciales sustanciales en el territorio de la Parte conforme a cuya ley está constituida u organizada.

Artículo 9-15. Medidas relativas al ambiente

1.   Nada de lo dispuesto en este capítulo se interpretará

como impedimento para que una Parte adopte, mantenga o ponga en ejecución cualquier medida, por lo demás compatible con este capítulo, que considere apropiada para asegurar que las actividades de inversión en su territorio se efectúen tomando en cuenta consideraciones en materia ambiental.

2.   Las Partes reconocen que es inadecuado alentar la inversión por medio de un relajamiento de las medidas internas aplicables a salud, seguridad o relativas al ambiente. En consecuencia, ninguna Parte debería renunciar a aplicar o de cualquier otro modo derogar, u ofrecer renunciar o derogar, dichas medidas como medio para inducir el establecimiento, la adquisición, la expansión o la conservación de la inversión de un inversionista en su territorio. Si una Parte estima que la otra Parte ha alentado una inversión de tal manera, podrá solicitar consultas con esa otra Parte y ambas consultarán con el fin de evitar incentivos de esa índole.

Sección C - Solución de controversias entre una Parte y un inversionista de la otra Parte

Artículo 9-16. Objetivo

Sin perjuicio de los derechos y obligaciones de las Partes establecidos en el capítulo 18 (Solución de controversias), esta sección establece un mecanismo para la solución de controversias en materia de inversión que asegura, tanto un trato igual entre inversionistas de las Partes de acuerdo con el principio de reciprocidad internacional, como un debido proceso legal ante un tribunal imparcial.

Artículo 9-17. Reclamación de un inversionista de una Parte, por cuenta propia

1.   De conformidad con esta sección un inversionista de una Parte podrá someter a arbitraje una reclamación en el sentido de que la otra Parte ha violado una obligación establecida en:

a)   la sección B o el artículo 14-04(2) (Empresas del Estado); o

b)   el artículo 14-03(4)(a) (Monopolios y empresas del Estado), cuando el monopolio ha actuado de manera incompatible con las obligaciones de la Parte de conformidad con la sección B;

y que el inversionista ha sufrido pérdidas o daños en virtud de esa violación o a consecuencia de ella.

2.   Un inversionista no podrá presentar una reclamación si han transcurrido más de tres años a partir de la fecha en la cual tuvo conocimiento por primera vez o debió haber tenido conocimiento de la presunta violación, así como conocimiento de que sufrió pérdidas o daños.

Artículo 9-18. Reclamación de un inversionista de una Parte, en representación de una empresa

1.   Un inversionista de una Parte, en representación de una empresa de la otra Parte que sea una persona jurídica propiedad del inversionista o que esté bajo su control directo o indirecto, podrá someter a arbitraje de conformidad con esta sección, una reclamación en el sentido de que la otra Parte ha violado una obligación establecida en:

a)   la sección B o el artículo 14-04(2) (Empresas del Estado); o

b)   el artículo 14-03(4)(a) (Monopolios y empresas del Estado), cuando el monopolio haya actuado de manera incompatible con las obligaciones de la Parte de conformidad con la sección B;

y que la empresa ha sufrido pérdidas o daños en virtud de esa violación o a consecuencia de ella.

2.   Un inversionista no podrá presentar una reclamación en representación de la empresa a la que se refiere el párrafo 1, si han transcurrido más de tres años a partir de la fecha en la cual la empresa tuvo conocimiento por primera vez, o debió tener conocimiento de la presunta violación, así como conocimiento de que sufrió pérdidas o daños.

3.   Cuando un inversionista presente una reclamación de conformidad con este artículo y, de manera paralela el inversionista o un inversionista que no tenga el control de una empresa, presente una reclamación en los términos del artículo 9-17 como consecuencia de los mismos actos que dieron lugar a la presentación de una reclamación de acuerdo con este artículo, y dos o más reclamaciones se sometan a arbitraje en los términos del artículo 9-21, el Tribunal establecido conforme al artículo 9-27, examinará conjuntamente dichas reclamaciones, salvo que el Tribunal determine que los intereses de una parte contendiente se verían perjudicados.

4.   Una inversión no podrá presentar una reclamación conforme a esta sección.

Artículo 9-19. Solución de una reclamación mediante consulta y negociación

Las partes contendientes intentarán primero dirimir la controversia por vía de consulta o negociación.

Artículo 9-20. Notificación de la intención de someter la reclamación a arbitraje

El inversionista contendiente notificará por escrito a la Parte contendiente su intención de someter una reclamación a arbitraje cuando menos 90 días antes de que se presente la reclamación, y la notificación señalará lo siguiente:

a)   el nombre y dirección del inversionista contendiente y cuando la reclamación se haya realizado conforme al artículo 9-18, incluirá el nombre y la dirección de la empresa;

b)   las disposiciones de este Tratado presuntamente incumplidas y cualquier otra disposición aplicable;

c)   las cuestiones de hecho y de derecho en que se funda la reclamación; y

d)   la reparación que se solicita y el monto aproximado de los daños reclamados.

Artículo 9-21. Sometimiento de la reclamación a arbitraje

1.   Siempre que hayan transcurrido seis meses desde que tuvieron lugar los actos que motivan la reclamación y sujeto a lo dispuesto en los párrafos 2 ó 3, un inversionista contendiente podrá someter la reclamación a arbitraje de acuerdo con:

a)   el Convenio del CIADI, siempre que tanto la Parte contendiente como la Parte del inversionista, sean Estados parte del mismo;

b)   las Reglas del Mecanismo Complementario del CIADI, cuando la Parte contendiente o la Parte del inversionista, pero no ambas, sea Parte del Convenio del CIADI; o

c)   las Reglas de Arbitraje de la CNUDMI.

2.   En el caso de una reclamación en conformidad con el artículo 9-17, el inversionista y la empresa, cuando sea una persona jurídica de su propiedad o que esté bajo su control directo o indirecto, no hayan sometido la misma reclamación ante un tribunal judicial o administrativo de la Parte contendiente.

3.   En el caso de una reclamación en conformidad con el artículo 9-18, tanto dicho inversionista como la empresa que sea una persona jurídica de su propiedad o que esté bajo su control directo o indirecto, no hayan sometido la misma reclamación ante un tribunal judicial o administrativo de la Parte contendiente.

4.   Las reglas arbitrales aplicables regirán el arbitraje salvo en la medida de lo modificado en esta sección.

Artículo 9-22. Condiciones previas al sometimiento de una reclamación al procedimiento arbitral

1.   Un inversionista contendiente podrá someter una reclamación al procedimiento arbitral de conformidad con el artículo 9-17, sólo si:

   a)   consiente someterse al arbitraje en los términos de los procedimientos establecidos en este Tratado; y

   b)   el inversionista y, cuando la reclamación se refiera a pérdida o daño en una participación en una empresa de la otra Parte que sea una persona jurídica propiedad del inversionista o que esté bajo su control directo o indirecto, la empresa renuncian a su derecho a iniciar cualquier procedimiento ante un tribunal administrativo o judicial conforme al derecho de la Parte contendiente u otros procedimientos de solución de controversias respecto a la medida de la Parte contendiente presuntamente violatoria de las disposiciones a las que se refiere el artículo 9-17, salvo los procedimientos en que se solicite la aplicación de medidas precautorias de carácter suspensivo, declaratorio o extraordinario, que no impliquen el pago de daños ante el tribunal administrativo o judicial, conforme a la legislación de la Parte contendiente.

2.   Un inversionista contendiente podrá someter una reclamación al procedimiento arbitral de conformidad con el artículo 9-18, sólo si tanto el inversionista como la empresa:

   a)   consienten en someterse a arbitraje en los términos de los procedimientos establecidos en este Tratado; y

   b)   renuncian a su derecho de iniciar cualquier procedimiento con respecto a la medida de la Parte contendiente que presuntamente sea una de las violaciones a las que se refiere el artículo 9-18 ante cualquier tribunal administrativo o judicial conforme a la legislación o derecho de una Parte u otros procedimientos de solución de controversias, salvo los procedimientos en que se solicite la aplicación de medidas precautorias de carácter suspensivo, declarativo o extraordinario, que no impliquen el pago de daños ante el tribunal administrativo o judicial, conforme a la legislación o derecho de la Parte contendiente.

3.   El consentimiento y la renuncia requeridos por este artículo se manifestarán por escrito, se entregarán a la Parte contendiente y se incluirán en el sometimiento de la reclamación a arbitraje.

4.   Sólo en el caso de que la Parte contendiente haya privado al inversionista contendiente del control en una empresa:

   a)   no se requerirá la renuncia de la empresa conforme al párrafo 1(b) o 2(b); y

   b)   no será aplicable el artículo 9-21(3).

Artículo 9-23. Consentimiento a arbitraje

1.   Cada Parte consiente en someter reclamaciones a arbitraje con apego a los procedimientos establecidos en este Tratado.

2.   El consentimiento a que se refiere el párrafo 1 y el sometimiento de una reclamación a arbitraje por parte de un inversionista contendiente cumplirá con los requisitos señalados en:

   a)   el Capítulo II del Convenio del CIADI (Jurisdicción del Centro) y las Reglas del Mecanismo Complementario que exigen el consentimiento por escrito de las partes;

   b)   el Artículo II de la Convención de Nueva York, que exige un acuerdo por escrito; y

   c)   el Artículo I de la Convención Interamericana, que requiere un acuerdo.

Artículo 9-24. Número de árbitros y método de nombramiento

Con excepción de lo que se refiere al Tribunal establecido conforme al artículo 9-27, y a menos que las partes contendientes acuerden otra cosa, el Tribunal estará integrado por tres árbitros. Cada una de las partes contendientes nombrará a uno. El tercer árbitro, quien será el presidente del Tribunal arbitral, será designado por acuerdo de las partes contendientes.

Artículo 9-25. Integración del Tribunal en caso de que una Parte no designe árbitro o las partes contendientes no logren un acuerdo en la designación del presidente del Tribunal arbitral

1.   El Secretario General nombrará a los árbitros en los procedimientos de arbitraje, de conformidad con esta sección.

2.   Cuando un Tribunal, que no sea el establecido de conformidad con el artículo 9-27, no se integre en un plazo de 90 días a partir de la fecha en que la reclamación se someta a arbitraje, el Secretario General, a petición de cualquiera de las partes contendientes, nombrará, a su discreción, al árbitro o árbitros no designados todavía, pero no al presidente del Tribunal quien será designado conforme a lo dispuesto en el párrafo 3.

3.   El Secretario General designará al presidente del Tribunal de entre los árbitros de la lista a la que se refiere el párrafo 4, asegurándose que el presidente del Tribunal no sea nacional de una de las Partes. En caso de que no se encuentre en la lista un árbitro disponible para presidir el Tribunal, el Secretario General designará, de la Lista de Árbitros del CIADI, al presidente del Tribunal arbitral, siempre que sea de nacionalidad distinta a la de cualquiera de las Partes.

4.   A la fecha de entrada en vigor de este Tratado, las Partes establecerán y mantendrán una lista de hasta 30 árbitros como posibles presidentes de Tribunal arbitral, que reúnan las cualidades establecidas en el Convenio y en las reglas contempladas en el artículo 9-21 y que cuenten con experiencia en derecho internacional y en materia de inversión. Los miembros de la lista serán designados por mutuo acuerdo.

Artículo 9-26. Consentimiento para la designación de árbitros

Para los propósitos del Artículo 39 del Convenio del CIADI y del Artículo 7 de la Parte C de las Reglas del Mecanismo Complementario, y sin perjuicio de objetar a un árbitro de conformidad con el artículo 9-25(3) o sobre base distinta a la nacionalidad:

a) la Parte contendiente acepta la designación de cada uno de los miembros de un Tribunal establecido de conformidad con el Convenio del CIADI o con las Reglas del Mecanismo Complementario;

b) un inversionista contendiente a que se refiere el artículo 9-17, podrá someter una reclamación a arbitraje o continuar el procedimiento conforme al Convenio del CIADI o a las Reglas del Mecanismo Complementario, únicamente a condición de que el inversionista contendiente manifieste su consentimiento por escrito sobre la designación de cada uno de los miembros del Tribunal; y

c) el inversionista contendiente a que se refiere el artículo 9-18(1) podrá someter una reclamación a arbitraje o continuar el procedimiento conforme al Convenio del CIADI o las Reglas del Mecanismo Complementario, únicamente a condición de que el inversionista contendiente y la empresa manifiesten su consentimiento por escrito sobre la designación de cada uno de los miembros del Tribunal.

Artículo 9-27. Acumulación de procedimientos

1. Un Tribunal establecido conforme a este artículo se instalará con apego a las Reglas de Arbitraje de la CNUDMI y procederá de conformidad con lo contemplado en dichas Reglas, salvo lo que disponga esta sección.

2. Cuando un Tribunal establecido conforme a este artículo determine que las reclamaciones sometidas a arbitraje de acuerdo con el artículo 9-21 plantean una cuestión en común de hecho o de derecho, el Tribunal, en interés de una resolución justa y eficiente, y habiendo escuchado a las partes contendientes, podrá asumir jurisdicción, conocer y resolver :

a) todas o parte de las reclamaciones, de manera conjunta; o

b) una o más de las reclamaciones sobre la base de que ello contribuirá a la resolución de las otras.

3. Una parte contendiente que pretenda obtener una orden de acumulación en los términos del párrafo 2, solicitará al Secretario General que instale un Tribunal y especificará en su solicitud:

a) el nombre de la Parte contendiente o de los inversionistas contendientes contra los cuales se pretenda obtener la orden de acumulación;

b) la naturaleza de la orden de acumulación solicitada; y

c) el fundamento en que se apoya la solicitud.

4.   Una parte contendiente entregará copia de su solicitud a la Parte contendiente o a los inversionistas contendientes contra quienes se pretende obtener la orden de acumulación.

5.   En un plazo de 60 días a partir de la fecha de la recepción de la solicitud, el Secretario General instalará un Tribunal integrado por tres árbitros. El Secretario General nombrará al presidente del Tribunal de la lista de árbitros a la que se refiere el artículo 9-25(4). En caso de que no se encuentre en la lista un árbitro disponible para presidir el Tribunal, el Secretario General designará, de la Lista de Árbitros del CIADI, al presidente del Tribunal quien no será nacional de ninguna de las Partes. El Secretario General designará a los otros dos integrantes del Tribunal de la lista a la que se refiere el artículo 9-25(4) y, cuando no estén disponibles en dicha lista, los seleccionará de la Lista de Árbitros del CIADI; de no haber disponibilidad de árbitros en esta lista, el Secretario General hará discrecionalmente los nombramientos faltantes. Uno de los miembros será nacional de la Parte contendiente y el otro miembro del Tribunal será nacional de la Parte de los inversionistas contendientes.

6.   Cuando se haya establecido un Tribunal conforme a este artículo, el inversionista contendiente que haya sometido una reclamación a arbitraje conforme al artículo 9-17 ó 9-18 y no haya sido mencionado en la solicitud de acumulación hecha de acuerdo con el párrafo 3, podrá solicitar por escrito al Tribunal que se le incluya en una orden formulada de acuerdo con el párrafo 2, y especificará en dicha solicitud:

   a)   el nombre y dirección del inversionista contendiente;

   b)   la naturaleza de la orden de acumulación solicitada; y

   c)   los fundamentos en que se apoya la solicitud.

7.   Un inversionista contendiente al que se refiere el párrafo 6, entregará copia de su solicitud a las partes contendientes señaladas en una solicitud hecha conforme al párrafo 3.

8.   Un Tribunal establecido conforme al artículo 9-21 no tendrá jurisdicción para resolver una reclamación, o parte de ella, respecto de la cual haya asumido jurisdicción un Tribunal establecido conforme a este artículo.

9.   A solicitud de una parte contendiente, un Tribunal establecido de conformidad con este artículo podrá, en espera de su decisión conforme al párrafo 2, disponer que los procedimientos de un Tribunal establecido de acuerdo al artículo 9-21 se aplacen a menos que ese último Tribunal haya suspendido sus procedimientos.

Artículo 9-28. Notificaciones

1.   Una Parte contendiente entregará al Secretariado en un plazo de 15 días a partir de la fecha en que se reciba por la Parte contendiente, una copia de:

   a)   una solicitud de arbitraje hecha conforme al párrafo 1 del Artículo 36 del Convenio del CIADI;

   b)   una notificación de arbitraje en los términos del Artículo 2 de la Parte C de las Reglas del Mecanismo Complementario del CIADI; o

c)   una notificación de arbitraje en los términos previstos por las Reglas de Arbitraje de la CNUDMI.

2.   Una Parte contendiente entregará al Secretariado copia de la solicitud formulada en los términos del artículo 9-27(3):

a)   en un plazo de 15 días a partir de la recepción de la solicitud en el caso de una petición hecha por el inversionista contendiente; y

b)   en un plazo de 15 días a partir de la fecha de la solicitud, en el caso de una petición hecha por la Parte contendiente.

3.   Una Parte contendiente entregará al Secretariado, copia de una solicitud formulada en los términos del artículo 9-27(6), en un plazo de 15 días a partir de la fecha de recepción de la solicitud.

4.   El Secretariado conservará un registro público de los documentos a los que se refieren los párrafos 1, 2 y 3.

5.   La Parte contendiente entregará a la otra Parte:

a)   notificación escrita de una reclamación que se haya sometido a arbitraje a más tardar 30 días después de la fecha de sometimiento de la reclamación a arbitraje; y

b)   copias de todos los escritos presentados en el procedimiento arbitral.

Artículo 9-29. Participación de una Parte

Previa notificación escrita a las partes contendientes, una Parte podrá someter a un Tribunal sobre cuestiones de interpretación de este Tratado.

Artículo 9-30. Documentación

1.   Una Parte tendrá, a su costa, derecho a recibir de la Parte contendiente una copia de:

a)   las pruebas ofrecidas al Tribunal; y

b)   los argumentos escritos presentados por las partes contendientes.

2.   Una Parte que reciba información conforme a lo dispuesto en el párrafo 1, dará tratamiento a la información como si fuera una Parte contendiente.

Artículo 9-31. Sede del arbitraje

Salvo que las partes contendientes acuerden otra cosa, un Tribunal llevará a cabo el arbitraje en territorio de una Parte que sea parte de la Convención de Nueva York, el cual será elegido de conformidad con:

a)   las Reglas del Mecanismo Complementario del CIADI, si el arbitraje se rige por esas reglas o por el Convenio del CIADI; o

b)   las Reglas de Arbitraje de la CNUDMI, si el arbitraje se rige por esas reglas.

Artículo 9-32. Derecho aplicable

1.   Un Tribunal establecido conforme a esta sección decidirá las controversias que se sometan a su consideración de conformidad con este Tratado y con las reglas aplicables del derecho internacional.

2.   La interpretación que formule la Comisión sobre una disposición de este Tratado, será obligatoria para un Tribunal establecido de conformidad con esta sección.

Artículo 9-33. Interpretación de los Anexos

1.   Cuando una Parte alegue como defensa que una medida presuntamente violatoria cae en el ámbito de una reserva o excepción consignada en el Anexo I, Anexo II, Anexo III o Anexo IV a petición de la Parte contendiente, el Tribunal solicitará a la Comisión una interpretación sobre ese asunto. La Comisión, en un plazo de 60 días a partir de la entrega de la solicitud, presentará por escrito al Tribunal su interpretación.

2.   Adicionalmente a lo señalado en el artículo 9-32(2), la interpretación de la Comisión sometida conforme al párrafo 1 será obligatoria para el Tribunal. Si la Comisión no somete una interpretación dentro de un plazo de 60 días, el Tribunal decidirá sobre el asunto.

Artículo 9-34. Dictámenes de expertos

Sin perjuicio de la designación de otro tipo de expertos cuando lo autoricen las reglas de arbitraje aplicables, el Tribunal, a petición de una parte contendiente, o por iniciativa propia a menos que las partes contendientes no lo acepten, podrá designar uno o más expertos para dictaminar por escrito cualquier cuestión de hecho relativa a asuntos ambientales, de salud, seguridad u otros asuntos científicos que haya planteado una parte contendiente en un procedimiento, de acuerdo a los términos y condiciones que acuerden las partes contendientes.

Artículo 9-35. Medidas provisionales de protección

Un Tribunal podrá ordenar una medida provisional de protección para preservar los derechos de una parte contendiente o para asegurar que la jurisdicción del Tribunal surta plenos efectos, incluso una orden para preservar las pruebas que estén en posesión o control de una parte contendiente, u órdenes para proteger la jurisdicción del Tribunal. Un Tribunal no podrá ordenar el embargo, ni la suspensión de la aplicación de la medida presuntamente violatoria a la que se refiere el artículo 9-17 ó 9-18. Para efectos de este artículo, se considerará que una recomendación constituye una orden.

Artículo 9-36. Laudo definitivo

1.   Cuando un Tribunal dicte un laudo definitivo desfavorable a una Parte, el Tribunal sólo podrá ordenar, por separado o en combinación:

a)   el pago de daños pecuniarios y los intereses que procedan;

b) la restitución de la propiedad, en cuyo caso el laudo dispondrá que la Parte contendiente podrá pagar daños pecuniarios, más los intereses que procedan, en lugar de la restitución.

2. Asimismo, un Tribunal podrá también ordenar el pago de costas de acuerdo con las reglas de arbitraje aplicables.

3. De conformidad con los párrafos 1 y 2, cuando la reclamación se haga con base en el artículo 9-18(1), el laudo:

a) que prevea la restitución de la propiedad, dispondrá que la restitución se otorgue a la empresa;

b) que conceda daños pecuniarios y, en su caso los intereses que procedan, dispondrá que la suma de dinero se pague a la empresa; y

c) dispondrá que el mismo se dicte sin perjuicio de cualquier derecho que cualquier persona tenga sobre la reparación conforme a la legislación interna aplicable.

4. Un Tribunal no podrá ordenar que una Parte pague daños que tengan carácter punitivo.

Artículo 9-37. Definitividad y ejecución del laudo

1. El laudo dictado por un Tribunal será obligatorio sólo para las partes contendientes y únicamente respecto del caso concreto.

2. Conforme a lo dispuesto en el párrafo 3 y al procedimiento de revisión aplicable a un laudo provisional, una parte contendiente acatará y cumplirá con el laudo sin demora.

3. Una parte contendiente no podrá solicitar la ejecución de un laudo definitivo en tanto:

a) en el caso de un laudo definitivo dictado conforme al Convenio del CIADI:

i. no hayan transcurrido 120 días desde la fecha en que se dictó el laudo y ninguna parte contendiente haya solicitado la revisión o anulación del mismo, o

ii. no hayan concluido los procedimientos de revisión o anulación; o

b) en el caso de un laudo definitivo conforme a las Reglas del Mecanismo Complementario del CIADI o las Reglas de Arbitraje de la CNUDMI:

i. no hayan transcurrido tres meses desde la fecha en que se dictó el laudo y ninguna parte contendiente haya iniciado un procedimiento para revisarlo, revocarlo o anularlo, o

ii. una corte no haya desechado o admitido una solicitud de reconsideración, revocación o anulación del laudo y esta resolución no pueda recurrirse.

4. Cada Parte dispondrá la debida ejecución de un laudo en su territorio.

5.   Cuando una Parte contendiente incumpla o no acate un laudo definitivo, la Comisión, a la entrega de una solicitud de una Parte cuyo inversionista fue parte en el arbitraje, integrará un grupo arbitral conforme al artículo 18-06 (Solicitud de integración del grupo arbitral). La Parte solicitante podrá invocar dichos procedimientos para obtener:

   a)   una determinación en el sentido de que el incumplimiento o desacato de los términos del laudo definitivo es contrario a las obligaciones de este Tratado; y

   b)   una recomendación en el sentido de que la Parte cumpla y acate el laudo definitivo.

6.   El inversionista contendiente podrá recurrir a la ejecución de un laudo arbitral conforme al Convenio del CIADI, la Convención de Nueva York o la Convención Interamericana, independientemente de que se hayan iniciado o no los procedimientos contemplados en el párrafo 5.

7.   Para los efectos del Artículo I de la Convención de Nueva York y del Artículo I de la Convención Interamericana, se considerará que la reclamación que se somete a arbitraje conforme a esta sección, surge de una relación u operación comercial.

Artículo 9-38. Disposiciones generales

Momento en que la reclamación se considera sometida a arbitraje

1.   Una reclamación se considera sometida a arbitraje en los términos de esta sección cuando:

   a)   la solicitud para un arbitraje conforme al párrafo 1 del Artículo 36 del Convenio del CIADI ha sido recibida por el Secretario General;

   b)   la notificación de arbitraje, de conformidad con el Artículo 2 de la Parte C de las Reglas del Mecanismo Complementario del CIADI, ha sido recibida por el Secretario General; o

   c)   la notificación de arbitraje contemplada en las Reglas de Arbitraje de la CNUDMI se ha recibido por la Parte contendiente.

Entrega de documentos

2.   La entrega de la notificación y otros documentos a una Parte se hará en el lugar designado por ella en el anexo 9-38(2).

Pagos conforme a contratos de seguro o garantía

3.   En un arbitraje conforme a lo previsto en esta sección, una Parte no aducirá como defensa, contrarreclamación, derecho de compensación, u otros, que el inversionista contendiente ha recibido o recibirá, de acuerdo a un contrato de seguro o garantía, indemnización u otra compensación por todos o por parte de los presuntos daños.

Publicación de laudos

4.   La publicación de laudos se realizará conforme al anexo 9-38(4).

Artículo 9-39. Exclusiones

1.   Sin perjuicio de la aplicabilidad o no aplicabilidad de las disposiciones de solución de controversias de esta sección o del capítulo 18 (Solución de controversias) a otras acciones realizadas por una Parte, de conformidad con el artículo 19-03 (Seguridad nacional), la resolución de una Parte que prohiba o restrinja la adquisición de una inversión en su territorio por un inversionista de la otra Parte o su inversión, de acuerdo con aquel artículo, no estará sujeta a dichas disposiciones.

2.   Las disposiciones de solución de controversias de esta sección y las del capítulo 18 (Solución de controversias) no se aplican a las cuestiones a que se refiere el anexo 9-39.

Sección D - Comité de Inversión y Comercio Transfronterizo de Servicios

Artículo 9-40. Comité de Inversión y Comercio Transfronterizo de Servicios

1.   Las Partes establecen un Comité de Inversión y Comercio Transfronterizo de Servicios, integrado por representantes de cada Parte, de acuerdo con el anexo 9-40.

2.   El Comité se reunirá por lo menos una vez al año, o en cualquier tiempo a solicitud de una Parte o de la Comisión.

3.   El Comité desempeñará, entre otras, las siguientes funciones:

   a)   vigilar la ejecución y administración de este capítulo y del capítulo 10 (Comercio transfronterizo de servicios);

   b)   discutir materias de servicios transfronterizos e inversión de interés bilateral; y

   c)   examinar bilateralmente temas relacionados con estas materias que se discuten en otros foros internacionales.

Anexo 9-10. Transferencias

1.   Para efectos de este anexo, se entenderá por:

crédito extranjero: cualquier tipo de financiamiento originado en mercados extranjeros, cualquiera que sea su naturaleza, forma o vencimiento;

existente: en vigor al 24 de octubre de 1996;

fecha de transferencia: la fecha de cierre en que los fondos que constituyen la inversión fueron convertidos a pesos chilenos, o la fecha de la importación del equipo y la tecnología;

inversión extranjera directa: una inversión de un inversionista de México, que no sea un crédito extranjero, destinado a:

a) establecer una persona jurídica chilena o para incrementar el capital de una persona jurídica chilena existente, con el propósito de producir un flujo adicional de bienes o servicios, excluyendo flujos meramente financieros; o

b) adquirir participación en la propiedad de una persona jurídica chilena y para participar en su administración, excluyendo las inversiones de carácter meramente financiero y que estén diseñadas sólo para adquirir acceso indirecto al mercado financiero de Chile;

Mercado Cambiario Formal: el mercado constituido por las entidades bancarias y otras instituciones autorizadas por la autoridad competente;

pagos de transacciones internacionales corrientes: "pagos de transacciones internacionales corrientes", tal como se definen en los Artículos del Convenio del Fondo Monetario Internacional y, para mayor certeza, no incluye pagos de capital en virtud de un préstamo realizado fuera de las fechas de vencimiento originalmente acordadas en el contrato de préstamo; y

persona jurídica chilena: una empresa constituida u organizada en Chile con fines de lucro, en una manera que se reconozca como persona jurídica de acuerdo a la legislación chilena.

2. Con el propósito de preservar la estabilidad de su moneda, Chile se reserva el derecho de:

a) mantener los requisitos existentes de que las transferencias desde Chile del producto de la venta de todo o parte de una inversión de un inversionista de México o de la liquidación parcial o total de la inversión no podrán realizarse hasta que haya transcurrido un plazo que no exceda de:

    i. en el caso de una inversión hecha conforme a la Ley 18.657, Ley Sobre Fondo de Inversión de Capitales Extranjeros, cinco años desde la fecha de transferencia a Chile, o

    ii. en todos los demás casos, sujeto a lo establecido en el literal c) iii), un año desde la fecha de transferencia a Chile;

b) aplicar la exigencia de mantener un encaje, de conformidad con el artículo 49 Nº 2 de la Ley 18.840, Ley Orgánica del Banco Central de Chile, a una inversión de un inversionista de México que no sea inversión extranjera directa y a créditos extranjeros relacionados con una inversión, siempre que tal exigencia de mantener un encaje no exceda el 30 por ciento del monto de la inversión o el crédito, según sea el caso;

c) adoptar:

i.   medidas que impongan una exigencia de mantener un encaje a que se refiere el literal b), por un periodo que no exceda de dos años desde la fecha de transferencia a Chile,

ii.   cualquier medida razonable que sea compatible con el párrafo 4 necesaria para implementar o evitar la elusión de las medidas tomadas de acuerdo a los literales a) o b), y

iii. medidas compatibles con el artículo 9-10 y con este anexo, que establezcan en el futuro programas especiales de inversión, de carácter voluntario, adicionales al régimen general para la inversión extranjera en Chile, con la excepción de que cualquiera de dichas medidas podrá restringir la transferencia desde Chile del producto de la venta de todo o parte de la inversión de un inversionista de México o de la liquidación total o parcial de la inversión por un período que no exceda de cinco años a partir de la fecha de transferencia a Chile; y

d)   aplicar, de conformidad con la Ley 18.840, medidas con respecto a transferencias relativas a la inversión de un inversionista de México que

i.   requieran que las operaciones de cambios internacionales para dichas transferencias se realicen en el Mercado Cambiario Formal,

ii.   requieran autorización para acceder al Mercado Cambiario Formal para adquirir monedas extranjeras, al tipo de cambio acordado por las partes involucradas en la operación. Este acceso se otorgará sin demora cuando tales transferencias sean:

A.   pagos de transacciones internacionales corrientes,

B.   producto de la venta de todo o parte, y de la liquidación parcial o total, de una inversión de un inversionista de México, o

C.   pagos hechos de conformidad a un préstamo, siempre que se realicen en las fechas de vencimiento originalmente acordadas en el contrato de préstamo, y

iii. requieran que monedas extranjeras sean convertidas a pesos chilenos, al tipo de cambio acordado por las partes involucradas en la operación, salvo las transferencias a que se refiere el inciso ii) (A) a (C), las que estarán eximidas de este requisito.

3.   Cuando Chile se proponga adoptar una medida de las que se refiere el párrafo 2(c), en cuanto fuera practicable:

a)   entregará a México, por adelantado, las razones por la medida que se propone adoptar, así como cualquier información que sea relevante en relación a la medida; y

b)   otorgará a México oportunidad razonable para comentar la medida que se propone adoptar.

4.   Una medida que sea compatible con este anexo, pero sea incompatible con el artículo 9-03, se tendrá como conforme con el artículo 9-03 siempre que, como lo requiere la legislación chilena, no discrimine entre inversionistas que realicen operaciones de la misma naturaleza.

5.   Este anexo se aplica a la Ley 18.840, al Decreto Ley 600 de 1974, a la Ley 18.657 y a cualquier otra ley que establezca en el futuro un programa especial de inversión, con carácter voluntario, que sea compatible con el párrafo 2(c)(iii) y a la continuación o pronta renovación de tales leyes, y a la reforma de tales leyes, en la medida que tal reforma no disminuya la conformidad entre la ley reformada y el artículo 9-10(1), tal como existía inmediatamente antes de la reforma.

Anexo 9-38(2). Lugar para la entrega

Para efectos del artículo 9-38(2), el lugar para la entrega de notificaciones y otros documentos bajo la sección C será:

1.   Para el caso de Chile:

> Dirección de Asuntos Jurídicos
> Ministerio de Relaciones Exteriores de la República de Chile
> Morandé 441
> Santiago,
> Chile

2.   Para el caso de México:

> Dirección General de Inversión Extranjera
> Secretaría de Comercio y Fomento Industrial
> Insurgentes Sur 1940, Piso 8,
> Colonia Florida, C.P. 01030, México, D.F.

Anexo 9-38(4). Publicación de laudos

Para efectos del artículo 9-38(4), la publicación de laudos se realizará:

1.   Para el caso en que Chile sea la Parte contendiente, ya sea Chile o un inversionista contendiente en el procedimiento de arbitraje podrá hacer público un laudo.

2.   Para el caso en que México sea la Parte contendiente, las reglas de procedimiento correspondientes se aplicarán con respecto a la publicación de un laudo.

Anexo 9-39. Exclusiones de las disposiciones de solución de controversias México

Las disposiciones relativas al mecanismo de solución de controversias previsto en el capítulo 18 (Solución de controversias), no se aplicarán a una decisión de la Comisión Nacional de Inversiones Extranjeras que resulte de someter a revisión una inversión conforme a las disposiciones del Anexo I, página I-M-F-4, relativa a si debe o no permitirse una adquisición que esté sujeta a dicha revisión.

Anexo 9-40. Integrantes del Comité de Inversión y Comercio Transfronterizo de Servicios

Para efectos del artículo 9-40, el Comité estará integrado:

1.   Para el caso de Chile, por la Dirección General de Relaciones Económicas Internacionales del Ministerio de Relaciones Exteriores, o su sucesora.

2.   Para el caso de México, por la Secretaría de Comercio y Fomento Industrial, o su sucesora.

* * *

ACUERDO MARCO PARA LA CREACIÓN DE LA ZONA DE LIBRE COMERCIO ENTRE EL MERCOSUR Y LA COMUNIDAD ANDINA[*]
[excerpts]

> The Framework Agreement for the Creation of the Free Trade Area between MERCOSUR and the Andean Community was signed on 30 September 1998. The signatories were Argentine, Brazil, Paraguay and Uruguay, member States of the Southern Common Market (MERCOSUR), on the one hand, and Bolivia, Colombia, Ecuador, Peru and Venezuela, member countries of the Cartagena Agreement, on the other hand. The Agreement entered into force on the date of signature.

Los Gobiernos de la República Argentina, de la República Federativa del Brasil, de la República del Paraguay y de la República Oriental del Uruguay, Estados Partes del Mercado Común del Sur -MERCOSUR- y los Gobiernos de la República de Bolivia, de la República de Colombia, de la República del Ecuador, de la República del Perú y de la República de Venezuela, Países Miembros del Acuerdo de Cartagena, en adelante denominados "las Partes Signatarias" del presente Acuerdo Marco, cuyas "Partes Contratantes" son el MERCOSUR y la Comunidad Andina,

CONSIDERANDO:

…

Que para contribuir a la expansión del comercio mundial y al eficiente funcionamiento de los mercados, es fundamental ofrecer a los agentes económicos reglas claras para el desarrollo del intercambio de bienes y servicios, así como de las inversiones recíprocas entre el MERCOSUR y la Comunidad Andina;

…

Convienen en celebrar el presente Acuerdo Marco:

TÍTULO I
OBJETIVOS

Artículo 1

El presente Acuerdo tiene por objetivos:

---

[*] *Source*: Comunidad Andina, Secretaria General (1998)."Acuerdo Marco para la Creación de la Zona de Libre Comercio entre el MERCOSUR y la Comunidad Andina ", SG/di 67, 21 de abril de 1998, mimeo; available also on the Internet (http://comunidandina.org/docs/mercosur.htm). [Note added by the editor.]

...

d)   Establecer un marco normativo para promover e impulsar las inversiones recíprocas entre los agentes económicos de las Partes Contratantes;

...

TÍTULO III
COOPERACIÓN ECONÓMICA Y COMERCIAL

Artículo 4

Para apoyar las acciones tendientes a incrementar los intercambios comerciales de bienes y servicios, las Partes Contratantes estimularán, entre otras iniciativas, las siguientes:

a)   La promoción de reuniones empresariales y otras actividades complementarias que amplíen las relaciones de comercio e inversión entre los sectores privados de ambas Partes Contratantes;

...

e)   La promoción de la complementación y de la integración industrial, con la finalidad de lograr el máximo aprovechamiento de los recursos disponibles, e incrementar el comercio de las Partes Contratantes;

f)   El examen de la posibilidad de suscribir entre las Partes Signatarias, nuevos Acuerdos de Promoción y Protección Recíproca de Inversiones, así como de Acuerdos para evitar la doble tributación; y;

...

TÍTULO IV
COMISIÓN NEGOCIADORA

Artículo 5

Para el logro de los objetivos del presente Acuerdo, las Partes Contratantes convienen en establecer una Comisión Negociadora por los Representantes Alternos ante la Comisión de la Comunidad Andina y del Grupo Ad Hoc del Grupo Mercado Común del MERCOSUR.

TÍTULO V
DISPOSICIONES VARIAS

Artículo 6

El presente Acuerdo entrará en vigor en la fecha de su firma.

Artículo 7

Las Partes Signatarias acuerdan mantener vigentes los Acuerdos de Alcance Parcial suscritos en el marco de la ALADI, hasta el 30 de septiembre de 1998. Los Acuerdos de Alcance Regional subsistirán en tanto no entre en vigencia al Acuerdo de Libre Comercio entre la Comunidad Andina y el MERCOSUR.

*   *   *

PART TWO

INVESTMENT-RELATED PROVISIONS IN ASSOCIATION AGREEMENTS, BILATERAL AND INTERREGIONAL COOPERATION AGREEMENTS

ANNEX A

Investment-related provisions in free trade agreements signed between the countries members of the European Free Trade Association and third countries and list of agreements signed (end-1999)

The countries members of the European Free Trade Association have signed free trade agreements that include investment-related provisions with the following countries and territories: Turkey (1991), Israel (1992), Poland (1992), Romania (1992), Bulgaria (1993), Hungary (1993), Czech Republic (1993), Slovak Republic (1993), Slovenia (1995), Estonia (1995), Latvia (1995), Lithuania (1995), Morocco (1997), and the Palestine Liberation Organization (PLO) (1998). The relevant investment-related provisions in these agreements are similar, with few variations, some of which are shown in the provisions from three agreements reproduced below.

AGREEMENT BETWEEN ICELAND, LIECHTENSTEIN, NORWAY AND SWITZERLAND, COUNTRIES MEMBERS OF THE EUROPEAN FREE TRADE ASSOCIATION AND THE REPUBLIC OF SLOVENIA[*]
[excerpts]

ARTICLE 17

Rules of competition concerning undertakings

1.   The following are incompatible with the proper functioning of this Agreement in so far as they may affect trade between an EFTA State and Slovenia:

(a)   all agreements between undertakings, decisions by associations of undertakings and concerted practices between undertakings which have as their object or effect the prevention, restriction or distortion of competition;

(b)   abuse by one or more undertakings of a dominant position in the territories of the States Parties to this Agreement as a whole or in a substantial part thereof.

2.   The provisions of paragraph 1 shall also apply to the activities of public undertakings, and undertakings for which the States Parties to this Agreement grant special or exclusive rights, in so far as the application of these provisions does not obstruct the performance, in law or in fact, of the particular public tasks assigned to them.

3. If a State Party to this Agreement considers that a given practice is incompatible with the provisions of paragraphs 1 and 2, it may take appropriate measures under the conditions and in accordance with the procedures laid down in Article 25 (Procedure for the application of safeguard measures).

ARTICLE 30

Services and Investment

1.   The States Parties to this Agreement recognize the growing importance of certain areas, such as services and investments. In their efforts to gradually develop and broaden their cooperation, in particular in the context of European integration, they will co-operate with the aim of achieving a gradual liberalization and mutual opening of markets for investments and trade in services, taking into account the results of the Uruguay Round as well as any relevant future work under the auspices of the World Trade Organization.

2.   The EFTA States and Slovenia will discuss this co-operation in the joint Committee with the aim of developing and deepening their relations under the Agreement.

*   *   *

---

[*]   *Source*: European Free Trade Association secretariat (1999). "Agreement between Iceland, Liechtenstein, Norway and Switzerland, Countries Members of the European Free Trade Association and the Republic of Slovenia"; available on the Internet (http://www.efta.int/structure/EFTA/efta-sec.cfm). [Note added by the editor.]

AGREEMENT BETWEEN ICELAND, LIECHTENSTEIN, NORWAY AND SWITZERLAND, COUNTRIES MEMBERS OF THE EUROPEAN FREE TRADE ASSOCIATION AND THE REPUBLIC OF LATVIA*
[excerpts]

ARTICLE 16

Rules of competition concerning undertakings

1.   The following are incompatible with the proper functioning of this Agreement in so far as they may affect trade between an EFTA State and Latvia:

(a)   all agreements between undertakings, decisions by associations of undertakings and concerted practices between undertakings which have as their object or effect the prevention, restriction or distortion of competition;

(b)   abuse by one or more undertakings of a dominant position in the territories of the States Parties to this Agreement as a whole or in a substantial part thereof.

2.   The provisions of paragraph 1 shall also apply to the activities of public undertakings, and undertakings for which the States Parties to this Agreement grant special or exclusive rights, in so far as the application of these provisions does not obstruct the performance, in law or in fact, of the particular public tasks assigned to them.

3.   If a State Party to this Agreement considers that a given practice is incompatible with the provisions of paragraphs 1 and 2, it may take appropriate measures under the conditions and in accordance with the procedures laid down in Article 24 (Procedure for the application of safeguard measures).

ARTICLE 29

Services and Investment

1.   The States Parties to this Agreement recognize the growing importance of certain areas, such as services and investments. In their efforts to gradually develop and broaden their cooperation, in particular in the context of European integration, they will co-operate with the aim of achieving a gradual liberalization and mutual opening of markets for investments and trade in services, taking into account the results of the Uruguay Round as well as any relevant future work under the auspices of the World Trade Organization. They will endeavour to accord to each others' operators treatment no less favourable than that accorded to other foreign operators in their territories on condition that a balance of rights and obligations as well as a balance of operating conditions exist between the individual States Parties to this Agreement.

---

*   *Source*: European Free Trade Association secretariat (1999). "Agreement between Iceland, Liechtenstein, Norway and Switzerland, Countries Members of the European Free Trade Association and the Republic of Latvia"; available on the Internet (http://www.efta.int/structure/EFTA/efta-sec.cfm). [Note added by the editor.]

2.   The EFTA States and Latvia will discuss this co-operation in the joint Committee with the aim of developing and deepening their relations under the Agreement.

*   *   *

AGREEMENT BETWEEN ICELAND, LIECHTENSTEIN, NORWAY AND SWITZERLAND, COUNTRIES MEMBERS OF THE EUROPEAN FREE TRADE ASSOCIATION AND THE KINGDOM OF MOROCCO*
[excerpts]

ARTICLE 14

Payments and Transfers

...

3.   No restrictive measures shall apply to transfers related to investments and in particular to the preparation of amounts invested or reinvested and of any kind revenues stemming therefrom.

...

ARTICLE 17

Rules of competition concerning undertakings

1.   The following are incompatible with the proper functioning of this Agreement in so far as they may affect trade between an EFTA State and Morocco:

(a)   all agreements between undertakings, decisions by associations of undertakings and concerted practices between undertakings which have as their object or effect the prevention, restriction or distortion of competition;

(b)   abuse by one or more undertakings of a dominant position in the territories of the States Parties to this Agreement as a whole or in a substantial part thereof.

2.   The provisions of paragraph 1 shall also apply to the activities of public undertakings, and undertakings for which the States Parties to this Agreement grant special or exclusive rights, in so far as the application of these provisions does not obstruct the performance, in law or in fact, of the particular public tasks assigned to them.

3.   If a State Party to this Agreement considers that a given practice is incompatible with the provisions of paragraphs 1 and 2, it may take appropriate measures under the conditions and in accordance with the procedures laid down in Article 25 (Procedure for the application of safeguard measures).

---

*   *Source*: European Free Trade Association secretariat (1999). "Agreement between Iceland, Liechtenstein, Norway and Switzerland, Countries Members of the European Free Trade Association and the Kingdom of Morocco"; available on the Internet (http://www.efta.int/structure/EFTA/efta-sec.cfm). [Note added by the editor.]

ARTICLE 28

Services and Investment

1.   The States Parties to this Agreement recognize the growing importance of certain areas, such as services and investments. In their efforts to gradually develop and broaden their cooperation, in particular in the context of Euro-Mediterranean integration, they will co-operate with the aim of achieving a gradual liberalization and mutual opening of markets for investments and trade in services, taking into account on-going work under the auspices of the WTO.

2.   The EFTA States and Morocco shall review developments in the services sectors with a view to considering liberalization measures between the parties.

3.   The EFTA States and Morocco will discuss this co-operation in the joint Committee with the aim of developing and deepening their relations under the Agreement.

*   *   *

ANNEX B

Investment-related provisions in association, partnership and cooperation agreements signed between the countries members of the European Community and third countries and list of agreements signed

(end-1999)

AGREEMENT ESTABLISHING AN ASSOCIATION BETWEEN THE EUROPEAN ECONOMIC COMMUNITY AND THE UNITED REPUBLIC OF TANZANIA, THE REPUBLIC OF UGANDA AND THE REPUBLIC OF KENYA[*]
[excerpts]

The Agreement Establishing an Association between the European Economic Community and the United Republic of Tanzania, the Republic of Uganda and the Republic of Kenya was signed on 24 September 1969. The agreement is no longer in force. Investment relations between the European Community and Kenya, Tanzania and Uganda are presently governed by the Fourth Convention of Lomé.

TITLE II

RIGHT OF ESTABLISHMENT AND SERVICES

Article 16

The Partner States of the East African Community shall ensure that, in the matter of the right of establishment and the provision of services, there shall be no discriminatory treatment, de jure or de facto, between nationals or between companies of Member States.

Article 17

Should one or more Partner States of the East African Community grant nationals or companies of a non-Member State more favourable treatment as regards the right of establishment or provision of services, such treatment shall be extended by the Partner State or States concerned to nationals or companies of the Member States, except where it arises out of regional agreements.

Nevertheless, nationals or companies of a Member State may not, for a specific activity, benefit in a Partner State of the East African Community from the provisions of this Article if the Member State to which they belong does not grant the nationals or companies of the Partner State of the East African Community concerned, as regards the right of establishment or provision of services, the same advantages for the activity in question as those obtained by the Partner State of the East African Community through an agreement with a non-Member State referred to in the preceding paragraph.

Article 18

Without prejudice to the provisions relating to movements of capital, the right of establishment within the meaning of this Agreement shall include the right to engage in and to

---

[*] *Source*: European Community (1969). "Agreement Establishing an Association between the European Economic Community and the United Republic of Tanzania, the Republic of Uganda and the Republic of Kenya", *Collection of the Agreements Concluded by the European Communities*, vol. 5 (1952-1975), (United Kingdom: European Communities), pp.531-579. [Note added by the editor.]

exercise self-employed activities: to set up and manage undertakings and, in particular, companies; and to set up agencies, branches or subsidiaries.

Article 19

Services within the meaning of this Agreement shall be deemed to be services normally provided against remuneration, provided that they are not governed by the provisions relating to trade, the right of establishment or movements of capital. Services shall include in particular activities of an industrial character, activities of a commercial character, artisan activities and activities of the liberal professions, excluding activities of employed persons.

Article 20

1. Companies within the meaning of this Agreement shall be deemed to be companies under civil or commercial law, including co-operative societies and other legal persons under public or private law, but not including non-profit-making bodies.

2. 'Company of a Member State or of a Partner State of the East African Community' shall mean any company constituted in accordance with the law of a Member State or of a Partner State of the East African Community and having its registered office, central administration or main establishment in a Member State or in a Partner State of the East African Community; nevertheless, should it have only its registered office in a Member State or in a Partner State of the East African Community, its business must have an effective and continuous link with the economy of that Member State or of that Partner State of the East African Community.

TITLE III

PAYMENTS AND CAPITAL

Article 21

The Member States and the Partner States of the East African Community shall authorize payments relating to trade in goods and in services, and also the transfer of such payments to the Partner State of the East African Community or to the Member State in which the creditor or the beneficiary is resident, in so far as the movement of goods and services has been liberalized in pursuance of this Agreement.

Article 22

The Partner States of the East African Community shall treat nationals and companies of Member States on an equal footing in respect of investments made by them, of capital movements and of current payments resulting therefrom, and also of transfers connected with such operations.

*   *   *

FRAMEWORK COOPERATION AGREEMENT BETWEEN THE EUROPEAN ECONOMIC COMMUNITY AND THE REPUBLICS OF COSTA RICA, EL SALVADOR, GUATEMALA, HONDURAS, NICARAGUA AND PANAMA*
[excerpts]

The Framework Cooperation Agreement between the European Economic Community and the Republics of Costa Rica, El Salvador, Guatemala, Honduras, Nicaragua and Panama was signed on 22 February 1993, and entered into force on 1 March 1999.

Article 8

Investment

1.   The Contracting Parties agree:

-     to promote, so far as their powers, rules and regulations and policies permit, an increase in mutually beneficial investment,

-     to endeavour to improve the climate for such investment by encouraging investment promotion and protection agreements between the Community's Member States and the Central American countries.

2.   In pursuit of these objectives, the Contracting parties agree to take measures to help promote and attract investment with a view to identifying new opportunities for such investment and encouraging the implementation thereof.

These measures shall include:

(a)   seminars, exhibitions and business missions;

(b)   training businessmen with a view to setting up investment projects;

(c)   technical assistance for joint investment;

(d)   measures under the European Community Investment Partners (ECIP) programme.

---

* *Source*: European Community (1999). "Framework Cooperation Agreement between the European Economic Community and the Republics of Costa Rica, El Salvador, Guatemala, Honduras, Nicaragua and Panama", *Official Journal of the European Communities*, L 63/39 of 12 March 1999, pp. 39-53. [Note added by the editor.]

185

3.   Cooperation in this field may involve public, private, national or multilateral bodies, including regional financial institutions, from both Central America and the Community.

*   *   *

FRAMEWORK AGREEMENT FOR COOPERATION BETWEEN THE EUROPEAN ECONOMIC COMMUNITY AND THE CARTAGENA AGREEMENT AND ITS MEMBER COUNTRIES, NAMELY, THE REPUBLIC OF BOLIVIA, THE REPUBLIC OF COLOMBIA, THE REPUBLIC OF ECUADOR, THE REPUBLIC OF PERU AND THE REPUBLIC OF VENEZUELA[*]
[excerpts]

The Framework Agreement for Cooperation between the European Economic Community and the Cartagena Agreement and Its member countries, namely, Bolivia, Colombia, Ecuador, Peru and Venezuela, was signed on 28 April 1993, and entered into force on 1 May 1998.

Article 3

Economic cooperation

1.   The Contracting Parties, taking into account their mutual interest and medium- and long-term economic objectives, undertake to establish between themselves economic cooperation of the widest possible scope, from which no field of activity is excluded in principle. The aims of such cooperation shall be in particular to:

...

(d)   encourage the flow of investment and the transfer of technology and reinforce investment protection;

...

Article 9

Investment

1.   The Contracting Parties agree:

-       to promote, so far as their powers, rules and regulations and respective policies permit, an increase in mutually beneficial investment,

---

[*] *Source*: European Community (1998). "Framework Agreement for Cooperation between the European Economic Community and the Cartagena Agreement and Its Member Countries, namely, the Republic of Bolivia, the Republic of Colombia, the Republic of Ecuador, the Republic of Peru and the Republic of Venezuela", *Official Journal of the European Communities*, Document 298 A0429 (01), L 127, 29 April 1998, pp. 11-25; available also on the Internet (http://europa.eu.int/search97cgi/s97_cg...emplate=EC_HTML-view.hts&hlnavigate=ALL). [Note added by the editor.]

- to improve the climate for such investment by seeking, in particular, agreements on investment promotion and protection between the Community's Member States and the Andean Pact countries based on the principles of non-discrimination and reciprocity.

2. In pursuit of these objectives, the Contracting Parties shall endeavour to stimulate investment promotion, *inter alia*, by means of:

- seminars, exhibitions and visits by company directors,

- training businessmen with a view to setting up investment projects,

- technical assistance necessary for joint investment,

- measures under the ECIP programme.

3. Cooperation in this field may involve public, private, national or multilateral bodies, including regional financial institutions such as 'Corporación Andina de Fomento' (CAF) and 'Fondo Latinoamericano de Reservas' (FLAR).

*   *   *

PARTNERSHIP AND COOPERATION AGREEMENT BETWEEN THE EUROPEAN COMMUNITIES AND THEIR MEMBER STATES AND UKRAINE *
[excerpts]

The Partnership and Cooperation Agreement between the European Communities and Their Member States on the one part, and Ukraine on the other part, was signed at Luxembourg on 14 June 1994. It entered into force on 1 March 1998. The Member States of the European Communities are: Austria, Belgium, Denmark, Finland, France, Germany, Greece, Ireland, Italy, Luxembourg, the Netherlands, Portugal, Spain, Sweden and the United Kingdom.

TITLE IV

PROVISIONS AFFECTING BUSINESS AND INVESTMENT

CHAPTER I

LABOUR CONDITIONS

Article 24

1.   Subject to the laws, conditions and procedures applicable in each Member State, the Community and the Member States shall endeavour to ensure that the treatment accorded to Ukrainian nationals, legally employed in the territory of a Member State shall be free from any discrimination based on nationality, as regards working conditions, remuneration or dismissal, as compared to its own nationals.

2.   Subject to the laws, conditions and procedures applicable in Ukraine, Ukraine shall endeavour to ensure that the treatment accorded to nationals of a Member State, legally employed in the territory of Ukraine shall be free from any discrimination based on nationality, as regards working conditions, remuneration or dismissal, as compared to its own nationals.

---

*   *Source*: European Communities (1998). "Partnership and Cooperation Agreement between the European Communities and Their Member States, and Ukraine", *Official Journal of the European Communities*, L 049, 19 February 1998, pp. 3-46; available also on the Internet (http://www.europa.eu.int/eur-lex/en/lif/dat/1998/en_298A0219_02.html). [Note added by the Editor.]

CHAPTER II

CONDITIONS AFFECTING THE ESTABLISHMENT AND OPERATION OF COMPANIES

Article 30

1.   (a)   The Community and its Member States shall grant for the establishment of Ukrainian companies in their territories treatment no less favourable than that accorded to companies of any third country, and this in conformity with their legislation and regulations.

(b)   Without prejudice to the reservations listed in Annex IV, the Community and its Member States shall grant to subsidiaries of Ukrainian companies established in their territories a treatment no less favourable than that granted to any Community company, in respect of their operation, and this in conformity with their legislation and regulations.

(c)   The Community and its Member States shall grant to branches of Ukrainian companies established in their territories a treatment no less favourable than that accorded to branches of companies of any third country, in respect of their operation, and this in conformity with their legislation and regulations.

2.   (a)   Without prejudice to the reservations listed in Annex V, Ukraine shall grant for the establishment of Community companies in its territory, a treatment no less favourable than that accorded to its own companies or to companies of any third country whichever is the better, and this in conformity with its legislation and regulations.

(b)   Ukraine shall grant to subsidiaries and branches of Community companies, established in its territory, treatment no less favourable than that accorded to its own companies or branches respectively or to companies or branches of any third country respectively, whichever is the better, in respect of their operations, and this in conformity with its legislation and regulations.

3.   The provisions of paragraphs 1 and 2 cannot be used so as to circumvent a Party's legislation and regulations applicable to access to specific sectors or activities by subsidiaries of companies of the other Party established in the territory of such first Party.

The treatment referred to in paragraph 1 and 2 shall benefit companies established in the Community and Ukraine respectively at the date of entry into force of this Agreement and companies established after that date once they are established.

Article 32

For the purposes of this Agreement:

(a)   A 'Community company' or a 'Ukrainian company' respectively, shall mean a company set up in accordance with the laws of a Member State or of Ukraine respectively and having its registered office or central administration or principal place of business in the territory of the Community or Ukraine respectively. However, should the company, set up in accordance with the laws of a Member State or Ukraine respectively, have only its registered office in the territory of the Community or Ukraine respectively, the company shall be considered a Community or Ukrainian company respectively if its operations possess a real and continuous link with the economy of one of the Member States or Ukraine respectively.

(b)   'Subsidiary` of a company shall mean a company which is effectively controlled by the first company.

(c)   'Branch` of a company shall mean a place of business not having legal personality which has the appearance of permanency, such as the extension of a parent body, has a management and is materially equipped to negotiate business with third parties so that the latter, although knowing that there will, if necessary, be a legal link with the parent body, the head office of which is abroad, do not have to deal directly with such parent body but may transact business at the place of business constituting the extension.

(d)   'Establishment` shall mean the right of Community or Ukrainian companies as referred to in (a) to take up economic activities by means of the setting-up of subsidiaries and branches in Ukraine or in the Community respectively.

(e)   'Operation` shall mean the pursuit of economic activities.

(f)   'Economic activities` shall mean activities of an industrial, commercial and professional character.

(g)   With regard to international maritime transport, including intermodal operations involving a sea leg, nationals of the Member States or of Ukraine, established outside the Community or Ukraine respectively, and shipping companies established outside the Community or Ukraine and controlled by nationals of a Member State or Ukrainian nationals respectively, shall also be beneficiaries of the provisions of this Chapter and Chapter III, if their vessels are registered in that Member State or in Ukraine respectively in accordance with their respective legislations.

Article 33

1.   Notwithstanding any other provisions of this Agreement, a Party shall not be prevented from taking measures for prudential reasons, including for the protection of investors, depositors, policyholders or persons to whom a fiduciary duty is owed by a financial service supplier, or to ensure the integrity and stability of the financial system. Where such measures do not conform with the provisions of this Agreement, they shall not be used as a means of avoiding the obligations of a Party under this Agreement.

2.   Nothing in this Agreement shall be construed to require a Party to disclose information relating to the affairs and accounts of individual customers or any confidential or proprietary information in the possession of public entities.

Article 34

The provisions of this Agreement shall not prejudice the application by each Party of any measure necessary to prevent the circumvention of its measures concerning third country access to its market, through the provisions of this Agreement.

Article 35

1.   Notwithstanding the provisions of Chapter I, a Community company or a Ukrainian company established in the territory of Ukraine or the Community respectively shall be entitled to employ, or have employed by one of its subsidiaries or branches, in accordance with the legislation in force in the host country of establishment, in the territory of Ukraine and the Community respectively, employees who are nationals of Community Member States and Ukraine respectively, provided that such employees are key personnel as defined in paragraph 2, and that they are employed exclusively by companies, subsidiaries or branches. The residence and work permits of such employees shall only cover the period of such employment.

2.   Key personnel of the above-mentioned companies herein referred to as 'organizations` are 'intracorporate transferees` as defined in (c) in the following categories, provided that the organization is a legal person and that the persons concerned have been employed by it or have been partners in it (other than as majority shareholders), for at least the year immediately preceding such movement:

(a)   Persons working in a senior position with an organization, who primarily direct the management of the establishment, receiving general supervision or direction principally from the board of directors or stockholders of the business or their equivalent, including:

- directing the establishment or a department or subdivision of the establishment,

- supervising and controlling the work of other supervisory, professional or managerial employees,

- having the authority personally to engage and dismiss or recommend engaging, dismissing or other personnel actions.

(b)   Persons working within an organization who possess uncommon knowledge essential to the establishment's service, research equipment, techniques or management. The assessment of such knowledge may reflect, apart from knowledge specific to the establishment, a high level of qualification referring to a type of work or trade requiring specific technical knowledge; including membership of an accredited profession.

(c)   An 'intracorporate transferee' is defined as a natural person working within an organization in the territory of a Party, and being temporarily transferred in the context of pursuit of economic activities in the territory of the other Party; the organization concerned must have its principal place of business in the territory of a Party and the transfer be to an establishment (branch, subsidiary) of that organization, effectively pursuing like economic activities in the territory of the other Party.

Article 36

1.   The Parties shall use their best endeavours to avoid taking any measures or actions which render the conditions for the establishment and operation of each other's companies more

restrictive than the situation existing on the day preceding the date of signature of the Agreement.

2.   The provisions of this Article are without prejudice to those of Article 44: the situations covered by such Article 44 shall be solely governed by its provisions to the exclusion of any other.

3.   Acting in the spirit of partnership and cooperation and in light of provisions contained in Article 51, the Government of Ukraine shall inform the Community of its intentions to submit new legislation or adopt new regulations which may render the conditions for the establishment or operation in Ukraine of subsidiaries and branches of Community companies more restrictive than the situation existing on the day preceding the date of signature of the Agreement. The Community may request Ukraine to communicate the drafts of such legislation or regulations and to enter into consultations about those drafts.

4.   Where new legislation or regulations introduced in Ukraine would result in rendering the conditions for establishment of Community companies into its territory and for the operation of subsidiaries and branches of Community companies established in Ukraine more restrictive than the situation xisting on the day of signature of the Agreement, such respective legislation or regulations shall not apply during three years following the entry into force of the relevant act to those subsidiaries and branches already established in Ukraine at the time of entry into force of the relevant act.

CHAPTER IV

GENERAL PROVISIONS

Article 41

1.   The provisions of this Title shall be applied subject to limitations justified on grounds of public policy, public security or public health.

2.   They shall not apply to activities which in the territory of either Party are connected, even occasionally, with the exercise of official authority.

Article 42

For the purpose of this Title, nothing in the Agreement shall prevent the Parties from applying their laws and regulations regarding entry and stay, work, labour conditions and establishment of natural persons and supply of services, provided that - in so doing - they do not apply them in a manner so as to nullify or impair the benefits accruing to any Party under the terms of a specific provision of the Agreement. This provision does not prejudice the application of Article 41.

Article 43

Companies which are controlled and exclusively owned by Ukrainian companies and Community companies jointly shall also be beneficiaries of the provisions of Chapters II, III and IV.

Article 44

Treatment granted by either Party to the other hereunder shall, as from the day one month prior to the date of entry into force of the relevant obligations of the General Agreement on Trade in Services (GATS), in respect of sectors or measures covered by the GATS, in no case be more favourable than that accorded by such first Party under the provisions of GATS and this in respect of each service sector, subsector and mode of supply.

Article 45

For the purposes of Chapters II, III and IV, no account shall be taken of treatment accorded by the Community, its Member States or Ukraine pursuant to commitments entered into in economic integration agreements in accordance with the principles of Article V of the GATS.

Article 46

1.   The most-favoured-nation treatment granted in accordance with the provisions of this Title shall not apply to the tax advantages which the Parties are providing or will provide in the future on the basis of agreements to avoid double taxation, or other tax arrangements.

2.   Nothing in this Title shall be construed to prevent the adoption or enforcement by the Parties of any measure aimed at preventing the avoidance or evasion of taxes pursuant to the tax provisions of agreements to avoid double taxation and other tax arrangements, or domestic fiscal legislation.

3.   Nothing in this Title shall be construed to prevent Member States or Ukraine from distinguishing, in the application of the relevant provisions of their fiscal legislation, between taxpayers who are not in identical situations, in particular as regards their place of residence.

Article 47

Without prejudice to Article 35, no provisions of Chapters II, III and IV hereof shall be interpreted as giving the right to:

- nationals of the Member States or of Ukraine respectively to enter, or stay in, the territory of Ukraine or the Community respectively in any capacity whatsoever, and in particular as a shareholder or partner in a company or manager or employed thereof or supplier or recipient of services,

- Community subsidiaries or branches of Ukrainian companies to employ or have employed in the territory of the Community nationals of Ukraine,

- Ukrainian subsidiaries or branches of Community companies to employ or have employed in the territory of Ukraine nationals of the Member States,

- Ukrainian companies or Community subsidiaries or branches of Ukrainian companies to supply Ukrainian persons to act for and under the control of other persons by temporary employment contracts,

- Community companies or Ukrainian subsidiaries or branches of Community companies to supply workers who are nationals of the Member States by temporary employment contracts.

TITLE V

CURRENT PAYMENTS AND CAPITAL

Article 48

1.   The Parties undertake to authorize in freely convertible currency, any payments on the current account of balance of payments between residents of the Community and of Ukraine connected with the movement of goods, services or persons made in accordance with the provisions of this Agreement.

2.   With regard to transactions on the capital account of balance of payments, from entry into force of this Agreement, the free movement of capital relating to direct investments made in companies formed in accordance with the laws of the host country and investments made in accordance with the provisions of Chapter II of Title IV, and the liquidation or repatriation of these investments and of any profit stemming therefrom shall be ensured.

3.   Without prejudice to paragraph 2 or to paragraph 5, as from entry into force of this Agreement, no new foreign exchange restrictions on the movement of capital and current payments connected therewith between residents of the Community and Ukraine shall be introduced and the existing arrangements shall not become more restrictive.

4.   The Parties shall consult each other with a view to facilitating the movement of forms of capital other than those referred to in paragraph 2 between the Community and Ukraine in order to promote the objectives of this Agreement.

5.   With reference to the provisions of this Article, until a full convertibility of Ukrainian currency within the meaning of Article VIII of the Articles of Agreement of the International Monetary Fund (IMF) is introduced, Ukraine may, in exceptional circumstances, apply exchange restrictions connected with the granting or taking-up of short- and medium-term financial credits to the extent that such restrictions are imposed on Ukraine for the granting of such credits and are permitted according to Ukraine's status under the IMF. Ukraine shall apply these restrictions in a non-discriminatory manner. They shall be applied in such a manner as to cause the least possible disruption to this Agreement. Ukraine shall inform the Cooperation Council promptly of the introduction of such measures and of any changes therein.

6.   Without prejudice to paragraphs 1 and 2, where, in exceptional circumstances, movements of capital between the Community and Ukraine cause, or threaten to cause, serious difficulties for the operation of exchange rate policy or monetary policy in the Community or Ukraine, the Community and Ukraine, respectively, may take safeguard measures with regard to movements of capital between the Community and Ukraine for a period not exceeding six months if such measures are strictly necessary.

TITLE VI

COMPETITION, INTELLECTUAL, INDUSTRIAL AND COMMERCIAL PROPERTY PROTECTION AND LEGISLATIVE COOPERATION

Article 49

1.　　The Parties agree to work to remedy or remove through the application of their competition laws or otherwise, restrictions on competition by enterprises or caused by State intervention in so far as they may affect trade between the Community and the Ukraine.

2.　　In order to attain the objectives mentioned in paragraph 1:

2.1.　　The Parties shall ensure that they have and enforce laws addressing restrictions on competition by enterprises within their jurisdiction.

2.2.　　The Parties shall refrain from granting State aid favouring certain undertakings or the production of goods other than primary products as defined in the GATT, or the provision of services, which distort or threaten to distort competition in so far as they affect trade between the Community and Ukraine.

2.3.　　Upon request by one Party, the other Party shall provide information on its aid schemes or on particular individual cases of State aid. No information needs to be provided which is covered by legislative requirements of the Parties on professional or commercial secrets.

2.4.　　In the case of State monopolies of a commercial character, the Parties declare heir readiness, as from the fourth year from the date of entry into force of this Agreement, to ensure that there is no discrimination between nationals of the Parties regarding the conditions under which goods are procured or marketed.

2.5.　　In the case of public undertakings or undertakings to which Member States or Ukraine grant exclusive rights, the Parties declare their readiness, as from the fourth year from the date of entry into force of this Agreement, to ensure that there is neither enacted nor maintained any measure distorting trade between the Community and Ukraine to an extent contrary to the Parties' respective interests. This provision shall not obstruct the performance, in law or fact, of the particular tasks assigned to such undertakings.

2.6.　　The period defined in paragraphs 2.4 and 2.5 may be extended by agreement of the Parties.

3.　　Consultations may take place within the Cooperation Committee at the request of the Community or Ukraine on the restrictions or distortions of competition referred to in paragraphs 1 and 2 and on the enforcement of their competition rules, subject to limitations imposed by laws regarding disclosure of information, confidentiality and business secrecy. Consultations may also comprise questions on the interpretation of paragraphs 1 and 2.

4.   The Parties with experience in applying competition rules shall give full consideration to providing other Parties, upon request and within available resources, technical assistance for the development and implementation of competition rules.

5.   The above provisions in no way affect the Parties' rights to apply adequate measures, notably those referred to in Article 19, in order to address distortions of trade in goods or services.

TITLE VII

ECONOMIC COOPERATION

Article 52

1.   The Community and Ukraine shall establish economic cooperation aimed at contributing to the process of economic reform and recovery and sustainable development of Ukraine. Such cooperation shall strengthen and develop economic links, to the benefit of both Parties.

Article 54

Investment promotion and protection

1.   Bearing in mind the respective powers and competences of the Community and the Member States, cooperation shall aim to establish a favourable climate for investment, both domestic and foreign, especially through better conditions for investment protection, the transfer of capital and the exchange of information on investment opportunities.

2.   The aims of this cooperation shall be in particular:

- the conclusion, where appropriate, between the Member States and Ukraine, of agreements for the promotion and protection of investment,

- the conclusion, where appropriate, between the Member States and Ukraine, of agreements to avoid double taxation,

- the creation of favourable conditions for attracting foreign investment into the Ukrainian economy,

- to establish stable and adequate business law and conditions, and to exchange information on laws, regulations and administrative practices in the field of investment,

- to exchange information on investment opportunities in the form of, inter alia, trade fairs, exhibitions, trade weeks and other events.

Article 73

Small and medium-sized enterprises

1.   The Parties shall aim to develop and strengthen small and medium-sized enterprises and their associations and cooperation between SMEs in the Community and Ukraine.

2.   Cooperation shall include technical assistance, in particular in the following areas:

- the development of a legislative framework for SMEs,

- the development of an appropriate infrastructure (an agency to support SMEs, communications, assistance to the creation of a fund of SMEs),

- the development of technology parks.

*   *   *

AGREEMENT ESTABLISHING AN ASSOCIATION BETWEEN THE EUROPEAN COMMUNITIES AND THEIR MEMBER STATES, OF THE ONE PART, AND THE REPUBLIC OF ESTONIA, OF THE OTHER PART*
[excerpts]

The Agreement Establishing an Association between the European Communities and Their Member States, of the One Part, and the Republic of Estonia, of the Other Part, was signed on 12 June 1995, and entered into force on 1 February 1998. The member States of the European Communities are: Austria, Belgium, Denmark, Finland, France, Germany, Greece, Ireland, Italy, Luxembourg, the Netherlands, Portugal, Spain, Sweden and the United Kingdom.

TITLE IV

MOVEMENT OF WORKERS, ESTABLISHMENT, SUPPLY OF SERVICES

CHAPTER II

ESTABLISHMENT

Article 43

1.   The Community and its Member States shall grant, except for the sectors included in Annex VII,

   (i)   from entry into force of this Agreement, treatment no less favourable than that accorded by Member States to their own companies or to any third country company, whichever is the better, with regard to the establishment of Estonian companies;

   (ii)   from entry into force of this Agreement, to subsidiaries and branches of Estonian companies, established in their territory, treatment no less favourable than that accorded by Member States to their own companies and branches or to subsidiaries and branches of any third country company established in their territory, whichever is the better, in respect of their operation;

   (iii) as from 31 December 1999, for the establishment of Estonian nationals and their operation, once established, treatment no less favourable than that accorded to Community nationals or to nationals of any third country, whichever is the better.

---

*   *Source*: European Communities (1998). "Agreement Establishing an Association between the European Communities and Their Member States, of the One Part, and the Republic of Estonia, of the Other Part", *Official Journal of the European Communities*, L 068, 9 March 1998, pp. 3-198. [Note added by the editor.]

2.   Estonia shall grant from the entry into force of this Agreement:

(i)   treatment no less favourable than that accorded to Estonian companies or to companies of any third country, whichever is the better, with regard to the establishment of Community companies;

(ii)   to subsidiaries and branches of Community companies, established in its territory, treatment no less favourable than that accorded to Estonian companies and branches, or to subsidiaries and branches of any third country company established in its territory, whichever is the better, in respect of their operation;

(iii)   for the establishment of Community nationals and their operation, once established, treatment no less favourable than that accorded to Estonian nationals or to nationals of any third country, whichever is the better.

Article 45

For the purposes of this Agreement:

(a)   a 'Community company' or an 'Estonian company' respectively shall mean a company set up in accordance with the laws of a Member State or of Estonia respectively and having its registered office or central administration or principal place of business within the Community or in the territory of Estonia respectively. However, should the company, set up in accordance with the laws of a Member State or Estonia respectively, have only its registered office within the Community or in the territory of Estonia respectively, the company shall be considered a Community or an Estonian company respectively if its operations possess a real and continuous link with the economy of one of the Member States or Estonia respectively;

(b)   'subsidiary' of a company shall mean a company which is effectively controlled by the first company.

(c)   'branch' of a company shall mean a place of business not having legal personality which has the appearance of permanency, such as the extension of a parent body, has a management and is materially equipped to negotiate business with third parties so that the latter, although knowing that there will if necessary be a legal link with the parent body, the head office of which is abroad, do not have to deal directly with such parent body but may transact business at the place of business constituting the extension;

(d)   'establishment' shall mean:

(i)   as regards nationals, the right to take up economic activities as self-employed persons and to set up undertakings, in particular companies, which they effectively control. Self-employment and business undertakings by nationals shall not extend to seeking or taking employment in the labour market or confer a right of access to the labour market of another Party. The provisions of this chapter do not apply to those who are not exclusively self-employed;

(ii) as regards Community or Estonian companies, the right to take up economic activities by means of the setting up of subsidiaries and branches in Estonia or in the Community respectively;

(e) 'operation' shall mean the pursuit of economic activities;

(f) 'economic activities' shall in principle include activities of an industrial, commercial and professional character and activities of craftsmen;

(g) 'Community national' and 'Estonian national' shall mean respectively a natural person who is a national of one of the Member States or of Estonia;

(h) with regard to international maritime transport, including inter-modal operations involving a sea leg, nationals of the Member States or of Estonia established outside the Community or Estonia respectively, and shipping companies established outside the Community or Estonia and controlled by nationals of a Member State or Estonian nationals respectively, shall also be beneficiaries of the provisions of Chapter II and Chapter III, if their vessels are registered in that Member State or in Estonia respectively in accordance with their respective legislation.

Article 46

1.   Subject to the provisions of Article 43, with the exception of financial services described in Annex VIII, each Party may regulate the establishment and operation of companies and nationals on its territory, insofar as these regulations do not discriminate against companies and nationals of the other Party in comparison with its own companies and nationals.

2.   In respect of financial services, notwithstanding any other provisions of this Agreement, a Party shall not be prevented from taking measures for prudential reasons, including for the protection of investors, depositors, policy holders or persons to whom a fiduciary duty is owed by a financial service supplier, or to ensure the integrity and stability of the financial system. Such measures shall not be used as a means of avoiding the Party's obligations under the Agreement.

3.   Nothing in the Agreement shall be construed to require a Party to disclose information relating to the affairs and accounts of individual customers or any confidential or proprietary information in the possession of public entities.

Article 47

1.   The provisions of Articles 43 and 46 do not preclude the application by a Party of particular rules concerning the establishment and operation in its territory of branches of companies of another Party not incorporated in the territory of the first Party, which are justified by legal or technical differences between such branches as compared with branches of companies incorporated in its territory or, as regards financial services, for prudential reasons.

2.   The difference in treatment shall not go beyond what is strictly necessary as a result of such legal or technical differences or, as regards financial services, for prudential reasons.

Article 48

1.   A 'Community company' or an 'Estonian company' established in the territory of Estonia or the Community respectively shall be entitled to employ, or have employed by one of its subsidiaries or branches, in accordance with the legislation in force in the host country of establishment, in the territory of Estonia and the Community respectively, employees who are nationals of Community Member States and Estonia respectively, provided that such employees are key personnel as defined in paragraph 2 of this Article, and that they are employed exclusively by companies, subsidiaries or branches.

The residence and work permits of such employees shall only cover the period of such employment.

2.   Key personnel of the above mentioned companies herein referred to as 'organisations` are 'intra-corporate transferees' as defined in (c) of this paragraph in the following categories, provided that the organisation is a juridical person and that the persons concerned have been employed by it or have been partners in it (other than as majority shareholders), for at least the year immediately preceding such movement:

(a)   persons working in a senior position with an organisation, who primarily direct the management of the establishment, receiving general supervision or direction principally from the board of directors or stockholders of the business or their equivalent, including:

   - directing the establishment or a department or subdivision of the establishment,

   - supervising and controlling the work of other supervisory, professional or managerial employees,

   - having the authority personally to recruit and dismiss or recommend recruiting, dismissing or other personnel actions;

(b)   persons working within an organisation who possess uncommon knowledge essential to the establishment's service, research equipment, techniques or management. The assessment of such knowledge may reflect, apart from knowledge specific to the establishment, a high level of qualification referring to a type of work or trade requiring specific technical knowledge, including membership of an accredited profession;

(c)   an 'intra-corporate transferee' is defined as a natural person working within an organisation in the territory of a Party, and being temporarily transferred in the context of pursuit of economic activities in the territory of the other Party; the organisation concerned must have its principal place of business in the territory of a Party and the transfer must be to an establishment (branch, subsidiary) of that organisation, effectively pursuing like economic activities in the territory of the other Party.

3.   The entry into and the temporary presence within the territory of the Community or Estonia of Estonian and Community nationals respectively shall be permitted, when these representatives of companies are persons working in a senior position, as defined in paragraph 2(a) above, within a company, and are responsible for the setting up of a Community subsidiary or branch of an Estonian company or of an Estonian subsidiary or branch of a Community company in a Community Member State or Estonia respectively when:

- those representatives are not engaged in making direct sales or supplying services, and

- the company has its principal place of business outside the Community or Estonia, respectively, and has no other representative, office, branch or subsidiary in that Community Member State or Estonia respectively.

Article 50

Up to the end of 1999, Estonia may introduce measures which derogate from the provisions of this Chapter as regards the establishment of Community companies and nationals if certain industries:

- are undergoing restructuring, or

- are facing serious difficulties, particularly where these entail serious social problems in Estonia, or

- face the elimination or a drastic reduction of the total market share held by Estonian companies or nationals in a given sector or industry in Estonia, or

-are newly emerging industries in Estonia.

Such measures:

- shall cease to apply at the latest on 31 December 1999,

- shall be reasonable and necessary in order to remedy the situation, and

- shall only relate to establishments in Estonia to be created after the entry into force of such measures and shall not introduce discrimination concerning the operations of Community companies or nationals already established in Estonia at the time of introduction of a given measure compared with Estonian companies or nationals.

While devising and applying such measures, Estonia shall grant whenever possible to Community companies and nationals a preferential treatment, and in no case a treatment less favourable than that accorded to companies or nationals from any third country.

Prior to the introduction of these measures, Estonia shall consult the Association Council and shall not put them into effect before a one-month period following the notification of the Association Council of the concrete measures to be introduced by Estonia, except where the threat of irreparable damage requires the taking of urgent measures in which case Estonia shall consult the Association Council immediately after their introduction.

CHAPTER IV

GENERAL PROVISIONS

Article 54

1.   The provisions of this Title shall be applied subject to limitations justified on grounds of public policy, public security or public health.

2.   They shall not apply to activities which in the territory of either Party are connected, even occasionally, with the exercise of official authority.

Article 55

For the purpose of this Title nothing in the Agreement shall prevent the Parties from applying their laws and regulations regarding entry and stay, work, labour conditions and establishment of natural persons and supply of services, provided that - in so doing - they do not apply them in a manner as to nullify or impair the benefits accruing to any Party under the terms of a specific provision of the Agreement.

Article 56

Companies which are controlled and exclusively owned by Estonian companies or nationals and Community companies or nationals jointly shall also be beneficiaries of the provisions of Chapters II, III and IV of this Title.

Article 57

1.   The most favoured nation treatment granted in accordance with the provisions of this Title shall not apply to the tax advantages which the Parties are providing or will provide in the future on the basis of agreements to avoid double taxation, or other tax arrangements.

2.   Nothing in this Title shall be construed to prevent the adoption or enforcement by the Parties of any measure aimed at preventing the avoidance or evasion of taxes pursuant to the tax provisions of agreements to avoid double taxation and other tax arrangements, or domestic fiscal legislation.

3.   Nothing in this Title shall be construed to prevent Member States or Estonia from distinguishing, in the application of the relevant provisions of their fiscal legislation, between taxpayers who are not in identical situations, in particular as regards their place of residence.

Article 58

The provisions of this Title shall be progressively adjusted by the Parties. In formulating recommendations to this effect, the Association Council shall take into account the respective obligations of the Parties under the General Agreement on Trade in Services (GATS), and in particular of its Article V.

Article 59

The provisions of this Agreement shall not prejudice the application by each Party of any measure necessary to prevent the circumvention of its measures concerning third country access to its market through the provisions of this Agreement.

TITLE V

PAYMENTS, CAPITAL, COMPETITION AND OTHER ECONOMIC PROVISIONS, APPROXIMATION OF LAWS

CHAPTER I

CURRENT PAYMENTS AND MOVEMENT OF CAPITAL

Article 60

The Parties undertake to authorise, in freely convertible currency, in accordance with the provisions of Article VIII of the Articles of Agreement of the International Monetary Fund, any payments and transfers on the current account of balance of payments between residents of the Community and Estonia.

Article 61

1.   With regard to transactions on the capital account of balance of payments, from entry into force of the Agreement, the Member States and Estonia respectively shall ensure the free movement of capital relating to direct investments made in companies formed in accordance with the laws of the host country and investments made in accordance with the provisions of Chapter II of Title IV, and the liquidation or repatriation of these investments and of any profit stemming therefrom.

Without prejudice to Article 43(1)(iii), complete free movement of capital relating to establishment and operations of self-employed persons, including the liquidation and repatriation of such investments, shall be ensured from entry into force of this Agreement.

2.   With regard to transactions on the capital account of balance of payments, from entry into force of this Agreement the Member States and Estonia respectively shall ensure the free movement of capital relating to portfolio investment. This shall also apply to the free movement of capital relating to credits related to commercial transactions or the provision of services in which a resident of one of the Parties is participating and to financial loans.

3.   Without prejudice to paragraph 1, the Member States and Estonia shall not introduce any new restrictions on the movement of capital and current payments connected therewith between residents of the Community and Estonia and shall not make the existing arrangements more restrictive.

4.   The Parties shall consult each other with a view to facilitating the movement of capital between the Community and Estonia in order to promote the objective of the present Agreement.

Article 62

1.   The Parties shall take measures permitting the creation of the necessary conditions for the further gradual application of Community rules on the free movement of capital.

2.   The Association Council shall examine ways of enabling Community rules on the movement of capital to be applied in full.

CHAPTER II

COMPETITION AND OTHER ECONOMIC PROVISIONS

Article 63

1.   The following are incompatible with the proper functioning of this Agreement, insofar as they may affect trade between the Community and Estonia:

(i)   all agreements between undertakings, decisions by associations of undertakings and concerted practices between undertakings which have as their object or effect the prevention, restriction or distortion of competition;

(ii)   abuse by one or more undertakings of a dominant position in the territories of the Community or of Estonia as a whole or in a substantial part thereof;

(iii)   any public aid, which distorts or threatens to distort competition by favouring certain undertakings or the production of certain goods.

2.   Any practices contrary to this Article shall be assessed on the basis of criteria arising from the application of the rules of Articles 85, 86 and 92 of the Treaty establishing the European Community or, for products covered by the ECSC Treaty, on the basis of corresponding rules of the ECSC Treaty including secondary legislation.

3.   The Association Council shall, by 31 December 1997, adopt by decision the necessary rules for the implementation of paragraphs 1 and 2.

Until these rules are adopted, the provisions of the Agreement on interpretation and application of Articles VI, XVI and XXIII of the GATT shall be applied as the rules for the implementation of paragraph 1(iii) and related parts of paragraph 2.

Article 64

1.   The Parties shall endeavour to avoid the imposition of restrictive measures including measures relating to imports for balance of payments purposes.

In the event of their introduction, the Party having introduced the same shall present to the other Party, as soon as possible, a time schedule for their removal.

2.   Where one or more Member State or Estonia is in serious balance of payments difficulties, or under imminent threat thereof, the Community or Estonia, as the case may be, may, in accordance with the conditions established under the GATT, adopt restrictive measures, including measures relating to imports, which shall be of limited duration and may not go beyond what is necessary to remedy the balance of payments situation. The Community or Estonia, as the case may be, shall inform the other Party forthwith.

3.   Any restrictive measures shall not apply to transfers related to investments and in particular to the repatriation of amounts invested or reinvested and of any kind of revenues stemming therefrom.

Article 65

With regard to public undertakings, and undertakings to which special or exclusive rights have been granted, the Association Council shall ensure that as from 1 January 1998, the principles of the Treaty establishing the European Community, notably Article 90, and the principles of the concluding document of the April 1990 Bonn meeting of the CSCE, notably entrepreneurs' freedom of decision, are upheld.

Article 67

1.   The Parties consider the opening up of the award of public contracts on the basis of non-discrimination and reciprocity, in particular in the GATT and WTO context, to be a desirable objective.

2.   The Estonian companies as defined in Article 45 of this Agreement, shall be granted access to contract award procedures in the Community pursuant to Community procurement rules under a treatment no less favourable than that accorded to Community companies as of the entry into force of this Agreement.

Community companies and branches of Community companies in the sense of Article 45 and subsidiaries of Community companies as described in Article 45 and in the forms of Article 56 shall be granted access to contract award procedures in Estonia under a treatment no less favourable than that accorded to Estonian companies as of the entry into force of this Agreement.

The provisions in this paragraph shall also apply to public contracts covered by Directive 93/38/EEC of 14 June 1993 once Estonia has introduced the appropriate legislation.

3.   As regards establishment, operations, supply of services between the Community and Estonia, as well as employment and movement of labour linked to the fulfilment of public contracts, the provisions of Article 36 to 59 of this Agreement are applicable.

TITLE VI

ECONOMIC COOPERATION

Article 73

Investment promotion and protection

1.   Cooperation shall aim at maintaining and, if necessary, improving a legal framework and a favourable climate for private investment and its protection, both domestic and foreign, which is essential to economic and industrial reconstruction and development in Estonia. The cooperation shall also aim to encourage and promote foreign investment and privatisation in Estonia.

2.   The particular aims of cooperation shall be:

- for Estonia to further develop and maintain a legal framework which favours and protects investment,

- the conclusion, where appropriate, with Member States of bilateral agreements for the promotion and protection of investment,

- to proceed with deregulation and to improve economic infrastructure,

- to exchange information on investment opportunities in the context of trade fairs, exhibitions, trade weeks and other events.

Assistance from the Community could be granted in the initial stage to agencies which promote inward investment.

3.   Estonia shall honour the rules on Trade-Related Aspects of Investment Measures (TRIMs).

Article 74

Small and medium-sized enterprises

1.   The Parties shall aim to develop and strengthen small and medium-sized enterprises (SMEs) and cooperation between SMEs in the Community and Estonia.

2.   They shall encourage the exchange of information and know-how by means of:

- improving, where appropriate, the legal, administrative, technical, tax and financial conditions necessary for the setting-up and expansion of SMEs and for cross-border cooperation,

- providing the specialised services required by SMEs (management training, accounting, marketing, quality control, etc.) and the strengthening of agencies providing such services,

...

*   *   *

AGREEMENT ESTABLISHING AN ASSOCIATION BETWEEN THE EUROPEAN COMMUNITIES AND THEIR MEMBER STATES, OF THE ONE PART, AND THE REPUBLIC OF LATVIA, OF THE OTHER PART[*]
[excerpts]

The Agreement Establishing an Association between the European Communities and Their Member States, of the One Part, and Latvia, of the Other Part, was signed at Luxembourg on 12 June 1995 and entered into force on 1 February 1998. The member States of the European Communities are: Austria, Belgium, Denmark, Finland, France, Germany, Greece, Ireland, Italy, Luxembourg, the Netherlands, Portugal, Spain, Sweden and the United Kingdom.

TITLE IV

MOVEMENT OF PEOPLE, ESTABLISHMENT, SUPPLY OF SERVICES

CHAPTER II

Establishment

Article 44

1.   The Community and its Member States shall grant, except for the sectors included in Annex XIV, from entry into force of this Agreement:

 (i)   treatment no less favourable than that accorded by Member States to their own companies or to any third country company, whichever is the better, with regard to the establishment of Latvian companies;

 (ii)   to subsidiaries and branches of Latvian companies, established in their territory, treatment no less favourable than that accorded by Member States to their own companies and branches or to subsidiaries and branches of any third country company established in their territory, whichever is the better, in respect of their operation.

2.   Latvia shall facilitate the setting up of operations on its territory by Community companies and nationals. To that end, it shall:

---

[*]   *Source*: European Communities (1998). "Agreement Establishing an Association between the European Communities and Their Member States, of the One Part, and the Republic of Latvia, of the Other Part", *Official Journal of the European Communities*, L 026, 2 February 1998, pp. 3-225. [Note added by the editor.]

(i)   grant, from entry into force of the Agreement, for the establishment of Community companies, treatment no less favourable than that accorded to its own companies or to companies of any third country, whichever is the better, save for the sectors referred to in Annex XV, where national treatment shall be granted at the latest by the end of the transitional period referred to in Article 3;

(ii)   grant, from entry into force of this Agreement, for the operation of branches and subsidiaries of Community companies, established in Latvia, treatment no less favourable than that accorded to its own companies or to subsidiaries and branches of any third country company established in its territory, whichever is the better.

3.   Latvia shall, during the transitional period referred to in paragraph 2(i) not adopt any measures or actions which introduce discrimination as regards the establishment and operations of Community companies and nationals in its territory in comparison to its own companies and nationals.

4.   The Association Council shall during the transitional period referred to in paragraph 2(i) examine regularly the possibility of accelerating the granting of national treatment in the sectors referred to in Annex XV. Amendments may be made to this Annex by decision of the Association Council.

Following the expiration of the transitional period referred to in Article 3, the Association Council may exceptionally, upon request of Latvia, and if the necessity arises, decide to prolong the duration of exclusion of certain areas or matters listed in Annex XV for a limited period of time.

5.   The treatment described in paragraphs 1 and 2 shall be applicable for the establishment and operation of nationals as from the end of the transitional period referred to in Article 3.

Article 45

1.   The provisions of this chapter shall not apply to air transport, inland waterways and maritime cabotage transport services.

2.   The Association Council may make recommendations for improving establishment and operations in the areas covered by paragraph 1.

Article 46

For the purposes of this Agreement:

a)   A "Community company" or a "Latvian company" respectively shall mean a company set up in accordance with the laws of a Member State or of Latvia respectively and having its registered office or central administration or principal place of business with in the Community or in the territory of Latvia respectively.

However, should the company, set up in accordance with the laws of a Member State or Latvia respectively, have only its registered office within the Community or in the territory of Latvia respectively, the company shall be considered a Community or Latvian company respectively if its operations possess a real and continuous link with the economy of one of the Member States or Latvia respectively.

b) "Subsidiary" of a company shall mean a company which is effectively controlled by the first company.

c) "Branch" of a company shall mean a place of business not having legal personality which has the appearance of permanency, such as the extension of a parent body, has a management and is materially equipped to negotiate business with third parties so that the latter, although knowing that there will if necessary be a legal link with the parent body, the head office of which is abroad, do not have to deal directly with such parent body but may transact business at the place of business constituting the extension.

d) "Establishment" shall mean:

   i) as regards nationals, the right to take up economic activities as self-employed persons and to set up undertakings, in particular companies, which they effectively control. Self-employment and business undertakings by nationals shall not extend to seeking or taking employment in the labour market or confer a right of access to the labour market of another Party.

   The provisions of this chapter do not apply to those who are not exclusively self-employed;

   ii) as regards Community or Latvian companies, the right to take up economic activities by means of the setting up of subsidiaries and branches in Latvia or in the Community respectively.

e) "Operation" shall mean the pursuit of economic activities.

f) "Economic activities" shall in principle include activities of an industrial, commercial and professional character and activities of craftsmen.

g) "Community national" and "Latvian national" shall mean respectively a natural person who is a national of one of the Member States or of Latvia.

h) With regard to international maritime transport, including intermodal operations involving a sea leg, nationals of the Member States or of Latvia established outside the Community or Latvia respectively, and shipping companies established outside the Community or Latvia and controlled by nationals of a Member State or Latvian nationals respectively, shall also be beneficiaries of the provisions of Chapter II and Chapter III, if their vessels are registered in that Member State or in Latvia respectively in accordance with their respective legislation.

Article 47

1.   Subject to the provisions of Article 43, with the exception of financial services described in Annex XVI, each Party may regulate the establishment and operation of companies and nationals on its territory, insofar as these regulations do not discriminate against companies and nationals of the other Party in comparison with its own companies and nationals.

2.   In respect of financial services, notwithstanding any other provisions of this Agreement, a Party shall not be prevented from taking measures for prudential reasons, including for the protection of investors, depositors, policy holders or persons to whom a fiduciary duty is owed by a financial service supplier, or to ensure the integrity and stability of the financial system. Such measures shall not be used as a means of avoiding the Party's obligations under the Agreement.

3.   Nothing in the Agreement shall be construed to require a Party to disclose information relating to the affairs and accounts of individual customers or any confidential or proprietary information in the possession of public entities.

Article 48

1.   The provisions of Article 44 and 47 do not preclude the application by a Party of particular rules concerning the establishment and operation in its territory of branches of companies of another Party not incorporated in the territory of the first Party, which are justified by legal or technical differences between such branches as compared with branches of companies incorporated in its territory or, as regards financial services, for prudential reasons.

2.   The difference in treatment shall not go beyond what is strictly necessary as a result of such legal or technical differences or, as regards financial services, for prudential reasons.

Article 49

1.   A "Community company" or a "Latvian company" established in the territory of Latvia or the Community respectively shall be entitled to employ, or have employed by one of its subsidiaries or branches, in accordance with the legislation in force in the host country of establishment, in the territory of Latvia and the Community respectively, employee who are nationals of Community Member States and Latvia respectively, provided that such employees are key personnel as defined in paragraph 2 of this Article, and that they are employed exclusively by companies, subsidiaries or branches.

The residence and work permits of such employees shall only cover the period of such employment.

2.   Key personnel of the above mentioned companies herein referred to as "organisations" are "intra-corporate transferees" as defined in (c) of this paragraph in the following categories, provided that the organisation in a juridical person and that the persons concerned have been employed by it or have been partners in it (other than as majority shareholders), for at least the year immediately preceding such movement:

(a)   Persons working in a senior position with an organisation, who primarily direct the management of the establishment, receiving general supervision or direction principally from the board of directors or stockholders of the business or their equivalent, including:

- directing the establishment or a department or sub-division of the establishment;

- supervising and controlling the work of other supervisory, professional or managerial employees;

- having the authority personally to recruit and dismiss or recommend recruiting, dismissing or other personnel actions.

(b)   Persons working within an organisation who possess uncommon knowledge essential to the establishment's service, research equipment, techniques or management. The assessment of such knowledge may reflect, apart from knowledge specific to the establishment, a high level of qualification referring to a type of work or trade requiring specific technical knowledge, including membership of an accredited profession.

(c)   An "intra-corporate transferee" is defined as a natural person working within an organisation in the territory of a Party, and being temporarily transferred in the context of pursuit of economic activities in the territory of the other Party; the organisation concerned must have its principal place of business in the territory of a Party and the transfer be to an establishment (branch, subsidiary) of that organisation, effectively pursuing like economic activities in the territory of the other Party.

3.   The entry into and the temporary presence within the territory of the Community or Latvia of Latvian and Community nationals respectively shall be permitted, when these representatives of companies are persons working in a senior position, as defined in paragraph 2(a) above, within a company, and are responsible for the setting up of a Community subsidiary or branch of a Latvian company or of a Latvian subsidiary or branch of a Community company in a Community Member State or Latvia respectively, when:

- those representatives are not engaged in making direct sales or supplying services, and

- the company has its principal place of business outside the Community or Latvia, respectively, and has no other representative, office, branch or subsidiary in that Community Member State or Latvia respectively.

Article 51

During the transitional period referred to in Article 3, Latvia may introduce measures which derogate from the provisions of this Chapter as regards the establishment of Community companies and nationals if certain industries:

- are undergoing restructuring, or

- are facing serious difficulties, particularly where these entail serious social problems in Latvia, or

- face the elimination or a drastic reduction of the total market share held by Latvian companies or nationals in a given sector or industry in Latvia, or

- are newly emerging industries in Latvia.

Such measures:

- shall cease to apply at the latest upon the expiration of the transitional period referred to in Article 3 and

- shall be reasonable and necessary in order to remedy the situation, and

- shall only relate to establishments in Latvia to be created after the entry into force of such measures and shall not introduce discrimination concerning the operations of Community companies or nationals already established in Latvia at the time of introduction of a given measure compared with Latvian companies or nationals.

While devising and applying such measures, Latvia shall grant whenever possible to Community companies and nationals a preferential treatment, and in no case a treatment less favourable than that accorded to companies or nationals from any third country.

Prior to the introduction of these measures, Latvia shall consult the Association Council and shall not put them into effect before a one-month period following the notification of the Association Council of the concrete measures to be introduced by Latvia, except where the threat of irreparable damage requires the talcing of urgent measures in which case Latvia shall consult the Association Council immediately after their introduction. Upon expiration of the transitional period referred to in Article 3, Latvia may introduce such measures only with the authorisation of the Association Council and under conditions determined by the latter.

CHAPTER IV

General Provisions

Article 55

1.   The provisions of this Title shall be applied subject to limitations justified on grounds of public policy, public security or public health.

2.   They shall not apply to activities which in the territory of either Party are connected, even occasionally, with the exercise of official authority.

Article 56

For the purpose of this Title nothing in the Agreement shall prevent the Parties from applying their laws and regulations regarding entry and stay, work labour conditions and establishment of natural persons and supply of services, provided that - in so doing - they do not apply them in a manner as to nullify or impair the benefits accruing to any Party under the terms of a specific provision of the Agreement.

Article 57

Companies which are controlled and exclusively owned by Latvian companies or nationals and Community companies or nationals jointly shall also be beneficiaries of the provisions of Chapters II, III and IV of this Title.

Article 58

1.   The Most Favoured Nation treatment granted in accordance with the provisions of this Title shall not apply to the tax advantages which the Parties are providing or will provide in the future on the basis of agreements to avoid double taxation, or other tax arrangements.

2.   Nothing in this Title shall be construed to prevent the adoption or enforcement by the Parties of any measure aimed at preventing the avoidance or evasion of taxes pursuant to the tax provisions of agreements to avoid double taxation and other tax arrangements, or domestic fiscal legislation.

3.   Nothing in this Title shall be construed to prevent Member States or Latvia from distinguishing, in the application of the relevant provisions of their fiscal legislation, between taxpayers who are not in identical situations, in particular as regards their place of residence.

Article 59

The provisions of this Title shall be progressively adjusted by the Parties. In formulating recommendations to this effect, the Association Council shall take into account the respective obligations of the Parties under the GATS, and in particular of its Article V.

Article 60

The provisions of this Agreement shall not prejudice the application by each Party of any measure necessary to prevent the circumvention of its measures concerning third country access to its market through the provisions of this Agreement.

TITLE V

PAYMENTS, CAPITAL, COMPETITION AND OTHER ECONOMIC PROVISIONS, APPROXIMATION OF LAWS

CHAPTER I

Current payments and movement of capital

Article 61

The Parties undertake to authorize, in freely convertible currency, in accordance to the provisions of Article VIII of the Articles of Agreement of the International Monetary Fund, any payments and transfers on the current account of balance of payments between residents of the Community and Latvia.

Article 62

1.   With regard to transactions on the capital account of balance of payments, from entry into force of the Agreement, the Member States and Latvia respectively shall ensure the free movement of capital relating to direct investments made in companies formed in accordance with the laws of the host country and investments made in accordance with the provisions of Chapter II of Title IV, and the liquidation or repatriation of these investments and of any profit stemming therefrom.

Without prejudice to Article 44, last paragraph, complete free movement of capital relating to establishment and operations of self employed persons, including the liquidation and repatriation of such investments, shall be ensured from entry into force of this Agreement.

2.   With regard to transactions on the capital account of balance of payments, from entry into force of this Agreement the Member States and Latvia respectively shall ensure the free movement of capital relating to portfolio investment. This shall also apply to the free movement of capital relating to credits related to commercial transactions or the provision of services in which a resident of one of the Parties is participating and to financial loans.

3.   Without prejudice to paragraph 1, the Member States and Latvia shall not introduce any new restrictions on the movement of capital and current payments connected therewith between residents of the Community and Latvia and shall not make the existing arrangements more restrictive.

4.   The Parties shall consult each other with a view to facilitating the movement of capital between the Community and Latvia in order to promote the objective of the present Agreement.

Article 63

1.   The Parties shall take measures permitting the creation of the necessary conditions for the further gradual application of Community rules on the free movement of capital.

2.   The Association Council shall examine ways of enabling Community rules on the movement of capital to be applied in full.

CHAPTER II

Competition and other economic provisions

Article 64

1.   The following are incompatible with the proper functioning of this Agreement, insofar as they may affect trade between the Community and Latvia:

(i)   all agreements between undertakings, decisions by associations of undertakings and concerted practices between undertakings which have as their object or effect the prevention, restriction or distortion of competition;

(ii)   abuse by one or more undertakings of a dominant position in the territories of the Community or of Latvia as a whole or in a substantial part thereof;

(iii)   any public aid, which distorts or threatens to distort competition by favouring certain undertakings or the production of certain goods.

2.   Any practices contrary to this Article shall be assessed on the basis of criteria arising from the application of themles of Articles 85, 86 and 92 of the Treaty establishing the European Community or, for products covered by the ECSC Treaty, on the basis of corresponding rules of the ECSC Treaty including secondary legislation.

3.   The Association Council shall, by 31 December 1997, adopt by decision the necessary rules for the implementation of paragraphs 1 and 2.

Until these rules are adopted, the provisions of this Agreement on interpretation and application of Articles VI, XVI and XXIII of the General Agreement on Tariffs and Trade shall be applied as the rules for the implementation of paragraphs 1 point (iii) and related parts of paragraph 2.

4.   (a)   For the purposes of applying the provisions of paragraph 1 point (iii), the Parties recognize that until 31 December 1999, any public aid granted by Latvia shall be assessed taking into account the fact that Latvia shall be regarded as an area identical to those areas of the Community described in Article 92(3)(a) of the Treaty establishing the European Community. The Association Council shall, taking into account the economic situation of Latvia, decide whether that period should be extended by further periods of five years.

        (b)   Each Party shall ensure transparency in the area of public aid, inter alia by reporting annually to the other Party on the total amount and the distribution of the aid given and by providing, upon request, information on aid schemes. Upon request by one Party, the other Party shall provide information on particular individual cases of public aid.

5.   With regard to products referred to in Chapters II and III of Title III:

- the provision of paragraph 1 point (iii) does not apply,

- any practices contrary to paragraph 1 point (i) should be assessed according to the criteria established by the Community on the basis of Articles 42 and 43 of the Treaty establishing the European Community and in particular of those established in Council Regulation No 26/1962.

6.   If the Community or Latvia considers that a particular practice is incompatible with the terms of the first paragraph of this Article, and

- is not adequately dealt with under the implementing rules referred to in paragraph 3, or

- in the absence of such rules, and if such practice causes or threatens to cause serious prejudice to the interests of the other Party or material injury to its domestic industry, including its services industry,

- it may take appropriate measures after consultation within the Association Council or after 30 working days following referral for such consultation.

In the case of practices incompatible with paragraph 1 point (iii) of this Article, such appropriate measures may, where the General Agreement on Tariffs and Trade applies thereto, only be adopted in conformity with the procedures and under the conditions laid down by the General Agreement on Tariffs and Trade and any other relevant instrument negotiated under its auspices which are applicable between the Parties.

7.   Notwithstanding any provisions to the contrary adopted in conformity with paragraph 3, the Parties shall exchange information taking into account the limitations imposed by the requirements of professional and business secrecy.

Article 65

1.   The Parties shall endeavour to avoid the imposition of restrictive measures including measures relating to imports for balance of payments purposes. In the event of their introduction, the Party having introduced the same shall present to the other Party, as soon as possible, a time schedule for their removal.

2.   Where one or more Member States or Latvia is in serious balance of payments difficulties, or under imminent threat thereof, the Community or Latvia, as the case may be, may, in accordance with the conditions established under the General Agreement on Tariffs and Trade, adopt restrictive measures, including measures relating to imports, which shall be of limited duration and may not go beyond what is necessary to remedy the balance of payments situation. The Community or Latvia, as the case may be, shall inform the other Party forthwith.

3.   Any restrictive measures shall not apply to transfers related to investments and in particular to the repatriation of amounts invested or reinvested and of any kind of revenues stemming therefrom.

Article 66

With regard to public undertakings, and undertakings to which special or exclusive rights have been granted, the Association Council shall ensure that as from 1 January 1998, the principles of the Treaty establishing the European Community, notably Article 90, and the relevant CSCE principles, in particular entrepreneurs' freedom of decision, are upheld.

TITLE VI

ECONOMIC COOPERATION

Article 74

Investment promotion and protection

1.   Cooperation shall aim at maintaining and, if necessary, improving a legal framework and a favourable climate for private investment and its protection, both domestic and foreign, which is essential to economic and industrial reconstruction and development in Latvia. The cooperation shall also aim to encourage and promote foreign investment and privatization in Latvia.

2.   The particular aims of cooperation shall be:

- for Latvia to establish a legal framework which favours and protects investment;

- the conclusion, where appropriate, with Member States of bilateral agreements for the promotion and protection on of investment;

- to proceed with deregulation and to improve economic infrastructure;

- to exchange information on investment opportunities in the context of trade fairs, exhibitions, trade weeks and other events.

Assistance from the Community could be granted in the initial stage to agencies which promote inward investment.

3.   Latvia shall honour the rules on Trade-Related Aspects of Investment Measures (TRIMs).

Article 75

Small and medium-sized enterprises

1.   The Parties shall aim to develop and strengthen small and medium-sized enterprises (SMEs) and cooperation between SMEs in the Community and Latvia.

2.   They shall encourage the exchange of information and know-how in the following areas:

- improving, where appropriate, the legal, administrative, technical, tax and financial conditions necessary for the setting-up and expansion of SMEs and for cross-border cooperation;

- the provision of the specialized services required by SMEs (management training, accounting, marketing, quality control, etc.) and the strengthening of agencies providing such services;

- the establishment of appropriate links with Community operators via European business cooperation networks, in order to improve the flow of information to SMEs and to promote cross-border cooperation.

3. The cooperation shall include the supply of technical assistance, in particular for the establishment of appropriate institutional back-up for SMEs at both national and regional level, regarding financial, training, advisory, technological and marketing services.

TITLE X

INSTITUTIONAL, GENERAL AND FINAL PROVISIONS

Article 119

Within the scope of this Agreement, each Party undertakes to ensure that natural and legal persons of the other Party have access free of discrimination in relation to its own nationals to the competent courts and administrative organs of the Parties to defend their individual rights and their property rights, including those concerning intellectual, industrial and commercial property.

Article 120

Nothing in this Agreement shall prevent a Contracting Party from taking any measures:

(a)   which it considers necessary to prevent the disclosure of information contrary to its essential security interests;

(b)   which relate to the production of, or trade in, arms, ammunition or war materials or to research, development or production indispensable for defence purposes, provided that such measures do not impair the conditions of competition in respect of products not intended for specifically military purposes;

(c)   which it considers essential to its own security in the event of serious internal disturbances affecting the maintenance of law and order, in time of war or serious international tension constituting threat of war or in order to carry out obligations it has accepted for the purpose of maintaining peace and international security;

(d)   which it considers necessary to respect its international obligations and commitments on the control of dual use industrial goods and technologies.

Article 121

1. In the fields covered by this Agreement and without prejudice to any special provisions contained therein:

- the arrangements applied by Latvia in respect of the Community shall not give rise to any discrimination between the Member States, their nationals, or their companies or branches,

- the arrangements applied by the Community in respect of Latvia shall not give rise to any discrimination between Latvian nationals or its companies or branches.

2.   The provisions of paragraph 1 are without prejudice to the right of the Parties to apply the relevant provisions of their fiscal legislation to tax payers who are not in identical situations as regards their place of residence.

*   *   *

EURO-MEDITERRANEAN AGREEMENT ESTABLISHING AN ASSOCIATION BETWEEN THE EUROPEAN COMMUNITIES AND THEIR MEMBER STATES, OF THE ONE PART, AND THE REPUBLIC OF TUNISIA, OF THE OTHER PART*
[excerpts]

The Euro-Mediterranean Agreement establishing an Association between the European Communities and Their Member States on the One Part, and Tunisia, on the Other Part, was signed in Brussels, on 17 July 1995. It entered into force on 1 March 1998. The Member States of the European Communities are: Austria, Belgium, Denmark, Finland, France, Germany, Greece, Ireland, Italy, Luxembourg, the Netherlands, Portugal, Spain, Sweden and the United Kingdom.

TITLE III

RIGHT OF ESTABLISHMENT AND SERVICES

Article 31

1.   The Parties agree to widen the scope of the Agreement to cover the right of establishment of one Party's firms on the territory of the other and liberalisation of the provision of services by one Party's firms to consumers of services in the other.

2.   The Association Council will make recommendations for achieving the objective described in paragraph 1.

In making such recommendations, the Association Council will take account of past experience of implementation of reciprocal most-favoured-nation treatment and of the respective obligations of each Party under the General Agreement on Trade in Services annexed to the Agreement establishing the WTO, hereinafter referred to as the 'GATS`, particularly those in Article V of the latter.

3.   The Association Council will make a first assessment of the achievement of this objective no later than five years after the Agreement enters into force.

---

* *Source*: European Communities (1998). "Euro-Mediterranean Agreement Establishing an Association between the European communities and Their Member States, of the One Part, and the Republic of Tunisia, of the Other Part", *Official Journal of the European Communities*, L 097, 30 March 1998, pp. 2-183. [Note added by the editor.]

Article 32

1.   At the outset, each of the Parties shall reaffirm its obligations under the GATS, particularly the obligation to grant reciprocal most-favoured-nation treatment in the service sectors covered by that obligation.

2.   In accordance with the GATS, such treatment shall not apply to:

(a)   advantages granted by either Party under the terms of an agreement of the type defined in Article V of the GATS or to measures taken on the basis of such an agreement;

(b)   other advantages granted in accordance with the list of exemptions from most-favoured-nation treatment annexed by either Party to the GATS.

TITLE IV

PAYMENTS, CAPITAL, COMPETITION AND OTHER ECONOMIC PROVISIONS

CHAPTER I

CURRENT PAYMENTS AND MOVEMENT OF CAPITAL

Article 33

Subject to the provisions of Article 35, the Parties undertake to allow all current payments for current transactions to be made in a freely convertible currency.

Article 34

1.   With regard to transactions on the capital account of balance of payments, the Community and Tunisia shall ensure, from the entry into force of this Agreement, that capital relating to direct investments in Tunisia in companies formed in accordance with current laws can move freely and that the yield from such investments and any profit stemming therefrom can be liquidated and repatriated.

2.   The Parties shall consult each other with a view to facilitating, and fully liberalising when the time is right, the movement of capital between the Community and Tunisia.

Article 35

Where one or more Member States of the Community, or Tunisia, is in serious balance of payments difficulties, or under threat thereof, the Community or Tunisia, as the case may be, may, in accordance with the conditions established under the General Agreement on Tariffs and Trade and Articles VIII and XIV of the Articles of Agreement of the International Monetary Fund, adopt restrictions on current transactions which shall be of limited duration and may not go beyond what is strictly necessary to remedy the balance of payments situation. The

Community or Tunisia, as the case may be, shall inform the other Party forthwith and shall submit to it as soon as possible a timetable for the elimination of the measures concerned.

CHAPTER II

COMPETITION AND OTHER ECONOMIC PROVISIONS

Article 36

1. The following are incompatible with the proper functioning of the Agreement, insofar as they may affect trade between the Community and Tunisia:

(a) all agreements between undertakings, decisions by associations of undertakings and concerted practices between undertakings which have as their object or effect the prevention, restriction or distortion of competition;

(b) abuse by one or more undertakings of a dominant position in the territories of the Community or of Tunisia as a whole or in a substantial part thereof;

(c) any official aid which distorts or threatens to distort competition by favouring certain undertakings or the production of certain goods, with the exception of cases in which a derogation is allowed under the Treaty establishing the European Coal and Steel Community.

2. Any practices contrary to this Article shall be assessed on the basis of criteria arising from the application of the rules of Articles 85, 86 and 92 of the Treaty establishing the European Community and, in the case of products falling within the scope of the European Coal and Steel Community, the rules of Articles 65 and 66 of the Treaty establishing that Community, and the rules relating to state aid, including secondary legislation.

3. The Association Council shall, within five years of the entry into force of this Agreement, adopt the necessary rules for the implementation of paragraphs 1 and 2.

Until these rules are adopted, the provisions of the Agreement on interpretation and application of Articles VI, XVI and XXIII of the General Agreement on Tariffs and Trade shall be applied as the rules for the implementation of paragraph 1(c) and related parts of paragraph 2.

4. (a) For the purposes of applying the provisions of paragraph 1(c), the Parties recognize that during the first five years after the entry into force of this Agreement, any State aid granted by Tunisia shall be assessed taking into account the fact that Tunisia shall be regarded as an area identical to those areas of the Community described in Article 92(3)(a) of the Treaty establishing the European Community.

During the same period of time, Tunisia may exceptionally, as regards ECSC steel products, grant State aid for restructuring purposes provided that:

- it leads to the viability of the recipient firms under normal market conditions at the end of the restructuring period,

- the amount and intensity of such aid are strictly limited to what is absolutely necessary in order to restore such viability and are progressively reduced,

- the restructuring programme is linked to a comprehensive plan for rationalising capacity in Tunisia.

The Association Council shall, taking into account the economic situation of Tunisia, decide whether the period should be extended every five years.

(b)   Each Party shall ensure transparency in the area of official aid, inter alia by reporting annually to the other Party on the total amount and the distribution of the aid given and by providing, upon request, information on aid schemes. Upon request by one Party, the other Party shall provide information on particular individual cases of official aid.

5.   With regard to products referred to in Chapter II of Title II:

- the provisions of paragraph 1(c) do not apply,

- any practices contrary to paragraph 1(a) shall be assessed according to the criteria established by the Community on the basis of Articles 42 and 43 of the Treaty establishing the European Community, and in particular those established in Council Regulation No 26/62.

6.   If the Community or Tunisia considers that a particular practice is incompatible with the terms of paragraph 1, and:

- is not adequately dealt with under the implementing rules referred to in paragraph 3, or

- in the absence of such rules, and if such practice causes or threatens to cause serious prejudice to the interest of the other Party or material injury to its domestic industry, including its services industry, it may take appropriate measures after consultation within the Association Committee or after 30 working days following referral to that Committee.

In the case of practices incompatible with paragraph 1(c) of this Article, such appropriate measures may, where the General Agreement on Tariffs and Trade applies thereto, only be adopted in accordance with the procedures and under the conditions laid down by the General Agreement on Tariffs and Trade and any other relevant instrument negotiated under its auspices which is applicable between the Parties.

7.   Notwithstanding any provisions to the contrary adopted in accordance with paragraph 3, the Parties shall exchange information taking into account the limitations imposed by the requirements of professional and business secrecy.

TITLE V

ECONOMIC COOPERATION

Article 50

Promotion and protection of investment

The aim of cooperation shall be to create a favourable climate for flows of investment, and to use the following in particular:

(a)   the establishment of harmonised and simplified procedures, co-investment machinery (especially to link small and medium-sized enterprises) and methods of identifying and providing information on investment opportunities;

(b)   the establishment, where appropriate, of a legal framework to promote investment, chiefly through the conclusion by Tunisia and the Member States of investment protection agreements and agreements preventing double taxation.

*   *   *

INTERREGIONAL FRAMEWORK COOPERATION AGREEMENT BETWEEN THE EUROPEAN COMMUNITY AND ITS MEMBER STATES, OF THE ONE PART, AND THE SOUTHERN COMMON MARKET AND ITS PARTY STATES, OF THE OTHER PART*
[excerpts]

The Interregional Framework Cooperation Agreement between the European Community and Its Member States, of the One Part, and the Southern Common Market and Its Party States, of the Other Part was signed on 15 and 31 December 1995, and entered into force on 1 July 1999. The member States of the European Communities are: Austria, Belgium, Denmark, Finland, France, Germany, Greece, Ireland, Italy, Luxembourg, the Netherlands, Portugal, Spain, Sweden and the United Kingdom.

TITLE III

ECONOMIC COOPERATION

Article 12

Promotion of investment

1.   Within the bounds of their spheres of competence, the Parties shall promote an attractive and stable climate for greater mutually beneficial investment.

2.   Such co-operation shall encompass measures including the following:

   (a)   promoting regular exchanges of information, the identification and dissemination of information on legislation and investment opportunities;

   (b)   promoting the development of a legal environment which is conducive to investment between the Parties, particularly, where applicable, through the conclusion between interested Community Member States and MERCOSUR Party States of bilateral agreements for the promotion and protection of investment and bilateral agreements to prevent double taxation;

   (c)   promoting joint ventures, particularly between small and medium-sized enterprises.

*   *   *

---

*   *Source*: European Communities (1999). "Interregional Framework Cooperation Agreement between the European Community and Its Member States, of the One Part, and the Southern Common Market and Its Party States, of the Other Part", *Official Journal of the European Communities*, L 112/66, 29 April 1999, pp. 66-77. [Note added by the editor.]

APPENDIX

Association, partnership and cooperation agreements signed between the European Community and its member States, on the one part, and third countries and groups of countries, on the other part, including investment-related provisions (end-1999)

Appendix. Association, partnership and cooperation agreements signed between the European Community, and its member States, on the one part, and third countries and groups of countries, on the other part, including investment-related provisions (end-1999)

Country/territory/group of countries	Date of signature	Date of entry into force
European Community and its member States		
Nigeria	16 July 1966[a]	…
African and Malagasy States[b]	29 July 1969[a]	…
East African States[c]	24 September 1969[a]	…
Malta	5 December 1970	1 April 1971
Austria	22 July 1972[a]	…
Israel	11 May 1975	1 July 1975
Algeria	26 April 1976	1 January 1978
Morocco	27 April 1976	1 November 1978
Egypt	18 January 1977	1 January 1979
Jordan	18 January 1977	1 January 1979
Syrian Arab Republic	18 January 1977	1 January 1978
Lebanon	3 May 1977	1 November 1978
ASEAN States[d]	7 March 1980	1 October 1980
Yugoslavia	2 April 1980	…
Zimbabwe	4 November 1980	…
China	21 May 1985	1 October 1985
Pakistan	23 July 1985	1 May 1986
States of the Gulf[e]	15 June 1988	1 January 1990
African, Carribean and the Pacific States[f]	15 December 1989	…
Argentina	2 April 1990	…
Uruguay	4 November 1991	1 January 1994
Hungary	16 December 1991	1 February 1994
(Poland)	(19 September 1989)[a]	…
Poland	16 December 1991	1 February 1994
San Marino	16 December 1991	nif
Albania	11 May 1992	1 December 1992
Mongolia	16 June 1992	1 March 1993
Brazil	26 June 1992	1 November 1995
EFTA States[g]	2 May 1992	17 March 1993
Macao	15 June 1992	1 January 1993
(Romania)	(22 October 1990)[a]	…
Romania	1 February 1993	1 February 1993
Central America[h]	22 February 1993[a]	…

/…

Country/territory/group of countries	Date of signature	Date of entry into force
European Community and its Member States		
(Bulgaria)	(8 May 1990)[a]	...
Bulgaria	8 March 1993	1 February 1995
Slovenia	5 April 1993	1 September 1993
Andean Group countries[i]	23 April 1993	1 May 1998
(Czechoslovakia)	(16 December 1991)[a]	...
Czech Republic	4 October 1993	1 February 1993
Slovakia	4 October 1993	1 February 1993
(India)	23 June 1981[a]	...
India	20 December 1993	1 August 1994
Ukraine	14 June 1994	nif
(Soviet Union)	(8 December 1989)[a]	
Russian Federation	25 June 1994	nif
(Sri Lanka)	(22 July 1975)[a]	
Sri Lanka	18 July 1994	...
Republic of Moldova	28 November 1994	nif
Kazakhstan	23 January 1995	nif
Kyrgyzstan	9 February 1995	nif
Belarus	6 March 1995	nif
(Turkey)	(12 September 1963)[a]	(1 December 1964)
Turkey	6 March 1995	...
(Latvia)	(11 May 1992)[a]	(1 February 1993)
Latvia	12 June 1995	1 February 1998
(Lithuania)	(11 May 1992)[a]	(1 February 1993)
Lithuania	12 June 1995	1 February 1998
(Estonia)	(11 May 1992)[a]	(1 March 1993)
Estonia	12 June 1995	1 February 1998
(Tunisia)	(25 April 1976)[a]	(1 November 1978)
Tunisia	17 July 1995	1 March 1998
Viet Nam	17 July 1995	1 June 1996
Nepal	20 November 1995	1 June 1996
MERCOSUR[j]	15 December 1995	1 July 1999
Armenia	22 April 96	nif
Azerbaijan	22 April 1996	nif
Georgia	22 April 1996	nif
Chile	21 June 1996	1 February 1999
Uzbekistan	21 June 1996	nif
Republic of Korea	28 October 1996	...
Cambodia	29 April 1997	...

/...

Country/territory/group of countries	Date of signature	Date of entry into force
European Community and its member States		
Lao People's Democratic Rep.	29 April 1997	1 December 1997
The FormerYugoslav Republic of Macedonia	18 December 1997	...
Turkmenistan	25 May 1998	nif
(Mexico)	(26 April 1991)	(1 November 1991)
Mexico	24 November 1999	nif

Source: UNCTAD, based on information provided by the Commission of the European Community.

... means information not available.

nif means not yet in force.

[a] no longer in force.

[b] Countries signatories to this agreement are: Dahomey (now Benin), Burundi, Upper Volta (now Burkina Faso), Cameroon, Central African Republic, Chad, Zaire (now the Democratic Republic of the Congo), Gabon, Côte d' Ivoire, Malagasy, Mali, Mauritania, Niger, Rwanda, Senegal, Somalia and Togo.

[c] Countries signatories to this agreement are: Kenya, United Republic of Tanzania and Uganda.

[d] Countries signatories to this agreement are: Brunei Darussalam, Cambodia, Indonesia, Lao People's Democratic Republic, Malaysia, Myanmar, the Philippines, Singapore, Thailand and Viet Nam.

[e] Countries parties to the Charter of the Cooperation Council for the Arab States of the Gulf are: Bahrain, Kuwait, Oman, Qatar, Saudi Arabia and United Arab Emirates.

[f] Countries parties to the Fourth ACP-EC Convention of Lomé are: African, Carribean and the Pacific countries, namely, Angola, Antigua and Barbuda, Bahamas, Barbados, Belize, Benin (formerly Dahomey), Botswana, Burkina Faso (formerly Upper Volta), Burundi, Cameroon, Cape Verde, Central African Republic, Chad, Comoros, Congo, the Democratic Republic of the Congo (formerly Zaire), Côte d'Ivoire, Djibouti, Dominica, Dominican Republic, Equatorial Guinea, Eritrea, Ethiopia, Fiji, Gabon, the Gambia, Ghana, Grenada, Guinea, Guinea-Bissau, Guyana, Haiti, Jamaica, Kenya, Kiribati, Lesotho, Liberia, Madagascar, Malawi, Mali, Mauritania, Mauritius, Mozambique, Namibia, Niger, Nigeria, Papua New Guinea, Rwanda, Saint Kitts and Nevis, Saint Lucia, Saint Vincent and the Grenadines, Sao Tome and Principe, Senegal, Seychelles, Sierra Leone, Solomon Islands, Sudan, Suriname, Swaziland, United Republic of Tanzania, Togo, Tonga, Trinidad and Tobago, Tuvalu, Uganda, Vanuatu, Western Samoa, Zambia, and Zimbabwe; and member countries of the European Community, namely, Austria, Belgium, Denmark, Finland, France, Germany, Greece, Ireland, Italy, Luxembourg, the Netherlands, Portugal, Spain, Sweden and the United Kingdom of Great Britain and Northern Ireland.

[g] Countries members to the European Free Trade Area are: Iceland, Liechtenstein, Norway and Switzerland.

[h] Countries Parties to the General Treaty on Central American Economic Integration are: Costa Rica, El Salvador, Guatemala, Honduras and Nicaragua.

[i] Countries members to the Andean Group are: Bolivia, Colombia, Ecuador, Peru and Venezuela.

[j] Countries members to the MERCOSUR are: Argentina, Brazil, Paraguay and Uruguay.

ANNEX C

Other bilateral investment-related agreements

AGREEMENT BETWEEN THE GOVERNMENT OF THE UNITED STATES OF AMERICA AND THE GOVERNMENT OF THE FEDERAL REPUBLIC OF GERMANY RELATING TO MUTUAL COOPERATION REGARDING RESTRICTIVE BUSINESS PRACTICES[*]

The Agreement between the Government of the United States of America and the Government of the Federal Republic of Germany Relating to Mutual Cooperation Regarding Restrictive Business Practices was signed on 23 June 1976. It entered into force on 11 September 1976.

The Government of the United States of America and the Government of the Federal Republic of Germany, considering that restrictive business practices affecting their domestic or international trade are prejudicial to the economic and commercial interests of their countries,

Convinced that action against these practices can be made more effective by the regularization of cooperation between their antitrust authorities, and

Having regard, in this respect, to their Treaty of Friendship, Commerce, and Navigation and to the Recommendations of the Council of the Organization for Economic Cooperation and development Concerning Cooperation Between Member Countries on Restrictive Business Practices Affecting International Trade adopted on October 5, 1967, and in July 3, 1973,

Have agreed as follows:

Article 1

For the purpose of this Agreement, the following terms shall have the meanings indicated:

(a)   "Antitrust laws" shall mean, in the United States of America, the Sherman Act (15 U.S.C. 1-11), the Clayton Act (15 U.S.C. 12 et seq.), and the Federal Trade Commission Act (15 U.S.C. 41 et seq.), and in the Federal Republic of Germany, the Act Against Restraints on Competition ("Gesetz gegen Wettbewerbsbeschr„nkungen") (BGB1. I 1974, 869) as those Acts have been and may from time to time be amended.

(b)   "Antitrust authorities" shall mean, in the United States of America, the Antitrust Division of the United States Department of Justice and the Federal Trade Commission, and, in the Federal Republic of Germany, the Federal Minister of

---

[*]   *Source*: Government of Germany and Government of the United States of America (1976). "Agreement between the Government of the United States of America and the Government of the Federal Republic of Germany Relating to Mutual Cooperation Regarding Restrictive Business Practices"; *Trade Regulation Reports*, vol. 4, Case No. 13,502 (Chicago: Commerce Clearing House); available also on the Internet (http://www.usdoj.gov/atr/public/international/docs/germany.us.txt). [Note added by the editor.]

Economics ("Bundesminister für Wirtschaft") and the Federal Cartel Office ("Bundeskartellamt") and successors in each country.

(c)   "Information" shall include reports, documents, memoranda, expert opinions, legal briefs and pleadings, decisions of administrative or judicial bodies, and other written or computerized records.

(d)   "Restrictive business practices" shall include all practices which may violate, or are regulated under, the antitrust laws of either party.

(e)   "Antitrust investigation or proceeding" shall mean any investigation or proceeding related to restrictive business practices and conducted by an antitrust authority under its antitrust laws.

Article 2

(1)   Each party agrees that its antitrust authorities will cooperate and render assistance to the antitrust authorities of the other party, to the extent set forth in this Agreement, in connection with:

(a)   antitrust investigations or proceedings,

(b)   studies related to competition policy and possible changes in antitrust laws, and

(c)   activities related to the restrictive business practice work of international organizations of which both parties are members.

(2)   Each party agrees that it will provide the other party with any significant information which comes to the attention of its antitrust authorities and which involves restrictive business practices which, regardless of origin, have a substantial effect on the domestic or international trade of such other party.

(3)   Each party agrees that, upon request of the other party, its antitrust authorities will obtain for and furnish such other party with such information as such other party may request in connection with a matter referred to in Article 2, paragraph 1, and will otherwise provide advice and assistance in connection therewith. Such advice and assistance shall include, but not necessarily be limited to, the exchange of information and a summary of experience relating to particular practices where either of the antitrust authorities of the requested party has dealt with or has information relating to a practice involved in the request. Such assistance shall also include the attendance of public officials of the requested party to give information, views or testimony in regard to any antitrust investigation or proceeding, legislation or policy, and the transmittal or the making available of documents and legal briefs and pleadings of the antitrust authorities of the requested party (or duly authenticated or certified copies thereof).

(4)   An antitrust authority of a party, in seeking to obtain information or interviews on a voluntary basis from a person or enterprise within the jurisdiction of the other party, may request such other party to transmit a communication seeking such information or interviews to such person or enterprise. In that event, the other party will transmit such communication and, if so

requested, will (if such is the case) notify such person or enterprise that the requested party has no objection to voluntary compliance with the request.

(5)   Each party agrees that, upon the request of an antitrust authority of the other party, its antitrust authorities will consult with the requesting party concerning possible coordination of concurrent antitrust investigations or proceedings in the two countries which are related or affect each other.

Article 3

(1)   Either party may decline, in whole or in part, to render assistance under Article 2 of this Agreement, or may comply with any request for such assistance subject to such terms and conditions as the complying party may establish, if such party determines that:

(a)   compliance would be prohibited by legal protections of confidentiality or by other domestic law of the complying party; or

(b)   compliance would be inconsistent with its security, public policy or other important national interests;

(c)   the requesting party is unable or unwilling to comply with terms or conditions established by the complying party, including conditions designed to protect the confidentiality of information requested; or

(d)   the requesting party would not be obligated to comply with such request, by reason of any grounds set forth in items (a), (b) or (c) above, if such request had been made by the requested party.

(2)   Neither party shall be obligated to employ compulsory powers in order to obtain information for, or otherwise provide advice and assistance to, the other party pursuant to this Agreement.

(3)   Neither party shall be obligated to undertake efforts in connection with this Agreement which are likely to require such substantial utilization of personnel or resources as to burden unreasonably its own enforcement duties.

Article 4

(1)   Each party agrees that it will act, to the extent compatible with its domestic law, security, public policy or other important national interests, so as not to inhibit or interfere with any antitrust investigation or proceeding of the other party.

(2)   Where the application of the antitrust laws of one party, including antitrust investigations or proceedings, will be likely to affect important interests of the other party, such party will notify such other party and will consult and coordinate with such other party to the extent appropriate under the circumstances.

Article 5

The confidentiality of information transmitted shall be maintained in accordance with the law of the party receiving such information, subject to such terms and conditions as may be established by the complying party furnishing such information. Each party agrees that it will use information received under this Agreement only for purposes of its antitrust authorities as set forth in Article 2, paragraph 1.

Article 6

(1)   The terms of this Agreement shall be implemented, and obligations under this Agreement shall be discharged, in accordance with the laws of the respective parties, by their respective antitrust authorities which shall develop appropriate procedures in connection therewith.

(2)   Requests for assistance pursuant to this Agreement shall be made or confirmed in writing, shall be reasonably specific and shall include the following information as appropriate:

(a)   the antitrust authority or authorities to whom the request is directed;

(b)   the antitrust authority or authorities making the request;

(c)   the nature of the antitrust investigation or proceeding, study or other activity involved;

(d)   the object of and reason for the request; and

(e)   the names and addresses of relevant persons or enterprises, if known.

Such requests may specify that particular procedures be followed or that a representative of the requesting party be present at requested proceedings or in connection with other requested actions.

(3)   The requesting party shall be advised, to the extent feasible, of the time, place and type of action to be taken by the requested party in response to any request for assistance under this Agreement.

(4)   If any such request cannot be fully complied with, the requested party shall promptly notify the requesting party of its refusal or inability to so comply, stating the grounds for such refusal, any terms or conditions which it may establish in connection therewith and any other information which it considers relevant to the subject of the request.

Article 7

All direct expenses incurred by the requested party in complying with a request for assistance under this Agreement shall, upon request, be paid or reimbursed by the requesting party. Such direct expenses may include fees of experts, costs of interpreters, travel and maintenance expenses of experts, interpreters and employees of antitrust authorities, transcript and reproduction costs, and other incidental expenses, but shall not include any part of the salaries of employees of antitrust authorities.

Article 8

This Agreement shall also apply to Land Berlin provided that the Government of the Federal Republic of Germany does not make a contrary declaration to the Government of the United States of America within three months of the date of entry into force of this Agreement.

Article 9

(1)   This Agreement shall enter into force one month from the date on which the parties shall have informed each other in an exchange of diplomatic notes that all the domestic legal requirements for such entry into force have been fulfilled.

(2)   This Agreement shall remain in force until terminated upon six months' notice given in writing by one of the parties to the other.

Done at Bonn, in duplicate, in the English and German languages, both texts being equally authentic, this twenty-third day of June, 1976.

*   *   *

AGREEMENT BETWEEN THE GOVERNMENT OF THE UNITED STATES OF AMERICA AND THE GOVERNMENT OF AUSTRALIA RELATING TO COOPERATION ON ANTITRUST MATTERS[*]

AND

AGREEMENT BETWEEN THE GOVERNMENT OF THE UNITED STATES OF AMERICA AND THE GOVERNMENT OF AUSTRALIA ON MUTUAL ANTITRUST ENFORCEMENT ASSISTANCE

The Agreement between the Government of the United States of America and the Government of Australia Relating to Cooperation on Antitrust Matters was signed on 29 June 1982. It entered into force upon signature. The Agreement between the Government of the United States of America and the Government of Australia on Mutual Antitrust Enforcement Assistance was signed on 27 April 1999. It entered into force on 5 November 1999.

The Government of the United States of America and the Government of Australia,

Recognizing that conflicts have arisen between the interests reflected in United States antitrust laws and policies and those reflected in Australian laws and policies, and that such conflicts may arise in the future;

Recognizing the need for such conflicts to be resolved with mutual respect for each other's sovereignty and with due regard for considerations of comity;

Considering that inter-governmental consultations may facilitate the resolution of such conflicts;

Desiring to establish an appropriate bilateral framework for conducting consultations; and

Considering that, in the absence of conflicts, cooperation between the Governments of the United States and Australia is desirable in the enforcement of antitrust laws,

Have agreed as follows:

---

[*] *Source*: Government of Australia and Government of the United States of America (1982). "Agreement between the Government of the United States of America and the Government of Australia Relating to Cooperation on Antitrust Matters", *Australian Treaty Series*, No. 13, 1982; *Trade Regulation Reports*, vol. 4, ƒ 13,502 (Chicago: Commerce Clearing House); available also on the Internet (http://usdoj.gov/atr/public/international/docs/austral.us.txt). [Note added by the editor.]

ARTICLE 1

Notification

1.   When the Government of Australia has adopted a policy that it considers may have antitrust implications for the United States, the Government of Australia may notify the Government of the United States of that policy. If practicable, such a notification shall be given before implementation of the policy by persons or enterprises.

2.   When the Department of Justice or Federal Trade Commission of the United States decides to undertake an antitrust investigation that may have implications for Australian laws, policies or national interests, the Government of the United States shall notify the Government of Australia of the investigation.

3.   A notification under paragraph 2 of this Article shall be effected promptly and, to the fullest extent possible under the circumstances of the particular case, prior to the convening of a grand jury or issuance of any civil investigative demand, subpoena or other compulsory process.

4.   The content of a notification made pursuant to paragraph 1 or 2 of this Article shall be sufficiently detailed to permit the notified Government to determine whether the matter may have implications for its laws, policies or national interests.

5.   Notifications undertaken in accordance with paragraphs 1 and 2 of this Article shall be transmitted through diplomatic channels.

ARTICLE 2

Consultations

1.   When it appears to the Government of Australia through notification pursuant to paragraph 2 of Article 1 that the Department of Justice or Federal Trade Commission of the United States has commenced, or is likely to commence, an antitrust investigation or legal proceeding that may have implications for Australian laws, policies or national interests, the Government of Australia shall communicate its concerns and may request consultations with the Government of the United States. The Government of the United States shall participate in such consultations.

2.   When it appears to the Government of the United States through notification pursuant to paragraph 1 of Article 1 that a policy of the Government of Australia may have significant antitrust implications under United States law, the Government of the United States shall communicate its concerns and may request consultations with the Government of Australia. The Government of Australia shall participate in such consultations.

3.   Either Party may seek consultations with respect to potential conflicts which come to its attention other than by notification.

4.   Both Parties during consultations shall seek to identify any respect in which:

(a)   implementation of the Australian policy has or might have implications for the United States in relation to the enforcement of its antitrust laws; and

(b)   the antitrust enforcement action by the Department of Justice or the Federal Trade Commission of the United States has or might have implications for Australian laws, policies or national interests.

5.   Both Parties during consultations shall seek earnestly to avoid a possible conflict between their respective laws, policies and national interests and for that purpose to give due regard to each other's sovereignty and to considerations of comity.

6.   In particular, in seeking to avoid conflict:

(a)   the Government of Australia shall give the fullest consideration to modifying any aspect of the policy which has or might have implications for the United States in relation to the enforcement of its antitrust laws. In this regard, consideration shall be given to any harm that may be caused by the implementation or continuation of the Australian policy to the interests protected by the United States antitrust laws; and

(b)   the Department of Justice or the Federal Trade Commission of the United States, as the case may be, shall give the fullest consideration to modifying or discontinuing its existing antitrust investigation or proceedings, or to modifying or refraining from contemplated antitrust investigations or proceedings.   In this regard, consideration shall be given to the interests of Australia with respect to the conduct to which the proceedings or contemplated proceedings, relate, or would relate, including, without limitation, Australia's interests in circumstances where that conduct:

(1)   was undertaken for the purpose of obtaining a permission or approval required under Australian law for the exportation from Australia of Australian natural resources or goods manufactured or produced in Australia;

(2)   was undertaken by an Australian authority, being an authority established by law in Australia, in the discharge of its functions in relation to the exportation from Australia of Australian natural resources or goods manufactured or produced in Australia;

(3)   related exclusively to the exportation from Australia to countries other than the United States, and otherwise than for the purpose of re-exportation to the United States, of Australian natural resources or goods manufactured or produced in Australia; or

(4)   consisted of representations to, or discussions with, the Government of Australia or an Australian authority in relation to the formulation or implementation of a policy of the Government of Australia with respect to the exportation from Australia of Australian natural resources or goods manufactured or produced in Australia.

7.   Each party during consultations shall provide as detailed an account as possible, under the particular circumstances, of the basis and nature of its antitrust investigation or proceeding, or its national policy and its implementation, as the case may be.

ARTICLE 3

Confidentiality

Documents and information provided by either Party in the course of notification or consultations under this Agreement shall be treated confidentially by the receiving Party unless the providing Party consents to disclosure or disclosure is compelled by law. The Government of the United States shall not, without the consent of the Government of Australia, use information or documents provided by the Government of Australia in the course of notification or consultations under this Agreement as evidence in any judicial or administrative proceeding under United States antitrust laws. The Government of the United States shall not, however, be foreclosed from pursuing an investigation of any conduct which is the subject of notification or consultations, or from initiating a proceeding based on evidence obtained from sources other than the Government of Australia.

ARTICLE 4

Procedure after Consultations

1.   When consultations have been held with respect to an Australian policy notified pursuant to paragraph 1 of Article 1, and the Department of Justice or the Federal Trade Commission of the United States, as the case may be, concludes that the implementation of that policy should not be a basis for action under United States antitrust laws, the Government of Australia may request a written memorialization of such conclusion and the basis for it. The Government of the United States shall, in the absence of circumstances making it inappropriate, provide such a written memorialization. When a written memorialization has been provided, the Government of the United States shall expeditiously consider requests by persons or enterprises for a statement of enforcement intentions with respect to proposed private conduct in implementation of the Australian policy, in accordance with the Department of Justice's Business Review Procedure or the Federal Trade Commission's Advisory Opinion Procedure, as may be appropriate in the case.

2.   If, through consultations pursuant to this Agreement, no means for avoiding a conflict between the laws, policies or national interests of the two Parties has been developed, each Party shall be free to protect its interests as it deems necessary.

ARTICLE 5

Cooperation in Antitrust Enforcement

1.   When a proposed investigation or enforcement action under the antitrust laws of one nation does not adversely affect the laws, policies or national interests of the other, each Party shall cooperate with the other in regard to that investigation or action, including through the

provision of information and administrative and judicial assistance to the extent permitted by applicable national law.

2.   The mere seeking by legal process of information or documents located in its territory shall not in itself be regarded by either Party as affecting adversely its significant national interests, or as constituting a basis for applying measures to prohibit the transmission of such information or documents to the authorities of the other Party, provided that in the case of United States legal process prior notice has been given of its issuance. Each Party shall, to the fullest extent possible under the circumstances of the particular case, provide notice to the other before taking action to prevent compliance with such legal process.

ARTICLE 6

Private Antitrust Suits in United States Courts

When it appears to the Government of Australia that private antitrust proceedings are pending in a United States court relating to conduct, or conduct pursuant to a policy of the Government of Australia, that has been the subject of notification and consultations under this Agreement, the Government of Australia may request the Government of the United States to participate in the litigation. The Government of the United States shall in the event of such request report to the court on the substance and outcome of the consultations.

ARTICLE 7

Entry into Force

This Agreement shall enter into force upon signature by both Parties, and shall remain in force unless terminated upon six months notice given in writing by one of the Parties to the other.

IN WITNESS WHEREOF, the undersigned, duly authorized thereto by their respective Government, have signed this Agreement.

DONE, in duplicate, at Washington this twenty-ninth day of June, 1982.

FOR THE GOVERNMENT OF

THE UNITED STATES OF AMERICA:

William French Smith
Attorney General

FOR THE GOVERNMENT

OF AUSTRALIA:

Peter Durack
Attorney General

*   *   *

AGREEMENT BETWEEN THE GOVERNMENT OF THE UNITED STATES OF AMERICA AND THE GOVERNMENT OF AUSTRALIA ON MUTUAL ANTITRUST ENFORCEMENT ASSISTANCE*

The Government of the United States of America and the Government of Australia (individually a "Party" or collectively the "Parties"), desiring to improve the effectiveness of the enforcement of the antitrust laws of both countries through cooperation and mutual legal assistance on a reciprocal basis, hereby agree as follows:

ARTICLE I

DEFINITIONS

Antitrust Authority
refers, in the case of the United States, to the United States Department of Justice or the United States Federal Trade Commission.

In the case of Australia, the term refers to the Australian Competition and Consumer Commission.

Antitrust Evidence
refers to information, testimony, statements, documents or copies thereof, or other things that are obtained, in anticipation of, or during the course of, an investigation or proceeding under the Parties' respective antitrust laws, or pursuant to the Parties' Mutual Assistance Legislation.

Antitrust Laws
refers, in the case of the United States, to the laws enumerated in subsection (a) of the first section of the Clayton Act, 15 U.S.C. 12(a), and to Section 5 of the Federal Trade Commission Act, 15 U.S.C. 45, to the extent that such Section 5 applies to unfair methods of competition.

In the case of Australia, the term refers to Part IV of the Trade Practices Act 1974; other provisions of that Act except Part X in so far as they relate to Part IV; Regulations made under that Act in so far as they relate to Part IV, except Regulations to the extent that they relate to Part X; and the Competition Code of the Australian States and Territories.

Central Authority
refers, in the case of the United States, to the Attorney General (or a person designated by the Attorney General), in consultation with the U.S. Federal Trade Commission. In the case of Australia, the term refers to the Australian Competition and Consumer Commission, in consultation with the Attorney General's Department.

---

* *Source*: Government of Australia and Government of the United States of America (1999). "Agreement between the Government of the United States of America and the Government of Australia on Mutual Antitrust Enforcement Assistance"; *Australian Treaty Series* 1999, No. 22; and *Federal Register Reports*, ƒ 264595 (Washington D.C.: World Laws); available also on the Internet (http://www.usdoj.gov/atr/public/international/docs/usaus7.htm). [Note added by the editor.]

Executing Authority

refers, in the case of the United States, to the Antitrust Authority designated to execute a particular request on behalf of a Party.

In the case of Australia, the term includes the Australian Competition and Consumer Commission and the Attorney General's Department.

Mutual Assistance Legislation

refers, in the case of the United States, to the International Antitrust Enforcement Assistance Act of 1994, 15 U.S.C. 6201-6212, Public Law No. 103-438, 108 Stat. 4597. In the case of Australia, the term refers to the Mutual Assistance in Business Regulation Act 1992 and the Mutual Assistance in Criminal Matters Act 1987, and Regulations made pursuant to those Acts.

Person or Persons

refers to any natural person or legal entity, including corporations, unincorporated associations, partnerships, or bodies corporate existing under or authorized by the laws of either the United States, its States, or its Territories, the laws of Australia, its States, or its Territories, or the laws of other sovereign states.

Request

refers to a request for assistance under this Agreement.

Requested Party

refers to the Party from which assistance is sought under this Agreement, or which has provided such assistance.

Requesting Party

refers to the Party seeking or receiving assistance under this Agreement.

ARTICLE II

OBJECT AND SCOPE OF ASSISTANCE

A.   The Parties intend to assist one another and to cooperate on a reciprocal basis in providing or obtaining antitrust evidence that may assist in determining whether a person has violated, or is about to violate, their respective antitrust laws, or in facilitating the administration or enforcement of such antitrust laws.

B.   Each Party's Antitrust Authorities shall, to the extent compatible with that Party's laws, enforcement policies, and other important interests, inform the other Party's Antitrust Authorities about activities that appear to be anticompetitive and that may be relevant to, or may warrant, enforcement activity by the other Party's Antitrust Authorities.

C.   Each Party's Antitrust Authorities shall, to the extent compatible with that Party's laws, enforcement policies, and other important interests, inform the other Party's Antitrust Authorities about investigative or enforcement activities taken pursuant to assistance provided under this Agreement that may affect the important interests of the other Party.

D.   Nothing in this Agreement shall require the Parties or their respective Antitrust Authorities to take any action inconsistent with their respective Mutual Assistance Legislation.

E.   Assistance contemplated by this Agreement includes but is not limited to:

    1.   disclosing, providing, exchanging, or discussing antitrust evidence in the possession of an Antitrust Authority;

    2.   obtaining antitrust evidence at the request of an Antitrust Authority of the other Party, including

        a.   taking the testimony or statements of persons or otherwise obtaining information from persons,

        b.   obtaining documents, records, or other forms of documentary evidence,

        c.   locating or identifying persons or things, and

        d.   executing searches and seizures, and disclosing, providing, exchanging, or discussing such evidence; and

    3.   providing copies of publicly available records, including documents or information in any form, in the possession of government departments and agencies of the national government of the Requested Party.

F.   Assistance may be provided whether or not the conduct underlying a request would constitute a violation of the antitrust laws of the Requested Party.

G.   Nothing in this Agreement shall prevent a Party from seeking assistance from or providing assistance to the other pursuant to other agreements, treaties, arrangements, or practices, including the Agreement Between the Government of Australia and the Government of the United States of America Relating to Cooperation on Antitrust Matters of June 29, 1982, either in place of or in conjunction with assistance provided pursuant to this Agreement.

H.   Except as provided by paragraphs C and D of Article VII, this Agreement shall be used solely for the purpose of mutual antitrust enforcement assistance between the Parties. The provisions of this Agreement shall not give rise to a right on the part of any private person to obtain, suppress, or exclude any evidence, or to impede the execution of a request made pursuant to this Agreement.

I.   Nothing in this Agreement compels a person to provide antitrust evidence in violation of any legally applicable right or privilege.

J.   Nothing in this Agreement affects the right of an Antitrust Authority of one Party to seek antitrust evidence on a voluntary basis from a person located in the territory of the other Party, nor does anything in this Agreement preclude any such person from voluntarily providing antitrust evidence to an Antitrust Authority.

ARTICLE III

REQUESTS FOR ASSISTANCE

A.   Requests for assistance under this Agreement shall be made by an Antitrust Authority of the Requesting Party. Such requests shall be made in writing and directed to the Central Authority of the Requested Party. With respect to the United States, the Attorney General, acting as the Central Authority, will upon receipt forward a copy of each request to the Federal Trade Commission.

B.   Requests shall include, without limitation:

1.   A general description of the subject matter and nature of the investigation or proceeding to which the request relates, including identification of the persons subject to the investigation or proceeding and citations to the specific antitrust laws involved giving rise to the investigation or proceeding; such description shall include information sufficient to explain how the subject matter of the request concerns a possible violation of the antitrust laws in question;

2.   The purpose for which the antitrust evidence, information, or other assistance is sought and its relevance to the investigation or proceeding to which the request relates. A request by the United States shall state either that the request is not made for the purpose of any criminal proceedings or that the request is made for a purpose that includes possible criminal proceedings. In the former case, the request shall contain a written assurance that antitrust evidence obtained pursuant to the request shall not be used for the purposes of criminal proceedings, unless such use is subsequently authorized pursuant to Article VII. In the latter case, the request shall indicate the relevant provisions of law under which criminal proceedings may be brought;

3.   A description of the antitrust evidence, information, or other assistance sought, including, where applicable and to the extent necessary and possible:

  (a)   the identity and location of any person from whom evidence is sought, and a description of that person's relationship to the investigation or proceeding which is the subject of the request;

  (b)   a list of questions to be asked of a witness;

  (c)   a description of documentary evidence requested; and

  (d)   with respect to searches and seizures, a precise description of the place or person to be searched and of the antitrust evidence to be seized, and information justifying such search and seizure under the laws of the Requested Party;

4.   Where applicable, a description of procedural or evidentiary requirements bearing on the manner in which the Requesting Party desires the request to be executed, which may include requirements relating to:

(a)   the manner in which any testimony or statement is to be taken or recorded, including the participation of counsel;

(b)   the administration of oaths;

(c)   any legal privileges that may be invoked under the law of the Requesting Party that the Requesting Party wishes the Executing Authority to respect in executing the request, together with an explanation of the desired method of taking the testimony or provision of evidence to which such privileges may apply; and

(d)   the authentication of public records;

5.   The desired time period for a response to the request;

6.   Requirements, if any, for confidential treatment of the request or its contents; and

7.   A statement disclosing whether the Requesting Party holds any proprietary interest that could benefit or otherwise be affected by assistance provided in response to the request; and

8.   Any other information that may facilitate review or execution of a request.

C.   Requests shall be accompanied by written assurances of the relevant Antitrust Authority that there have been no significant modifications to the confidentiality laws and procedures described in Annex A hereto.

D.   An Antitrust Authority may modify or supplement a request prior to its execution if the Requested Party agrees.

ARTICLE IV

LIMITATIONS ON ASSISTANCE

A.   The Requested Party may deny assistance in whole or in part if that Party's Central Authority or Executing Authority, as appropriate, determine that:

1.   A request is not made in accordance with the provisions of this Agreement;

2.   Execution of a request would exceed the Executing Authority's reasonably available resources;

3.   Execution of a request would not be authorized by the domestic law of the Requested Party;

4.   execution of a request would be contrary to the public interest of the Requested Party.

5.   Before denying a request, the Central Authority or the Executing Authority of the Requested Party, as appropriate, shall consult with the Central Authority of the Requesting Party and the Antitrust Authority that made the request to determine whether assistance may be given in whole or in part, subject to specified terms and conditions.

6.   If a request is denied in whole or in part, the Central Authority or the Executing Authority of the Requested Party, as appropriate, shall promptly inform the Central Authority of the Requesting Party and the Antitrust Authority that made the request and provide an explanation of the basis for denial.

ARTICLE V

EXECUTION OF REQUESTS

A.   After receiving a request, the Central Authority shall promptly provide the Requesting Party an initial response that includes, when applicable, an identification of the Executing Authority (Authorities) for the Request.

B.   The Central Authority of the United States, the Attorney General of Australia, or, once designated, the Executing Authority of either Party may request additional information concerning the request or may determine that the request will be executed only subject to specified terms and conditions. Without limitation, such terms and conditions may relate to

(1)   the manner or timing of the execution of the request, or

(2)   the use or disclosure of any antitrust evidence provided. If the Requesting Party accepts assistance subject to such terms and conditions, it shall comply with them.

C.   A request shall be executed in accordance with the laws of the Requested Party. The method of execution specified in the request shall be followed, unless it is prohibited by the law of the Requested Party or unless the Executing Authority otherwise concludes, after consultation with the Authority that made the request, that a different method of execution is appropriate.

D.   The Executing Authority shall, to the extent permitted by the laws and other important interests of the Requested Party, facilitate the participation in the execution of a request of such officials of the Requesting Party as are specified in the request.

ARTICLE VI

CONFIDENTIALITY

A.   Except as otherwise provided by this paragraph and Article VII, each Party shall, to the fullest extent possible consistent with that Party's laws, maintain the confidentiality of any request and of any information communicated to it in confidence by the other Party under this Agreement. In particular:

1.   The Requesting Party may ask that assistance be provided in a manner that maintains the confidentiality of a request and/or its contents. If a request cannot be executed in that manner, the Requested Party shall so inform the Requesting Party, which shall then determine the extent to which it wishes the request to be executed; and

2.   Antitrust evidence obtained pursuant to this Agreement shall be kept confidential by both the Requesting Party and the Requested Party, except as provided in paragraph E of this Article and Article VII.

       Each Party shall oppose, to the fullest extent possible consistent with that Party's laws, any application by a third party for disclosure of such confidential information.

B.   By entering into this Agreement, each Party confirms that:

1.   The confidentiality of antitrust evidence obtained under this Agreement is ensured by its national laws and procedures pertaining to the confidential treatment of such evidence, and that such laws and procedures as are set forth in Annex A to this Agreement are sufficient to provide protection that is adequate to maintain securely the confidentiality of antitrust evidence provided under this Agreement; and

2.   The Antitrust Authorities designated herein are themselves subject to the confidentiality restrictions imposed by such laws and procedures.

3.   Unauthorized or illegal disclosure or use of information communicated in confidence to a Party pursuant to this Agreement shall be reported immediately to the Central Authority and the Executing Authority of the Party that provided the information; the Central Authorities of both Parties, together with the Executing Authority that provided the information, shall promptly consult on steps to minimize any harm resulting from the disclosure and to ensure that unauthorized or illegal disclosure or use of confidential information does not recur. The Executing Authority that provided the information shall give notice of such unauthorized or illegal disclosure or use to the person, if any, that provided such information to the Executing Authority.

4.   Unauthorized or illegal disclosure or use of information communicated in confidence under this Agreement is a ground for termination of the Agreement by the affected Party, in accordance with the procedures set out in Article XIII.C.

5.   Nothing in this Agreement shall prevent disclosure, in an action or proceeding brought by an Antitrust Authority of the Requesting Party for a violation of the antitrust laws of the Requesting Party, of antitrust evidence provided hereunder to a defendant or respondent in that action or proceeding, if such disclosure is required by the law of the Requesting Party. The Requesting Party shall notify the Central Authority of the Requested Party and the Executing Authority that provided the information at least ten days in advance of any such proposed

disclosure, or, if such notice cannot be given because of a court order, then as promptly as possible.

ARTICLE VII

LIMITATIONS ON USE

A.   Except as provided in paragraphs C and D of this Article, antitrust evidence obtained pursuant to this Agreement shall be used or disclosed by the Requesting Party solely for the purpose of administering or enforcing the antitrust laws of the Requesting Party.

B.   Antitrust evidence obtained pursuant to this Agreement may be used or disclosed by a Requesting Party to administer or enforce its antitrust laws only

(1)   in the investigation or proceeding specified in the request in question and

(2)   for the purpose stated in the request, unless the Executing Authority that provided such antitrust evidence has given its prior written consent to a different use or disclosure; when the Requested Party is Australia, such consent shall not be given until the Executing Authority has obtained any necessary approval from the Attorney General.

C.   Antitrust evidence obtained pursuant to this Agreement may be used or disclosed by a Requesting Party with respect to the administration or enforcement of laws other than its antitrust laws only if (1) such use or disclosure is essential to a significant law enforcement objective and (2) the Executing Authority that provided such antitrust evidence has given its prior written consent to the proposed use or disclosure. In the case of the United States, the Executing Authority shall provide such consent only after it has made the determinations required for such consent by its mutual assistance legislation.

D.   Antitrust evidence obtained pursuant to this Agreement that has been made public consistently with the terms of this Article may thereafter be used by the Requesting Party for any purpose consistent with the Parties' mutual assistance legislation.

ARTICLE VIII

CHANGES IN APPLICABLE LAW

A.   The Parties shall provide to each other prompt written notice of actions within their respective States having the effect of significantly modifying their antitrust laws or the confidentiality laws and procedures set out in Annex A to this Agreement.

B.   In the event of a significant modification to a Party's antitrust laws or confidentiality laws and procedures set out in Annex A to this Agreement, the Parties shall promptly consult to determine whether this Agreement or Annex A to this Agreement should be amended.

ARTICLE IX

TAKING OF TESTIMONY AND PRODUCTION OF DOCUMENTS

A.   A person requested to testify and produce documents, records, or other articles pursuant to this Agreement may be compelled to appear and testify and produce such documents, records, and other articles, in accordance with the requirements of the laws of the Requested Party. Every person whose attendance is required for the purpose of giving testimony pursuant to this Agreement is entitled to such fees and allowances as may be provided for by the law of the Requested Party.

B.   Upon request by the Requesting Party, the Executing Authority shall furnish information in advance about the date and place of the taking of testimony or the production of evidence pursuant to this Agreement.

C.   The Executing Authority shall, to the extent permitted by the laws and other important interests of the Requested Party, permit the presence during the execution of the request of persons specified in the request, and shall, to the extent permitted by the laws and other important interests of the Requested Party, allow such persons to question the person giving the testimony or providing the evidence.

D.   The Executing Authority shall, to the extent permitted by the laws of the Requested Party, comply with any instructions of the Requesting Party with respect to any claims of legal privilege, immunity, or incapacity under the laws of the Requesting Party.

E.   The Executing Authority shall, to the extent permitted by the laws of the Requested Party, permit a person whose testimony is to be taken pursuant to this Article to have counsel present during the testimony.

F.   A Requesting Party may ask the Requested Party to facilitate the appearance in the Requesting Party's territory of a person located in the territory of the Requested Party, for the purpose of being interviewed or giving testimony. The Requesting Party shall indicate the extent to which the person's expenses will be paid. Upon receiving such a request, the Executing Authority shall invite the person to appear before the appropriate authority in the territory of the Requesting Party. The Executing Authority shall promptly inform the Requesting Party of the person's response.

G.   Antitrust evidence consisting of testimony or documentary evidence provided by the Requested Party pursuant to this Agreement shall be authenticated in accordance with the requirements of the law of the Requesting Party, in so far as such requirements would not violate the laws of the Requested Party.

ARTICLE X

SEARCH AND SEIZURE

A.   Where a request is to be executed by means of the search and seizure of antitrust evidence, the request shall include such information as is necessary to justify such action under the laws of the Requested Party. The Central Authorities shall confer, as needed, on alternative, equally effective procedures for compelling or obtaining the antitrust evidence that is the subject of a request.

B.   Upon request, every official of a Requested Party who has custody of antitrust evidence seized pursuant to this Agreement shall certify the continuity of custody, the identity of the antitrust evidence, and the integrity of its condition; the Requested Party shall furnish such certifications in the form specified by the Requesting Party.

ARTICLE XI

RETURN OF ANTITRUST EVIDENCE

At the conclusion of the investigation or proceeding specified in a request, the Central Authority or the Antitrust Authority of the Requesting Party shall return to the Central Authority or the Antitrust Authority of the Requested Party from which it obtained antitrust evidence all such evidence obtained pursuant to the execution of a request under this Agreement, along with all copies thereof, in the possession or control of the Central Authority or Antitrust Authority of the Requesting Party; provided, however, that antitrust evidence that has become evidence in the course of judicial or administrative proceedings or that has properly entered the public domain is not subject to this requirement.

ARTICLE XII

COSTS

Unless otherwise agreed, the Requested Party shall pay all costs of executing a request, except for the fees of expert witnesses, the costs of translation, interpretation, and transcription, and the allowances and expenses related to travel to the territory of the Requested Party, pursuant to Articles IX and X, by officials of the Requesting Party.

ARTICLE XIII

ENTRY INTO FORCE AND TERMINATION

A.   This Agreement shall enter into force upon notification by each Party to the other through diplomatic channels that it has completed its necessary internal procedures.

B.   Assistance under this Agreement shall be available in investigations or proceedings under the Parties' antitrust laws concerning conduct or transactions occurring before as well as after this Agreement enters into force.

C.   As stated in Article VI.D of this Agreement, a Party may unilaterally elect to terminate this Agreement upon the unauthorized or illegal disclosure or use of confidential antitrust evidence provided hereunder; provided, however, that neither Party shall make such an election until after it has consulted with the other Party, pursuant to Article VI.C, regarding steps to minimize any harm resulting from the unauthorized or illegal disclosure or use of information communicated in confidence under this Agreement, and steps to ensure that such disclosure or use does not recur. Termination shall take effect immediately upon notice or at such future date as may be determined by the terminating Party.

D.   On termination of this Agreement, the Parties agree, subject to Article VI.E and Article VII, to maintain the confidentiality of any request and information communicated to them in confidence by the other Party under this Agreement prior to its termination; and to return, in accordance with the terms of Article XI, any antitrust evidence obtained from the other Party under this Agreement; provided, however, that any such request or information that has become public in the course of public judicial or administrative proceedings is not subject to this requirement.

E.   In addition to the procedure set forth in paragraph C of this Article, either Party may terminate this Agreement by means of written notice through diplomatic channels. Termination shall take effect 30 days after the date of receipt of such notification.

        IN WITNESS WHEREOF, the undersigned, being duly authorized by their respective Governments, have signed this Agreement.

        DONE at Washington, this 27th day of April, 1999, in duplicate, in the English language.

For The Government of   **For The Government of**
The United States of America: **Australia:**

Janet Reno   Peter Costello

Date: April 27, 1999   Date: April 27, 1999

Robert Pitofsky
Date: April 27, 1999

*   *   *

AGREEMENT BETWEEN THE GOVERNMENT OF THE UNITED STATES OF AMERICA AND THE GOVERNMENT OF CANADA REGARDING THE APPLICATION OF THEIR COMPETITION AND DECEPTIVE MARKETING PRACTICE LAWS[*]

> The Agreement between the Government of the United States of America and the Government of Canada Regarding the Application of Their Competition and Deceptive Marketing Practice Laws was signed in Washington on 1 August 1995, and in Ottawa on 3 August 1995. It entered into force on the latter date.

The Government of the United States of America and the Government of Canada (hereinafter referred to as "Parties");

Having regard to their close economic relations and cooperation within the framework of the North American Free Trade Agreement ("NAFTA");

Noting that the sound and effective enforcement of their competition laws is a matter of importance to the efficient operation of markets within the free trade area and to the economic welfare of the Parties' citizens;

Having regard to their commitment in Chapter 15 of NAFTA to the importance of cooperation and coordination among their competition authorities to further effective competition law enforcement in the free trade area;

Recognizing that coordination of enforcement activities may, in appropriate cases, result in a more effective resolution of the Parties' respective concerns than would be attained through independent action;

Having regard to the fact that the effective enforcement of their laws relating to deceptive marketing practices is also a matter of importance to the efficient operation of markets within the free trade area, and having regard to the potential benefits of increased cooperation between the Parties in the enforcement of those laws;

Noting that from time to time differences may arise between the Parties concerning the application of their competition laws to conduct or transactions that implicate the important interests of both Parties;

Noting further their commitment to give careful consideration to each others important interest in the application of their competition laws; and

---

[*] *Source*: The Government of Canada and the Government of the United States of America (1996). "Agreement between the Government of the United States of America and the Government of Canada Regarding the Application of Their Competition and Deceptive Marketing Practice Laws", *International Legal Materials,* vol. 35 (1996), pp. 309-323; available also on the Internet (http://www.sice.oas.org/cp%5Fcomp/english/cpa/cpa1%5Fe.stm). [Note added by the editor.]

Having regard to the long history of cooperation between the Parties in matters relating to competition law, including the bilateral Understandings of 1959, 1969 and 1984, as well as the 1986 Recommendations of the Council of the OECD Concerning Cooperation Between Member Countries on Restrictive Business Practices Affecting International Trade;

Have agreed as follows:

Article I
Purpose and Definitions

1.   The purpose of this Agreement is to promote cooperation and coordination between the competition authorities of the Parties, to avoid conflicts arising from the application of the Parties' competition laws and to minimize the impact of differences on their respective important interests, and, in addition, to establish a framework for cooperation and coordination with respect to enforcement of deceptive marketing practices laws.

2.   For the purposes of this Agreement, the following terms shall have the following definitions:

  (a)   "Anticompetitive activity(ies)" means any conduct or transaction that may be subject to penalties or other relief under the competition laws a Party;

  (b)   "Competition authority(ies)" means

    (i)   for Canada, the Director of Investigation and Research;

    (ii)   for the United States of America, the United States Department of Justice and the Federal Trade Commission;

  (c)   "Competition law(s)" means

    (i)   for Canada, the *Competition Act*, R.S.C. 1985, c. C-34, except sections 52 through 60 of that Act;

    (ii)   for the United States of America, the *Sherman Act* (15 U.S.C. §§ 1-7), the *Clayton Act* (15 U.S.C. §§ 12-27), the *Wilson Tariff Act* (15 U.S.C. §§ 8-11) and the *Federal Trade Commission Act* (15 U.S.C. §§ 41-58), to the extent that it applies to unfair methods of competition,

    as well as any amendments thereto, and such other laws or regulations as the Parties may from time to time agree in writing to be a "competition law" for the purposes of this Agreement; and

  (d)   "Enforcement activity(ies)" means any investigation or proceeding conducted by a Party in relation to its competition laws.

3.   Any reference in this Agreement to a specific provision in either Party's competition law shall be interpreted as referring to that provision as amended from time to time and to any

successor provision thereof. Each Party shall promptly notify the other of any amendments to its competition laws.

Article II
Notification

1.   Each Party shall, subject to Article X(1), notify the other Party in the manner provided by this Article and Article XII with respect to its enforcement activities that may affect important interests of the other Party.

2.   Enforcement activities that may affect the important interests of the other Party and therefore ordinarily require notification include those that:

   (a)   are relevant to enforcement activities of the other Party;

   (b)   involve anticompetitive activities, other than mergers or acquisitions, carried out in whole or in part in the territory of the other Party, except where the activities occurring in the territory of the other Party are insubstantial;

   (c)   involve mergers or acquisitions in which

   -        one or more of the parties to the transaction, or

   -        a company controlling one or more of the parties to the transaction.

   is a company incorporated or organized under the laws of the other Party or of one of its provinces or states;

   (d)   involve conduct believed to have been required, encouraged or approved by the other Party;

   (e)   involve remedies that expressly require or prohibit conduct in the territory of the other Party or are otherwise directed at conduct in the territory of the other Party; or

   (f)   involve the seeking of information located in the territory of the other Party, whether by personal visit by officials of a Party to the territory of the other Party or otherwise.

3.   Notification pursuant to this Article shall ordinarily be given as soon as a Party's competition authorities become aware that notifiable circumstances are present, and in any event in accordance with paragraphs 4 through 7 of this Article.

4.   Where notifiable circumstances are present with respect to mergers or acquisitions, notification shall be given not later than

   (a)   in the case of the United States of America, the time its competition authorities seek information or documentary material concerning the proposed transaction pursuant to the *Hart-Scott-Rodino Antitrust Improvements Act of 1976* (15 U.S.C.

18a(e), the *Federal Trade Commission Act* (15 U.S.C. 49, 57b-1) or the *Antitrust Civil Process Act* (15 U.S.C. 1312); and

(b)   in the case of Canada, the time its competition authorities issue a written request for the information under oath or affirmation, or obtain an order under section 11 of the *Competition Act*, with respect to the transaction.

5.   When the competition authorities of a Party request that a person provide information, documents or other records located in the territory of the other Party, or request oral testimony in a proceeding or participation in a personal interview by a person located in the territory of the other Party, notification shall be given:

(a)   if compliance with a request for written information, documents or other records is voluntary, at or before the time that the request is made;

(b)   if compliance with a request for written information, documents or other records is compulsory, at least seven (7) days prior to the request, (or, when seven (7) days' notice cannot be given, as promptly as circumstances permit); and

(c)   in the case of oral testimony or personal interviews, at or before the time arrangements for the interview or testimony are made.

Notification is not required with respect to telephone contacts with a person in the territory of the other Party where (i) that person is not he subject of an investigation, (ii) the contact seeks only an oral response on a voluntary basis (although the availability and possible voluntary provision of documents may be discussed) and (iii) the other Party's important interests do not appear to be otherwise implicated, unless the other Party requests otherwise in relation to a particular matter.

Notification is not required for each subsequent request for information in relation to the same matter unless the Party seeking information becomes aware of new issues bearing on the important interests of the other Party, or the other Party requests otherwise in relation to a particular matter.

6.   The Parties acknowledge that officials of either Party may visit the territory of the other Party in the course of conducting investigations pursuant to their respective competition laws. Such visits shall be subject to notification pursuant to this Article and the consent of the notified Party.

7.   Notification shall also be given at least seven (7) days in advance of each of the following where notifiable circumstances are present:

(a)   (i)   in the case of the United States of America, the issuance of a complaint, the filing of a civil action seeking a temporary restraining order or preliminary injunction or the initiation of criminal proceedings;

        (ii)   in the case of Canada, the filing of an application with the Competition Tribunal, an application under Part IV of the *Competition Act* or the initiation of criminal proceedings;

    (b)   the settlement of a matter by way of an undertaking, an application F.O. a consent order or the filing or issuance of a proposed consent order or decree; and

    (c)   the issuance of a business review or advisory opinion that will ultimately be made public by the competition authorities.

When seven (7) days' notice cannot be given, notice shall be given as promptly as circumstances permit.

8.   Each Party shall also notify the other whenever its competition authorities intervene or otherwise publicly participate in a regulatory or judicial proceeding that is not initiated by the competition authorities if the issue addressed in the intervention or participation may affect hte other Party's important interests. Such notification shall be made at the time of the intervention or participation or as soon thereafter as possible.

9.   Notifications shall be sufficiently detailed to enable the notified Party to make an initial evaluation of the effect of the enforcement activity on its own important interests, and shall include the nature of the activities under investigation and the legal provisions concerned. Where possible, notifications shall include the names and locations of the persons involved. Notifications concerning a proposed undertaking, consent order or decree shall either include or, as soon as practicable be followed by, copies of the proposed undertaking, order or decree and any competitive impact statement or agreed statement of facts relating to the matter.

Article III
Enforcement Cooperation

1.   (a)   The Parties acknowledge that it is in their common interest to cooperate in the detection of anticompetitive activities and the enforcement of their competition laws to the extent compatible with their respective laws and important interests, and within their reasonably available resources.

    (b)   The Parties further acknowledge that it is in their common interest to share information which will facilitate the effective application of their competition laws and promote better understanding of each other's enforcement policies and activities.

2.   The Parties will consider adopting such further arrangements as may be feasible and desirable to enhance cooperation in the enforcement of their competition laws.

3.   Each Party's competition authorities will, to the extent compatible with that Party's laws, enforcement policies and other important interests,

    (a)   assist the other Party's competition authorities, upon request, in locating and securing evidence and witnesses, and in securing voluntary compliance with requests for information, in the requested Party's territory;

    (b)   inform the other Party's competition authorities with respect to enforcement activities involving conduct that may also have an adverse effect on competition within the territory of the other Party;

(c)   provide to the other Party's competition authorities, upon request, such information within its possession as the requesting Party's competition authorities may specify that is relevant to the requesting Party's enforcement activities; and

(d)   provide the other Party's competition authorities with any significant information that comes to their attention about anticompetitive activities that may be relevant to, or may warrant, enforcement activity by the other Party's competition authorities.

4.   Nothing in this Agreement shall prevent the Parties from seeking or providing assistance to one another pursuant to other agreements, treaties, arrangements or practices between them.

Article IV
Coordination With Regard to Related Matters

1.   Where both Parties' competition authorities are pursuing enforcement activities with regard to related matters, they will consider coordination of their enforcement activities. In such matters, the Parties may invoke such mutual assistance arrangements as may be in force from time to time.

2.   In considering whether particular enforcement activities should be coordinated, either in whole or in part, the Parties' competition authorities shall take into account the following factors, among others:

(a)   the effect of such coordination on the ability of both Parties to achieve their respective enforcement objectives;

(b)   the relative abilities of the Parties' competition authorities to obtain information necessary to conduct the enforcement activities;

(c)   the extent to which either Party's competition authorities can secure effective relief against the anticompetitive activities involved;

(d)   the possible reduction of cost to the Parties and to the persons subject to enforcement activities; and

(e)   the potential advantages of coordinated remedies to the Parties and to the persons subject to the enforcement activities.

3.   In any coordination arrangement, each Party's competition authorities shall seek to conduct their enforcement activities consistently with the enforcement objectives of the other Party's competition authorities.

4.   In the case of concurrent or coordinated enforcement activities, the competition authorities of each Party shall consider, upon request by the competition authorities of the other Party and where consistent with the requested Party's enforcement interests, ascertaining whether persons that have provided confidential information in connection with those enforcement activities will consent to the sharing of such information between the Parties' competition authorities.

5.   Either Party's competition authorities may at any time notify the other Party's competition authorities that they intend to limit or terminate coordinated enforcement and pursue their enforcement activities independently and subject to the other provisions of this Agreement.

Article V
Cooperation Regarding Anticompetitive Activities in the Territory of One Party That Adversely Affect the Interests of the Other Party

1.   The Parties note that anticompetitive activities may occur within the territory of one Party that, in addition to violating that Party's competition laws, adversely affect important interests of the other Party. The Parties agree that it is in their common interest to seek relief against anticompetitive activities of this nature.

2.   If a Party believes that anticompetitive activities carried out in the territory of the other Party adversely affect its important interests, the first Party may request that the other Party's competition authorities initiate appropriate enforcement activities. The request shall be as specific as possible about the nature of the anticompetitive activities and their effects on the interests of the Party, and shall include an offer of such further information and other cooperation as the requesting Party's competition authorities are able to provide.

3.   The requested Party's competition authorities shall carefully consider whether to initiate enforcement activities, or to expand ongoing enforcement activities, with respect to the anticompetitive activities identified in the request. The requested Party's competition authorities shall promptly inform the requesting Party of its decision. If enforcement activities are initiated, the requested Party's competition authorities shall advise the requesting Party of their outcome and, to the extent possible, of significant interim developments.

4.   Nothing in this Article limits the discretion of the requested Party's competition authorities under its competition laws and enforcement policies as to whether to undertake enforcement activities with respect to the anticompetitive activities identified in a request, or precludes the requesting Party's competition authorities from undertaking enforcement activities with respect to such anticompetitive activities.

Article VI
Avoidance of Conflicts

1.   Within the framework of its own laws and to the extent compatible with its important interests, each Party shall, having regard to the purpose of this Agreement as set out in Article I, give careful consideration to the other Party's important interests throughout all phases of its enforcement activities, including decisions regarding the initiation of an investigation or proceeding, the scope of an investigation or proceeding and the nature of the remedies or penalties sought in each case.

2.   When a Party informs the other that a specific enforcement activity may affect the first Party's important interests, the second Party shall provide timely notice of developments of significance to those interests.

3.   While an important interest of a Party may exist in the absence of official involvement by the Party with the activity in question, it is recognized that such interest would normally be reflected in antecedent laws, decisions or statements of policy by its competent authorities.

4.   A Party's important interests may be affected at any stage of enforcement activity by the other Party. The Parties recognize the desirability of minimizing any adverse effects of their enforcement activities on each other's important interests, particularly in the choice of remedies. Typically, the potential for adverse impact on one Party's important interests arising from enforcement activity by the other Party is less at the investigative stage and greater at the stage at which conduct is prohibited or penalized, or at which other forms of remedial orders are imposed.

5.   Where it appears that one Party's enforcement activities may adversely affect the important interests of the other Party, each Party shall, in assessing what measures it will take, consider all appropriate factors, which may include but are not limited to:

(i)   the relative significance to the anticompetitive activities involved of conduct occurring within one Party's territory as compared to conduct occurring within that of the other;

(ii)   the relative significance and foreseeability of the effects of the anticompetitive activities on one Party's important interests as compared to the effects on the other Party's important interests;

(iii)   the presence or absence of a purpose on the part of those engaged in the anticompetitive activities to affect consumers, suppliers or competitors within the enforcing Party's territory;

(iv)   the degree of conflict or consistency between the first Party's enforcement activities (including remedies) and the other Party's laws or other important interests;

(v)   whether private persons, either natural or legal, will be placed under conflicting requirements by other Parties;

(vi)   the existence or absence of reasonable expectations that would be furthered or defeated by the enforcement activities;

(vii)   the location of relevant assets;

(viii)   the degree to which a remedy, in order to be effective, must be carried out within the other Party's territory; and

(ix)   the extent to which enforcement activities of the other Party with respect to the same persons, including judgements or undertakings resulting from such activities, would be affected.

Article VII
Cooperation and Coordination With Respect to Enforcement of Deceptive Marketing Practices Laws

1.   For the purposes of this Agreement, "deceptive marketing practices law(s)" means:

(a)   for Canada, sections 52 through 60 of the *Competition Act*;

(b)   for the United States of America, the *Federal Trade Commission Act* (15 U.S.C. §§ 41-58), to the extent that it applies to unfair or deceptive acts or practices;

as well as any amendments thereto, and such other laws or regulations as the Parties may from time to time agree in writing to be a "deceptive marketing practices law" for purposes of this Agreement. Each Party shall promptly notify the other of any amendments to its deceptive marketing practices laws.

2.   The Parties note that conduct occurring in the territory of one Party may contribute to violations of the deceptive marketing practices laws of the other Party and that it is in their common interest for the Director of Investigation and Research and the Federal Trade Commission to cooperate in the enforcement of those laws. The Parties further note that the Director of Investigation and Research and the Federal Trade Commission have in the past cooperated with each other and coordinated their activities with respect to deceptive marketing practices matters on an informal basis. The Parties wish to establish a more formal framework for continuing and broadening such cooperation and coordination.

3.   The Director of Investigation and Research and the Federal Trade Commission shall, to the extent compatible with their laws, enforcement policies and other important interests:

(a)   use their best efforts to cooperate in the detection of deceptive marketing practices;

(b)   inform each other as soon as practicable of investigations and proceedings involving deceptive marketing practices occurring or originating in the territory of the other Party, or that affect consumers or markets in the territory of the other Party;

(c)   share information relating to the enforcement of their deceptive marketing practices laws; and

(d)   in appropriate cases, coordinate their enforcement against deceptive marketing practices with a transborder dimension.

4.   In furtherance of these objectives, the Director of Investigation and Research and the Federal Trade Commission shall jointly study further measures to enhance the scope and effectiveness of information sharing, cooperation and coordination in the enforcement of deceptive marketing practices laws.

5.   Nothing in this Article shall prevent the Parties from seeking or providing assistance to one another with respect to the enforcement of their deceptive marketing practices laws pursuant to other agreements, treaties, arrangements or practices between them.

6.   Articles II, III, IV, V and VI shall not apply to deceptive marketing practices.

Article VIII
Consultations

1.   Either Party may request consultations regarding any matter relating to this Agreement. The request for consultations shall indicate the reasons for the request and whether any procedural time limits or other constraints require that consultations be expedited. Each Party shall consult promptly when so requested with the view to reaching a conclusion that is consistent with the principles set forth in this Agreement.

2.   Consultations under this Article shall take place at the appropriate level as determined by each Party.

3.   During consultations under this Article, each Party shall provide to the other as much information as it is able in order to facilitate the broadest possible discussion regarding the relevant aspects of the matter that is the subject of consultations. Each Party shall carefully consider the representations of the other Party in light of the principles set out in this Agreement and shall be prepared to explain the specific results of its application of those principles to the matter that is the subject of consultations.

Article IX
Semi-Annual Meetings

Officials of the Parties' competition authorities shall meet at least twice a year to:

(a)   exchange information on their current enforcement efforts and priorities in relation to their competition and deceptive marketing practices laws;

(b)   exchange information on economic sectors of common interest;

(c)   discuss policy changes that they are considering; and

(d)   discuss other matters of mutual interest relating to the application of their competition and deceptive marketing practices laws and the operation of this Agreement.

Article X
Confidentiality of Information

1.   Notwithstanding any other provision of this Agreement, neither Party is required to communicate information to the other Party if such communication is prohibited by the laws of the Party possessing the information or would be incompatible with that Party's important interests.

2.   Unless otherwise agreed by the Parties, each Party shall, to the fullest extent possible, maintain the confidentiality of any information communicated to it in confidence by the other Party under this Agreement. Each Party shall oppose, to the fullest extent possible consistent with that Party's laws, any application by a third party for disclosure of such confidential information.

3.   The degree to which either Party communicates information to the other pursuant to this Agreement may be subject to and dependent upon the acceptability of the assurances given by the other Party with respect to confidentiality and with respect to the purposes for which the information will be used.

4.   (a)   Notifications and consultations pursuant to Articles II and VIII of this Agreement and other communications between the Parties in relation thereto shall be deemed to be confidential.

      (b)   Party may not, without the consent of the other Party, communicate to its state or provincial authorities information received from the other Party pursuant to notifications or consultations under this Agreement. The Party providing the information shall consider requests for consent sympathetically, taking into account the other Party's reasons for seeking disclosure, the risk, if any, that disclosure would pose for its enforcement activities, and any other relevant considerations.

      (c)   The notified Party may, after the notifying Party's competition authorities have advised a person who is the subject of a notification of the enforcement activities referred to in the notification, communicate the fact of the notification to, and consult with that person concerning the subject of the notification. The notifying Party shall, upon request, promptly inform the notified Party of the time at which the person has, or will be, advised of the enforcement activities in question.

5.   Subject to paragraph 2, information communicated in confidence by a Party's competition authorities to the competition authorities of the other Party in the context of enforcement cooperation or coordination pursuant to Articles III, IV or V of this Agreement shall not be communicated to third parties or to other agencies of the receiving competition authorities' government, without the consent of the competition authorities that provided the information. A Party's competition authorities may, however, communicate such information to the Party's law enforcement officials for the purpose of competition law enforcement.

6.   Information communicated in confidence by a Party's competition authorities to the competition authorities of the other Party in the context of enforcement cooperation or coordination pursuant to Articles III, IV or V of this Agreement shall not be used for purposes other than competition law enforcement, without the consent of the competition authorities that provided the information.

7.   Subject to paragraph 2, information communicated in confidence between the Director of Investigation and Research and the Federal Trade Commission in the context of enforcement cooperation or coordination pursuant to Article VII of this Agreement shall not be communicated to third parties or to other agencies of the receiving agency's government, without the consent of the agency that provided the information. The receiving agency of a Party may, however, communicate such information to the Party's law enforcement officials for the purpose of enforcement of deceptive marketing practices laws.

8.   Information communicated in confidence between the Director of Investigation and Research and the Federal Trade Commission in the context of enforcement cooperation or coordination pursuant to Article VII of this Agreement shall not be used for purposes other than

enforcement of deceptive marketing practices laws, without the consent of the agency that provided the information.

Article XI
Existing Laws

Nothing in this Agreement shall require a Party to take any action, or to refrain from acting, in a manner that is inconsistent with its existing laws, or require any change in the laws of the Parties or of their respective provinces or states.

Article XII
Communications Under This Agreement

Communications under this Agreement may be carried out by direct communication between the competition authorities of the Parties. Notifications under Article II and requests under Articles V(2) and VIII(1) shall, however, be confirmed promptly in writing through customary diplomatic channels and shall refer to the initial communication between the competition authorities and repeat the information supplied therein.

Article XIII
Entry into Force and Termination

1.   This Agreement shall enter into force upon signature.

2.   This Agreement shall remain in force until 60 days after the date on which either Party notifies the other Party in writing that it wishes to terminate this Agreement.

IN WITNESS WHEREOF, the undersigned, being duly authorized by their respective Governments, have signed this Agreement.

DONE at Washington, in duplicate, this 1st day of August, 1995, and at Ottawa, this 3rd day of August, 1995, in the English and French languages, each text being equally authentic.

FOR THE GOVERNMENT OF THE   FOR THE GOVERNMENT OF
UNITED STATES OF AMERICA   CANADA

*   *   *

AGREEMENT BETWEEN THE GOVERNMENT OF THE UNITED STATES OF AMERICA AND THE GOVERNMENT OF JAPAN CONCERNING COOPERATION ON ANTICOMPETITIVE ACTIVITIES[*]

The Agreement between the Government of the United States of America and the Government of Japan Concerning Cooperation on Anticompetitive Activities was signed on 7 October 1999. It entered into force upon signature.

The Government of the United States of America and the Government of Japan (hereinafter referred to as "Parties"):

Recognizing that the world's economies are becoming increasingly interrelated, in particular the economies of the United States of America and Japan;

Noting that the sound and effective enforcement of competition laws of each country is a matter of importance to the efficient functioning of their respective markets and to trade between them;

Noting that the sound and effective enforcement of competition laws of each country would be enhanced by cooperation and, where appropriate, coordination between the Parties in the application of those laws;

Noting that from time to time differences may arise between the Parties concerning the application of the competition laws of each country;

Noting their commitment to give careful consideration to the important interests of each Party in the application of the competition laws of each country; and

Having regard to Article XVIII of the Treaty of Friendship, Commerce and Navigation between the United States of America and Japan signed on April 2, 1953, to the Recommendation of the Council of the Organization for Economic Co-operation and Development Concerning Cooperation Between Member Countries on Anticompetitive Practices Affecting International Trade, as revised July 27 and 28, 1995, and to the Recommendation of the Council of the Organization for Economic Co-operation and Development Concerning Effective Action Against Hard Core Cartels adopted on March 25, 1998;

Have agreed as follows:

---

[*] *Source:* Government of Japan and Government of the United States of America (1999). "Agreement between the Government of the United States of America and the Government of Japan Concerning Cooperation on Anticompetitive Activities"; *Trade Regulation Reports*, vol. 4, ƒ 13,507 (Chicago: Commerce Clearing House); available also on the Internet (http://www.usdoj.gov/atr/public/international/docs/3740.htm). [Note added by the editor.]

ARTICLE I

1.   The purpose of this Agreement is to contribute to the effective enforcement of the competition laws of each country through the development of cooperative relationships between the competition authorities of each Party. The competition authorities of the Parties shall, in accordance with the provisions of this Agreement, cooperate with and provide assistance to each other in their enforcement activities, to the extent compatible with their respective Party's important interests.

2.   For the purposes of this Agreement,

(a)   the term "anticompetitive activity(ies)" means any conduct or transaction that may be subject to penalties or relief under the competition laws of either country;

(b)   the term "competition authority(ies)" means:

(i)   for the United States of America, the United States Department of Justice and the Federal Trade Commission; and

(ii)   for Japan, the Fair Trade Commission;

(c)   the term "competition law(s)" means:

(i)   for the United States of America, the *Sherman Act* (15 U.S.C. 1-7), the *Clayton Act* (15 U.S.C. 12-27), the *Wilson Tariff Act* (15 U.S.C. 8-11), and the *Federal Trade Commission Act* (15 U.S.C. 41-58) to the extent that it applies to unfair methods of competition, and their implementing regulations; and

(ii)   for Japan, *the Law Concerning Prohibition of Private Monopoly and Maintenance of Fair Trade* (Law No. 54 of April 14, 1947) (hereinafter referred to as "the Antimonopoly Law") and its implementing regulations.

(d)   the term "enforcement activity (ies)" means any investigation or proceeding conducted by a Party in relation to the competition laws of its country. However, (i) the review of business conduct or routine filings and (ii) research, studies or surveys with the objective of examining the general economic situation or general conditions in specific industries are not included.

ARTICLE II

1.   The competition authority of each Party shall notify the competition authority of the other Party with respect to the enforcement activities of the notifying Party that the notifying competition authority considers may affect the important interests of the other Party.

2.   Enforcement activities that may affect the important interests of the other Party include those that:

(a)   are relevant to enforcement activities of the other Party;

(b)   are against a national or nationals of the other country, or against a company or companies incorporated or organized under the applicable laws and regulations within the territory of the other country;

(c)   involve anticompetitive activities, other than mergers or acquisitions, carried out in any substantial part in the territory of the other country;

(d)   involve mergers or acquisitions in which

-- one or more of the parties to the transaction, or

-- a company controlling one or more of the parties to the transaction, is a company incorporated or organized under the applicable laws and regulations within the territory of the other country;

(e)   involve conduct considered by the notifying competition authority to have been required, encouraged or approved by the other Party; or

(f)   involve relief that requires or prohibits conduct in the territory of the other country.

Notification pursuant to paragraph 1 of this Article shall be given as promptly as possible when the competition authority of a Party becomes aware that enforcement activities of its Party may affect the important interests of the other Party, and in any event in accordance with paragraphs 4 and 5 of this Article.

4.   Where notification is required pursuant to paragraph 1 of this Article with respect to mergers or acquisitions, such notification shall be given not later than:

(a)   for the competition authorities of the United States of America, the time either one seeks information or documentary material concerning the proposed transaction pursuant to the *Hart-Scott-Rodino Antitrust Improvements Act of* 1976 (15 U.S.C. 18a(e)), the *Federal Trade Commission Act* (15 U.S.C. 49, 57b-1) or the *Antitrust Civil Process Act* (15 U.S.C. 1312).

(b)   for the competition authority of Japan, the earlier of

    (i)   the time it seeks production of documents, reports or other information concerning the proposed transaction pursuant to the Antimonopoly Law; or

    (ii)   the time it advises a party to the transaction that the transaction as originally proposed raises serious questions under the Antimonopoly Law; provided, however, that if at the time of such advice the transaction has not been publicly disclosed by a party to the transaction, notification shall be made as soon as possible after the time at which the transaction or proposed transaction is publicly disclosed by a party to the transaction.

5.   Where notification is required pursuant to paragraph 1 of this Article with respect to matters other than mergers or acquisitions, notification shall be given as far in advance of the following actions as is practically possible:

    (a)   for the Government of the United States of America,

        (i)   the initiation of criminal proceedings;

        (ii)   the initiation of a civil or administrative action, including the seeking of a temporary restraining order or preliminary injunction;

        (iii)   the entry of a proposed consent decree or a proposed cease and desist order; and

        (iv)   the issuance of a business review or advisory opinion that will ultimately be made public by the competition authority.

    (b)   for the Government of Japan,

        (i)   the filing of a criminal accusation;

        (ii)   the filing of a complaint seeking an urgent injunction;

        (iii)   the issuance of a recommendation or the decision to initiate a hearing;

        (iv)   the issuance of a surcharge payment order when no prior recommendation with respect to the payer has been issued;

        (v)   the issuance of a reply to a prior consultation that will ultimately be made public by the competition authority; and

        (vi)   the issuance of a warning.

6.   The competition authority of each Party shall also notify the competition authority of the other Party if it initiates a survey which the notifying competition authority considers may affect the important interests of the other Party.

7.   The competition authority of each Party shall also notify the competition authority of the other Party whenever the notifying competition authority publicly participates, in connection with the competition laws or policy issues, in an administrative, regulatory or judicial proceeding in its country that is not initiated by the competition authority, if the notifying competition authority considers that the issue addressed may affect the important interests of the other Party. Such notification shall be made at the time of the participation or as soon thereafter as possible.

8.   Each Party shall notify the other Party if it initiates a civil action in the courts of the other country against a private party for monetary damages or other relief based on a violation of the competition laws of the other country.

9.   Notifications shall be sufficiently detailed to enable the notified competition authority to make an initial evaluation of the effect on its Party's important interests.

10.   (a)   The competition authority of each Party shall promptly notify the competition authority of the other Party of any amendment to the competition laws of its country.

        (b)   The competition authority of each Party shall provide the competition authority of the other Party with copies of its publicly-released guidelines, regulations or policy statements that it issues in relation to the competition laws of its country.

        (c)   The competition authority of each Party shall provide the competition authority of the other Party with copies of its proposed guidelines, regulations or policy statements in relation to the competition laws of its country that are made generally available to the public, and, when it provides the general public with opportunities to submit comments on such guidelines, regulations or policy statements, receive and pay due consideration to the comments submitted by the other Party prior to finalizing such guidelines, regulations or policy statements.

ARTICLE III

1.   The competition authority of each Party shall render assistance to the competition authority of the other Party in its enforcement activities to the extent consistent with the laws and regulations of the country of the assisting Party and the important interests of the assisting Party, and within its reasonably available resources.

2.   The competition authority of each Party shall, to the extent consistent with the laws and regulations of its country and the important interests of its Party:

        (a)   inform the competition authority of the other Party with respect to its enforcement activities involving anticompetitive activities that the informing competition authority considers may also have an adverse effect on competition within the territory of the other country;

        (b)   provide the competition authority of the other Party with any significant information, within its possession and that comes to its attention, about anticompetitive activities that the providing competition authority considers may be relevant to, or may warrant, enforcement activities by the competition authority of the other Party; and

        (c)   provide the competition authority of the other Party, upon request and in accordance with the provisions of this Agreement, with information within its possession that is relevant to the enforcement activities of the competition authority of the other Party.

ARTICLE IV

1.   Where the competition authorities of both Parties are pursuing enforcement activities with regard to related matters, they shall consider coordination of their enforcement activities.

2.   In considering whether particular enforcement activities should be coordinated, the competition authorities of the Parties should take into account the following factors, among others:

(a)   the effect of such coordination on their ability to achieve the objectives of their enforcement activities;

(b)   the relative abilities of the competition authorities of the Parties to obtain information necessary to conduct the enforcement activities;

(c)   the extent to which the competition authority of either Party can secure effective relief against the anticompetitive activities involved;

(d)   the possible reduction of cost to the Parties and to the persons subject to the enforcement activities; and

(e)   the potential advantages of coordinated relief to the Parties and to the persons subject to the enforcement activities.

3.   In any coordinated enforcement activity, the competition authority of each Party shall seek to conduct its enforcement activities with careful consideration to the objectives of the enforcement activities by the competition authority of the other Party.

4.   Where the competition authorities of both Parties are pursuing enforcement activities with regard to related matters, the competition authority of each Party shall consider, upon request by the competition authority of the other Party and where consistent with the important interests of the requested Party, inquiring whether persons who have provided confidential information in connection with those enforcement activities will consent to the sharing of such information with the competition authority of the other Party.

5.   Subject to appropriate notification to the competition authority of the other Party, the competition authority of either Party may, at any time, limit or terminate the coordination of enforcement activities and pursue their enforcement activities independently.

ARTICLE V

1.   If the competition authority of a Party believes that anticompetitive activities carried out in the territory of the other country adversely affect the important interests of the former Party, such competition authority, taking into account the importance of avoiding conflicts regarding jurisdiction and taking into account that the competition authority of the other Party may be in a position to conduct more effective enforcement activities with regard to such anticompetitive activities, may request that the competition authority of the other Party initiate appropriate enforcement activities. The request shall be as specific as possible about the nature of the anticompetitive activities and their effect on the important interests of the Party of the requesting competition authority, and shall include an offer of such further information and other cooperation as the requesting competition authority is able to provide.

2.   The requested competition authority shall carefully consider whether to initiate enforcement activities, or whether to expand ongoing enforcement activities, with respect to the

anticompetitive activities identified in the request. The requested competition authority shall inform the requesting competition authority of its decision as soon as practically possible. If enforcement activities are initiated, the requested competition authority shall inform the requesting competition authority of their outcome and, to the extent possible, of significant interim developments.

ARTICLE VI

1.   Each Party shall give careful consideration to the important interests of the other Party throughout all phases of its enforcement activities, including decisions regarding the initiation of enforcement activities, the scope of enforcement activities and the nature of penalties or relief sought in each case.

2.   When either Party informs the other Party that specific enforcement activities by the latter Party may affect the former's important interests, the latter Party shall endeavor to provide timely notice of significant developments of such enforcement activities.

3.   Where either Party considers that enforcement activities by a Party may adversely affect the important interests of the other Party, the Parties should consider the following factors, in addition to any other factor that may be relevant in the circumstances in seeking an appropriate accommodation of the competing interests:

(a)   the relative significance to the anticompetitive activities of conduct or transactions occurring within the territory of the country of the enforcing Party as compared to conduct or transactions occurring within the territory of the other country;

(b)   the relative impact of the anticompetitive activities on the important interests of the respective Parties;

(c)   the presence or absence of evidence of an intention on the part of those engaged in the anticompetitive activities to affect consumers, suppliers, or competitors within the territory of the country of the Party conducting the enforcement activities;

(d)   the extent to which the anticompetitive activities substantially lessencompetition in the market of each country;

(e)   the degree of conflict or consistency between the enforcement activities by a Party and the laws of the other country, or the policies or important interests of the other Party;

(f)   whether private persons, either natural or legal, will be placed under conflicting requirements by both Parties;

(g)   the location of relevant assets and parties to the transaction;

(h)   the degree to which effective penalties or relief can be secured by the enforcement activities of the Party against the anticompetitive activities; and

(i)   the extent to which enforcement activities by the other Party with respect to the same persons, either natural or legal, would be affected.

ARTICLE VII

1.   The Parties may hold, as necessary, consultations through the diplomatic channel on any matter which may arise in the implementation of this Agreement.

2.   A request for consultations under this Article shall be communicated through the diplomatic channel.

ARTICLE VIII

1.   The competition authorities of the Parties shall consult with each other, upon request of either Party's competition authority, on any matter which may arise in connection with this Agreement.

2.   The competition authorities of the Parties shall meet at least once a year to:

(a)   exchange information on their current enforcement efforts and priorities in relation to the competition laws of each country;

(b)   exchange information on economic sectors of common interest;

(c)   discuss policy changes that they are considering; and

(d)   discuss other matters of mutual interest relating to the application of the competition laws of each country.

ARTICLE IX

1.   (a)   Information, other than publicly available information, communicated by a Party to the other Party pursuant to this Agreement shall only be used by the receiving Party for the purpose specified in Article 1, paragraph 1 of this Agreement, unlessthe Party providing the information has approved otherwise.

(b)   Information, other than publicly available information, provided by a competition authority or a relevant law enforcement authority pursuant to this Agreement shall not be communicated to a third party or other authorities, unless the competition authority or the relevant law enforcement authority providing the information has approved otherwise.

2.   Notwithstanding paragraph 1(b) of this Article, unless otherwise notified by the competition authority providing the information, the competition authority receiving the information communicated pursuant to this Agreement may provide the information to its Party's relevant law enforcement authorities, for the purpose of competition law enforcement, which may use such information under the conditions stipulated in Article X of this Agreement.

3.   Each Party shall, consistent with the laws and regulations of its country, maintain the confidentiality of any information communicated to it in confidence by the other Party pursuant to this Agreement, unless the latter Party consents to the disclosure of such information.

4.   Each Party may limit the information it communicates to the other Party when the latter Party is unable to give the assurance requested by the Party with respect to confidentiality or with respect to the limitations of purposes for which the information will be used.

5.   Notwithstanding any other provision of this Agreement, neither Party is required to communicate information to the other Party if such communication is prohibited by the laws or regulations of the country of the Party possessing the information or such communication would be incompatible with its important interests.

6.   This Article shall not preclude the use or disclosure of information to the extent that there is an obligation to do so under the laws and regulations of the country of the Party receiving the information. Such Party shall, wherever possible, give advance notice of any such use or disclosure to the Party which provided the information.

ARTICLE X

1.   Information communicated by a Party to the other Party pursuant to this Agreement, except publicly available information, shall not be presented to a grand jury or to a court or a judge in criminal proceedings.

2.   In the event that information communicated by a Party to the other Party pursuant to this Agreement, except publicly available information, is needed for presentation to a grand jury or to a court or a judge in criminal proceedings, that Party shall submit a request for such information to the other Party through the diplomatic channel or other channel established in accordance with the law of the requested Party. The requested Party will make, upon request, its best efforts to respond promptly to meet any legitimate deadlines indicated by the requesting Party.

ARTICLE XI

1.   This Agreement shall be implemented by the Parties in accordance with the laws and regulations in force in each country and within the available resources of their respective competition authorities.

2.   Detailed arrangements to implement this Agreement may be made between the competition authorities of the Parties.

3.   Nothing in this Agreement shall prevent the Parties from seeking or providing assistance to one another pursuant to other bilateral or multilateral agreements or arrangements between the Parties.

4.   Nothing in this Agreement shall be construed to prejudice the policy or legal position of either Party regarding any issue related to jurisdiction.

5.   Nothing in this Agreement shall be construed to affect the rights and obligations of either Party under other international agreements or under its laws.

ARTICLE XII

Unless otherwise provided in this Agreement, communications under this Agreement may be directly carried out between the competition authorities of the Parties. Notifications under Article II (except paragraph 8) and requests under Article V, paragraph 1 of this Agreement, however, shall be confirmed in writing through the diplomatic channel. The confirmation shall be made as promptly as practically possible after the communication concerned between the competition authorities of the Parties.

ARTICLE XIII

1.   This Agreement shall enter into force upon signature.

2.   Either Party may terminate this Agreement by giving two months written notice to the other Party through diplomatic channel.

3.   The Parties shall review the operation of this Agreement not more than five years from the date of its entry into force.

IN WITNESS WHEREOF, the undersigned, being duly authorized by their respective Governments, have signed this Agreement.

DONE at Washington, this seventh day of October, 1999, in duplicate, in the English and Japanese languages, both texts being equally authentic.

FOR THE GOVERNMENT OF   THE GOVERNMENT OF

THE UNITED STATES OF AMERICA: JAPAN:

*   *   *

AGREEMENT BETWEEN THE GOVERNMENT OF THE UNITED STATES OF AMERICA AND THE GOVERNMENT OF THE FEDERATIVE REPUBLIC OF BRAZIL REGARDING COOPERATION BETWEEN THEIR COMPETITION AUTHORITIES IN THE ENFORCEMENT OF THEIR COMPETITION LAWS[*]

The Agreement between the Government of the United States of America and the Government of the Federative Republic of Brazil regarding Cooperation between Their Competition Authorities in the Enforcement of Their Competition Laws was signed on 26 October 1999. As of 31 October 1999 it had not entered into force.

The Government of the United States of America and the Government of the Federative Republic of Brazil (hereinafter referred to as "parties"),

Desiring to enhance the effective enforcement of their competition laws through cooperation between their competition authorities;

Having regard to their close economic relations and noting that the sound and effective enforcement of their competition laws is a matter of crucial importance to the efficient operation of markets and to the economic welfare of the citizens of their respective countries;

Recognizing that cooperation and coordination in competition law enforcement activities may result in a more effective resolution of the Parties' respective concerns than would be attained through independent action;

Further recognizing that technical cooperation between the Parties' competition authorities will contribute to improving and strengthening their relationship; and

Noting the Parties' commitment to give careful consideration to each other's important interests in the application of their competition laws,

Have agreed as follows:

---

[*] *Source*: Government of Brazil and Government of the United States of America (1999). "Agreement between the Government of the United States of America and the Government of the Federative Republic of Brazil regarding Cooperation between Their Competition Authorities in the Enforcement of Their Competition Laws"; available also on the Internet (http://www.usdoj.gov/atr/public/international/37776.htm). [Note added by the editor.]

ARTICLE I

PURPOSE AND DEFINITIONS

1.   The purpose of this Agreement is to promote cooperation, including both enforcement and technical cooperation, between the competition authorities of the Parties, and to ensure that the Parties give careful consideration to each other's important interests in the application of their competition laws.

2.   For the purposes of this Agreement, the following terms shall have the following definitions:

    a.   "anticompetitive practice(s)" means any conduct or transaction that may be subject to penalties or other relief under the competition laws of a Party;

    b.   "competition authority(ies)" means

        i.   for Brazil, the Administrative Council for Economic Defense (CADE) and the Secretariat for Economic Law Enforcement (SDE) in the Ministry of Justice; the Secretariat for Economic Monitoring (SEAE) in the Ministry of Finance;

        ii.   for the United States of America, the United States Department of Justice and the Federal Trade Commission;

    c.   "competition law(s)" means

        i.   for Brazil, Federal Laws 8884/94 and 9021/95; and Provisional Measure 1.567/97;

        ii.   for the United States of America, the Sherman Act (15 U.S.C. §§ 1-7), the Clayton Act (15 U.S.C.§§12-27), the Wilson Tariff Act (15 U.S.C. §§ 8-11), and the Federal Trade Commission Act (15 U.S.C. §§ 41-58), to the extent that it applies to unfair methods of competition, as well as any amendments thereto;

    d.   "enforcement activity(ies)" means any investigation or proceeding conducted by a Party in relation to its competition laws;

3.   Each Party shall promptly notify the other of any amendments to its competition laws and of such other new laws or regulations that the Party considers to be part of its competition legislation.

ARTICLE II

NOTIFICATION

1.   Each Party shall, subject to Article IX, notify the other party in the manner provided by this Article and Article XI with respect to enforcement activities specified in this Article.

Notifications shall identify the nature of the practices under investigation and the legal provisions concerned, and shall ordinarily be given as promptly as possible after a Party's competition authorities become aware that notifiable circumstances are present.

2.   Enforcement activities to be notified pursuant to this Article are those that:

   a.   to enforcement activities of the other Party;

   b.   involve anticompetitive practices, other than mergers or acquisitions, carried out in whole or in substantial part in the territory of the other Party;

   c.   involve mergers or acquisitions in which one or more of the parties to the transaction, or a company controlling one or more of the parties to a transaction, is a company incorporated or organized under the laws of the other Party or of one of its states;

   d.   involve conduct believed to have been required, encouraged, or approved by the other Party;

   e.   involve remedies that expressly require or prohibit conduct in the territory of the other Party or are otherwise directed at conduct in the territory of the other Party; or

   f.   involve the seeking of information located in the territory of the other Party.

3.   The Parties acknowledge that officials of either Party may visit the territory of the other Party in the course of conducting investigations pursuant to their respective competition laws. Such visits shall be subject to notification pursuant to this Article and the consent of the notified Party.

ARTICLE III

ENFORCEMENT COOPERATION

1.   The Parties agree that it is in their common interest to cooperate in the detection of anticompetitive practices and the enforcement of their competition laws, and to share information that will facilitate the effective application of those laws and promote better understanding of each other's competition enforcement policies and activities, to the extent compatible with their respective laws and important interests, and within their reasonably available resources.

2.   Nothing in this Agreement shall prevent the Parties from seeking or providing assistance to one another pursuant to other agreements, treaties, arrangements or practices between them.

ARTICLE IV

COOPERATION REGARDING ANTICOMPETITIVE PRACTICES IN THE TERRITORY OF ONE PARTY THAT MAY ADVERSELY AFFECT THE INTERESTS OF THE OTHER PARTY

1.   The Parties agree that it is in their common interest to secure the efficient operation of their markets by enforcing their respective competition laws in order to protect their markets from anticompetitive practices. The Parties further agree that it is in their common interest to seek relief against anticompetitive practices that may occur in the territory of one Party that, in addition to violating that Party's competition laws, adversely affect the interest of the other Party in securing the efficient operation of the other Party's markets.

2.   If a Party believes that anticompetitive practices carried out in the territory of the other Party adversely affect its important interests, the first Party may, after prior consultation with the other Party, request that the other Party's competition authorities initiate appropriate enforcement activities. The request shall be as specific as possible about the nature of the anticompetitive practices and their effects on the important interests of the requesting Party, and shall include an offer of such further information and other cooperation as the requesting Party's competition authorities are able to provide.

3.   The requested Party's competition authorities shall carefully consider whether to initiate or to expand enforcement activities with respect to the anticompetitive practices identified in the request, and shall promptly inform the requesting Party of its decision. If enforcement activities are initiated or expanded, the requested Party's competition authorities shall advise the requesting Party of their outcome and, to the extent possible, of significant interim developments.

4.   Nothing in this Article limits the discretion of the requested Party's competition authorities under its competition laws and enforcement policies as to whether to undertake enforcement activities with respect to the anticompetitive practices identified in a request, nor precludes the requesting Party's competition authorities from undertaking enforcement activities with respect to such anticompetitive practices.

ARTICLE V

COORDINATION WITH REGARD TO RELATED MATTERS

1.   Where both Parties' competition authorities are pursuing enforcement activities with regard to related matters, they will consider coordination of their enforcement activities.

2.   In any coordination arrangement, each Party's competition authorities will seek to conduct their enforcement activities consistently with the enforcement objectives of the other Party's competition authorities.

ARTICLE VI

AVOIDANCE OF CONFLICTS; CONSULTATIONS

1.   Each Party shall, within the framework of its own laws and to the extent compatible with its important interests, give careful consideration to the other Party's important interests throughout all phases of its enforcement activities, including decisions regarding the initiation of an investigation or proceeding, the scope of an investigation or proceeding, and the nature of the remedies or penalties sought in each case.

2.   Either Party may request consultations regarding any matter relating to this Agreement. The request for consultations shall indicate the reasons for the request and whether any procedural time limits or other constraints require that consultations be expedited. Each Party shall consult promptly when so requested with a view to reaching a conclusion that is consistent with the purpose of this Agreement.

ARTICLE VII

TECHNICAL COOPERATION ACTIVITIES

The Parties agree that it is in their common interest for their competition authorities to work together in technical cooperation activities related to competition law enforcement and policy. These activities will include, within their competition agencies' reasonably available resources: exchanges of information pursuant to Article III of this Agreement; exchanges of competition agency personnel for training purposes at each other's competition agencies; participation of competition agency personnel as lecturers or consultants at training courses on competition law and policy organized or sponsored by each other's competition authorities; and such other forms of technical cooperation as the Parties' competition authorities agree are appropriate for purposes of this Agreement.

ARTICLE VIII

MEETINGS OF COMPETITION AUTHORITIES

Officials of the Parties' competition authorities shall meet periodically to exchange information on their current enforcement efforts and priorities in relation to their competition laws.

ARTICLE IX

CONFIDENTIALITY

1.   Notwithstanding any other provision of this Agreement, neither Party is required to communicate information to the other Party if such communication is prohibited by the laws of the Party possessing the information or would be incompatible with that Party's important interests.

2.   Unless otherwise agreed by the Parties, each Party shall, to the fullest extent possible, maintain the confidentiality of any information communicated to it in confidence by the other Party under this Agreement. Each Party shall oppose, to the fullest extent possible consistent

with that Party's laws, any application by a third party for disclosure of such confidential information.

ARTICLE X

EXISTING LAWS

Nothing in this Agreement shall require a Party to take any action, or to refrain from acting, in a manner that is inconsistent with its existing laws, or require any change in the laws of the Parties or of their respective states.

ARTICLE XI

COMMUNICATIONS UNDER THIS AGREEMENT

Communications under this Agreement may be carried out by direct communication between the competition authorities of the Parties. Notifications under Article II and requests under Articles IV.2 and VI.2 shall, however, be confirmed promptly in writing through customary diplomatic channels and shall refer to the initial communication between the competition authorities and repeat the information supplied therein.

ARTICLE XII

ENTRY INTO FORCE AND TERMINATION

1. This Agreement shall enter into force on the date on which the Parties exchange diplomatic notes informing each other that they have completed all applicable requirements for its entry into force.

2. This Agreement may be amended by the mutual agreement of the Parties. An amendment shall enter into force in the manner set forth in paragraph 1 for entry into force of this Agreement.

3. This Agreement shall remain in force for an indefinite period of time, unless one Party notifies the other Party in writing that it wishes to terminate the Agreement. In that case, the Agreement shall terminate 60 days after such written notice is given.

IN WITNESS WHEREOF, the undersigned, being duly authorized by their respective Governments, have signed this Agreement.

DONE at Washington, DC, this 26th day of October, 1999, in the English and Portuguese languages, each text being equally authentic.

FOR THE GOVERNMENT OF
THE UNITED STATES OF
AMERICA:

FOR THE GOVERNMENT OF
THE FEDERATIVEREPUBLIC
OF BRAZIL:

*　　*　　*

Part Three

Prototype Bilateral Investment Treaties and list of Bilateral Investment Treaties

(July-1995 — end-1998)

AGREEMENT FOR THE
PROMOTION AND PROTECTION OF INVESTMENTS
BETWEEN THE ARAB REPUBLIC OF EGYPT
AND* _____

The Government of the Arab Republic of Egypt and the Government of _____ hereinafter referred to as the "Contracting Parties".

Desiring to create favourable conditions for greater, economic co-operation between them, and in particular for investment by investors of one Contracting Party in the territory of the other Contracting Party.

Recognizing that the encouragement and reciprocal protection of such investments will be conducive to the stimulation of business initiatives and will increase prosperity in the territories of the Contracting Parties.

Have agreed as follows:

Article 1

Definitions

For the purpose of this Agreement

1.   The term "investment" shall comprise every kind of asset invested by a natural or juridical person including the Government of a Contracting Party, in the territory of the other Contracting Party in accordance with the laws and regulations of that Party.

Without restricting the generality of the foregoing the term "investment" shall include:

a)   movable and immovable property as well as any other property rights in rem such as mortgages, guarantees, pledges, usufruct and similar rights;

b)   shares, stocks and debentures, or other rights or interests in such companies;

c)   claims to money, or to any performance having economic value associated with an investment;

d)   intellectual property rights including copyrights, trademarks, patents, industrial designs, technical processes, know-how, trade, juridical rights and goodwill;

---

* *Source*: Government of Egypt, General Authority for Investments and Free Zones. [Note added by the editor.]

e)   Any rights conferred by laws or under contract and any licences and permits granted pursuant to law, including the concession to search for, extract, cultivate and exploit natural resources. A change in the form in which assets are invested does not affect their character as investments.

2.   The term "investor" shall mean any natural or juridical person, including the Government of a Contracting Party who invests in the territory of the other Contracting Party.

a)   "Natural person" means with respect to either Contracting Party a natural person holding the nationality of that Party in accordance with its laws.

b)   "Juridical person" means, with respect to either Contracting Party, any entity established in accordance with, and recognized as a juridical person by its laws: such as public institutions; corporations; foundations; private companies; firms; establishments and other organisations; and having permanent residence in the territory of one of the Contracting Party.

3.   The term "returns" refers to income deriving from an investment in accordance with the definition contained above and includes, in particular, profits, dividends and interests.

4.   The term "territory" designates the land territory, air space and territorial waters of each of the Contracting Parties, as well as the exclusive economic zone and the continental shelf that extends outside the limits of the territorial waters of each of the Parties, over which they have jurisdiction and sovereign rights pursuant to international law.

Article 2

Promotion and Protection of Investments

1.   Each Contracting Party shall encourage and create favourable conditions for investors of the other Contracting Party to invest in its territory, and subject to its right to exercise powers conferred by its laws, shall admit such investment.

2.   Investments of investors of each Contracting Party shall at all times be accorded fair and equitable treatment and shall enjoy adequate protection and security in the territory of the other Contracting Party no less than that enjoyed by its nationals. Neither Contracting Party shall in any way impair by unreasonable or discriminatory measures the management, maintenance, use, enjoyment disposal of investments in its territory of investors of the other Contracting Party.

3.   The Contracting Parties may periodically consult between themselves concerning investment opportunities within the territory of each other in various sectors of the economy, to determine where investments may be most beneficial, in the interest of both Contracting Parties.

Article 3

Treatment of Investment

1.   Investment of investors of one Contracting Party in the territory of the other Contracting Party and also the returns therefrom shall receive treatment which is fair and equitable and not less favourable than that accorded in respect of the investments of investors of any third state.

2.   Each Contracting Party shall in its territory accord to investors of the other Contracting Party as regards the management, use, enjoyment or disposal of their investment, treatment which is fair and equitable and not less favourable than that which is accorded to investors of any third state.

3.   The treatment mentioned above shall not apply to any advantage or privilege accorded to investors of a third state by either Contracting Party based on the membership of that Party in a Customs Union, Common Market, Free Trade Zone, economic multilateral or international agreement, or based on an agreement concluded between that Party and a third state on Avoidance of Double Taxation or based on cross-border trade arrangement.

Article 4

Compensation for Losses

Investors of one Contracting Party whose investments in the territory of the other Contracting Party suffer losses owing to war or other armed conflicts, revolution, a state of national emergency, revolt, insurrection or riot in the territory of the latter Contracting Party shall be accorded by the latter Contracting Party, as regards restitution, indemnification, compensation or other settlement, treatment no less favourable than that which the latter Contracting Party grants to investors of any third state. Any payment made under this Article shall be prompt, adequate, effective and freely transferable.

Article 5

Nationalization and Expropriation

The nationalization, expropriation or any other measure of similar characteristics or effects that may be applied by the authorities of one Contracting Party against the investments in its own territory of investors of the other Contracting Party must be applied exclusively for reasons of public interest pursuant to the law, and shall in no case be discriminatory. The Contracting Party adopting such measures shall pay to the investor or his legal beneficiary adequate indemnity in convertible currency without unjustified delay.

Article 6

Transfer

1.   With regard to the investments made in its territory each Contracting Party shall grant to investors of the other Contracting Party the right to transfer freely the income deriving from and other payments related thereto, including particularly, but not exclusively, the following:

a)   Investment returns, as defined, in Article (1);

b)   The indemnities provided for under Article 4 and 5;

c)   The proceeds of the sale or liquidation, in full or partial, of an investment; in relation to investment,

d)   The salaries, wages and other compensation received by the nationals of one Contracting Party who have obtained in the territory of the other, Contracting Party the corresponding work permits in accordance with existing laws and regulations.

2.   Transfers shall be effected without delay in freely convertible foreign currencies subject to existing laws and regulations.

Article 7

Subrogation

In case one Contracting Party has granted any guarantee against non-commercial risks in respect to investments by its investor in the territory to such investors under the said guarantee, the other Contracting Party shall recognize the transfer of the right of such investor to the first mentioned Contracting Party, and the subrogation of that Contracting Party shall not exceed the original rights of such investors.

Article 8

Settlement of Investment Disputes

1.   Any dispute which may arise between a Contracting Party and an investor of other Contracting Party, shall be notified in writing, including detailed information, by the investor to the host Party of the investment, and shall, if possible, be settled amicably.

2.   If the dispute cannot be settled in this way within six months from the date of the written notification mentioned in paragraph (1), it may be submitted upon request of either Party to the dispute, either to:

a)   The competent courts of the Contracting Party in whose territory the investment was made;

b)   The International Center for the Settlement of Investment Disputes (ICSID) created by the Convention on the Settlement of Investment Disputes between States and Nationals of other State opened for signature, in Washington D.C. on 18 March 1965, once both Contracting Parties herein become member states thereof ; or

c)   The Ad-hoc Court of arbitration established under the Arbitration rules of Procedure of the United Nations Commission for International Trade Law.

d)   Regional Center for International Commercial Arbitration in Cairo.

3.   The dispute shall be settled in accordance with:

a)   The Provisions of this agreement;

b)   The National law of the Contracting Party in whose territory the investment was made; and

c)   Principles of International law.

4.   The decisions shall be final and binding on the Parties to the dispute. Each Contracting Party shall execute them in accordance with its laws.

Article 9

Settlement of Disputes between the Contracting Parties

1.   Disputes between the Contracting Parties concerning the interpretation or application of this Agreement shall be settled through negotiations.

2.   If the dispute cannot be so settled within six months from start of the negotiation, it shall upon the request of either Contracting Party, be submitted to an arbitral tribunal, in accordance with the provisions of this article.

3.   The Arbitral Tribunal shall be constituted in the following way:

Each Contracting Party shall appoint an arbitrator and these two arbitrators shall then select a national of a third State who shall act as chairman, the arbitrators shall be appointed within three months and the Chairman within five months from the date on which either of the two Contracting Parties informed the other Contracting Party of its intention to submit the dispute to arbitration.

4.   It within the periods specified in paragraph (3) of this Article, the necessary appointments have not been made, either Contracting Party may, in the absence of any other agreement, invite the President of the International Court of Justice to make any necessary appointments. If the President is a national of either Contracting Party or if he is otherwise prevented from discharging the said function, the Vice-President shall be invited to make the necessary appointments. If the Vice-President is a national of either Contracting Party or if he too is prevented from discharging the said function, the member of the International Court of Justice next in seniority, who is not a national of either Contracting Party shall be invited to make the necessary appointments.

5.   The Arbitral Tribunal shall issue its decision on the basis of the rules contained in this Agreement and in other agreements in force between the Contracting Parties, as well as of the principles of the International Law.

6.   The Arbitral Tribunal shall determine its own procedure and shall reach its decision by a majority of votes. Such decision shall be final and binding on both Contracting Parties. Each Contracting Party shall bear the cost of its own arbitrator and its Counsel in the arbitral proceedings, the cost of the Chairman and the remaining costs shall be borne in equal parts by both Contracting Parties.

Article 10

Entry into force

The Contracting Parties shall notify each other when the legal requirements for the entry into force of this Agreement have been fulfilled. The Agreement shall enter into force thirty days after the date of the last notification.

Article 11

Duration and Termination

This Agreement shall remain in force for a period of ten years, and shall continue in force thereafter for another similar period, or periods, unless terminated in writing by either Contracting Party twelve months before its expiration.

In witness hereof, the undersigned, duly authorized thereto by their respective Governments, have signed this Agreement.

Done in _____ on ………………..\199… in two original languages.
Both texts being equally authentic.

For the Government of
The Arab Republic of Egypt

For the Government of
_____

*   *   *

October 1999

Accord entre le Gouvernement de la Republique Française et le Gouvernement de _____ sur l'Encouragement et la Protection Reciproques des Investissements[*]

Le Gouvernement de la République française et le Gouvernement de _____ ci-après dénommés "les Parties contractantes",

Désireux de renforcer la coopération économique entre les deux Etats et de créer des conditions favorables pour les investissements français en ... et ... en France,

Persuadés que l'encouragement et la protection de ces investissements sont propres à stimuler les transferts de capitaux et de technologie entre les deux pays, dans l'intérêt de leur développement économique,

Sont convenus des dispositions suivantes:

ARTICLE 1

Définitions

Pour l'application du présent accord :

1.   Le terme "investissement" désigne tous les avoirs, tels que les biens, droits et intérêts de toutes natures et, plus particulièrement mais non exclusivement:

    a)   les biens meubles et immeubles, ainsi que tous autres droits réels tels que les hypothèques, privilèges, usufruits, cautionnements et tous droits analogues ;

    b)   les actions, primes d'émission et autres formes de participation, même minoritaires ou indirectes, aux sociétés constituées sur le territoire de l'une des Parties contractantes ;

    c)   les obligations, créances et droits à toutes prestations ayant valeur économique;

    d)   les droits de propriété intellectuelle, commerciale et industrielle tels que les droits d'auteur, les brevets d'invention, les licences, les marques déposées, les modèles et maquettes industrielles, les procédés techniques, le savoir-faire, les noms déposés et la clientèle ;

---

[*] *Source*: Government of France, Ministry of Foreign Affairs. [Note added by the editor.]

e) les concessions accordées par la loi ou en vertu d'un contrat, notamment les concessions relatives à la prospection, la culture, l'extraction ou l'exploitation de richesses naturelles, y compris celles qui se situent dans la zone maritime des Parties contractantes.

Il est entendu que lesdits avoirs doivent être ou avoir été investis conformément à la législation de la Partie contractante sur le territoire ou dans la zone maritime de laquelle l'investissement est effectué, avant ou après l'entrée en vigueur du présent accord.

Aucune modification de la forme d'investissement des avoirs n'affecte leur qualification d'investissement, à condition que cette modification ne soit pas contraire à la législation de la Partie contractante sur le territoire ou dans la zone maritime de laquelle l'investissement est réalisé.

2. Le terme de "nationaux" désigne les personnes physiques possédant la nationalité de l'une des Parties contractantes.

3. Le terme de "sociétés" désigne toute personne morale constituée sur le territoire de l'une des Parties contractantes, conformément à la législation de celle-ci et y possédant son siège social, ou contrôlée directement ou indirectement par des nationaux de l'une des Parties contractantes, ou par des personnes morales possédant leur siège social sur le territoire de l'une des Parties contractantes et constituées conformément à la législation de celle-ci.

4. Le terme de "revenus" désigne toutes les sommes produites par un investissement, telles que bénéfices, redevances ou intérêts, durant une période donnée.

Les revenus de l'investissement et, en cas de réinvestissement, les revenus de leur réinvestissement jouissent de la même protection que l'investissement.

5. Le présent accord s'applique au territoire de chacune des Parties contractantes ainsi qu'à la zone maritime de chacune des Parties contractantes, ci-après définie comme la zone économique et le plateau continental qui s'étendent au-delà de la limite des eaux territoriales de chacune des Parties contractantes et sur lesquels elles ont, en conformité avec le Droit international, des droits souverains et une juridiction aux fins de prospection, d'exploitation et de préservation des ressources naturelles.

6. Aucune disposition du présent Accord ne sera interprétée comme empêchant l'une des Parties contractantes de prendre toute disposition visant à régir les investissements réalisés par des investisseurs étrangers et les conditions d'activités desdits investisseurs, dans le cadre de mesures destinées à préserver et à encourager la diversité culturelle et linguistique.

ARTICLE 2

Champ de l'accord

Pour l'application du présent Accord, il est entendu que les Parties contractantes sont responsables des actions ou omissions de leurs collectivités publiques, et notamment de leurs Etats fédérés, régions, collectivités locales ou de toute autre entité sur lesquels la Partie contractante excerce une tutelle, la représentation ou la responsabilité de ses relations internationales ou sa souveraineté.

ARTICLE 3

Encouragement et admission des investissements

Chacune des Parties contractantes encourage et admet, dans le cadre de sa législation et des dispositions du présent accord, les investissements effectués par les nationaux et sociétés de l'autre Partie sur son territoire et dans sa zone maritime.

ARTICLE 4

Traitement juste et équitable

Chacune des Parties contractantes s'engage à assurer, sur son territoire et dans sa zone maritime, un traitement juste et équitable, conformément aux principes du Droit international, aux investissements des nationaux et sociétés de l'autre Partie et à faire en sorte que l'exercice du droit ainsi reconnu ne soit entravé ni en droit, ni en fait. En particulier, bien que non exclusivement, sont considérées comme des entraves de droit ou de fait au traitement juste et équitable, toute restriction à l'achat et au transport de matières premières et de matières auxiliaires, d'énergie et de combustibles, ainsi que de moyens de production et d'exploitation de tout genre, toute entrave à la vente et au transport des produits à l'intérieur du pays et à l'étranger, ainsi que toutes autres mesures ayant un effet analogue.

Les Parties contractantes examineront avec bienveillance, dans le cadre de leur législation interne, les demandes d'entrée et d'autorisation de séjour, de travail, et de circulation introduites par des nationaux d'une Partie contractante, au titre d'un investissement réalisé sur le territoire ou dans la zone maritime de l'autre Partie contractante.

ARTICLE 5

Traitement national et traitement de la Nation la plus favorisée

Chaque Partie contractante applique, sur son territoire et dans sa zone maritime, aux nationaux ou sociétés de l'autre Partie, en ce qui concerne leurs investissements et activités liées à ces investissements, un traitement non moins favorable que celui accordé à ses nationaux ou sociétés, ou le traitement accordé aux nationaux ou sociétés de la Nation la plus favorisée si celui-ci est plus avantageux. A ce titre, les nationaux autorisés à travailler sur le territoire et dans la zone maritime de l'une des Parties contractantes doivent pouvoir bénéficier des facilités matérielles appropriées pour l'exercice de leurs activités professionnelles.

Ce traitement ne s'étend toutefois pas aux privilèges qu'une Partie contractante accorde aux nationaux ou sociétés d'un Etat tiers, en vertu de sa participation ou de son association à une zone de libre échange, une union douanière, un marché commun ou toute autre forme d'organisation économique régionale.

Les dispositions de cet Article ne s'appliquent pas aux questions fiscales.

ARTICLE 6

Dépossession et indemnisation

1.   Les investissements effectués par des nationaux ou sociétés de l'une ou l'autre des Parties contractantes bénéficient, sur le territoire et dans la zone maritime de l'autre Partie contractante, d'une protection et d'une sécurité pleines et entières.

2.   Les Parties contractantes ne prennent pas de mesures d'expropriation ou de nationalisation ou toutes autres mesures dont l'effet est de déposséder, directement ou indirectement, les nationaux et sociétés de l'autre Partie des investissements leur appartenant, sur leur territoire et dans leur zone maritime, si ce n'est pour cause d'utilité publique et à condition que ces mesures ne soient ni discriminatoires, ni contraires à un engagement particulier.

Toutes les mesures de dépossession qui pourraient être prises doivent donner lieu au paiement d'une indemnité juste et préalable dont le montant, égal à la valeur réelle des investissements concernés, doit être évalué par rapport à une situation économique normale et antérieure à toute menace de dépossession.

Cette indemnité, son montant et ses modalités de versement sont fixés au plus tard à la date de la dépossession. Cette indemnité est effectivement réalisable, versée sans retard et librement transférable. Elle produit, jusqu'à la date de versement, des intérêts calculés au taux d'intérêt de marché approprié.

3.   Les nationaux ou sociétés de l'une des Parties contractantes dont les investissements auront subi des pertes dues à la guerre ou à tout autre conflit armé, révolution, état d'urgence national ou révolte survenu sur le territoire ou dans la zone maritime de l'autre Partie contractante, bénéficieront, de la part de cette dernière, d'un traitement non moins favorable que celui accordé à ses propres nationaux ou sociétés ou à ceux de la Nation la plus favorisée.

ARTICLE 7

Libre transfert

Chaque Partie contractante, sur le territoire ou dans la zone maritime de laquelle des investissements ont été effectués par des nationaux ou sociétés de l'autre Partie contractante, accorde à ces nationaux ou sociétés le libre transfert:

a)   des intérêts, dividendes, bénéfices et autres revenus courants;

b) des redevances découlant des droits incorporels désignés au paragraphe 1, lettres d) et e) de l'Article 1;

c) des versements effectués pour le remboursement des emprunts régulièrement contractés ;

d) du produit de la cession ou de la liquidation totale ou partielle de l'investissement, y compris les plus-values du capital investi ;

e) des indemnités de dépossession ou de perte prévues à l'Article 5, paragraphes 2 et 3 ci-dessus.

Les nationaux de chacune des Partes contractantes qui ont été autorisés à travailler sur le territoire ou dans la zone maritime de l'autre Partie contractante, au titre d'un investissement agréé, sont également autorisés à transférer dans leur pays d'origine une quotité appropriée de leur rémunération.

Les transferts visés aux paragraphes précédents sont effectués sans retard au taux de change normal officiellement applicable à la date du transfert.

Lorsque, dans des circonstances exceptionnelles, les mouvements de capitaux en provenance ou à destination de pays tiers causent ou menacent de causer un déséquilibre grave pour la balance des paiements, chacune des Parties contractantes peut temporairement appliquer des mesures de sauvegarde relatives aux transferts, pour autant que ces mesures soient strictement nécessaires, appliquées sur une base équitable, non-discriminatoire et de bonne foi et qu'elles n'excèdent pas une période de six mois.

ARTICLE 8

Règlement des différends entre un investisseur et une Partie contractante

Tout différend relatif aux investissements entre l'une des Parties contractantes et un national ou une société de l'autre Partie contractante est réglé à l'amiable entre les deux parties concernées.

Si un tel différend n'a pas pu être réglé dans un délai de six mois à partir du moment où il a été soulevé par l'une ou l'autre des parties au différend, il est soumis à la demande de l'une ou l'autre de ces parties, de manière inconditionnelle et nonobstant toute autre disposition contractuelle ou renonciation à l'arbitrage international, à l'arbitrage du Centre international pour le règlement des différends relatifs aux investissements (C.I.R.D.I.), créé par la Convention pour le règlement des différends relatifs aux investissements entre Etats et ressortissants d'autres Etats, signée à Washington le 18 mars 1965.

Dans le cas où le différend est de nature à engager la responsabilité pour les actions ou omissions de collectivités publiques ou d'organismes dépendants de l'une des deux Parties contractantes, au sens de l'article 2 du présent accord, ladite collectivité publique ou ledit organisme sont tenus de donner leur consentement de manière inconditionnelle au recours à l'arbitrage du Centre international pour le règlement des différends relatifs aux investissements (C.I.R.D.I.), au sens de l'article 25 de la Convention pour le règlement des différends relatifs aux investissements entre Etats et ressortissants d'autres Etats, signée à Washington le 18 mars 1965.

ARTICLE 9

Garantie et subrogation

1.   Dans la mesure où la réglementation de l'une des Parties contractantes prévoit une garantie pour les investissements effectués à l'étranger, celle-ci peut être accordée, dans le cadre d'un examen cas par cas, à des investissements effectués par des nationaux ou sociétés de cette Partie sur le territoire ou dans la zone maritime de l'autre Partie.

2.   Les investissements des nationaux et sociétés de l'une des Parties contractantes sur le territoire ou dans la zone maritime de l'autre Partie ne pourront obtenir la garantie visée à l'alinéa ci-dessus que s'ils ont, au préalable, obtenu l'agrément de cette dernière Partie.

3.   Si l'une des Parties contractantes, en vertu d'une garantie donnée pour un investissement réalisé sur le territoire ou dans la zone maritime de l'autre Partie, effectue des versements à l'un de ses nationaux ou à l'une de ses sociétés, elle est, de ce fait, subrogée dans les droits et actions de ce national ou de cette société.

4.   Lesdits versements n'affectent pas les droits du bénéficiaire de la garantie à recourir au C.I.R.D.I. ou à poursuivre les actions introduites devant lui jusqu'à l'aboutissement de la procédure.

ARTICLE 10

Engagement spécifique

Les investissements ayant fait l'objet d'un engagement particulier de l'une des Parties contractantes à l'égard des nationaux et sociétés de l'autre Partie contractante sont régis, sans préjudice des dispositions du présent accord, par les termes de cet engagement dans la mesure où celui-ci comporte des dispositions plus favorables que celles qui sont prévues par le présent accord. Les dispositions de l'article 7 du présent Accord s'appliquent même en cas d'engagement spécifique prévoyant la renonciation à l'arbitrage international ou désignant une instance arbitrale différente de celle mentionnée à l'article 7 du présent Accord.

ARTICLE II

Règlement des différends entre Parties contractantes

1.   Les différends relatifs à l'interprétation ou à l'application du présent accord, à l'exclusion des différends relatifs aux investissements mentionnés à l'Article 8 du présent Accord, doivent être réglés, si possible, par la voie diplomatique.

2.   Si dans un délai de six mois à partir du moment où il a été soulevé par l'une ou l'autre des Parties contractantes, le différend n'est pas réglé, il est soumis, à la demande de l'une ou l'autre Partie contractante, à un tribunal d'arbitrage.

3.   Ledit tribunal sera constitué pour chaque cas particulier de la manière suivante: chaque Partie contractante désigne un membre, et les deux membres désignent, d'un commun accord, un ressortissant d'un Etat tiers qui est nommé Président du tribunal par les deux Parties contractantes. Tous les membres doivent être nommés dans un délai de deux mois à compter de la date à laquelle une des Parties contractantes a fait part à l'autre Partie contractante de son intention de soumettre le différend à arbitrage.

4.   Si les délais fixés au paragraphe 3 ci-dessus n'ont pas été observés, l'une ou l'autre Partie contractante, en l'absence de tout autre accord, invite le Secrétaire général de l'Organisation des Nations-Unies à procéder aux désignations nécessaires. Si le Secrétaire général est ressortissant de l'une ou l'autre Partie contractante ou si, pour une autre raison, il est empêché d'exercer cette fonction, le Secrétaire général adjoint le plus ancien et ne possédant pas la nationalité de l'une des Parties contractantes procède aux désignations nécessaires.

5.   Le tribunal d'arbitrage prend ses décisions à la majorité des voix. Ces décisions sont définitives et exécutoires de plein droit pour les Parties contractantes.

Le tribunal fixe lui-même son règlement. Il interprète la sentence à la demande de l'une ou l'autre Partie contractante. A moins que le tribunal n'en dispose autrement, compte tenu de circonstances particulières, les frais de la procédure arbitrale, y compris les vacations des arbitres, sont répartis également entre les Parties Contractantes.

ARTICLE 12

Entrée en vigueur et durée

Chacune des Parties notifiera à l'autre l'accomplissement des procédures internes requises pour l'entrée en vigueur du présent accord, qui prendra effet un mois après le jour de la réception de la dernière notification.

L'accord est conclu pour une durée initiale de dix ans. Il restera en vigueur après ce terme, à moins que l'une des Parties ne le dénonce par la voie diplomatique avec préavis d'un an.

A l'expiration de la période de validité du présent accord, les investissements effectués pendant qu'il était en vigueur continueront de bénéficier de la protection de ses dispositions pendant une période supplémentaire de vingt ans.

*   *   *

AGREEMENT BETWEEN
THE GOVERNMENT OF THE REPUBLIC OF INDONESIA
AND THE GOVERNMENT OF _____
CONCERNING THE PROMOTION AND PROTECTION
OF INVESTMENTS[*]

The Government of the Republic of Indonesia and the Government of _____ (hereinafter referred to as "Contracting Parties");

Bearing in mind the friendly and co-operative relations existing between the two countries and their peoples;

Intending to create favourable conditions for investments by nationals of one Contracting Party on the basis of sovereign equality and mutual benefit; and

Recognizing that the Agreement on the Promotion and Protection of such Investments will be conducive to the stimulation of investment activities in both countries;

Have agreed as follows:

Article I

Definitions

For the purpose of this Agreement:

1.   The term "investments" shall mean any kind of asset invested by investors of one Contracting Party in the territory of the other Contracting Party, in conformity with the laws and regulations of the latter, including, but not exclusively;

      a.   movable and immovable property as well as other rights such as mortgages, privileges, and guarantees and any other similar rights;

      b.   rights derived from shares, bonds or any other form of interest in companies or joint venture in the territory of the other Contracting Party;

      c.   claims to money or to any performance having a financial value;

      d.   intellectual property rights, technical processes, goodwill and know-how;

---

[*] *Source* : Government of Indonesia, Department of Foreign Affairs. [Note added by the editor.]

e. business concessions conferred by law or under contract related to investment including concessions to search for or exploit natural resources.

Any alteration of the form in which assets are invested shall not affect their character as an investment, provided that such alteration has also been approved or admitted under Article II.

2. The term "investors" shall comprise with regard, to either Contracting Party:

(i) natural persons having the nationality of that Contracting Party;

(ii) legal persons constituted under the law of that Contracting Party;

3. The term "without delay" shall be deemed to be fulfilled if a transfer is made within such period as is normally required by international financial practices.

4. "Territory" shall mean:

a. In respect of the Republic-of Indonesia:
    The Territory of the Republic of Indonesia as defined in its laws.

b. In respect of ....:

Article II

Promotion and Protection of Investments

1. Either Contracting Party shall encourage and create favourable conditions for investors of the other Contracting Party to invest in its territory, and shall admit such capital in accordance with its laws and regulations.

2. Investments of investors of either Contracting Party shall at all times be accorded fair and equitable treatment and shall enjoy adequate protection and security in the territory of the other Contracting Party.

Article III

Most-Favoured-Nation Provisions

1. Each Contracting Party shall ensure fair and equitable treatment of the investments of investors of the other Contracting Party and shall not impair, by unreasonable or discriminatory measures, the operation, management, maintenance, use, enjoyment or disposal thereof by those investors. Each Contracting Party shall accord to such investment adequate physical security and protection.

2.   More particularly, each Contracting Party shall accord to such investments treatment which in any case shall not be less favourable than that accorded to investments of investors of any third state.

3.   If a Contracting Party has accorded special advantages to investors of any third state by virtue of agreements establishing customs unions, economic unions, monetary unions or similar institutions, or on the basis of interim agreements leading to such unions of institutions, that Contracting Party shall not be obliged to accord such advantages to' investors of the other Contracting Party.

Article IV

Expropriation

Each Contracting Party shall not take any measures of expropriation, nationalization or any other dispossession, having effect equivalent to nationalization or expropriation against the investments of an investor of the other Contracting Party except under the following conditions:

(a)   the measures are taken for a lawful purpose or public purpose and under process of law;

(b)   the measures are non discriminatory;

(c)   the measures are accompanied by provisions for the payment of prompt, adequate and effective compensatiom Such compensation shall amount to the fair market value without delay before the measure of dispossession became public knowledge. Such- market value shall be determined in accordance with internationally acknowledged practices and methods or, where such fair market value cannot be determined, it sable be such reasonable amount as may be mutually agreed between the Contracting Parties hereto, and it shall be freely transferable in freely usable currencies from the Contracting Party.

Article V

Compensation for Losses

1.   Investors of one Contracting Party, whose investments in the territory of the other Contracting Party suffer losses owing to war or other armed conflict, revolution, a state of investor emergency, revolt, insurrection or riot in the territory of the latter Contracting Party, shall be accorded by the latter Contracting Party treatment, as regards restitutions, indemnification. compensation or other settlement.

2.   The treatment shall not be less favourable than that which the latter Contracting Party accords to investors or investors of any third state.

Article VI

Transfer

Either Contracting Party shall guarantee within the scope of its laws and regulations, in respect to investments by investors of the other Contracting Party grant to those investors without delay, the transfer of:

a.   profits, interests, dividends and other current income;

b.   funds necessary:

   (i)   for the acquisition of raw or auxiliary materials, semi fabricated or finished products, or

   (ii)   to replace capital assets in order to safeguard the continuity of an investment;

c.   additional funds necessary for the development of an investment;

d.   funds in repayment of loans;

e.   royalties or fees;

f.   earnings of natural persons;

g.   the proceeds of sale or liquidation of the investment;

h.   compensation for losses;

i.   compensation for expropriation.

2.   Such transfer shall be made at the prevailing rate of exchange on the date of transfer with respect to current transaction in the currency to be transferred.

Article VII

Subrogation

If the investments of an investor of the one Contracting Party are insured against non-commercial risks under a system established by law, any subrogation of the insurer or re-insurer to the rights of the said investor pursuant to the terms of such insurance shall be recognized by the other Contracting Party, provided, however, that the insurer or the re-insurer shall not be entitled to exercise any rights other than the rights which the investor would have been entitled to exercise.

Article VIII

Settlement of Disputes between Investors and the Contracting Party

1.   Any dispute between a Contracting Party and an investor of the other Contracting Party, concerning an investment of the latter in the territory of the former, shall be settled amicably through consultations and negotiations.

2.   If such a dispute cannot be settled within a period of six months from the date of a written notification either party requested amicable settlement, the dispute shall, at the request of the investor concerned, be submitted either to the judicial procedures provided by the Contracting Party concerned or to international arbitration or conciliation.

3.   In case that the dispute is submitted to arbitration or conciliation the investor shall be entitled to refer the dispute to:

a.   The International Center for Settlement of Investment Disputes for settlement by conciliation or arbitration under the Convention on the Settlement of Investment Disputes between States and Nationals of other States, opened for signature at Washington, D.C, on 18 March 1965, in case both Contracting Parties have become the parties to the Convention; or

b.   An ad hoc tribunal to be established under the arbitration rules of the United Nations Commissions on International Trade Law (UNCITRAL).

Article IX

Settlement of Disputes between the Contracting Parties Concerning Interpretation and Application of the Agreement

Disputes between the Contracting Parties concerning the interpretation or application of this Agreement should, if possible, be settled through diplomatic channels.

Article X

Applicability of this Agreement

1.   This Agreement shall apply to investments by investors of .... in the territory of the Republic of Indonesia which have been previously granted admission in accordance with the Law No. 1 of 1967 concerning Foreign Investment and any law amending or replacing it, and to investments by Investors of the Republic of Indonesia in the territory of .... which have been granted admission in accordance with ....

2.   The provisions of this Agreement shall not apply to any dispute, claim or difference which arose before its entry into force.

Article XI

Application of other Provisions

If the provisions of law of either Contracting Party or obligations under international law existing at present or established hereafter between the Contracting Parties in addition to the present Agreement contain a regulation, whether general or specific, entitling investments by investors of the other Contracting Party to a treatment more favourable than is provided for by the present Agreement, such regulation shall to the extent that it is more favourable prevail over the present Agreement.

Article XII

Consultation and Amendment

1.   Either Contracting Party may request that consultations be held on any matter concerning this Agreement. The other Party shall accord sympathetic consideration to the proposal and shall afford adequate opportunity for such consultations.

2.   This Agreement may be amended at any time, if deemed necessary, by mutual consent of both Contracting Parties.

Article XIII

Entry into Force, Duration and Termination

1.   The present Agreement shall enter into force three months after the date of the latest notification by which Contracting Parties have notified each other that their constitutional requirements for the entry into force of this Agreement have been fulfilled.

2.   This Agreement shall remain in force for a period of ten (10) years and shall continue in force thereafter for similar period unless either Contracting Party notifies the other Contracting Party in writing of its intention to terminate this Agreement one year before its expiration.

3.   With respect to investments made prior to the date of termination of this Agreement, the provisions of this Agreement shall continue to be effective for a period of ten (10) years from the date of termination.

IN WITNESS WHEREOF, the undersigned, duly authorized thereto by their respective Governments, have signed this Agreement.

Done in duplicate at Jakarta on .... in Indonesian, ...and English languages. All texts are equally authentic. If there is any divergence concerning the interpretation, the English text shall prevail.

FOR THE GOVERNMENT OF   FOR THE GOVERNMENT OF
THE REPUBLIC OF INDONESIA   ....

*   *   *

AGREEMENT

BETWEEN

THE GOVERNMENT OF JAMAICA

AND THE GOVERNMENT OF _____

CONCERNING

THE PROMOTION AND RECIPROCAL PROTECTION OF INVESTMENTS[*]

The Government of Jamaica and the Government of _____,

(Hereinafter referred to as the "Contracting Parties").

Desiring to intensify economic co-operation between the two countries;

INTENDING to create favourable conditions for investments by investors of either country in the territory of the other.

RECOGNISING that the protection of such investments are conducive to the stimulation of individual business initiative and will increase prosperity in both Contracting Parties;

Have agreed as follows:

ARTICLE 1

Definitions

For the purposes of this Agreement:

1.   The term "investments" means every kind of asset established or acquired, including changes in the form of such investment invested by an investor of one Contracting Party in the territory of the other Contracting Party, in accordance with the national laws of the Contracting Party in whose territory the investment is made and in particular, though not exclusively includes:

   a)   movable and immovable property as well as any other property rights, such as mortgages, liens and pledges;

   b)   shares in companies and other kinds of interests in companies;

   c)   claims to money or to any performance under contract having an economic value;

   d)   intellectual property rights, such as copyrights, patents, utility models, industrial designs, trade and business secrets, technical processes and goodwill;

---

[*] *Source*: Government of Jamaica, Attorney General's Department. [Note added by the editor.]

e)   business concessions under public law, including rights to search for, cultivate, extract and exploit natural resources.

2.   The term "returns" means the amounts yielded by an investment over any given period such as profit dividends, interest, royalties, fees and other current income.

3.   The term "investors" means:

a)   any natural person who is a national of a Contracting Party in accordance with its laws;

b)   any legal person constituted in accordance with the laws and regulations of a Contracting Party and having its seat in the territory of that Contracting Party, whether or not for pecuniary profit.

4.   The term " nationals" means:

in respect of Jamaica:
physical persons, who are citizens of Jamaica according to its laws.

in respect of the _____:

5.   term "territory" means: the territory under sovereignty or jurisdiction of each Contracting Party and also includes their relevant maritime areas and airspace.

The provisions of this Agreement shall not apply to the investments made by natural persons who are nationals of one Contracting Party in the territory of the other Contracting Party if such persons, not having entered that territory as investors, have been residents in the latter Contracting Party for more than two years, unless it is proved that the investment was admitted into its territory from abroad.

ARTICLE 2

Promotion of Investments

1.   Each Contracting Party shall, within the framework of its national policies, encourage and create favourable conditions for investors of the other Contracting Party to invest capital in its territory, and they shall consult with each other as to the most effective ways to achieve that purpose.

2.   Each Contracting Party shall admit such investments subject to its laws and regulations.

ARTICLE 3

Protection of Investments

1.   Each Contracting Party shall at all times ensure fair and equitable treatment of the investments by investors of the other Contracting Party and shall not impair the management, maintenance, use, enjoyment or disposal thereof through unjustified or discriminatory measures.

2.   Each Contracting Party, once it has admitted investments in its territory by investors of the other Contracting Party shall grant full legal protection to such investments and shall accord them treatment which is not less favourable than that accorded to investments by its own investors or by investors of third States.

3.   Notwithstanding the provisions of Paragraph 2) of this Article, the treatment of the most favoured nation shall not apply to privileges which either Contracting Party accords to investors of a third State because of its membership in, or association with a free trade area, customs union, common market or regional agreement.

4.   The provisions of Paragraph 2) of this Article shall not be construed so as to oblige one Contracting Party to extend to investors of the other Contracting Party the benefit of any treatment, preference or privilege resulting from an international agreement, relating wholly or mainly to taxation.

ARTICLE 4

Expropriation and Compensation

1.   Neither of the Contracting Parties shall take any measure of nationalisation or expropriation or any other measure having the same effect against investments in its territory belonging to investors of the other Contracting Party, unless the measures are taken in the public interest, on a non-discriminatory basis and under due process of law. The measures shall be accompanied by provisions for the payment of prompt, adequate and effective compensation. Such compensation shall amount to the market value of the expropriated investment immediately before the expropriation or before the impending expropriation was publicly announced, shall include interest from the date of expropriation at a normal commercial rate, shall be paid without delay and shall be effectively realisable and freely transferable. In determining the compensation, due consideration shall be given to any factors which might have affected the value before the measures were publicly announced.

2.   Investors of either Contracting Party who suffer losses of their investments in the territory of the other Contracting Party due to war or other armed conflict, a state of national emergency, revolt, insurrection or riot shall be accorded with respect to restitution, indemnification, compensation or other settlement, a treatment which is no less favourable than that accorded to its own investors or to investors of any third State.

ARTICLE 5

Transfer of Funds

1.   Each Contracting Party shall grant investors of the other Contracting Party the unrestricted right to transfer payments related to investment, in particular, though not exclusively of:

   a)   the capital and additional sums necessary for the maintenance and development of the investments;

b)   the returns;

c)   the proceeds from a total or partial sale or liquidation of an investment, provided, however, that in periods of exceptional balance of payments difficulties, transfers may be phased over a three year period;

d)   the earnings of nationals of one Contracting Party who are allowed to work in connection with an investment in the territory of the other;

e)   compensations provided for in Article 4.

2.   Transfers shall be effected without delay, in freely convertible currency, at the normal applicable exchange rate at the date of the transfer, in accordance with the procedures established by the Contracting Party in whose territory the investment was made, which procedures shall not impair the substance of the rights set forth in this Article.

ARTICLE 6

Subrogation

1.   If a Contracting Party or any agency designated by it makes a payment to any of its investors under a guarantee or insurance it has contracted in respect of an investment, the other Contracting Party shall recognise the validity of the subrogation in favour of the former Contracting Party or its agency to any right or title held by the investor. The Contracting Party or any agency thereof shall, within the limits of subrogation be entitled to exercise the same rights which the investor would have been entitled to exercise.

2.   In the case of subrogation as defined in Paragraph 1) above, the investor shall not pursue a claim unless authorised to do so by the Contracting Party or its agency.

3.   As regards the transfer of payments, Article 4 and 5 shall, mutatis mutandis, apply to any such assigned right or claim.

ARTICLE 7

More Favourable Treatment

If the laws of either Contracting Party or obligations under international law existing at present or established hereafter between the Contracting Parties in addition to this Agreement contain a provision, whether general or specific, entitling investments by investors of the other Contracting Party to a treatment more favourable than is provided for by this Agreement, such provision shall, to the extent that it is more favourable prevail over this Agreement.

ARTICLE 8

Scope of Application

This Agreement shall apply to all investments made before or after its entry into force by investors of either Contracting Party in the territory of the other Contracting Party which have been or are made in accordance with the laws and regulations of the latter Contracting Party.

ARTICLE 9

Settlement of Disputes between the Contracting Parties

1. Disputes between the Contracting Parties concerning the interpretation or application of this Agreement shall as far as possible be settled through diplomatic channels.

2. If a dispute cannot thus be settled within six months from the beginning of the negotiations it shall upon the request of either Contracting Party be submitted to an arbitral tribunal.

3. Such arbitral tribunal shall be constituted <u>ad hoc</u> as follows: each Contracting Party shall appoint one member, and these two members shall agree upon a national of a third State as their chairman to be appointed by the governments of the two Contracting Parties. Such members shall be appointed within two months, and such chairman within three months from the date on which either Contracting Party has notified the other Contracting Party that it intends to submit the dispute to an arbitral tribunal.

4. If the necessary appointments have not been made within the periods specified in Paragraph 3) above either Contracting Party may, in the absence of any other arrangement, invite the President of the International Court of Justice to make any necessary appointments. If the President is a national of either Contracting Party or if he is otherwise prevented from discharging the said function, the Vice President shall be invited to make the necessary appointments. If the Vice President is a national of either Contracting Party or if he too is prevented from discharging the said function, the member of the Court next in seniority, who is not a national of either Contracting Party, shall be invited to make the necessary appointments.

5. The arbitral tribunal shall reach its decisions by a majority of votes. Such decisions shall be binding. Each Contracting Party shall bear the cost of its own member of the tribunal and of its representatives in the arbitration proceedings. The cost of the Chairman and the remaining costs shall be borne in equal parts by the Contracting Parties. The arbitral tribunal may make a different decision concerning costs. In all other respects, the tribunal shall determine its own procedure.

ARTICLE 10

Settlement of Investment Disputes between a Contracting Party and an Investor of the other Contracting Party

1. Disputes between a Contracting Party and investors of the other Contracting Party concerning an investment of such in the territory of the former Contracting Party shall as far as possible be settled amicably between the parties concerned.

2.   If the dispute cannot thus be settled within six months following the date on which the dispute has been raised by either party, it may be submitted to:

a)   the competent tribunal of the Contracting Party in whose territory the investment was made, or

b)   international arbitration according to the provisions of Paragraph 3.

3.   The arbitration tribunal shall decide in accordance with the provisions of this Agreement, the laws of the Contracting Party involved in the dispute, including its rules on conflict of law, the terms of any specific agreement concluded in relation to such an investment and the relevant principles of international law.

4.   The award shall be binding on the parties and shall not be subject to any appeal or remedy other than that provided for in the said Convention. The award shall be enforceable in accordance with the domestic law of the Contracting Party in which the investment in question is situated.

5.   Neither Contracting Party shall pursue diplomatic channels in a dispute unless:

(i)   where the dispute was referred to the International Centre for the Settlement of Investment Disputes (ICSID) created by the Convention on the Settlement of Investment. Disputes between States and Nationals of other States opened for signature in Washington D.C. on 18th March 1965, the Secretary General of the Centre, a Conciliation Commission or an arbitral tribunal constituted by it, decides that the dispute is not within the jurisdiction of the Centre; or

(ii)   the other Contracting Party fails to comply with or abide by a final award, rendered by an arbitration tribunal.

ARTICLE 11

General Exceptions

1.   Investments in cultural industries are exempt from the provisions of this Agreement. "Cultural Industries", means natural persons or enterprises engaged in any of the following activities:

a)   the publication, distribution or sale of books, magazines, periodicals or newspapers in print or machine readable form but not including the sole activity of printing or typesetting any of the foregoing;

b)   the production, distribution, sale or exhibition of film or video recordings.

c)   the production, distribution, sale or exhibition of audio or video music recording;

d)   the publication, distribution, sale or exhibition of music in print or machine readable form, or

e) radio communications in which the transmission are intended for direct reception by the general public, and all radio, television or cable broadcasting undertakings and all Satellite programming and broadcasting network services.

2. Notwithstanding any other provision of the Agreement, a contracting Party shall not be prevented from taking prudential measures with respect to financial services, including measures for the protection of investors, depositors, policy holders or persons to whom a fiduciary duty is owed by an enterprise providing financial services, or to ensure the integrity and stability of its financial system.

3. Where such measures do not conform with the provisions of the Agreement, they shall not be used as a means of avoiding the Contracting Party's commitments or obligations under the Agreement.

ARTICLE 12

Entry into force, duration and termination

1. This Agreement shall enter into force on the first day of the second month following the date on which the Contracting Parties notify each other in writing that their constitutional requirements for the entry into force of this Agreement have been fulfilled. It shall remain in force for a period of ten years. Thereafter it shall remain in force until the expiration of twelve months from the date that either Contracting Party in writing notifies the other Contracting Party of its decision to terminate this Agreement.

2. In respect of investments made prior to the date when the notice of termination of this Agreement becomes effective, the provisions of Articles 1 to 9 shall remain in force for a further period of ten years from the date.

IN WITNESS THEREOF the undersigned, duly authorised thereto by their respective Governments, have signed this Agreement.

Done at _____ on this ....day of ......, in duplicate in the English language.

....

For the Government of Jamaica   For the Government of ....

*   *   *

AGREEMENT BETWEEN THE GOVERNMENT OF MALAYSIA AND THE GOVERNMENT OF _____ FOR THE PROMOTION AND PROTECTION OF INVESTMENTS*

The Government of Malaysia and the Government of _____ hereinafter referred to as the "Contracting Parties";

Desiring to expand and strengthen economic and industrial cooperation on a long term basis, and in particular, to create favourable conditions for investments by investors of one Contracting Party in the territory of the other Contracting Party;

Recognizing the need to protect investments by investors of both Contracting Parties and to stimulate the flow of investments and individual business initiative with a view to promoting the economic prosperity of both Contracting Parties;

Have agreed as follows:

ARTICLE 1

Definitions

1.   For the purpose of this Agreement:

(a)   "Investments" means every kind of asset and in particular, though not exclusively, includes:

> (i)   movable and immovable property and any other property rights such as mortgages, liens or pledges;

> (ii)   shares, stocks and debentures of companies or interests in the property of such companies;

> (iii)   a claim to money or a claim to any performance having financial value;

> (iv)   Intellectual and industrial property rights, including rights with respect to copyrights, patents, trademarks, tradenames, industrial designs, trade secrets, technical processes and know-how and goodwill;

> (v)   business concessions conferred by law or under contract, including concessions to search for, cultivate, extract, or exploit natural resources;

(b)   "investor" means:

---

* *Source*: Government of Malaysia, Ministry of International Trade and Industry. [Note added by the editor.]

(i)   any natural person possessing the citizenship of or permanently residing in the territory of a Contracting Party in accordance with its laws; or

(ii)   any corporation, partnership, trust, joint-venture, organisation, association or enterprise incorporated or duly constituted in accordance with applicable laws of that Contracting Party;

(c)   "territory" means:

(i)   with respect to Malaysia, all land territory comprising the Federation of Malaysia, the territorial sea, its bed and subsoil and airspace above;

(ii)   with respect to the...
....
....

(d)   "freely usable currency" means the United States dollar, pound sterling, Deutschemark, French franc, Japanese yen or any other currency that is widely used to make payments for international transactions and widely traded in the international principal exchange markets.

2   (a)   The term "investments" referred to in paragraph 1(a) shall only refer to all investments that are made in accordance with the laws, regulations and national policies of the Contracting Parties.

(b)   Any alteration of the form in which assets are invested shall not affect their classification as investments, provided that such alteration is not contrary to the approval, if any, granted in respect of the assets originally invested.

ARTICLE 2

Promotion and Protection of Investments

1.   Each Contracting Party shall encourage and create favourable conditions for investors of the other Contracting Party to invest capital in its territory and, in accordance with its laws, regulations and national policies, shall admit such investments.

2.   Investments of investors of each Contracting Party shall at all times be accorded equitable treatment and shall enjoy full and adequate protection and security in the territory of the other Contracting Party.

ARTICLE 3

Most-Favoured-Nation Provisions

1.   Investments made by investors of either Contracting Party in the territory of the other Contracting Party shall receive treatment which is fair and equitable, and not less favourable than that accorded to investments made by investors of any third State.

2.   The provisions of this Agreement relative to the granting of treatment not less favourable than that accorded to the investors of any third State shall not be construed so as to oblige one Contracting Party to extend to the investors of the other the benefit of any treatment, preference or privilege resulting from:

(a)   any existing or future customs union or free trade area or a common market or a monetary union or similar international agreement or other forms of regional cooperation to which either of the Contracting Parties is or may become a party; or the adoption of an agreement designed to lead to the formation or extension of such a union or area within a reasonable length of time; or

(b)   any international agreement or arrangement relating wholly or mainly to taxation or any domestic legislation relating wholly or mainly to taxation.

ARTICLE 4

Compensation for Losses

Investors of one Contracting Party whose investments in the territory of the other Contracting Party suffer losses owing to war or other armed conflict, revolution, a state of national emergency, revolt, insurrection or riot in the territory of the latter Contracting Party shall be accorded by the latter Contracting Party treatment, as regards restitution, indemnification, compensation or other settlement, no less favourable than that which the latter Contracting Party accords to investors of any third State.

ARTICLE 5

Expropriation

Neither Contracting Party shall take any measures of expropriation or nationalization against the investments of an Investor of the other Contracting Party except under the following conditions:

(a)   the measures are taken for a lawful or public purpose and under due process of law;

(b)   the measures are non-discriminatory;

(c)   the measures are accompanied by provisions for the payment of prompt, adequate and effective compensation. Such compensation shall amount to the market value of the investments affected immediately before the measure of dispossession became public knowledge, and it shall be freely transferable in freely usable currencies from the Contracting Party. Any unreasonable delay in payment of compensation shall carry an interest at prevailing commercial rate as agreed upon by both parties unless such rate is prescribed by law.

ARTICLE 6

Transfers

1.   Each Contracting Party shall, subject to its laws and regulations allow without unreasonable delay the transfer in any freely usable currency:

  (a)   the net profits, dividends, royalties, technical fees, interest and other current income, accruing from any investment of the investors of the other Contracting Party;

  (b)   the proceeds from the total or partial liquidation of any investment made by investors of the other Contracting Party;

  (c)   funds in repayment of borrowings/ loans given by investors of one Contracting Party to the investors of the other Contracting Party which both Contracting Parties have recognised as investment; and

  (d)   the net earnings and other compensations of national of one Contracting Party who are employed and allowed to work in connection with an investment in the territory of the other Contracting Party.

2.   The exchange rates applicable to such transfers in the paragraph 1 of this Article shall be the rate of exchange prevailing at the time of remittance.

3.   The Contracting Parties undertake to accord to the transfers referred to in paragraph 1 of this Article a treatment as favourable as that accorded to transfer originating from investments made by investors of any third State.

ARTICLE 7

Settlement of Investment Disputes Between
a Contracting Party and an Investor
of the Other Contracting Party

1.   Each Contracting Party consents to submit to the International Centre for the Settlement of Investment Disputes (hereinafter referred to as □the Centre") for the settlement by conciliation or arbitration under the Convention on the Settlement of Investment Disputes between States and Nationals of other States opened for signature at Washington D.C. on 18 March 1965 any dispute arising between that Contracting Party and an investor of the other Contracting Party which involves:

  (a)   an obligation entered into by that Contracting Party with the investor of the other Contracting Party regarding an Investment by such investor; or

  (b)   an alleged breach of any right conferred or created by this Agreement with respect to an investment by such Investor.

2.   A company which is incorporated or constituted under the laws in force in the territory of one Contracting Party and in which before such a dispute arises the majority of shares are owned by investors of the other Contracting Party shall in accordance with Article 25(2)(b) of the Convention be treated for the purpose of this Convention as a company of the other Contracting Party.

3.   (a)   If any dispute referred to in paragraph 1 should arise, the Contracting Party and the investor concerned shall seek to resolve the dispute through consultation and negotiation. If the dispute cannot thus be resolved within three (3) months, then if the investor concerned also consents in writing to submit the dispute to the Centre for settlement by conciliation or arbitration under the Convention, either party to the dispute may institute proceedings by addressing a request to that effect to the Secretary-General of the Centre as set forth in Articles 28 and 36 of the Convention, provided that the investor concerned has not submitted the dispute to the courts of justice or administrative tribunals or agencies of competent jurisdiction of the Contracting Party that is party to the dispute.

        (b)   In the event of disagreement as to whether conciliation or arbitration is the more appropriate procedure, the opinion of the investor concerned shall prevail. The Contracting Party which is a party to the dispute shall not raise as an objection, defence, or right of set-off at any stage of the proceedings or enforcement of an award the fact that the investor which is the other party to the dispute has received or will receive, pursuant to an insurance or guarantee contract, an indemnity or other compensation for all or part of his or its losses and damages.

4.   Neither Contracting Party shall pursue through diplomatic channels any dispute referred to the Centre unless:

        (a)   the Secretary-General of the Centre, or a conciliation commission or an arbitral tribunal constituted by it, decides that the dispute is not within the jurisdiction of the Centre; or

        (b)   the other Contracting Party should fail to abide by or to comply with any award rendered by an arbitral tribunal.

ARTICLE 8

Settlement of Disputes Between the Contracting Parties

1.   Disputes between the Contracting Parties concerning the interpretation or application of this Agreement should, if possible, be settled through diplomatic channels.

2.   If a dispute between the Contracting Parties cannot thus be settled, it shall upon the request of either Contracting Party be submitted to an arbitral tribunal.

3.   Such an arbitral tribunal shall be constituted for each individual case in the following way. Within two months of the receipt of the request for arbitration, each Contracting Party shall appoint one member of the tribunal. Those two members shall then select a national of a third

State who on approval by the two Contracting Parties shall be appointed Chairman of the tribunal. The Chairman shall be appointed within two (2) months from the date of appointment of the other two members.

4.   If within the periods specified in paragraph 3 of this Article the necessary appointments have not been made, either Contracting Party may, in the absence of any other agreement, invite the President of the International Court of Justice to make the necessary appointments. If the President is a national of either Contracting Party or if he is otherwise prevented from discharging the said function, the Vice-President shall be invited to make the necessary appointments. If the Vice-President is a national of either Contracting Party or if he too is prevented from discharging the said function, the member of the International Court of Justice next in seniority who is not a national of either Contracting Party shall be invited to make the necessary appointments.

5.   The arbitral tribunal shall reach its decision by a majority of votes. Such decision shall be binding on both Contracting Parties. Each Contracting Party shall bear the cost of its own member of the tribunal and of its representation in the arbitral proceedings; the cost of the Chairman and the remaining costs shall be borne in equal parts by the Contracting Parties. The tribunal may, however, in its decision direct that a higher proportion of costs shall be borne by one of the two Contracting Parties, and this award shall be binding on both Contracting Parties. The tribunal shall determine its own procedure.

ARTICLE 9

Subrogation

If a Contracting Party or its designated agency makes a payment to any of its investors under a guarantee it has granted in respect of an investment, the other Contracting Party shall, without prejudice to the rights of the former Contracting Party under Article 7, recognize the transfer of any right or title of such investors to the former Contracting Party or its designated agency and the subrogation of the former Contracting Party or its designated agency to any right or title.

ARTICLE 10

Application to Investments

This Agreement shall apply to investments made in the territory of either Contracting Party in accordance with its laws, regulations or national policies by investors of the other Contracting Party prior to as well as after the entry into force of this Agreement.

ARTICLE 11

Amendment

This agreement may be amended by mutual consent of both Contracting Parties at any time after it is in force. Any alteration or modification of this Agreement shall be done without prejudice to the rights and obligations arising from this Agreement prior to the date of such alteration or modification until such rights and obligations are fully implemented.

ARTICLE 12

Entry into Force, Duration and Termination

1.   This Agreement shall enter into force thirty (30) days after the later date on which the Governments of the Contracting Parties have notified each other that their constitutional requirements for the entry into force of this Agreement have been fulfilled. The later date shall refer to the date on which the last notification letter is sent.

2.   This Agreement shall remain in force for a period of ten (10) years, and shall continue in force, unless terminated in accordance with paragraph 3 of this Article.

3.   Either Contracting Party may by giving one (1) year's written notice to the other Contracting Party, terminate this Agreement at the end of the initial ten (10) year period or anytime thereafter.

4.   With respect to investments made or acquired prior to the date of termination of this Agreement, the provisions of all of the other Articles of this Agreement shall continue to be effective for a period of ten (10) years from such date of termination.

IN WITNESS WHEREOF, the undersigned, duly authorised thereto by their respective Governments, have signed this Agreement.

Done in duplicate at _____ this _____ day of _____ in Bahasa Malaysia _____ and the English Language, all texts being equally authentic. In case of any divergence of interpretation, the English text shall prevail.

FOR THE GOVERNMENT OF   FOR THE GOVERNMENT OF
       MALAYSIA   _____

*   *   *

Standard text March 1997 (rev.2)

Agreement on Encouragement and Reciprocal Protection of Investments between _____ and the Kingdom of the Netherlands[*]

The _____
and
the Kingdom of the Netherlands,

hereinafter referred to as the Contracting Parties,

Desiring to strengthen their traditional ties of friendship and to extend and intensify the economic relations between them, particularly with respect to investments by the nationals of one Contracting Party in the territory of the other Contracting Party,

Recognising that agreement upon the treatment to be accorded to such investments will stimulate the flow of capital and technology and the economic development of the Contracting Parties and that fair and equitable treatment of investment is desirable,

Have agreed as follows:

Article 1

For the purposes of this Agreement:

(a)   the term "investments" means every kind of asset and more particularly, though not exclusively:

(i)   movable and immovable property as well as any other rights *in rem* in respect of every kind of asset;

(ii)   rights derived from shares, bonds and other kinds of interests in companies and joint ventures;

(iii)   claims to money, to other assets or to any performance having an economic value;

(iv)   rights in the field of intellectual property, technical processes, goodwill and know-how;

(v)   rights granted under public law or under contract, including rights to prospect, explore, extract and win natural resources.

(b)   the term "nationals" shall comprise with regard to either Contracting Party:

---

[*] *Source*: Government of the Netherlands, Ministry of Economic Affairs. [Note added by the editor.]

(i)   natural persons having the nationality of that Contracting Party;

(ii)   legal persons constituted under the law of that Contracting Party;

(iii)   legal persons not constituted under the law of that Contracting Party but controlled, directly or indirectly, by natural persons as defined in (i) or by legal persons as defined in (ii).

(c)   The term "territory" means:

the territory of the Contracting Party concerned and any area adjacent to the territorial sea which, under the laws applicable in the Contracting Party concerned, and in accordance with international law, is the exclusive economic zone or continental shelf of the Contracting Party concerned, in which that Contracting Party exercises jurisdiction or sovereign rights.

Article 2

Either Contracting Party shall, within the framework of its laws and regulations, promote economic cooperation through the protection in its territory of investments of nationals of the other Contracting Party. Subject to its right to exercise powers conferred by its laws or regulations, each Contracting Party shall admit such investments.

Article 3

1.   Each Contracting Party shall ensure fair and equitable treatment of the investments of nationals of the other Contracting Party and shall not impair, by unreasonable or discriminatory measures, the operation, management, maintenance, use, enjoyment or disposal thereof by those nationals. Each Contracting Party shall accord to such investments full physical security and protection.

2.   More particularly, each Contracting Party shall accord to such investments treatment which in any case shall not be less favourable than that accorded either to investments of its own nationals or to investments of nationals of any third State, whichever is more favourable to the national concerned.

3.   If a Contracting Party has accorded special advantages to nationals of any third State by virtue of agreements establishing customs unions, economic unions, monetary unions or similar institutions, or on the basis of interim agreements leading to such unions or institutions, that Contracting Party shall not be obliged to accord such advantages to nationals of the other Contracting Party.

4.   Each Contracting Party shall observe any obligation it may have entered into with regard to investments of nationals of the other Contracting Party.

5.   If the provisions of law of either Contracting Party or obligations under international law existing at present or established hereafter between the Contracting Parties in addition to the present Agreement contain a regulation, whether general or specific, entitling investments by nationals of the other Contracting Party to a treatment more favourable than is provided for by the present Agreement, such regulation shall, to the extent that it is more favourable, prevail over the present Agreement.

Article 4

With respect to taxes, fees, charges and to fiscal deductions and exemptions, each Contracting Party shall accord to nationals of the other Contracting Party who are engaged in any economic activity in its territory, treatment not less favourable than that accorded to its own nationals or to those of any third State who are in the same circumstances, whichever is more favourable to the nationals concerned. For this purpose, however, there shall not be taken into account any special fiscal advantages accorded by that Party:

a)   under an agreement for the avoidance of double taxation; or

b)   by virtue of its participation in a customs union, economic union or similar institution; or

c)   on the basis of reciprocity with a third State.

Article 5

The Contracting Parties shall guarantee that payments relating to an investment may be transferred. The transfers shall be made in a freely convertible currency, without restriction or delay. Such transfers include in particular though not exclusively:

a)   profits, interests, dividends and other current income;

b)   funds necessary :

   (i)   for the acquisition of raw or auxiliary materials, semi-fabricated or finished products, or

   (ii)   to replace capital assets in order to safeguard the continuity of an investment;

c)   additional funds necessary for the development of an investment;

d)   funds in repayment of loans;

e)   royalties or fees;

f)   earnings of natural persons;

g)   the proceeds of sale or liquidation of the investment;

h)   payments arising under Article 7.

Article 6

Neither Contracting Party shall take any measures depriving, directly or indirectly, nationals of the other Contracting Party of their investments unless the following conditions are complied with:

a) the measures are taken in the public interest and under due process of law;

b) the measures are not discriminatory or contrary to any undertaking which the Contracting Party which takes such measures may have given;

c) the measures are taken against just compensation. Such compensation shall represent the genuine value of the investments affected, shall include interest at a normal commercial rate until the date of payment and shall, in order to be effective for the claimants, be paid and made transferable, without delay, to the country designated by the claimants concerned and in the currency of the country of which the claimants are nationals or in any freely convertible currency accepted by the claimants.

Article 7

Nationals of the one Contracting Party who suffer losses in respect of their investments in the territory of the other Contracting Party owing to war or other armed conflict, revolution, a state of national emergency, revolt, insurrection or riot shall be accorded by the latter Contracting Party treatment, as regards restitution, indemnification, compensation or other settlement, no less favourable than that which that Contracting Party accords to its own nationals or to nationals of any third State, whichever is more favourable to the nationals concerned.

Article 8

If the investments of a national of the one Contracting Party are insured against non-commercial risks or otherwise give rise to payment of indemnification in respect of such investments under a system established by law, regulation or government contract, any subrogation of the insurer or re-insurer or Agency designated by the one Contracting Party to the rights of the said national pursuant to the terms of such insurance or under any other indemnity given shall be recognised by the other Contracting Party.

Article 9

Each Contracting Party hereby consents to submit any legal dispute arising between that Contracting Party and a national of the other Contracting Party concerning an investment of that national in the territory of the former Contracting Party to the International Centre for Settlement of Investment Disputes for settlement by conciliation or arbitration under the Convention on the Settlement of Investment Disputes between States and Nationals of other States, opened for signature at Washington on 18 March 1965. A legal person which is a national of one Contracting Party and which before such a dispute arises is controlled by nationals of the other Contracting Party shall, in accordance with Article 25 (2) (b) of the Convention, for the purpose of the Convention be treated as a national of the other Contracting Party.

Article 10

The provisions of this Agreement shall, from the date of entry into force thereof, also apply to investments which have been made before that date.

Article 11

Either Contracting Party may propose to the other Party that consultations be held on any matter concerning the interpretation or application of the Agreement. The other Party shall accord sympathetic consideration to the proposal and shall afford adequate opportunity for such consultations.

Article 12

1.   Any dispute between the Contracting Parties concerning the interpretation or application of the present Agreement, which cannot be settled within a reasonable lapse of time by means of diplomatic negotiations, shall, unless the Parties have otherwise agreed, be submitted, at the request of either Party, to an arbitral tribunal, composed of three members. Each Party shall appoint one arbitrator and the two arbitrators thus appointed shall together appoint a third arbitrator as their chairman who is not a national of either Party.

2.   If one of the Parties fails to appoint its arbitrator and has not proceeded to do so within two months after an invitation from the other Party to make such appointment, the latter Party may invite the President of the International Court of Justice to make the necessary appointment.

3.   If the two arbitrators are unable to reach agreement, in the two months following their appointment, on the choice of the third arbitrator, either Party may invite the President of the International Court of Justice to make the necessary appointment.

4.   If, in the cases provided for in the paragraphs (2) and (3) of this Article, the President of the International Court of Justice is prevented from discharging the said function or is a national of either Contracting Party, the Vice-President shall be invited to make the necessary appointments. If the Vice-President is prevented from discharging the said function or is a national of either Party the most senior member of the Court available who is not a national of either Party shall be invited to make the necessary appointments.

5.   The tribunal shall decide on the basis of respect for the law. Before the tribunal decides, it may at any stage of the proceedings propose to the Parties that the dispute be settled amicably. The foregoing provisions shall not prejudice settlement of the dispute <u>ex aequo et bono</u> if the Parties so agree.

6.   Unless the Parties decide otherwise, the tribunal shall determine its own procedure.

7.   The tribunal shall reach its decision by a majority of votes. Such decision shall be final and binding on the Parties.

Article 13

As regards the Kingdom of the Netherlands, the present Agreement shall apply to the part of the Kingdom in Europe, to the Netherlands Antilles and to Aruba, unless the notification provided for in Article 14, paragraph (1) provides otherwise.

Article 14

1.   The present Agreement shall enter into force on the first day of the second month following the date on which the Contracting Parties have notified each other in writing that their constitutionally required procedures have been complied with, and shall remain in force for a period of fifteen years.

2.   Unless notice of termination has been given by either Contracting Party at least six months before the date of the expiry of its validity, the present Agreement shall be extended tacitly for periods of ten years, whereby each Contracting Party reserves the right to terminate the Agreement upon notice of at least six months before the date of expiry of the current period of validity.

3.   In respect of investments made before the date of the termination of the present Agreement, the foregoing Articles shall continue to be effective for a further period of fifteen years from that date.

4.   Subject to the period mentioned in paragraph (2) of this Article, the Kingdom of the Netherlands shall be entitled to terminate the application of the present Agreement separately in respect of any of the parts of the Kingdom.

IN WITNESS WHEREOF, the undersigned representatives, duly authorised thereto, have signed the present Agreement.

DONE in two originals at, _____, on _____, in the _____, Netherlands and English languages, the three texts being authentic. In case of difference of interpretation the English text will prevail.

For _____   **For the Kingdom of the Netherlands:**

*   *   *

AGREEMENT BETWEEN THE GOVERNMENT
OF THE DEMOCRATIC SOCIALIST REPUBLIC OF SRI LANKA
AND THE GOVERNMENT OF ————————
FOR THE PROMOTION AND PROTECTION
OF INVESTMENTS *

THE Government of the Democratic Socialist Republic of Sri Lanka and the Government of ……………….. (hereinafter referred to as the "Contracting Parties");.

DESIRING to create conditions favourable for greater investment by investors of one Contracting Party in the territory of the other Contracting Party;

RECOGNIZING that the encouragement and reciprocal protection under international agreement of such investments will be conducive to the stimulation of individual business initiative and will increase prosperity in both States;

HAVE agreed as follows:

ARTICLE 1

DEFINITIONS

1.   The term "investment" means every kind of property or asset invested by an investor of one Contracting Party in the territory of the other Contracting Party in accordance with the laws and regulations of the Contracting Party (hereinafter referred to as the host Contracting Party) in particular though not exclusively includes:

(a)   movable and immovable property and any other rights such as mortgages liens or pledges;

(b)   shares, stocks and debentures of companies or any other similar forms of interests in such companies;

(c)   claims to money or any performance under contract, having a financial value;

(d)   industrial and intellectual property rights such as patents, utility models, industrial designs or models, trade marks and names, know-how and goodwill;

(e)   business concessions conferred by law or under contract including concessions to search for, cultivate, extract and exploit natural resources;

---

* *Source*: Government of Sri-Lanka, Ministry of Foreign Affairs. [Note added by the editor.]

2.   The term "investor" with regard to either Contracting Party means the following persons who invest in the territory of the other Contracting Party:

    (a)   natural persons who, having the nationality of one Contracting Party, in accordance with its laws and are not nationals of the other Contracting Party.

    (b)   legal entities of either Contracting Party which are formed and incorporated under the laws of one Contracting Party and have their seat together with their substantial economic activities in the territory of that same Contracting Party.

3.   The term "nationals" means

    (a)   in respect of the Republic of Sri Lanka :
         persons who are citizens of Sri Lanka according to its laws;

    (b)   in respect of the Government of ....

4.   The term "returns" means the amounts legally yielded by an investment such as profit derived from investment, financial costs, dividends, royalties and fees.

5.   The term "territory" means the territory under sovereignty or jurisdiction of each Contracting Party, and also includes their relevant maritime areas.

ARTICLE 2

PROMOTION AND PROTECTION OF INVESTMENTS

1.   Each Contracting Party shall, subject to its rights to exercise powers conferred by its laws, encourage and create favourable conditions for nationals and companies of the other Contracting Party to invest in its territory, and subject to the same rights, shall admit such investments.

2.   Investments of nationals or companies of either Contracting Party shall at all times be accorded fair and equitable treatment and shall enjoy full protection and security in the territory of the other Contracting Party. Neither Contracting Party shall in any way impair by unreasonable or discriminatory measures the management, maintenance, use, enjoyment or disposal of investments in its territory of nationals or companies of the other Contracting Party.

ARTICLE 3

MOST-FAVOURED-NATION PROVISION

1.   Neither Contracting Party shall in its territory subject investments admitted in accordance with the provisions of Article 2 or returns of nationals or companies of the other Contracting Party to treatment less favourable than that which it accords to investments or returns of its own nationals or companies or to investments or returns of nationals or companies of any third State.

2.   Neither Contracting Party shall in its territory subject nationals or companies of the other Contracting Party, as regards their management, use, enjoyment or disposal of their investments, to treatment less favourable than that which it accords to its own nationals or companies or to nationals or companies of any third State.

ARTICLE 4

EXCEPTIONS

The provisions of this Agreement relative to the grant of treatment not less favourable than that accorded to the nationals or companies of either Contracting Party or of any third State shall not be construed so as to oblige one Contracting Party to extend to the nationals or companies of the other Contracting Party the benefit of any treatment or preference which may be extended by the former Contracting Party by virtue of:

(a)   the formation or extension of a customs or a free trade area or a common external tariff area or a monetary union or a regional association for economic co-operation; or

(b)   the adoption of an agreement designed to lead to the formation or extension of such a union or area within a reasonable length of time; or

(c)   any arrangement with a third State or States in the same geographical region designed to promote regional co-operation in the economic, social, labour, industrial or monetary fields within the framework of specific projects; or

(d)   any international agreement or arrangement, or any domestic legislation relating wholly or mainly to taxation.

ARTICLE 5

COMPENSATION FOR LOSSES

Investors of either Contracting Party whose investments suffer losses due to war or any armed conflict, revolution or similar state of emergency in the territory of the other Contracting Party shall be accorded by the other Contracting Party treatment no less favourable than that accorded to its own investors or to investors of any other third country whichever is the most favourable treatment as regards compensation, restitution and indemnification in relation to such losses. Resulting payments shall be freely transferable.

ARTICLE 6

EXPROPRIATION

1.   Investments by nationals or companies of either Contracting Party shall enjoy full protection and security in the territory of the other Contracting Party.

2.   Investments by nationals or companies of either Contracting Party shall not be expropriated, nationalized or directly or indirectly subjected to any other measure the effects of which would be tantamount to expropriation or nationalization in the territory of the other Contracting Party except for a public purpose and against prompt and effective compensation. Such compensation shall be equivalent to the value of the expropriated investment immediately before the date on which the actual or threatened expropriation, nationalization or comparable measure became publicly known and shall include interest at a normal commercial rate until the date of payment. The compensation shall be paid without delay and shall be effectively realizable and freely transferable. Provision shall have been made in an appropriate manner at or prior to the time of expropriation, nationalization or comparable measure for the determination and payment of such compensation. The national or company affected shall have a right to prompt preview by a judicial or other independent authority of the Contracting Party making the expropriation, of this or its case and of the valuation of his or its investment in accordance with the principles set out in this paragraph.

3.   Nationals or companies of either Contracting Party whose investments suffer losses in the territory of the other Contracting Party owing to war or other armed conflict, revolution, a state of national emergency, or revolt, shall be accorded treatment no less favourable by such other Contracting Party than that which the latter Contracting Party accords to its own nationals or companies as regards restitution, indemnification, compensation or other valuable consideration. Such payments shall be freely transferable.

4.   Nationals or companies of either Contracting Party shall enjoy most-favoured-nation treatment in the territory of the other Contracting Party in respect of the matters provided for in this Article.

ARTICLE 7

REPATRIATION OF INVESTMENT

Each Contracting Party shall in respect of investments guarantee to nationals or companies of the other Contracting Party the free transfer of their capital and of the returns from it, subject to the right of each Contracting Party in exceptional balance of payments difficulties to exercise equitably and in good faith powers conferred by its laws; in conformity with its responsibilities and commitments as a member of the International Monetary Fund.

ARTICLE 8

SETTLEMENT OF INVESTMENT DISPUTES BETWEEN
A CONTRACTING PARTY AND AN INVESTOR OF THE OTHER
CONTRACTING PARTY

1. Any dispute between a Contracting Party and an investor of the other Contracting Party shall be notified in writing including a detailed information by the investor to the host party of the investment, and shall, if possible, be settled amicably.

2. If the dispute cannot be settled in this way within six months from the date of the written notification mentioned in paragraph 1 above, it may be submitted upon request of the investor either to:

(a) The competent tribunal of the Contracting Party in whose territory the investment was made ; or

(b) the International Centre for the Settlement of Investment Disputes (ICSID) established by the convention the settlement of investment disputes between States and Nationals of the other states opened for signature in Washington D.C. on 18th March 1965; or

(c) the Regional Centre for International Commercial Arbitration in Cairo;

(d) the Regional Centre for Arbitration - Kuala Lumpur;

(e) The International Arbitration Institute of Stockholm Chamber of Commerce; or

(f) the Ad-hoc Court of Arbitration established under the arbitration rules of procedures of the United Nations Commission for International Trade Law.

3. The arbitration tribunal shall decide in accordance with:

- The provisions of this agreement;

- The national law of the Contracting Party in whose territory the investment was made;

- Principles of International Law;

4. The arbitration decision shall be final and binding for the parties in the dispute. Each Contracting Party shall execute them in accordance with its laws.

ARTICLE 9

DISPUTES BETWEEN THE CONTRACTING PARTIES

1.	Disputes between the Contracting Parties concerning the interpretation or application of this Agreement should, if possible, be settled through diplomatic channels.

2.	If a dispute between the Contracting Parties cannot thus be settled, it shall upon the request of either Contracting Party be submitted to an arbitral tribunal.

3.	Such an arbitral tribunal shall be constituted for each individual case in the following way. Within two months of the receipt of the request for arbitration, each Contracting Party shall appoint one member of the tribunal. Those two members shall then select a national of a third State who on approval by the two Contracting Parties shall be appointed Chairman of the tribunal. The Chairman shall be appointed within two months from the date of appointment of the other two members.

4.	If within the periods specified in paragraph 3 of this article the necessary appointments have not been made, either contracting Party may, in the absence of any other agreement, invite the President of the International Court of Justice to make any necessary appointments. If the President is a national of either Contracting Party or if he is otherwise prevented from discharging the said function, the Vice President shall be invited to make the necessary appointments. If the Vice President is a national of either Contracting Party or if he too is prevented from discharging the said function, the member of the International Court of Justice next in seniority who is not a national of either Contracting Party shall be invited to make the necessary appointments.

5.	The arbitral tribunal shall reach its decision by a majority of votes. Such decision shall be binding on both Contracting Parties. Each Contracting Party shall bear the cost of its own member of the tribunal and of its representation in the arbitral proceedings; the cost of the Chairman and the remaining costs shall be borne in equal parts by the Contracting Parties. The tribunal may however in its decision direct that a higher proportion of costs shall be borne by one of the two Contracting Parties, and this award shall be binding on both Contracting Parties. The tribunal shall determine its own procedure.

ARTICLE 10

SUBROGATION

If either Contracting Party or its designated agency makes a payment to its own investors under an insurance agreement or guarantee agreement against non-commercial risks it has accorded in respect of investment in the territory of the other Contracting Party, the latter Contracting Party shall recognize:

(a)	the assignment, whether under the law or pursuant to a legal transaction in that country, of any right or claim from the party indemnified to the former Contracting Party or its designated Agency; and

(b)   that the former Contracting Party or its designated Agency is entitled by virtue of subrogation to exercise the rights and enforce the claims of such a party, provided that such Contracting Party shall not be entitled under this paragraph to exercise any rights other than such rights as the national or company would have been entitled to exercise.

The former Contracting Party (or its designated Agency) shall accordingly if it so desires be entitled to assert any such right or claim to the same extent as its predecessor in title either before a Court or tribunal in the territory of the latter Contracting Party or in any other circumstances. If the former Contracting Party acquires amounts in the lawful currency of the other Contracting Party or credits thereof by assignment under the terms of an indemnity, the former Contracting Party shall be accorded in respect thereof treatment not less favourable than that accorded to the funds of companies or nationals of the latter Contracting Party or of any third State deriving from investment activities similar to those in which the party indemnified was engaged. Such amounts and credits shall be freely available to the former Contracting Party concerned for the purpose of meeting its expenditure in the territory of the other Contracting Party.

ARTICLE 11

ENTRY INTO FORCE

This Agreement shall be ratified and shall enter into force on the exchange of instruments of ratification.

ARTICLE 12

APPLICABILITY OF THE AGREEMENT

This Agreement shall also apply to the investments made prior to its entry into force by nationals or companies of either Contracting Party in the territory of the other Contracting Party, consistent with the host Contracting Party's laws.

ARTICLE 13

DURATION AND TERMINATION

This Agreement shall remain in force for a period of ten years. Thereafter it shall continue in force until the expiration of twelve months from the date on which either Contracting Party shall have given written notice of termination to the other. Provided that in respect of investments made whilst the Agreement is in force, its provisions shall continue in effect with respect to such investments for a period of ten years after the date of termination and without prejudice to the application thereafter of the rules of general international law.

IN WITNESS WHEREOF, the undersigned, duly authorised thereto by their respective Governments, have signed this Agreement.

Done in duplicate at .... this ....day of .... in the Sinhalase, …….. and English languages, all texts being equally authentic. In the event of divergence of interpretation the English text shall prevail.

For the Government   **For the Government**

of Democratic Socialist   **of** _____

Republic of Sri Lanka

*   *   *

ANNEX

Bilateral investment treaties concluded between mid-1995 and end-1998[*]

---

[*] The list of BITs up to the middle of 1995 is contained in *volume III* of this *Compendium;* the list of BITs up to 31 December 1996 is contained in UNCTAD (1996), *Bilateral Investment Treaties in the Mid-1990s* (Geneva and New York: United Nations), United Nations publication, Sales No. E.98.II.D.8.

Bilateral investment treaties concluded between mid-1995 and end-1998

Country/territory	Date of signature	Date of entry into force
Albania		
Denmark	05 September 1995	...
Hungary	24 January 1996	01 April 1998
Israel	29 January 1996	18 February 1997
Finland	24 June 1997	20 February 1999
Slovenia	23 October 1997	...
Macedonia, the Former Yugoslav Republic of	04 December 1997	03 April 1998
Portugal	11 September 1998	...
Algeria		
Germany	11 March 1996	...
Mali	11 July 1996	16 February 1999
Jordan	01 August 1996	05 June 1997
China	17 October 1996	...
Viet Nam	21 October 1996	...
Egypt	29 March 1997	...
Niger	16 March 1998	...
Turkey	03 June 1998	...
Bulgaria	25 October 1998	...
Mozambique	12 December 1998	...
Angola		
Italy	10 July 1997	...
Cape Verde	30 September 1997	15 December 1997
Portugal	24 October 1997	...
Antigua and Barbuda		
Germany	05 November 1998	05 November 1998
Argentina		
Israel	23 July 1995	10 April 1997
Ukraine	09 August 1995	06 May 1997
Australia	23 August 1995	11 January 1997
Indonesia	07 November 1995	...

/...

Country/territory	Date of signature	Date of entry into force
Cuba	30 November 1995	01 June 1997
Lithuania	14 March 1996	01 September 1998
El Salvador	09 May 1996	08 January 1999
Panama	10 May 1996	22 June 1998
Viet Nam	03 June 1996	01 June 1997
Morocco	13 June 1996	...
Czech Republic	27 September 1996	23 July 1998
Mexico	13 November 1996	22 June 1998
Guatemala	21 April 1998	...
Russian Federation	25 June 1998	...
South Africa	23 July 1998	...
Nicaragua	10 August 1998	...

Armenia

France	04 November 1995	21 June 1997
Germany	21 December 1995	...
Turkmenistan	19 March 1996	...
Georgia	04 June 1996	...
Canada	08 May 1997	29 March 1999
Italy	23 July 1998	...

Australia

Argentina	23 August 1995	11 January 1997
Peru	07 December 1995	02 February 1997
Chile	09 July 1996	...
Pakistan	07 February 1998	...
Lithuania	24 November 1998	...

Austria

Romania	15 May 1996	01 July 1997
Lithuania	28 June 1996	01 July 1997
Hong Kong, China	11 October 1996	01 January 1998
Ukraine	08 November 1996	01 December 1997
Kuwait	16 November 1996	22 September 1998
South Africa	28 November 1996	01 January 1998
Bulgaria	22 January 1997	01 November 1997
Croatia	19 February 1997	...
Bolivia	04 April 1997	...
Chile	08 September 1997	...

/...

Country/territory	Date of signature	Date of entry into force
Mexico	29 June 1998	...
Azerbaijan		
Pakistan	09 October 1995	...
Germany	22 December 1995	29 July 1998
United Kingdom	04 January 1996	11 December 1996
Georgia	08 March 1996	10 July 1996
Uzbekistan	27 May 1996	02 November 1996
Kazakhstan	16 September 1996	...
Italy	25 September 1996	...
Iran, Islamic Republic of	28 October 1996	...
Ukraine	21 March 1997	09 December 1997
United States	01 August 1997	...
Poland	26 August 1997	...
Kyrgyzstan	28 August 1997	28 August 1997
Lebanon	11 February 1998	...
France	01 September 1998	...
Bahrain		
Egypt	04 October 1997	...
Bangladesh		
Pakistan	24 October 1995	...
China	12 September 1996	...
Philippines	08 September 1997	01 August 1998
Indonesia	09 February 1998	22 April 1999
Poland	08 July 1998	...
Japan	10 November 1998	...
Barbados		
Italy	25 October 1995	21 July 1997
Cuba	19 February 1996	13 August 1998
Canada	29 May 1996	17 January 1997
China	20 July 1998	...
Belarus		
Iran, Islamic Republic of	14 July 1995	...

/...

Country/territory	Date of signature	Date of entry into force
Italy	25 July 1995	12 August 1997
Turkey	08 August 1995	20 February 1997
Ukraine	14 December 1995	11 June 1997
Bulgaria	21 February 1996	11 November 1997
Yugoslavia	06 March 1996	25 January 1997
Czech Republic	14 October 1996	09 April 1998
Pakistan	22 January 1997	...
Egypt	20 March 1997	...
Republic of Korea	22 April 1997	09 August 1997
Latvia	03 March 1998	21 December 1998
Cyprus	29 May 1998	03 September 1998

Belgium / Luxembourg

Estonia	24 January 1996	11 December 1996
Romania	04 March 1996	...
Latvia	27 March 1996	04 April 1999
Moldova, Republic of	21 May 1996	...
Hong Kong, China	07 October 1996	...
Tunisia	08 January 1997	...
Lithuania	15 October 1997	...
India	31 October 1997	...
Philippines	14 January 1998	...
Venezuela	17 March 1998	...
Kazakhstan	16 April 1998	...
Uzbekistan	17 April 1998	...
Pakistan	23 April 1998	...
Cuba	19 May 1998	...
Gabon	27 May 1998	...
South Africa	14 August 1998	...
Mexico	27 August 1998	...

Belize

Cuba	08 April 1998	16 April 1999

Bolivia

Romania	09 October 1995	16 March 1997
Republic of Korea	01 April 1996	04 June 1997
Austria	04 April 1997	...
United States	17 April 1998	...

/...

Country/territory	Date of signature	Date of entry into force
Bosnia and Herzegovina		
Croatia	26 February 1996	...
Iran, Islamic Republic of	27 July 1996	...
Turkey	21 January 1998	...
Egypt	11 March 1998	...
Netherlands	13 May 1998	...
Qatar	01 June 1998	...
Botswana		
Malaysia	31 July 1997	...
Switzerland	26 June 1998	...
Brazil		
Venezuela	04 July 1995	...
Republic of Korea	01 September 1995	...
Germany	21 September 1995	...
Cuba	26 June 1997	...
Netherlands	25 November 1998	...
Brunei Darussalam		
Germany	30 March 1998	...
Oman	08 June 1998	...
Bulgaria		
Spain	05 September 1995	22 April 1998
United Kingdom	11 December 1995	24 June 1997
Yugoslavia	13 February 1996	09 January 1997
Belarus	21 February 1996	11 November 1997
Moldova, Republic of	17 April 1996	11 June 1997
Morocco	22 May 1996	...
Croatia	25 June 1996	20 February 1998
Viet Nam	19 September 1996	15 May 1998
Austria	22 January 1997	01 November 1997
Kuwait	17 June 1997	16 September 1998
Finland	03 October 1997	16 April 1999
Egypt	15 March 1998	...
Uzbekistan	24 June 1998	...

/...

Country/territory	Date of signature	Date of entry into force
Slovenia	30 June 1998	...
Algeria	25 October 1998	...
India	29 October 1998	...
Iran, Islamic Republic of	13 November 1998	...
Italy	05 December 1998	05 December 1998
Cuba	15 December 1998	...

Burkina Faso

Germany	22 October 1996	...
Malaysia	23 April 1998	...

Cambodia

China	19 July 1996	...
Switzerland	12 October 1996	...
Singapore	04 November 1996	...
Republic of Korea	10 February 1997	12 March 1997

Cameroon

China	10 May 1997	...

Canada

Trinidad and Tobago	11 September 1995	08 July 1996
Philippines	10 November 1995	01 November 1996
South Africa	27 November 1995	...
Romania	17 April 1996	...
Ecuador	29 April 1996	06 June 1997
Barbados	29 May 1996	17 January 1997
Venezuela	01 July 1996	28 January 1998
Panama	12 September 1996	13 February 1998
Egypt	13 November 1996	03 November 1997
Thailand	17 January 1997	24 September 1998
Croatia	03 February 1997	...
Lebanon	11 April 1997	...
Armenia	08 May 1997	29 March 1999
Uruguay	29 October 1997	...
Costa Rica	18 March 1998	...

/...

Country/territory	Date of signature	Date of entry into force
Cape Verde		
Cuba	22 May 1997	22 May 1997
Italy	12 June 1997	...
Angola	30 September 1997	15 December 1997
China	27 April 1998	...
Chad		
Egypt	14 March 1998	...
Chile		
Romania	04 July 1995	27 July 1997
Poland	05 July 1995	...
Paraguay	07 August 1995	17 December 1997
Uruguay	26 October 1995	22 April 1999
Ukraine	30 October 1995	29 August 1997
Philippines	20 November 1995	06 August 1997
United Kingdom	08 January 1996	21 April 1997
Cuba	10 January 1996	...
Australia	09 July 1996	...
Greece	10 July 1996	...
Costa Rica	11 July 1996	...
Republic of Korea	06 September 1996	...
El Salvador	08 November 1996	29 March 1997
Guatemala	08 November 1996	...
Nicaragua	08 November 1996	...
Panama	08 November 1996	...
Honduras	11 November 1996	...
Hungary	10 March 1997	...
Austria	08 September 1997	...
Turkey	21 August 1998	...
Tunisia	23 October 1998	...
South Africa	12 November 1998	...
Netherlands	30 November 1998	...
China		
Yugoslavia	18 December 1995	...
Saudi Arabia	29 February 1996	01 May 1997
Mauritius	04 May 1996	08 June 1997

/...

Country/territory	Date of signature	Date of entry into force
Zimbabwe	21 May 1996	01 March 1998
Lebanon	13 June 1996	10 July 1997
Zambia	21 June 1996	...
Cambodia	19 July 1996	...
Bangladesh	12 September 1996	...
Algeria	17 October 1996	...
Syrian Arab Republic	09 December 1996	...
Gabon	09 May 1997	...
Cameroon	10 May 1997	...
Nigeria	12 May 1997	...
Sudan	30 May 1997	...
Macedonia, the Former Yugoslav Republic of	09 June 1997	01 November 1997
Congo, Democratic Republic of	18 December 1997	...
South Africa	30 December 1997	01 April 1998
Yemen	16 February 1998	...
Qatar	09 April 1998	...
Cape Verde	27 April 1998	...
Ethiopia	11 May 1998	...
Barbados	20 July 1998	...

Congo, Democratic Republic of

China	18 December 1997	...
Egypt	18 December 1998	...

Costa Rica

Chile	11 July 1996	...
Spain	08 July 1997	...
Paraguay	29 January 1998	...
Canada	18 March 1998	...
Czech Republic	21 October 1998	...

Côte d'Ivoire

Ghana	04 November 1997	...

Croatia

Slovakia	12 February 1996	05 February 1997
Turkey	12 February 1996	21 April 1998

/...

Country/territory	Date of signature	Date of entry into force
Bosnia and Herzegovina	26 February 1996	...
Czech Republic	05 March 1996	15 May 1997
Hungary	15 May 1996	...
Russian Federation	20 May 1996	...
France	03 June 1996	05 March 1998
Bulgaria	25 June 1996	20 February 1998
United States	13 July 1996	...
Greece	18 October 1996	21 October 1998
Switzerland	30 October 1996	...
Italy	05 November 1996	12 June 1998
Canada	03 February 1997	...
Austria	19 February 1997	...
Kuwait	08 March 1997	02 July 1998
United Kingdom	11 March 1997	16 April 1998
Germany	21 March 1997	...
Spain	21 July 1997	17 September 1998
Egypt	27 October 1997	...
Slovenia	12 December 1997	...
Ukraine	15 December 1997	...
Netherlands	28 April 1998	01 June 1999
Yugoslavia	18 August 1998	...

Cuba

Country/territory	Date of signature	Date of entry into force
Viet Nam	12 October 1995	01 October 1996
Argentina	30 November 1995	01 June 1997
South Africa	08 December 1995	07 April 1997
Lebanon	14 December 1995	07 January 1999
Chile	10 January 1996	...
Romania	27 January 1996	22 May 1997
Barbados	19 February 1996	13 August 1998
Germany	30 April 1996	22 November 1998
Greece	18 June 1996	18 October 1997
Switzerland	28 June 1996	07 November 1997
Venezuela	11 December 1996	...
Slovakia	22 March 1997	05 December 1997
France	25 April 1997	...
Lao People's Democratic Republic	28 April 1997	10 June 1998
Ecuador	06 May 1997	01 June 1998
Cape Verde	22 May 1997	22 May 1997
Jamaica	31 May 1997	...
Brazil	26 June 1997	...

/...

357

Country/territory	Date of signature	Date of entry into force
Namibia	27 June 1997	...
Indonesia	19 September 1997	...
Malaysia	26 September 1997	...
Turkey	22 December 1997	...
Belize	08 April 1998	16 April 1999
Belgium / Luxembourg	19 May 1998	...
Portugal	08 July 1998	...
Bulgaria	15 December 1998	...

Cyprus

Russian Federation	11 April 1997	...
Seychelles	28 May 1998	19 March 1999
Belarus	29 May 1998	03 September 1998
Israel	13 October 1998	...
Egypt	21 October 1998	...

Czech Republic

Kuwait	08 January 1996	21 January 1997
Italy	22 January 1996	01 November 1997
Croatia	05 March 1996	15 May 1997
Ireland	28 June 1996	01 August 1997
Malaysia	09 September 1996	03 December 1998
Uruguay	26 September 1996	...
Argentina	27 September 1996	23 July 1998
Kazakhstan	08 October 1996	02 April 1998
India	11 October 1996	06 February 1998
Belarus	14 October 1996	09 April 1998
Tunisia	06 January 1997	08 July 1998
Uzbekistan	15 January 1997	06 April 1998
Lebanon	19 September 1997	...
Jordan	20 September 1997	...
Israel	23 September 1997	16 March 1999
Yugoslavia	13 October 1997	...
Viet Nam	25 November 1997	09 July 1998
Mongolia	13 February 1998	...
Korea, Democratic People's Republic of	27 February 1998	...
Indonesia	17 September 1998	...
Costa Rica	21 October 1998	...
Paraguay	21 October 1998	...

/...

Country/territory	Date of signature	Date of entry into force
South Africa	14 December 1998	...
Denmark		
Albania	05 September 1995	...
India	06 September 1995	28 August 1996
South Africa	22 February 1996	23 April 1997
Tunisia	28 June 1996	11 April 1997
Pakistan	18 July 1996	25 September 1996
Korea, Democratic People's Republic of	10 September 1996	25 December 1997
Zimbabwe	25 October 1996	02 February 1999
Philippines	25 September 1997	19 April 1998
Lao People's Democratic Republic	09 September 1998	09 May 1999
Djibouti		
Egypt	21 July 1998	...
Malaysia	03 August 1998	...
Dominican Republic		
Ecuador	26 June 1998	...
Ecuador		
Germany	21 March 1996	12 February 1999
Romania	21 March 1996	18 July 1997
Russian Federation	25 April 1996	...
Canada	29 April 1996	06 June 1997
Spain	26 June 1996	18 June 1997
Cuba	06 May 1997	01 June 1998
Dominican Republic	26 June 1998	...
Egypt		
Poland	01 July 1995	17 January 1998
Uganda	04 November 1995	...
Netherlands	17 January 1996	01 March 1998
Sri Lanka	11 March 1996	10 March 1998
Lebanon	16 March 1996	06 February 1997
Republic of Korea	18 March 1996	25 May 1997

/...

Country/territory	Date of signature	Date of entry into force
Jordan	08 May 1996	...
Turkey	04 October 1996	...
Canada	13 November 1996	03 November 1997
Belarus	20 March 1997	...
Algeria	29 March 1997	...
India	09 April 1997	...
Malaysia	14 April 1997	...
Morocco	14 April 1997	...
Singapore	15 April 1997	01 March 1998
Latvia	24 April 1997	03 June 1998
Syrian Arab Republic	28 April 1997	...
Slovakia	30 April 1997	...
United Republic of Tanzania	30 April 1997	...
Viet Nam	06 September 1997	...
Russian Federation	23 September 1997	...
Bahrain	04 October 1997	...
Croatia	27 October 1997	...
Gabon	22 December 1997	...
Niger	04 March 1998	...
Senegal	05 March 1998	...
Guinea	06 March 1998	...
Mali	09 March 1998	...
Bosnia and Herzegovina	11 March 1998	...
Ghana	11 March 1998	...
Chad	14 March 1998	...
Bulgaria	15 March 1998	...
Oman	25 March 1998	...
Palestine Liberation Organization	28 April 1998	...
Djibouti	21 July 1998	...
Cyprus	21 October 1998	...
Slovenia	28 October 1998	...
South Africa	28 October 1998	...
Mozambique	08 December 1998	...
Congo, Democratic Republic of	18 December 1998	...

El Salvador

Argentina	09 May 1996	08 January 1999
Peru	13 June 1996	15 December 1996
Taiwan Province of China	30 August 1996	25 February 1997
Chile	08 November 1996	29 March 1997
Germany	11 December 1997	03 April 1998

/...

Country/territory	Date of signature	Date of entry into force
Paraguay	30 January 1998	08 November 1998
Republic of Korea	07 July 1998	...

Eritrea

| Italy | 06 February 1996 | ... |

Estonia

Lithuania	07 September 1995	20 June 1996
Belgium / Luxembourg	24 January 1996	11 December 1996
Latvia	07 February 1996	23 May 1996
Italy	20 March 1997	...
Greece	17 April 1997	07 July 1998
Turkey	03 June 1997	...
Spain	11 November 1997	01 July 1998

Ethiopia

Kuwait	14 September 1996	...
China	11 May 1998	...
Switzerland	26 June 1998	07 December 1998
Malaysia	22 October 1998	...

Finland

Moldova, Republic of	25 August 1995	21 June 1997
Kuwait	10 March 1996	21 May 1997
United Arab Emirates	12 March 1996	15 May 1997
Indonesia	13 March 1996	07 June 1997
Poland	25 November 1996	11 March 1998
Albania	24 June 1997	20 February 1999
Lebanon	25 August 1997	...
Oman	27 September 1997	20 February 1999
Bulgaria	03 October 1997	16 April 1999
Philippines	25 March 1998	16 April 1999
Slovenia	01 June 1998	...
South Africa	14 September 1998	...

France

| South Africa | 11 October 1995 | 22 June 1997 |

/...

Country/territory	Date of signature	Date of entry into force
Armenia	04 November 1995	21 June 1997
Hong Kong, China	30 November 1995	30 May 1997
Morocco	13 January 1996	...
Croatia	03 June 1996	05 March 1998
Qatar	08 September 1996	...
Lebanon	28 November 1996	...
Georgia	03 February 1997	...
Cuba	25 April 1997	...
India	02 September 1997	...
Moldova, Republic of	08 September 1997	...
Tunisia	20 October 1997	18 January 1999
Macedonia, the Former Yugoslav Republic of	28 January 1998	...
Kazakhstan	03 February 1998	...
Slovenia	11 February 1998	...
Nicaragua	13 February 1998	...
Honduras	27 April 1998	...
Guatemala	27 May 1998	...
Namibia	25 June 1998	...
Azerbaijan	01 September 1998	...
Mexico	12 November 1998	...

Gabon

China	09 May 1997	...
Egypt	22 December 1997	...
Belgium / Luxembourg	27 May 1998	...
Germany	15 September 1998	...

Georgia

Uzbekistan	04 September 1995	...
Iran, Islamic Republic of	26 September 1995	...
Azerbaijan	08 March 1996	10 July 1996
Turkmenistan	20 March 1996	21 November 1996
Armenia	04 June 1996	...
Kazakhstan	17 September 1996	...
France	03 February 1997	...
Kyrgyzstan	22 April 1997	28 October 1997
Italy	15 May 1997	...
Moldova, Republic of	05 December 1997	...
Romania	11 December 1997	12 June 1998

/...

Country/territory	Date of signature	Date of entry into force
Netherlands	03 February 1998	...

Germany

India	10 July 1995	13 July 1998
South Africa	11 September 1995	10 April 1998
Brazil	21 September 1995	...
Zimbabwe	29 September 1995	...
Armenia	21 December 1995	...
Azerbaijan	22 December 1995	29 July 1998
Hong Kong, China	31 January 1996	19 February 1998
Algeria	11 March 1996	...
Ecuador	21 March 1996	12 February 1999
Cuba	30 April 1996	22 November 1998
Kenya	03 May 1996	...
Nicaragua	06 May 1996	...
Venezuela	14 May 1996	16 October 1998
Qatar	14 June 1996	19 January 1999
Romania	25 June 1996	12 December 1998
Lao People's Democratic Republic	09 August 1996	24 March 1999
Macedonia, the former Yugoslav Republic	10 September 1996	...
Burkina Faso	22 October 1996	...
Saudi Arabia	29 October 1996	09 January 1999
Lebanon	18 March 1997	25 March 1999
Croatia	21 March 1997	...
Philippines	18 April 1997	...
United Arab Emirates	21 June 1997	...
Kyrgyzstan	28 August 1997	06 September 1998
Turkmenistan	28 August 1997	...
El Salvador	11 December 1997	03 April 1998
Brunei Darussalam	30 March 1998	...
Mexico	25 August 1998	...
Gabon	15 September 1998	...
Antigua and Barbuda	05 November 1998	05 November 1998

Ghana

Malaysia	08 November 1996	18 April 1997
Côte d'Ivoire	04 November 1997	...
Egypt	11 March 1998	...
Italy	25 June 1998	...

/...

Country/territory	Date of signature	Date of entry into force
South Africa	09 July 1998	...
Greece		
Latvia	20 July 1995	09 February 1998
Cuba	18 June 1996	18 October 1997
Chile	10 July 1996	...
Lithuania	19 July 1996	10 July 1997
Croatia	18 October 1996	21 October 1998
Uzbekistan	01 April 1997	08 May 1998
Estonia	17 April 1997	07 July 1998
Romania	23 May 1997	11 June 1998
Slovenia	29 May 1997	...
Yugoslavia	25 June 1997	08 May 1998
Lebanon	24 July 1997	...
Moldova, Republic of	23 March 1998	...
Guatemala		
Chile	08 November 1996	...
Argentina	21 April 1998	...
France	27 May 1998	...
Guinea		
Yugoslavia	22 October 1996	15 July 1998
Malaysia	07 November 1996	24 February 1997
Egypt	06 March 1998	...
Honduras		
United States	01 July 1995	...
Taiwan Province of China	26 February 1996	...
Chile	11 November 1996	...
France	27 April 1998	...
Hong Kong, China		
New Zealand	06 July 1995	05 August 1995
Italy	28 November 1995	02 February 1998
France	30 November 1995	30 May 1997
Germany	31 January 1996	19 February 1998

/...

Country/territory	Date of signature	Date of entry into force
Belgium / Luxembourg	07 October 1996	...
Austria	11 October 1996	01 January 1998
Japan	15 May 1997	18 June 1997
Republic of Korea	30 June 1997	30 July 1997
United Kingdom	30 July 1998	12 April 1999

Hungary

Albania	24 January 1996	01 April 1998
Croatia	15 May 1996	...
Slovenia	15 October 1996	...
Chile	10 March 1997	...
Singapore	17 April 1997	01 January 1999

Iceland

Latvia	11 June 1998	01 May 1999

India

Germany	10 July 1995	13 July 1998
Malaysia	01 August 1995	...
Denmark	06 September 1995	28 August 1996
Turkmenistan	20 September 1995	...
Netherlands	06 November 1995	01 December 1996
Italy	23 November 1995	26 March 1998
Tajikistan	13 December 1995	...
Israel	29 January 1996	18 February 1997
Republic of Korea	26 February 1996	07 May 1996
Poland	07 October 1996	31 December 1997
Czech Republic	11 October 1996	06 February 1998
Kazakhstan	09 December 1996	...
Sri Lanka	22 January 1997	13 February 1998
Viet Nam	08 March 1997	...
Oman	02 April 1997	...
Switzerland	04 April 1997	...
Egypt	09 April 1997	...
Kyrgyzstan	16 May 1997	10 April 1998
France	02 September 1997	...
Spain	30 September 1997	15 December 1998
Belgium / Luxembourg	31 October 1997	...
Romania	17 November 1997	...

/...

Country/territory	Date of signature	Date of entry into force
Mauritius	04 September 1998	...
Turkey	17 September 1998	...
Bulgaria	29 October 1998	...

Indonesia

Kyrgyzstan	19 July 1995	23 April 1997
Suriname	28 October 1995	...
Argentina	07 November 1995	...
Pakistan	08 March 1996	03 December 1996
Finland	13 March 1996	07 June 1997
Ukraine	11 April 1996	22 June 1997
Sri Lanka	10 June 1996	...
Uzbekistan	27 August 1996	27 April 1997
Jordan	12 November 1996	...
Turkey	25 February 1997	...
Mongolia	04 March 1997	13 April 1999
Mauritius	05 March 1997	29 August 1998
Morocco	14 March 1997	...
Romania	27 June 1997	...
Syrian Arab Republic	27 June 1997	...
Cuba	19 September 1997	...
Bangladesh	09 February 1998	22 April 1999
Sudan	10 February 1998	...
Thailand	17 February 1998	05 November 1998
Yemen	20 February 1998	...
Czech Republic	17 September 1998	...

Iran, Islamic Republic of

Belarus	14 July 1995	...
Tajikistan	18 July 1995	...
Georgia	27 September 1995	...
Philippines	08 October 1995	...
Pakistan	08 November 1995	27 June 1998
Kazakhstan	16 January 1996	03 April 1999
Turkmenistan	23 January 1996	...
Yemen	29 February 1996	...
Ukraine	21 May 1996	...
Bosnia and Herzegovina	27 July 1996	...
Kyrgyzstan	31 July 1996	31 July 1996
Zimbabwe	21 September 1996	...

/...

Country/territory	Date of signature	Date of entry into force
Azerbaijan	28 October 1996	...
Turkey	21 December 1996	...
Lebanon	28 October 1997	...
South Africa	03 November 1997	...
Syrian Arab Republic	05 February 1998	...
Switzerland	08 March 1998	...
Poland	02 October 1998	...
Republic of Korea	31 October 1998	...
Bulgaria	13 November 1998	...

Ireland

Czech Republic	28 June 1996	01 August 1997

Israel

Argentina	23 July 1995	10 April 1997
Kazakhstan	27 December 1995	19 February 1997
Albania	29 January 1996	18 February 1997
India	29 January 1996	18 February 1997
Turkey	14 March 1996	27 August 1998
Moldova, Republic of	22 June 1997	16 March 1999
Czech Republic	23 September 1997	16 March 1999
Uruguay	30 March 1998	...
Slovenia	13 May 1998	...
Romania	03 August 1998	...
Cyprus	13 October 1998	...

Italy

Belarus	25 July 1995	12 August 1997
Barbados	25 October 1995	21 July 1997
India	23 November 1995	26 March 1998
Hong Kong, China	28 November 1995	02 February 1998
Czech Republic	22 January 1996	01 November 1997
Eritrea	06 February 1996	...
Russian Federation	09 April 1996	06 January 1997
Jordan	21 July 1996	...
Saudi Arabia	10 September 1996	22 May 1998
Kenya	16 September 1996	...
Azerbaijan	25 September 1996	...
Croatia	05 November 1996	12 June 1998

/...

Country/territory	Date of signature	Date of entry into force
Macedonia, the Former Yugoslav Republic of	26 February 1997	...
Estonia	20 March 1997	...
Georgia	15 May 1997	...
Latvia	21 May 1997	02 March 1999
South Africa	09 June 1997	...
Cape Verde	12 June 1997	...
Angola	10 July 1997	...
Pakistan	19 July 1997	...
Uzbekistan	17 September 1997	...
Moldova, Republic of	19 September 1997	...
Lebanon	07 November 1997	...
Uganda	12 December 1997	...
Ghana	25 June 1998	...
Armenia	23 July 1998	...
Slovakia	30 July 1998	...
Bulgaria	05 December 1998	05 December 1998

Jamaica

Cuba	31 May 1997	...

Japan

Hong Kong, China	15 May 1997	18 June 1997
Pakistan	10 March 1998	...
Bangladesh	10 November 1998	...
Russian Federation	13 November 1998	...

Jordan

Egypt	08 May 1996	...
Italy	21 July 1996	...
Algeria	01 August 1996	05 June 1997
Indonesia	12 November 1996	...
United States	02 July 1997	...
Czech Republic	20 September 1997	...
Poland	04 October 1997	...
Netherlands	17 November 1997	01 August 1998
Morocco	16 June 1998	...

/...

Country/territory	Date of signature	Date of entry into force
Kazakhstan		
United Kingdom	23 November 1995	23 November 1995
Israel	27 December 1995	19 February 1997
Iran, Islamic Republic of	16 January 1996	03 April 1999
Republic of Korea	20 March 1996	26 December 1996
Romania	25 April 1996	05 April 1997
Malaysia	27 May 1996	...
Azerbaijan	16 September 1996	...
Georgia	17 September 1996	...
Czech Republic	08 October 1996	02 April 1998
India	09 December 1996	...
Uzbekistan	02 June 1997	08 September 1997
Kuwait	31 August 1997	...
France	03 February 1998	...
Belgium / Luxembourg	16 April 1998	...
Kenya		
Germany	03 May 1996	...
Italy	16 September 1996	...
Korea, Democratic People's Republic of		
Denmark	10 September 1996	25 December 1997
Russian Federation	28 November 1996	...
Macedonia, the Former Yugoslav Republic of	15 December 1997	30 April 1998
Romania	23 January 1998	...
Malaysia	04 February 1998	17 October 1998
Czech Republic	27 February 1998	...
Slovakia	27 October 1998	17 April 1999
Switzerland	14 December 1998	...
Kuwait		
Czech Republic	08 January 1996	21 January 1997
Finland	10 March 1996	21 May 1997
Ethiopia	14 September 1996	...
Austria	16 November 1996	22 September 1998
Croatia	08 March 1997	02 July 1998
Bulgaria	17 June 1997	16 September 1998

/...

Country/territory	Date of signature	Date of entry into force
Kazakhstan	31 August 1997	...
Mongolia	15 March 1998	...
Switzerland	31 October 1998	...

Kyrgyzstan

Indonesia	19 July 1995	23 April 1997
Malaysia	20 July 1995	...
Pakistan	26 August 1995	...
Iran, Islamic Republic of	31 July 1996	31 July 1996
Uzbekistan	24 December 1996	06 February 1997
Georgia	22 April 1997	28 October 1997
India	16 May 1997	10 April 1998
Azerbaijan	28 August 1997	28 August 1997
Germany	28 August 1997	06 September 1998

Lao People's Democratic Republic

Viet Nam	14 January 1996	23 June 1996
Republic of Korea	15 May 1996	14 June 1996
Germany	09 August 1996	24 March 1999
Sweden	29 August 1996	01 January 1997
Switzerland	04 December 1996	04 December 1996
Russian Federation	06 December 1996	...
Singapore	24 March 1997	26 March 1998
Cuba	28 April 1997	10 June 1998
Denmark	09 September 1998	09 May 1999

Latvia

Greece	20 July 1995	09 February 1998
Portugal	27 September 1995	17 July 1997
Spain	26 October 1995	14 March 1997
Viet Nam	06 November 1995	20 February 1996
Estonia	07 February 1996	23 May 1996
Lithuania	07 February 1996	23 July 1996
Belgium / Luxembourg	27 March 1996	04 April 1999
Uzbekistan	23 May 1996	29 January 1997
Republic of Korea	23 October 1996	26 January 1997
Turkey	18 February 1997	03 March 1999
Egypt	24 April 1997	03 June 1998
Italy	21 May 1997	02 March 1999

/...

Country/territory	Date of signature	Date of entry into force
Ukraine	24 July 1997	30 December 1997
Belarus	03 March 1998	21 December 1998
Slovakia	09 April 1998	30 October 1998
Iceland	11 June 1998	01 May 1999
Singapore	07 July 1998	18 March 1999

Lebanon

Cuba	14 December 1995	07 January 1999
Spain	22 February 1996	...
Egypt	16 March 1996	06 February 1997
China	13 June 1996	10 July 1997
France	28 November 1996	...
Syrian Arab Republic	12 January 1997	13 October 1998
Germany	18 March 1997	25 March 1999
Russian Federation	08 April 1997	...
Canada	11 April 1997	...
Morocco	03 July 1997	...
Greece	24 July 1997	...
Finland	25 August 1997	...
Czech Republic	19 September 1997	...
Iran, Islamic Republic of	28 October 1997	...
Italy	07 November 1997	...
Azerbaijan	11 February 1998	...
Malaysia	26 February 1998	...
Tunisia	24 June 1998	...

Lithuania

Estonia	07 September 1995	20 June 1996
Viet Nam	27 September 1995	...
Latvia	07 February 1996	23 July 1996
Argentina	14 March 1996	01 September 1998
Austria	28 June 1996	01 July 1997
Greece	19 July 1996	10 July 1997
Belgium / Luxembourg	15 October 1997	...
United States	14 January 1998	...
Portugal	27 May 1998	...
Slovenia	13 October 1998	...
Australia	24 November 1998	...

/...

Country/territory	Date of signature	Date of entry into force
Macedonia, the Former Yugoslav Republic of		
Turkey	09 September 1995	27 October 1997
Slovenia	05 June 1996	...
Yugoslavia	04 September 1996	22 July 1997
Germany	10 September 1996	...
Switzerland	26 September 1996	06 May 1997
Malawi		
Malaysia	05 September 1996	...
Malaysia		
Pakistan	17 July 1995	30 November 1995
Kyrgyzstan	20 July 1995	...
Mongolia	27 July 1995	14 January 1996
India	03 August 1995	...
Uruguay	09 August 1995	...
Peru	13 October 1995	25 December 1995
Kazakhstan	27 May 1996	...
Romania	25 June 1996	08 May 1997
Malawi	05 September 1996	...
Czech Republic	09 September 1996	03 December 1998
Guinea	07 November 1996	24 February 1997
Ghana	08 November 1996	18 April 1997
Egypt	14 April 1997	...
Botswana	31 July 1997	...
Cuba	26 September 1997	...
Macedonia, the Former Yugoslav Republic of	11 November 1997	17 March 1999
Korea, Democratic People's Republic of	04 February 1998	17 October 1998
Yemen	11 February 1998	...
Lebanon	26 February 1998	...
Turkey	26 February 1998	...
Burkina Faso	23 April 1998	...
Sudan	02 August 1998	...
Djibouti	03 August 1998	...
Ethiopia	22 October 1998	...

/...

Country/territory	Date of signature	Date of entry into force
Mali		
Algeria	11 July 1996	16 February 1999
Egypt	09 March 1998	...
Mauritius		
China	04 May 1996	08 June 1997
Mozambique	14 February 1997	...
Indonesia	05 March 1997	29 August 1998
Pakistan	03 April 1997	...
Portugal	12 December 1997	12 December 1997
South Africa	17 February 1998	17 February 1998
India	04 September 1998	...
Switzerland	26 November 1998	...
Mexico		
Switzerland	10 July 1995	14 March 1996
Argentina	13 November 1996	22 June 1998
Netherlands	13 May 1998	...
Austria	29 June 1998	...
Germany	25 August 1998	...
Belgium / Luxembourg	27 August 1998	...
France	12 November 1998	...
Moldova, Republic of		
Finland	25 August 1995	21 June 1997
Ukraine	29 August 1995	20 May 1996
Netherlands	26 September 1995	01 May 1997
Uzbekistan	21 November 1995	17 January 1997
Switzerland	30 November 1995	29 November 1996
United Kingdom	19 March 1996	30 July 1998
Bulgaria	17 April 1996	11 June 1997
Belgium / Luxembourg	21 May 1996	...
Israel	22 June 1997	16 March 1999
France	08 September 1997	...
Italy	19 September 1997	...
Georgia	05 December 1997	...
Russian Federation	17 March 1998	...
Greece	23 March 1998	...

/...

Country/territory	Date of signature	Date of entry into force
Mongolia		
Singapore	24 July 1995	14 January 1996
Malaysia	27 July 1995	14 January 1996
Romania	06 November 1995	15 August 1996
Poland	08 November 1995	21 March 1996
Russian Federation	29 November 1995	...
Switzerland	29 January 1997	...
Indonesia	04 March 1997	13 April 1999
Czech Republic	13 February 1998	...
Kuwait	15 March 1998	...
Turkey	16 March 1998	...
Morocco		
France	13 January 1996	...
Bulgaria	22 May 1996	...
Argentina	13 June 1996	...
Indonesia	14 March 1997	...
Egypt	14 April 1997	...
Lebanon	03 July 1997	...
Spain	11 December 1997	...
Jordan	16 June 1998	...
Mozambique		
Portugal	28 May 1996	...
Mauritius	14 February 1997	...
South Africa	06 May 1997	...
United States	01 December 1998	...
Egypt	08 December 1998	...
Algeria	12 December 1998	...
Myanmar		
Philippines	17 February 1998	11 September 1998
Namibia		
Cuba	27 June 1997	...
France	25 June 1998	...

/...

Country/territory	Date of signature	Date of entry into force
Netherlands		
Moldova, Republic of	26 September 1995	01 May 1997
India	06 November 1995	01 December 1996
Egypt	17 January 1996	01 March 1998
Uzbekistan	14 March 1996	01 July 1997
Slovenia	24 September 1996	01 August 1998
Zimbabwe	11 December 1996	01 May 1998
Jordan	17 November 1997	01 August 1998
Georgia	03 February 1998	...
Croatia	28 April 1998	01 June 1999
Tunisia	11 May 1998	...
Bosnia and Herzegovina	13 May 1998	...
Mexico	13 May 1998	...
Macedonia, the Former Yugoslav Republic of	07 July 1998	01 June 1999
Brazil	25 November 1998	...
Chile	30 November 1998	...
New Zealand		
Hong Kong, China	06 July 1995	05 August 1995
Nicaragua		
United States	01 July 1995	...
Germany	06 May 1996	...
Chile	10 November 1996	...
United Kingdom	04 December 1996	...
France	13 February 1998	...
Argentina	10 August 1998	...
Switzerland	30 November 1998	...
Niger		
Egypt	04 March 1998	...
Algeria	16 March 1998	...
Nigeria		
China	12 May 1997	...
Republic of Korea	27 March 1998	01 February 1999

/...

Country/territory	Date of signature	Date of entry into force
Norway		
Russian Federation	04 October 1995	21 May 1998
Oman		
Sweden	13 July 1995	06 June 1996
United Kingdom	25 November 1995	21 May 1996
India	02 April 1997	...
Finland	27 September 1997	20 February 1999
Pakistan	09 November 1997	...
Egypt	25 March 1998	...
Brunei Darussalam	08 June 1998	...
Yemen	20 September 1998	...
Pakistan		
Romania	10 July 1995	08 August 1996
Switzerland	11 July 1995	06 May 1996
Malaysia	17 July 1995	30 November 1995
Kyrgyzstan	23 August 1995	...
Azerbaijan	09 October 1995	...
Bangladesh	24 October 1995	...
United Arab Emirates	05 November 1995	...
Iran, Islamic Republic of	08 November 1995	27 June 1998
Indonesia	08 March 1996	03 December 1996
Tunisia	18 April 1996	...
Syrian Arab Republic	25 April 1996	...
Denmark	18 July 1996	25 September 1996
Portugal	11 October 1996	14 December 1996
Belarus	22 January 1997	...
Mauritius	03 April 1997	...
Italy	19 July 1997	...
Oman	09 November 1997	...
Sri Lanka	20 December 1997	...
Australia	07 February 1998	...
Japan	10 March 1998	...
Belgium / Luxembourg	23 April 1998	...
Palestine Liberation Organization		
Egypt	28 April 1998	...

/...

Country/territory	Date of signature	Date of entry into force
Panama		
Argentina	10 May 1996	22 June 1998
Canada	12 September 1996	13 February 1998
Chile	08 November 1996	...
Spain	10 November 1997	31 July 1998
Uruguay	18 February 1998	...
Paraguay		
Chile	07 August 1995	17 December 1997
Venezuela	05 September 1996	14 November 1997
Costa Rica	29 January 1998	...
El Salvador	30 January 1998	08 November 1998
Czech Republic	21 October 1998	...
Peru		
Malaysia	13 October 1995	25 December 1995
Australia	07 December 1995	02 February 1997
Venezuela	12 January 1996	18 September 1997
El Salvador	13 June 1996	15 December 1996
Philippines		
Thailand	30 September 1995	06 September 1996
Iran, Islamic Republic of	08 October 1995	...
Canada	10 November 1995	01 November 1996
Chile	20 November 1995	06 August 1997
Switzerland	31 March 1997	23 April 1999
Germany	18 April 1997	...
Bangladesh	08 September 1997	01 August 1998
Russian Federation	12 September 1997	...
Denmark	25 September 1997	19 April 1998
Belgium / Luxembourg	14 January 1998	...
Myanmar	17 February 1998	11 September 1998
Finland	25 March 1998	16 April 1999
Poland		
Egypt	01 July 1995	17 January 1998
Chile	05 July 1995	...

/...

Country/territory	Date of signature	Date of entry into force
Mongolia	08 November 1995	21 March 1996
Slovenia	28 June 1996	...
Yugoslavia	03 September 1996	23 January 1997
India	07 October 1996	31 December 1997
Finland	25 November 1996	11 March 1998
Macedonia, the Former Yugoslav Republic of	28 November 1996	22 April 1997
Azerbaijan	26 August 1997	...
Jordan	04 October 1997	...
Bangladesh	08 July 1998	...
Iran, Islamic Republic of	02 October 1998	...

Portugal

Slovakia	10 July 1995	...
Latvia	27 September 1995	17 July 1997
Mozambique	28 May 1996	...
Pakistan	11 October 1996	14 December 1996
Slovenia	14 May 1997	...
Sao Tome and Principe	18 July 1997	...
Uruguay	25 July 1997	...
Angola	24 October 1997	...
Mauritius	12 December 1997	12 December 1997
Lithuania	27 May 1998	...
Cuba	08 July 1998	...
Albania	11 September 1998	...

Qatar

Romania	06 June 1996	27 April 1997
Germany	14 June 1996	19 January 1999
France	08 September 1996	...
China	09 April 1998	...
Bosnia and Herzegovina	01 June 1998	...
Sudan	03 June 1998	...
Senegal	10 June 1998	...

Republic of Korea

South Africa	07 July 1995	28 June 1997
Tajikistan	14 July 1995	13 August 1995
Sweden	30 August 1995	18 June 1997

/...

Country/territory	Date of signature	Date of entry into force
Brazil	01 September 1995	...
India	26 February 1996	07 May 1996
Egypt	18 March 1996	25 May 1997
Kazakhstan	20 March 1996	26 December 1996
Bolivia	01 April 1996	04 June 1997
Lao People's Democratic Republic	15 May 1996	14 June 1996
Chile	06 September 1996	...
Latvia	23 October 1996	26 January 1997
Ukraine	16 December 1996	03 November 1997
Cambodia	10 February 1997	12 March 1997
Belarus	22 April 1997	09 August 1997
Hong Kong, China	30 June 1997	30 July 1997
Nigeria	27 March 1998	01 February 1999
El Salvador	07 July 1998	...
Yugoslavia	26 July 1998	...
Iran, Islamic Republic of	31 October 1998	...
United Republic of Tanzania	18 December 1998	...

Romania

Country/territory	Date of signature	Date of entry into force
Chile	04 July 1995	27 July 1997
Pakistan	10 July 1995	08 August 1996
United Kingdom	13 July 1995	10 January 1996
Bolivia	09 October 1995	16 March 1997
Tunisia	16 October 1995	08 August 1997
Mongolia	06 November 1995	15 August 1996
Yugoslavia	28 November 1995	16 May 1997
Slovenia	24 January 1996	24 November 1996
Cuba	27 January 1996	22 May 1997
Belgium / Luxembourg	04 March 1996	...
Ecuador	21 March 1996	18 July 1997
Canada	17 April 1996	...
Kazakhstan	25 April 1996	05 April 1997
Austria	15 May 1996	01 July 1997
Qatar	06 June 1996	27 April 1997
Uzbekistan	06 June 1996	30 May 1997
Germany	25 June 1996	12 December 1998
Malaysia	25 June 1996	08 May 1997
Greece	23 May 1997	11 June 1998
Indonesia	27 June 1997	...
India	17 November 1997	...
Georgia	11 December 1997	12 June 1998

/...

Country/territory	Date of signature	Date of entry into force
Korea, Democratic People's Republic of	23 January 1998	...
Israel	03 August 1998	...

Russian Federation

Norway	04 October 1995	21 May 1998
Yugoslavia	11 October 1995	19 July 1996
Mongolia	29 November 1995	...
Italy	09 April 1996	06 January 1997
Ecuador	25 April 1996	...
Croatia	20 May 1996	...
Korea, Democratic People's Republic of	28 November 1996	...
Lao People's Democratic Republic	06 December 1996	...
Lebanon	08 April 1997	...
Cyprus	11 April 1997	...
Philippines	12 September 1997	...
Egypt	23 September 1997	...
Macedonia, the Former Yugoslav Republic of	21 October 1997	09 July 1998
Turkey	15 December 1997	...
Uzbekistan	22 December 1997	...
Moldova, Republic of	17 March 1998	...
Argentina	25 June 1998	...
Japan	13 November 1998	...
Ukraine	17 November 1998	...

Sao Tome and Principe

Portugal	18 July 1997	...

Saudi Arabia

China	29 February 1996	01 May 1997
Italy	10 September 1996	22 May 1998
Germany	29 October 1996	09 January 1999

Senegal

Taiwan Province of China	24 October 1997	...
Egypt	05 March 1998	...

/...

Country/territory	Date of signature	Date of entry into force
South Africa	05 June 1998	...
Qatar	10 June 1998	...

Seychelles

| Cyprus | 28 May 1998 | 19 March 1999 |

Singapore

Mongolia	24 July 1995	14 January 1996
Cambodia	04 November 1996	...
Lao People's Democratic Republic	24 March 1997	26 March 1998
Egypt	15 April 1997	01 March 1998
Hungary	17 April 1997	01 January 1999
Latvia	07 July 1998	18 March 1999

Slovakia

Portugal	10 July 1995	...
Turkmenistan	17 November 1995	10 March 1999
Yugoslavia	07 February 1996	16 July 1998
Croatia	12 February 1996	05 February 1997
Cuba	22 March 1997	05 December 1997
Egypt	30 April 1997	...
Latvia	09 April 1998	30 October 1998
Italy	30 July 1998	...
Korea, Democratic People's Republic of	27 October 1998	17 April 1999

Slovenia

Switzerland	09 November 1995	20 March 1997
Romania	24 January 1996	24 November 1996
Macedonia, the Former Yugoslav Republic of	05 June 1996	...
Poland	28 June 1996	...
United Kingdom	03 July 1996	27 March 1999
Netherlands	24 September 1996	01 August 1998
Hungary	15 October 1996	...
Portugal	14 May 1997	...
Greece	29 May 1997	...
Albania	23 October 1997	...

/...

Country/territory	Date of signature	Date of entry into force
Croatia	12 December 1997	...
France	11 February 1998	...
Israel	13 May 1998	...
Finland	01 June 1998	...
Bulgaria	30 June 1998	...
Lithuania	13 October 1998	...
Egypt	28 October 1998	...

South Africa

Republic of Korea	07 July 1995	28 June 1997
Germany	11 September 1995	10 April 1998
France	11 October 1995	22 June 1997
Canada	27 November 1995	...
Cuba	08 December 1995	07 April 1997
Denmark	22 February 1996	23 April 1997
Austria	28 November 1996	01 January 1998
Mozambique	06 May 1997	...
Italy	09 June 1997	...
Iran, Islamic Republic of	03 November 1997	...
China	30 December 1997	01 April 1998
Mauritius	17 February 1998	17 February 1998
Sweden	25 May 1998	...
Senegal	05 June 1998	...
Ghana	09 July 1998	...
Argentina	23 July 1998	...
Belgium / Luxembourg	14 August 1998	...
Finland	14 September 1998	...
Spain	30 September 1998	...
Egypt	28 October 1998	...
Chile	12 November 1998	...
Czech Republic	14 December 1998	...

Spain

Bulgaria	05 September 1995	22 April 1998
Latvia	26 October 1995	14 March 1997
Venezuela	02 November 1995	10 September 1997
Lebanon	22 February 1996	...
Ecuador	26 June 1996	18 June 1997
Costa Rica	08 July 1997	...
Croatia	21 July 1997	17 September 1998

/...

Country/territory	Date of signature	Date of entry into force
India	30 September 1997	15 December 1998
Panama	10 November 1997	31 July 1998
Estonia	11 November 1997	01 July 1998
Morocco	11 December 1997	...
Ukraine	26 February 1998	...
South Africa	30 September 1998	...

Sri Lanka

Thailand	03 January 1996	14 May 1996
Egypt	11 March 1996	10 March 1998
Indonesia	10 June 1996	...
India	22 January 1997	13 February 1998
Pakistan	20 December 1997	...

Sudan

China	30 May 1997	...
Indonesia	10 February 1998	...
Qatar	03 June 1998	...
Malaysia	02 August 1998	...

Suriname

Indonesia	28 October 1995	...

...

Swaziland

Taiwan Province of China	03 March 1998	...

Sweden

Oman	13 July 1995	06 June 1996
Ukraine	15 August 1995	01 March 1997
Republic of Korea	30 August 1995	18 June 1997
Lao People's Democratic Republic	29 August 1996	01 January 1997
Venezuela	25 November 1996	05 January 1998
Turkey	11 April 1997	08 October 1998
Uruguay	17 June 1997	...
Zimbabwe	06 October 1997	...
Macedonia, the Former Yugoslav Republic of	07 May 1998	01 October 1998

/...

Country/territory	Date of signature	Date of entry into force
South Africa	25 May 1998	...

Switzerland

Mexico	10 July 1995	14 March 1996
Pakistan	11 July 1995	06 May 1996
Slovenia	09 November 1995	20 March 1997
Moldova, Republic of	30 November 1995	29 November 1996
Cuba	28 June 1996	07 November 1997
Zimbabwe	15 August 1996	...
Macedonia, the Former Yugoslav Republic of	26 September 1996	06 May 1997
Cambodia	12 October 1996	...
Croatia	30 October 1996	...
Lao People's Democratic Republic	04 December 1996	04 December 1996
Mongolia	29 January 1997	...
Philippines	31 March 1997	23 April 1999
India	04 April 1997	...
Thailand	17 November 1997	...
Iran, Islamic Republic of	08 March 1998	...
Botswana	26 June 1998	...
Ethiopia	26 June 1998	07 December 1998
Kuwait	31 October 1998	...
United Arab Emirates	03 November 1998	...
Mauritius	26 November 1998	...
Nicaragua	30 November 1998	...
Korea, Democratic People's Republic of	14 December 1998	...

Syrian Arab Republic

Pakistan	25 April 1996	...
Yemen	09 October 1996	...
China	09 December 1996	...
Lebanon	12 January 1997	13 October 1998
Egypt	28 April 1997	...
Indonesia	27 June 1997	...
United Arab Emirates	26 November 1997	...
Iran, Islamic Republic of	05 February 1998	...

/...

Country/territory	Date of signature	Date of entry into force

Country/territory	Date of signature	Date of entry into force
Taiwan Province of China		
Honduras	26 February 1996	...
Thailand	30 April 1996	30 April 1996
El Salvador	30 August 1996	25 February 1997
Senegal	24 October 1997	...
Swaziland	03 March 1998	...
Tajikistan		
Republic of Korea	14 July 1995	13 August 1995
Iran, Islamic Republic of	18 July 1995	...
India	13 December 1995	...
United Arab Emirates	17 December 1995	...
Turkey	06 May 1996	...
Poland	28 November 1996	22 April 1997
Italy	26 February 1997	...
China	09 June 1997	01 November 1997
Russian Federation	21 October 1997	09 July 1998
Malaysia	11 November 1997	17 March 1999
Albania	04 December 1997	03 April 1998
Korea, Democratic People's Republic of	15 December 1997	30 April 1998
France	28 January 1998	...
Ukraine	02 March 1998	...
Sweden	07 May 1998	01 October 1998
Netherlands	07 July 1998	01 June 1999
Thailand		
Philippines	30 September 1995	06 September 1996
Sri Lanka	03 January 1996	14 May 1996
Taiwan Province of China	30 April 1996	30 April 1996
Canada	17 January 1997	24 September 1998
Switzerland	17 November 1997	...
Indonesia	17 February 1998	05 November 1998
Tonga		
United Kingdom	22 October 1997	22 October 1997

/...

Country/territory	Date of signature	Date of entry into force
Trinidad and Tobago		
Canada	11 September 1995	08 July 1996
Tunisia		
Romania	16 October 1995	08 August 1997
United Arab Emirates	10 April 1996	...
Pakistan	18 April 1996	...
Denmark	28 June 1996	11 April 1997
Czech Republic	06 January 1997	08 July 1998
Belgium / Luxembourg	08 January 1997	...
France	20 October 1997	18 January 1999
Netherlands	11 May 1998	...
Lebanon	24 June 1998	...
Chile	23 October 1998	...
Turkey		
Belarus	08 August 1995	20 February 1997
Macedonia, the Former Yugoslav Republic of	09 September 1995	27 October 1997
Croatia	12 February 1996	21 April 1998
Israel	14 March 1996	27 August 1998
Tajikistan	06 May 1996	...
Egypt	04 October 1996	...
Ukraine	27 November 1996	21 May 1998
Iran, Islamic Republic of	21 December 1996	...
Latvia	18 February 1997	03 March 1999
Indonesia	25 February 1997	...
Sweden	11 April 1997	08 October 1998
Estonia	03 June 1997	...
Russian Federation	15 December 1997	...
Cuba	22 December 1997	...
Bosnia and Herzegovina	21 January 1998	...
Malaysia	26 February 1998	...
Mongolia	16 March 1998	...
Algeria	03 June 1998	...
Chile	21 August 1998	...
India	17 September 1998	...

/...

Country/territory	Date of signature	Date of entry into force
Turkmenistan		
India	20 September 1995	...
Slovakia	17 November 1995	10 March 1999
Uzbekistan	16 January 1996	02 August 1996
Iran, Islamic Republic of	23 January 1996	...
Armenia	19 March 1996	...
Georgia	20 March 1996	21 November 1996
Germany	28 August 1997	...
Ukraine	29 January 1998	...
Uganda		
Egypt	04 November 1995	...
Italy	12 December 1997	...
United Kingdom	24 April 1998	24 April 1998
Ukraine		
Argentina	09 August 1995	06 May 1997
Sweden	15 August 1995	01 March 1997
Moldova, Republic of	29 August 1995	20 May 1996
Chile	30 October 1995	29 August 1997
Belarus	14 December 1995	11 June 1997
Indonesia	11 April 1996	22 June 1997
Iran, Islamic Republic of	21 May 1996	...
Austria	08 November 1996	01 December 1997
Turkey	27 November 1996	21 May 1998
Republic of Korea	16 December 1996	03 November 1997
Azerbaijan	21 March 1997	09 December 1997
Latvia	24 July 1997	30 December 1997
Croatia	15 December 1997	...
Turkmenistan	29 January 1998	...
Spain	26 February 1998	...
Macedonia, the Former Yugoslav Republic of	02 March 1998	...
Russian Federation	17 November 1998	...
United Arab Emirates		
Pakistan	05 November 1995	...
Tajikistan	17 December 1995	...

/...

387

Country/territory	Date of signature	Date of entry into force
Finland	12 March 1996	15 May 1997
Tunisia	10 April 1996	...
Germany	21 June 1997	...
Syrian Arab Republic	26 November 1997	...
Switzerland	03 November 1998	...

United Kingdom

Romania	13 July 1995	10 January 1996
Kazakhstan	23 November 1995	23 November 1995
Oman	25 November 1995	21 May 1996
Bulgaria	11 December 1995	24 June 1997
Azerbaijan	04 January 1996	11 December 1996
Chile	08 January 1996	21 April 1997
Moldova, Republic of	19 March 1996	30 July 1998
Slovenia	03 July 1996	27 March 1999
Nicaragua	04 December 1996	...
Croatia	11 March 1997	16 April 1998
Tonga	22 October 1997	22 October 1997
Uganda	24 April 1998	24 April 1998
Hong Kong, China	30 July 1998	12 April 1999

United Republic of Tanzania

Egypt	30 April 1997	...
Republic of Korea	18 December 1998	...

United States

Honduras	01 July 1995	...
Nicaragua	01 July 1995	...
Croatia	13 July 1996	...
Jordan	02 July 1997	...
Azerbaijan	01 August 1997	...
Lithuania	14 January 1998	...
Bolivia	17 April 1998	...
Mozambique	01 December 1998	...

Uruguay

Malaysia	09 August 1995	...
Chile	26 October 1995	22 April 1999

/...

Country/territory	Date of signature	Date of entry into force
Czech Republic	26 September 1996	...
Venezuela	20 May 1997	...
Sweden	17 June 1997	...
Portugal	25 July 1997	...
Canada	29 October 1997	...
Panama	18 February 1998	...
Israel	30 March 1998	...

Uzbekistan

Georgia	04 September 1995	...
Moldova, Republic of	21 November 1995	17 January 1997
Turkmenistan	16 January 1996	02 August 1996
Netherlands	14 March 1996	01 July 1997
Viet Nam	28 March 1996	06 March 1998
Latvia	23 May 1996	29 January 1997
Azerbaijan	27 May 1996	02 November 1996
Romania	06 June 1996	30 May 1997
Indonesia	27 August 1996	27 April 1997
Kyrgyzstan	24 December 1996	06 February 1997
Czech Republic	15 January 1997	06 April 1998
Greece	01 April 1997	08 May 1998
Kazakhstan	02 June 1997	08 September 1997
Italy	17 September 1997	...
Russian Federation	22 December 1997	...
Belgium / Luxembourg	17 April 1998	...
Bulgaria	24 June 1998	...

Venezuela

Brazil	04 July 1995	...
Spain	02 November 1995	10 September 1997
Peru	12 January 1996	18 September 1997
Germany	14 May 1996	16 October 1998
Canada	01 July 1996	28 January 1998
Paraguay	05 September 1996	14 November 1997
Sweden	25 November 1996	05 January 1998
Cuba	11 December 1996	...
Uruguay	20 May 1997	...
Belgium / Luxembourg	17 March 1998	...

/...

Country/territory	Date of signature	Date of entry into force
Viet Nam		
Cuba	12 October 1995	01 October 1996
Latvia	06 November 1995	20 February 1996
Lao People's Democratic Republic	14 January 1996	23 June 1996
Uzbekistan	28 March 1996	06 March 1998
Argentina	03 June 1996	01 June 1997
Bulgaria	19 September 1996	15 May 1998
Algeria	21 October 1996	...
India	08 March 1997	...
Egypt	06 September 1997	...
Czech Republic	25 November 1997	09 July 1998
Yemen		
Iran, Islamic Republic of	29 February 1996	...
Syrian Arab Republic	09 October 1996	...
Malaysia	11 February 1998	...
China	16 February 1998	...
Indonesia	20 February 1998	...
Oman	20 September 1998	...
Yugoslavia		
Russian Federation	10 October 1995	19 July 1996
Romania	28 November 1995	16 May 1997
China	18 December 1995	...
Slovakia	07 February 1996	16 July 1998
Bulgaria	13 February 1996	09 January 1997
Belarus	06 March 1996	25 January 1997
Poland	03 September 1996	23 January 1997
Macedonia, the Former Yugoslav Republic of	04 September 1996	22 July 1997
Zimbabwe	19 September 1996	22 July 1997
Guinea	22 October 1996	15 July 1998
Greece	25 June 1997	08 May 1998
Czech Republic	13 October 1997	...
Republic of Korea	26 July 1998	...
Croatia	18 August 1998	...

/...

Country/territory	Date of signature	Date of entry into force
Zambia		
China	21 June 1996	...
Zimbabwe		
Germany	29 September 1995	...
China	21 May 1996	01 March 1998
Switzerland	15 August 1996	...
Yugoslavia	19 September 1996	22 July 1997
Iran, Islamic Republic of	21 September 1996	...
Denmark	25 October 1996	02 February 1999
Netherlands	11 December 1996	01 May 1998
Sweden	06 October 1997	...

Source: UNCTAD database on BITs.

Note: ... means information not available.

Country/territory	Date of signature	Date of entry into force

PART FOUR

NON-GOVERNMENTAL INSTRUMENTS

DRAFT CONVENTION ON INVESTMENTS ABROAD[*]

(ABS-SHAWCROSS DRAFT CONVENTION)

> Proposals for the negotiation of a multilateral agreement to protect private foreign investment have been made from time to time since the end of the First World War. One of the most significant early efforts was launched by groups of European business people, and lawyers, under the leadership of Hermann Abs, Chairperson of the Deutsche Bank in Germany, and Lord Shawcross, former Attorney-General of the United Kingdom. The initiative began in 1957 when the Society to Advance the Protection of Foreign Investments, an organization of German business people, with headquarters in Cologne, published a draft instrument entitled International Convention for the Mutual Protection of Private Property Rights in Foreign Countries. That version was subsequently revised and, in April 1959, a Draft Convention on Investments Abroad was issued. The Draft Convention, which was under consideration by the Organisation for European Economic Co-operation, was not adopted. The Draft Convention was accompanied by a commentary by the authors. The commentary has not been included in this volume.

The High Contracting Parties:

believing that peace, security, and progress in the world can only be attained and ensured by fruitful co-operation between all peoples on a basis of international law and mutual confidence;

appreciating also the importance of encouraging commercial relations and promoting the flow of capital for economic activity and development; and considering the contribution which may be made towards these-ends by a restatement of principles of conduct relating to foreign investments; have resolved for this purpose to conclude the present Convention.

Article I

Each Party shall at all times ensure fair and equitable treatment to the property of the nationals of the other Parties. Such property shall be accorded the most constant protection and security within the territories shall not in any way be impaired by unreasonable or discriminatory measures.

Article II

Each Party shall at all times ensure the observance of any undertakings, which it may have given in relation to investments made by nationals of any other Party.

---

[*] *Source*: Abs, Herman and Hartley Shawcross (1960). "Draft Convention on Investments Abroad", *in* "The proposed convention to protect private foreign investment: a round table", *Journal of Public Law* (presently *Emory Law Journal*), vol. 1, Spring 1960, pp. 115-118. [Note added by the editor.]

Article III

No Party shall take any measures against nationals of another Party to deprive them directly or indirectly of their property except under due process of law and provided that such measures are not discriminatory or contrary to undertakings given by that Party and are accompanied by the payment of just and effective compensation. Adequate provision shall have been made at or prior to the time of deprivation for the prompt determination and payment of such compensation, which shall represent the genuine value of the property affected, be made in transferable form, and be paid without undue delay.

Article IV

Any breach of this Convention shall entail the obligation to make full reparation. The Parties shall not recognise or enforce within their territories any measures conflicting with the principles of this Convention and affecting the property of nationals of any of the Parties until reparation is made or secured.

Article V

No Party may take measures derogating from the present Convention unless it is involved in war, hostilities, or other public emergency, which threatens its life; and such measures shall be limited in extent and duration to those strictly required by the exigencies of the situation. Nothing in this Article shall be construed as superseding the generally accepted laws of war.

Article VI

The provisions of this Convention shall not prejudice the application of any present or future treaty or municipal law under which more favourable treatment is accorded to nationals of any of the Parties.

Article VII

1. Any dispute as to the interpretation or application of the present Convention may, with the consent of the interested Parties, be submitted to an Arbitral Tribunal set up in accordance with the provisions of the Annex to this Convention. Such consent may take the form of specific agreements or of unilateral declarations. In the absence of such consent or of agreement for settlement by other specific means, the dispute may be submitted by either Party to the International Court of Justice.

2. A national of one of the Parties claiming that he has been injured by measures in breach of this Convention may institute proceedings against the Party responsible for such measures before the Arbitral Tribunal referred to in paragraph 1 of this Article, provided that the Party against which the claim is made has declared that it accepts the jurisdiction of the said Arbitral Tribunal in respect of claims by nationals of one or more Parties, including the Party concerned.

Article VIII

If a Party against which a judgement or award is given fails to comply with the terms thereof, the other Parties shall be entitled, individually or collectively, to take such measures as are strictly required to give effect to that judgement or award.

Article IX

For the purposes of this Convention,

a.   "nationals" in relation to a Party includes (i) companies which under the municipal law of that Party are considered national companies of that Party and (ii) companies in which nationals of that Party have directly or indirectly a controlling interest. "Companies" includes both juridical persons recognised as such by the law of a Party and associations even if they do not possess legal personality.

b.   "property" includes all property, rights, and interests, whether held directly or indirectly. A member of a company shall be deemed to have an interest in the property of the company.

Article X

Final clauses relating to ratification, entry into force, accession, deposit, etc.

ANNEX RELATING TO THE ARBITRAL TRIBUNAL

1.   The Arbitral Tribunal referred to in Article VII of the Convention shall consist of three persons appointed as follows: one arbitrator shall be appointed by each of the parties to the arbitration proceedings; a third arbitrator (hereinafter sometimes called "the Umpire") shall be appointed by agreement of the parties or, if they shall not agree, by the President of the International Court of Justice, or failing appointment by him, by the Secretary-General of the United Nations. If either of the parties shall fail to appoint an arbitrator, such arbitrator shall be appointed by the Umpire. In case any arbitrator appointed in accordance with this Article shall resign, die, or become unable to act, a, successor arbitrator shall be appointed in the same manner as herein prescribed for the appointment of the original arbitrator and such successor shall have all the powers and duties of such original arbitrator.

2.   Arbitration proceedings may be instituted upon notice by the party instituting such proceedings (whether a Party to the Convention or a national of a Party to the Convention, as the case may be) to the other-party. Such notice shall contain a statement setting forth the nature of the relief sought, and the name of the arbitrator appointed by the party instituting such proceedings. Within 30 days after the giving of such notice, the adverse party shall notify the party instituting proceedings of the name of the arbitrator appointed by such adverse party.

3.   If, within 60 days after the giving of such notice instituting the arbitration proceedings, the parties shall not have agreed upon an Umpire, either party may request the appointment of an Umpire as provided in, Article 1 of this Annex.

4.   The Arbitral Tribunal shall convene at such time and place as shall be fixed by the Umpire. Thereafter, the Arbitral Tribunal shall determine where and when it shall sit.

5.   Subject to the provisions of this Annex and except as the parties shall otherwise agree, the Arbitral Tribunal, shall decide all questions relating to its competence and, shall determine its

procedure and all questions relating to costs. All decisions of the Arbitral Tribunal shall be by majority vote.

6. The Arbitral Tribunal shall afford to all parties a fair hearing and shall render its award in writing. Such award may be rendered by default. An award signed by the majority of the Arbitral Tribunal shall constitute the award of such Tribunal. A signed counterpart of the award shall be transmitted to each party. Any such award rendered in accordance with the provisions of this Annex shall be final and binding upon the parties and shall be published. Each party shall abide by and comply with any such award rendered by the Arbitral Tribunal.

*   *   *

Draft NGO Charter on Transnational Corporations[*]

(The People's Action Network to Monitor Japanese TNCs)

The Draft NGO Charter on Transnational Corporations was drafted by the People's Action Network to Monitor Japanese Transnational Corporations Abroad (PAN) and published in January 1998, to serve as guidelines for overseas operations of Japanese corporations.

I. Introduction

Aim of Charter

1.   Foreign investments by corporations from the East Asian region including Japan, Hong Kong, South Korea and Taiwan as well as from other transnational based in other countries, have been flowing into Asia, the current hotbed of economic growth. These investments have seriously affected the local economies, cultures and the lives of the people in the host countries.

While it is explained that investments by transnationals contribute to economic growth and increased employment in the host countries, such investments have also been the root cause of human rights violations, unfair labour practices, exportation of industrial pollution, environmental destruction, over-exploitation of natural resources and cultural conflicts.

2.   The problems relating to transnational corporations are primarily due to the managerial responsibilities of the corporations themselves. I however, at the same time, there are no legal or binding criteria or regulations on the investments by transnational corporations in the host countries, in the home countries and in the international arena.

There have been numerous guidelines, statements, and declarations on transnational corporation's activities by international organisations such as ILO and OECD, and by government or regional organisations. Even the corporations themselves have issued guidelines. However, none of them has legal binding power and most of them are limited to guidelines on business principles.

3.   This draft charter was developed by citizens' groups, labour organisations and other NGOs working on the issues of transnational corporations in Asia. In reflecting their work on these issues, the draft charter has incorporated the code of conduct on transnational corporations and the guideline on monitoring transnational corporations (TNC) by citizens and workers at the international level.

---

[*]   *Source*: People's Action Network to Monitor Japanese TNCs (1998). "NGO Charter on Transnational Corporations (Draft)", *Asian Labour Update n. 26*, October 1997-January 1998; available on the Internet (http://citinv.it/associazioni/COORDNS/archivio/strategie/NGO_charter.html). [Note added by the editor.]

With ever-increasing investments in Asia by TNCs, the monitoring of their activities by NGOs is becoming increasingly important. Therefore, this draft charter primarily aims at establishing criteria to monitor TNCs by concerned NGOs.

II. Code of Conduct for Transnational Corporations

<u>Principles of conduct for transnational corporations</u>

1.   When investing or doing business in the recipient country, transnational corporations must not only contribute to the interests of the host country's government and its business partners, but also provide benefits to the society and public interest of the host country. The business operations of the TNC must be in harmony and coordinated with the local economy and culture. The TNC should make every possible effort to help develop the economic and social independence of the host country.

2.   When planning to do business in the host country, the TNC shall stipulate its basic principles and guidelines for conducting business overseas. Such principles and guidelines must be disclosed in a fully open manner both inside and outside of the company. In particulars the TNC shall ensure access of information to all the rank and file of the company regarding the company's business and activities. At the same time, the TNC shall conduct periodic inspection of its business conduct in reference to its guidelines and principles and the results of the inspection must be publicised.

<u>Conforming with international criteria/guidelines while respecting the sovereignty of the recipient country</u>

3.   As a matter of course, the TNC when doing business in any country shall strictly observe the laws, regulations and administrative orders/practices of a country. However, when a country's laws and regulations in regards to pollution controls, environmental conservation/protection, consumer protection and the basic labour rights are not up to par with international standards, the corporation shall follow the relevant international regulations.

<u>Respecting and upholding basic human rights and freedom of thoughts and beliefs</u>

4.   The TNC when conducting business must respect the basic human rights and fully observe the relevant international standards such as the ILO Charter and the Universal Declaration of Human Rights. In particular, no TNC shall exercise any form of discrimination based on race, gender, religion, language, ethnic group or nationality. At the same time, the TNC shall not discriminate against any individual or group based on philosophy, beliefs or political positions/opinions.

<u>Respecting social and cultural values and customs</u>

5.   The TNC must fully respect and place priority on the social and cultural values and customs and traditions of the locality where it operates. It shall not carry out production, manufacturing or sales activities nor provide services or goods that are deemed by the national or local government and citizens to negatively affect the cultural and traditional values and customs in the locality where it operates.

Ban on political and illegal activities such as bribes

6.   The TNC shall not be involved in or conduct any political and illegal activity wherever it operates including bribes to local and/or national governments, to political or administrative figures, or to specific groups or organisations. It shall not unfairly purchase public or private entities for its own benefit.

Information disclosure

7.   The TNC must publicise, through appropriate means, to the public of the country where it operates, information on the company's entire organisational structure, details of its business activities, and financial and non-financial management conditions. Such information shall be regularly publicised every six months in general or in exceptional cases, every year.

The information publicised shall include at least the following:

(1)   Names and addresses of the local corporation and the investing corporations including the parent company, the form and breakdown of the investments, the fond or nature of the business relationship such as technology transfers and related local and overseas business entities;

(2)   The contents of the major businesses, the financial statements including the balance sheet and the revenue statement and other relevant information of the local corporation;

(3)   The number of employees, working conditions and the information on the labour and management relationship of the local corporation and;

(4)   The pricing policy for merchandise/commodity transfers among the affiliates and other related companies.

8.   The TNC must provide all relevant information on its business activities when required by the local governments, authorities and general public of the place where it operates as well as its labour union.

Guarantee of the three basic labour rights

9.   Regardless the country or region where the TNC operates, it must respect the three major labour rights of works, i.e. the right to organise, bargain and strike. In respecting such labour rights, the following must be specially observed:

(1)   Workers shall be free from any intervention in voluntarily organising themselves into a labour union. Management shall not dismiss, or force a worker to resign or discriminatively treat any individual worker on the grounds that he/she organised or attempted to organise a labour union

(2)   When so requested by the workers representatives who were chosen by the workers, management shall come to the negotiating table in good faith. Management shall observe the following requirements during negotiations:

(i)   Management shall provide the relevant and necessary information on the entire business operations of the company when requested by the workers representatives.

(ii)   Management shall assign a manager who is responsible or has decision-making authority on the issues being negotiated; and

(iii)   Management shall not resort to any forms of threats, such as closure of the plant/factory in response to the workers demands.

(3)   The TNC must guarantee its workers the right to strike or engage in talks to settle labour disputes. The TNC shall not dismiss or unfairly treat any of its employees or workers on the grounds he/she organised or participated in a strike or labour meeting at work. The TNC shall not use violence or any forms of oppression to disperse a labour strike or any labour dispute.

Employment, working conditions and labour-management relations

10.   The TNC shall not exert any form of unfair discrimination against an employee/worker regarding recruitment, employment, job allocation, promotions or any other treatment while making efforts to expand and stabilize employment opportunities in the country it operates. When doing so, the following provisions must be taken into account:

(1)   In order to stabilize and expand employment opportunities, the corporate shall operate on the principle of maximizing local supply of raw materials, parts and facilities while placing priority on local business entities when establishing its business agreements/contracts.

(2)   In making significant changes in its business activities that would have a major impact on employment conditions, the management of the TNC shall submit to the workers and the representatives of the workers organisation a notice of change at the earliest stage possible so that there is enough time for consultation and making any alterations to the plans if necessary. Especially in the case of closures of plants/factories involving massive lay-offs or dismissals, the TNC is required to submit an early notice of such plan and provide sufficient time for negotiations with the workers or their representatives.

(3)   When employing/recruiting, allocating jobs, providing education and training, and promoting employees/workers, the management of the TNC shall adopt the principle of equal employment opportunities and treatment while ensuring no form of discrimination. At the same time, the management shall fully respect the social, cultural and religious customs of the locality where it operates.

11.   In order to contribute to improved employment standards and working conditions in the country where it operates, the TNC shall make conscious efforts to ensure the highest level of working conditions and the optimum labour-management relationship. When doing so, it shall into account the followings:

(1)   The wages and working conditions shall be the highest level among the business entities of the same or similar industry in the country or region it operates. In terms of the labour-management relationship, the TNC shall seek the highest prevailing level.

(2)   Regarding occupational safety, health and hygiene, the TNC shall strictly conform to the relating laws and regulations of the country where it operates as well as to the relevant international conventions, treaties and recommendations. Even within the territory of the country that has not ratified the relevant international agreements or conventions, the TNC shall adopt the relevant standards incorporated within them in the attempt to maintain the highest level of occupational safety and health. In particular, responsible education and appropriate information must be provided to the workers and local residents respectively on safety, health and hygiene related to the company's business operation.

Consumer protection

12.   The TNC, taking full consideration of the effects its business has on the daily consumption patterns and conditions in the place where it operates, shall fully comply with the national and local laws and regulations regarding consumer protection (within the country it operates) as well as with the relevant international standards and regulations. When doing so, the following provisions shall be taken into account:

(1)   Prohibition of the supply of goods and services that a) may harm consumers' health, threaten their safety or impose undesirable effects on them; and b) impose considerable impact on the traditional consumption patterns and lifestyles.

(2)   Consumers shall be clearly and effectively informed the accurate information on the nature and details of the goods and services to be manufactured or sold as well as all the available information on the safety and health regarding such goods and services.

(3)   False and erroneous advertisements shall be illegal.

Protection of nature, the environment and natural resources

13.   The TNC shall take full account of its effect and impact on the environment and natural resources and fully conform to national/local laws and regulations regarding protection of the environment and the ecosystem, and the conservation of natural resources in the country/region where it operates while conforming to the relevant international standards. When doing so, the TNC shall observe the following:

(1)   Implement an environmental assessment and follow up with a review.

(2)   Establish an environmental/conservation policy and guideline and develop a pro-environmental management system.

(3)   Freely disclose information on the company's environmental policy.

14.   When any environmental destruction or other negative impact due primarily to the operations of the TNC, it shall take the appropriate measures including compensation for the damage caused by the environmental damage and restore the environment to its original state.

Responsibility in resolving a dispute

15.   In the case of labour-management disputes and problems with local residents over the TNC's business operations, the TNC shall, as the responsibility of an investor company or as a parent company, make positive efforts to resolve the dispute or problem. When doing so, the TNC shall observe the following:

(1)   Sincerely and honestly respond to demands for information on the TNC's business operations and to questions regarding disputes or problems from the labour union, workers association, local residents, local/national governments or authorities.

(2)   Be fully receptive to the demands for negotiations set forth by the labour union or residents.

Domestic employee issue

16.   The TNC shall not close a plant or factory, or reduce/dismiss employees/workers of low work skills on the grounds that the company is going to transfer its operations overseas or is going to invest overseas. The TNC shall not make foreign investments or transfer its business overseas if it leads to destabilised employment conditions at home. When making such moves overseas, the management of the TNC shall consult with its labour union before implementing such a plan. The TNC shall submit information and data on the following subjects to the labour union for preliminary consultation:

(1)   Aims and purposes of deploying business operations overseas and the details of such plans.

(2)   Current and medium-term plans on production, sales, purchases, capital funding and employment for the planned overseas business.

(3)   Production and employment plans of the currently operating business in the respective country.

III. TNC Monitoring Activities

1.   In monitoring TNCs, it is necessary to establish an organization(s) and system to monitor TNCs on a daily basis and to strengthen national and international networks both in the parent countries of the TNCs (i.e. investors) and the affiliated countries (i.e. recipients of the TNC's investment).

2.   TNC monitoring requires closer cooperation among NGOs in various sectors and of different backgrounds. In particular, it requires stronger links and networks between citizens organisations and labour unions/organisations. International cooperation and the network of NGOs between the investors countries and the host countries are especially important.

Responsibility and roles of the NGOs in the investor's countries

3.   In the investors' countries, it is required for NGOs to conduct daily research on the movements/trends of TNCs based in their own country. When any problem relating to TNC operations is confirmed, the NGO shall immediately contact the head office of the TNC and the

relevant authorities for confirmation and submit the necessary demands and proposals for a solution.

4.   In the investors countries, the NGOs shall provide the necessary information including the managerial data when they are requested by labour unions, residents or citizens organisations or other NGOs working on issues in the host countries.

5.   When the NGOs receive requests for support actions from NGOs in other countries working on the problems relating to a TNC based in their country, they shall plan and carry out the following support actions. However, in such cases, they shall adopt the principle of developing responses to direct requests from the NGO in the other country who is directly involved with the problems relating to the TNC. They shall acquire accurate and clear information on the chronology of events and other details on the issues of dispute or problems the other party is involved in.

(1)   Confirm and clarify the details of the dispute or problems by contacting the head office of the TNC, the relevant authorities and related organisations.

(2)   When the dispute or problem is confirmed on their side, the following initiatives shall be taken;

        i)   Present the demands for a solution to the TNC management and/or perform protest actions if necessary.

        ii)   Develop closer communications and cooperation for the solution among the relevant authorities and organisations and;

        iii)   Organise a campaign within their country.

6.   Standing on the principle that a settlement to the dispute must be carried out through direct negotiations with the parties involved, the NGOs in the investor countries shall press the TNC head office to work for a solution as the responsibility of the investor. When the representatives of the directly-involved party such as the labour union and the local residents association visit the country to seek negotiations with the TNC's head office, the NGOs shall offer their full support. Such support shall be provided on the understanding of the following principles:

(1)   The TNC shall fully respect the decision of the representatives on the agenda, the demands and agreements regarding the negotiations with the TNC head office, as they are the directly involved party. (The negotiations shall be carried out based on the decisions and responsibility of the mission of the representatives).

(2)   The TNC shall fully respect the decision of the host NGOs, i.e. the supporting group in the investor's country regarding how and what to support and organize for the representative's mission.

Roles of NGOs in recipient countries

7.   The NGOs in the countries where the TNC has made investments, may inform and request for the necessary cooperation to the NGOs in the countries where the head offices of the

TNCs are located when human rights violations, environmental destruction and other similar problems have occurred due to or in relation to the TNC's business.

<u>International support and solidarity actions</u>

8.   The strengthened global NGO network is required to effectively monitor and regulate the TNCs. As a first step for such a network, the directory of NGOs working on and are involved with TNC issues in Asia shall be completed while strengthening the communications among them.

9.   In terms of logistics and desirable formation of the international support and solidarity on the problems caused by TNCs, labour unions/workers associations have developed their own networks and rules as a result of their experiences in dealing with many cases. However, NGO in other sectors need to build up and share the lessons from actual cases in the various countries to serve as a guideline.

10.   In the international support and solidarity actions relating to TNC issues, the following shall be taken into account with special attention:

(1)   Provide and inform accurate information.

(2)   Respect the demands of the directly-involved parties while conforming to the integrated strategy and objectives as a shared group.

(3)   Develop and grow based on face-to-face support and solidarity actions.

*   *   *

INTERNATIONAL AGREEMENT ON INVESTMENT[*]

(CONSUMER UNITY & TRUST SOCIETY)

The Consumer Unity & Trust Society (CUTS) prepared a first draft of an International Agreement on Investment for discussions at the UNCTAD Round Table between Ambassadors and NGOs on a Possible Multilateral Framework on Investment, jointly organized with the United Nations Non-governmental Liaison Service in Geneva on 10 June 1998. The draft lays out what, according to CUTS, an equitable alternative international agreement on investment should look like. CUTS considered that the draft provided a good basis for starting discussions, although it could be improved. CUTS made this effort to help the international community in developing investment instruments that would promote social justice, equity, transparency, predictability and accountability.

1. GENERAL PROVISIONS

PREAMBLE

The Contracting Parties to this Agreement,

Recognizing the growing importance of international investment in the world economy and its contribution to development in their countries;

Wishing to establish a well-defined multilateral framework of principles and rules for international investment with a view to the expansion of such investment flows under conditions of transparency, predictability and progressive liberalization and as a means of promoting the economic growth of all Contracting Parties and the development of developing countries;

Desiring the early achievement of progressively higher levels of liberalization of investment flows through successive rounds of multilateral negotiations aimed at promoting the interests of all parties and beneficiaries on a mutually advantageous basis and at securing an overall balance of rights and obligations between and among investors and host countries, while giving due respect to national policy objectives;

Recognizing the right of Contracting Parties to regulate, and to introduce new regulations, on a non-discriminatory basis, on the manner and flow of investments within their territories in order to meet national policy objectives and, given asymmetries existing with respect to the degree of development and market regulation in different countries, the particular need of developing countries to exercise this right;

---

[*]   *Source*: Consumer Unity & Trust Society (CUTS), Centre for International Trade, Economics and Environment (1998). "International Agreement on Investment" (1st draft prepared and presented in June 1998), *Multilateralisation of Sovereignty--Proposals for Multilateral Frameworks for Investment,* Annex (Jaipur, India: CUTS), pp. 85-119. [Note added by the editor.]

Recognizing that investment, as an engine of economic growth, has a vital role in ensuring sustainable economic growth and development, when accompanied by appropriate policies at the domestic and international levels governing the interests of environment, consumers, labour, citizens and culture;

Renewing their commitment to the international covenants and principles enunciated at several international events, such as the Agenda 21 adopted at the Earth Summit, the Copenhagen Declaration of World Summit on Social Development, Bejing Declaration at the Womens' Summit etc. and to observance of the UN Charter on Human Rights and Covenants on Social, Economic and Political Rights, the Tripartite Declaration of Principles concerning Multilateral Enterprises and Social Policy, the UN Guidelines on Consumer Protection etc.;

Reiterating their support for the United Nations Guidelines for Transnational Investment, as fundamental principles of behaviour of firms and contracting parties between and among each other;

Affirming their decision to create a free-standing independent agreement operating under an independent secretariat of the International Agreement on Investment;

Hereby agree as follows:

II. SCOPE AND APPLICATION

DEFINITIONS

1. "Investor" means:

    (i)   a natural person who has the nationality of, or who is permanently residing in, the territory of a Contracting Party in accordance with its applicable law; or

    (ii) a legal person or any other entity constituted or organised under the applicable law of a Contracting Party, whether or not for profit, and whether private or government owned or controlled, and includes a corporation, trust, partnership1 , joint venture, association or organisation <u>as recognised under the law</u> of the <u>Contracting Party</u> in whose <u>territory</u> the investment is made.2

2. "Investment" means:

    (a)   Every kind of asset owned or controlled, directly or indirectly, by an investor, including:

        (i)   an enterprise (being a legal person or any other entity constituted or organised under the applicable law of the Contracting Party, whether or not for profit, and whether private or government owned or controlled, and includes a corporation, trust, partnership, branch, joint venture, association or organisation);

        (ii) shares, stocks or other forms of equity participation in an enterprise, and rights derived therefrom;

(iii)   bonds, debentures, loans to and other form of debt of an enterprise and rights derived therefrom;

(iv)   rights under contracts, including turnkey, construction, management, production or revenue-sharing contracts;

(v)   claims to money and claims to performance;

(vi)   intellectual property rights;

(vii)   rights conferred pursuant to law or contract, including rights conferred by licenses, authorisations, and permits.

(viii)   any other tangible and intangible, movable and immovable property, and any related property rights, such as leases, mortgages, liens and pledges, unless such assets lack the characteristics of an investment.

(b)   "Investment" does not include:

(i)   public debt, debt securities of and loans to a state enterprise or Contracting Party;

(ii)   financial assets, unless the respective claims are assets of an enterprise mentioned in paragraph(a) (i);

(iii)   derivatives where the underlying asset is not regarded as an investment;

(iv)   real estate or other property, tangible or intangible (including rights associated therewith)3, not acquired in the expectation or used for the purpose of economic benefit or other business purposes;

(v)   movable or immovable property, and any related rights, acquired for personal use.

EXPLANATORY NOTE: "Investor"

(a)   The definition of "Investor" covers natural persons as well as legal persons or any other entity constituted or organised under the applicable law of a Contracting Party. It also clarifies that the legal entity may be one organised for profit for it may be one which is not organised for profit such as, charitable institutions or societies. Again, the legal entity may be private or it may be owned or controlled by the Government. It includes *inter alia*:

(i)   a Corporation,

(ii)   a Trust,

(iii)   a Partnership,

(iv)   Sole proprietorship,

(v)   Joint Venture,

(vi)   Association,

vii)   Organisation.

See Article 1 (ii) of "Investment" .

It may be mentioned that in law, a concern which belongs to a single living person is not an artificial entity. It is that very living person itself. It is not distinct from that person.

(b)   It should also be pointed out that a joint venture does not automatically become an artificial legal person, separate from its Constituent members. For example, if company 'A' and company 'B' agree to form a joint venture, then they may or may not form a new company 'C' to operate the joint venture. If they form a new company 'C', then there is born another legal entity. But if they do not form a new company 'C', then no new legal entity will emerge, and company 'A' and company 'B' will be regarded as having formed a partnership. Of course, this is subject to any statutory prohibition that may be operative in this regard, in the country concerned, in its law relating to companies or law relating to partnerships. The words "as recognised under the law of the Contracting Party in whose territory the investment is made", have been used for this reason.

EXPLANATORY NOTE: "INVESTMENT"

The definition of the word "Investment", is intended to be comprehensive. See the words-

"Every kind of asset, controlled directly or indirectly by an investor". The inclusive part of the definition, seeks to cover several specific types of assets-tangible and intangible.

3. "Territory" means:

(a)   the land territory, internal waters, and the territorial sea of a Contracting Party, and, in the case of a Contracting Party which is an archipelagic state, its archipelagic waters; and

(b)   the maritime areas beyond the territorial sea with respect to which a Contracting Party exercises sovereign rights or jurisdiction in accordance with international law, as reflected particularly in the 1982 United Nations Convention on the Law of the Sea.

EXPLANATORY NOTE: "TERRITORY"

The definition is self-explanatory.

APPLICATION

APPLICATION TO OVERSEAS TERRITORIES

A Contracting Party may, at any time, declare in writing to the Depositary that this Agreement shall apply to all or to one or more of the territories for the international relations of which it is responsible. Such declaration, made prior to or upon ratification, accession or acceptance, shall take effect upon entry into force of this Agreement for that State. A subsequent declaration shall take effect with respect to the territory or territories concerned on the ninetieth day following receipt of the declaration by the Depositary.

A Party may at any time declare in writing to the Depositary, that this Agreement shall cease to apply to all or to one more of the territories for the international relations of which it is responsible. Such declaration shall take effect upon the expiry of one year from the date of receipt of the declaration by the Depositary, with the same effect regarding existing investment as withdrawal of a Party.

III. TREATMENT OF INVESTORS AND INVESTMENTS

NATIONAL TREATMENT AND MOST FAVOURED NATION TREATMENT

1.1   Each Contracting Party shall accord to investors of another Contracting Party and to their investments, treatment no less favourable than the treatment which it accords, in like circumstances, to its own investor and their investments with respect to the establishment, acquisition, expansion, operation, management, maintenance, use, enjoyment and sale or other disposition of investment.

1.2   Each Contracting Party shall accord to investors of another Contracting Party and to their investments, treatment no less favourable than the treatment which it accords, in like circumstances to investors of any other Contracting Party or of a non-Contracting Party, and to the investments of investors of any other Contracting Party or of a non-Contracting Party, with respect to the establishment, acquisition, expansion, operation, management, maintenance, use, enjoyment, and sale or other disposition of investment.

1.3   Each Contracting Party shall accord to investors of another Contracting Party and to their investments the better of the treatment required by Article 1.1 and 1.2, whichever is the more favourable to those investors or investments.

1.4   <u>Nothing in paragraphs 1. 1 to 1.3 shall apply to measures adopted by a Contracting Party for compelling reasons connected with its national interest.</u>

EXPLANATORY NOTE:

NATIONAL TREATMENT AND MOST FAVOURED NATION TREATMENT

Article 1.1 of the draft requires each Contracting Party to accord, to investors of another Contracting Party and to their investments, non-discriminatory treatment, that is to say, treatment no less favourable than the treatment accorded by the Contracting Party to its own investors in the like circumstances. The guarantee extends to all the stages ex post investment including the sale or its disposition.

Article 1.2 in the draft provides for most favoured nation treatment and Article 1.3 requires that the better of the treatments envisaged by Article 1.1 and Article 1.2 shall be accorded to the investors.

However, the total prohibition of discrimination between investors, would not be acceptable to certain Contracting Parties, particularly, developing countries. Such countries may, for economic reasons or on socio-cultural considerations, find it necessary to make a discrimination between national and foreign investors, intended to take care of this aspect.

1.5   <u>THE PROVISIONS OF THIS ARTICLE SHALL BE SUBJECT TO THOSE OF ARTICLES 1.A TO 1.K</u>

1.A ENTRY AND ESTABLISHMENT

A Contracting Party shall have the right to impose, on the entry of, and establishment and conduct of business by, investors, restrictions where such restrictions are:

(i)   non-discriminatory in nature;

(ii)   based on vital social, economic or cultural considerations; and

(iii)   mandatory by national legislation or policy of the Contracting Party.

EXPLANATORY NOTE:

The legislature or the executive of a Contracting Party should be able to exclude an investor or type of investor, if such investment is not acceptable, for certain specific reasons. For example, a foreign investor should not acquire the right to produce large quantities of alcoholic liquor, in a country where there is a large segment of the population opposed to drinking alcoholic liquor on religious grounds and national regulations severely limit its production.

(iv)   Entry and establishment have to remain subject to the industrial policy and other policy instruments as per the Contracting Party's preference.

1.B NATIONAL TREATMENT WITHOUT DISCRIMINATION

A Contracting Party shall have freedom to discriminate between an investor of the Contracting Party and an investor of another Contracting Party, where such discrimination is considered absolutely necessary for:

(i)   promoting or maintaining any public utility project in the Contracting Party's territory;

(ii)   for maintaining national security or public order;

(iii)   for preserving public health;

(iv)   for preserving the culture of the Contracting Party;

(v)   protection of consumers against fraud or unfair practices; or

(vi)   for protecting other vital national considerations.

EXPLANATORY NOTE:

Absolute freedom to foreign investors may sometimes damage national cultural values or impair the protection of other national considerations.

Examples can be drawn from the harm that may be caused by unrestricted exhibition of films or unrestricted performance or display of other audio visual or visual entertainment material.

A Contracting State should therefore be allowed to discriminate, for justifiable cause, based on its vital interests of security, public order, consumer protection, of **infant industry**, considerations of unutilised capacity, other economic objectives and preservation of national culture and deep-rooted values.

It may be pointed out that the Treaty of Rome permits (in substance) discrimination against foreign industries, for reasons based on cultural considerations. Again, under the TRIPs Agreement, "public order" is a reasonable ground, justifying compulsory licensing or total denial of **patent** rights.

Besides the above, a country should be allowed to support or subsidise domestic projects in the nature of public works or public utilities. It is vital that investors who invest, should remain permanently in the host country and should not pack off when, for any reason, the going gets tough.

1.C INVESTMENT REGULATIONS: STAND-STILL AND ROLL BACK

A Contracting Party shall be free to adopt or continue (with or without modifications) such restrictive measures in regard to investment as are considered necessary in the national interest. However, a Contracting Party shall use its best endeavours to limit such measures to the absolute minimum.

EXPLANATORY NOTE:

(i)   Under a draft, which totally prohibits regulations discriminations that are discriminatory will have to be cancelled ("rolled back"), and there will be a bar against any further amendments of a discriminatory nature ("stand-still").

(ii)   This would imply, *inter alia*, that the existing national restrictions will have to be deleted.

(iii)   In particular, a total prohibition would invalidate national legislation (if discriminatory) relating to-

      (a)   agriculture;

      (b)   bank frauds (by foreign banks);

      (c)   environment; and

      (d)   health.

(iv)   In view of this, a better alternative would be to frame the relevant provisions in the "best endeavour clause" form. It may be mentioned that the APEC treaty (investment clause), leaves the decisions, in most cases, to "best endeavour clause".

1D TRANSFER OF FUNDS (BALANCE OF PAYMENTS ASPECT)

A Contracting Party shall be free to adopt or continue (with or without modifications) such measures in regard to investments as are considered necessary in the interest of the economy of the Contracting Party, including the rectification or avoidance of an unfavourable position regarding balance of payments. The Contracting Party shall, however, use its best endeavour to limit such measures to the absolute minimum.

EXPLANATORY NOTE:

(i)   Under an unrestricted draft, foreign investors will have the right to all money accruing to them from the investment. These would include-

      (a)   profits;

      (b)   sale proceeds;

      (c)   proceeds of liquidation;

      (d)   amounts received for technical and managerial services; and

      (e)   royalties from intellectual property (the list is illustrative only).

As a consequence, there will be ruled out (for example) restrictions based on the position of a State regarding balance of payments.

(ii)   An unfettered right of the foreign investor to transfer all money would seriously impair the economy of a country whose financial position, for the time being, is critical.

(iii)   Besides this, an unfettered right for the foreign investor would at times itself operate, in practice in a <u>discrimination manner</u> against domestic enterprises and local communities. It may be mentioned that even the WTO accords accept Balance of Payments position, as a basis for special provision (for developing countries).

(iv)   Hence, a "best endeavour clause" would be a proper solution in regard to freedom of transfer of funds.

1.E <u>HUMAN RIGHTS AND CULTURE</u>

A Contracting Party shall be free to adopt or continue (with or without modification), such measures as are required for securing conformity with international treaties, conventions and agreements relating to-

(a)   human rights; and

(b)   cultural protection.

EXPLANATORY NOTE:

International obligations (undertaken by various countries) regarding human rights and cultural protection should be expressly saved.

These are important obligations, which business must observe. A specific provision on the point is needed.

If all countries are signatories to the UN Convention on human rights and cultural protection, then the same must form part of the Investments agreements also, so as to avoid a situation where under human rights etc. may be diluted to suit investors.

1.F <u>CONSUMER PROTECTION</u>

A Contracting Party shall have freedom to adopt or continue (with or without modifications) such measures as are required to ensure compliance with UN Guidelines for consumer protection as amended or revised from time to time, including, in particular, UN Guidelines dealing with the following matters-

(a)   physical safety (including product re-call and product liability);

(b)   economic interests, including competition principles;

(c)   standards;

(d)   essential goods and services;

(e)   health and basic needs;

(f)   redressal of grievances; and

(g)   education and information for the consumer.

EXPLANATORY NOTE:

(i)   There are in existence UN Guidelines for Consumer Protection, 1985 (currently under revision). If investors seek the highest standard agreement on investment, they must be prepared to provide the highest standards of consumer protection. The guidelines developed and accepted by the international community should be followed in maintaining the highest standards of consumer protection. The areas covered include the matters enumerated in the above draft.

1.G RESTRICTIVE BUSINESS PRACTICES

A Contracting Party shall have freedom to adopt or continue (with or without modifications) measures that are required to check anti-competitive business practices, to the extent to which such measures are in substantial conformity with the UNCTAD Code, known as the Set of Multilaterally Agreed Equitable Principles and Rules for the Control of Restrictive Business Practices 1980, as revised from time to time.

EXPLANATORY NOTE:

(i)   There is in existence an UNCTAD set/code on Restrictive Business Practices, known as the UNCTAD Set of Multilaterally Agreed Equitable Principles and Rules for the Control of Restrictive Business Practices 1980.

(ii)   It is desirable that investors should comply with the provisions of the UNCTAD Codes, so as to adhere to the highest standards of competition principles. It may be mentioned that these principles provide protection both to rivals and to consumers.

(iii)   These provisions include the curbing of anti-competitive practices, such as:

     (a)   tied selling;

     (b)   resale price maintenance;

     (c)   exclusive dealing;

     (d)   reciprocal exclusivity;

     (e)   refusal to deal;

     (f)   differential pricing;

     (g)   predatory pricing;

     (h)   cartelisation; and

     (i)   mergers, amalgamations and takeovers.

1.H WORKER PROTECTION (ILO TRIPARTITE DECLARATION)

A Contracting Party shall be entitled to adopt or continue (with or without modifications) such measures as are required to secure conformity with the ILO Tripartite Declaration of Principles concerning Multinational Enterprises and Social Policy 1971, as revised or amended from time to time.

EXPLANATORY NOTE:

(i)   Investment regimes should be consistent with international conventions relating to Workers' Protection. A good model is the Tripartite Declaration of Principles Concerning Multinational Enterprises and Social Policy 1971, adopted by the ILO. This Declaration incorporates adequate guidelines on the basis of the relevant ILO Conventions.

(ii)   Guidelines given in the Tripartite Declaration cover-

    (a)   employment;

    (b)   training;

    (c)   conditions of work and life; and

    (d)   industrial relations.

There may also be need to give workers the right to negotiate work contracts. It should also be ensured that workers in the host country get full protection and decent wages which are not less favourable than those prevailing in the home countries of the investors.

1.I NOTIFICATION OF OPERATIONAL GUIDELINES AND MANDATORY STANDARDS

(i)   Each investor shall keep-

    (a)   the Contracting Party in whose territory the investment is made; and

    (b)   the MAI Secretariat, informed about the operational guidelines and mandatory standards formulated by the investor from time to time for being followed in its branches and units.

(ii)   The MAI Secretariat shall communicate to Contracting States the information received by it under paragraph 1.I (i)(b) above, by issuing periodical circulars as and when needed.

EXPLANATORY NOTE:

(i)   It appears desirable to require investors to notify the MAI Central Secretariat and the host Governments, of all mandatory standards and operational guidelines issued within the investor organisation so as to apply to all its branches and units.

(ii)   Such a requirement would achieve a variety of objectives--

    (a)   It would ensure transparency and allay suspicions on the part of citizens in the host country;
    (b)   It would make available to all concerned the benefit of expertise developed by the investor organisation.

(iii)   Notification by the investor to the MAI Central Secretariat as proposed above, would enable the latter to index the information received from various investors. Notification by the investor to the host country would enable the latter to make the standards etc. available to business persons of the host country.

1.J TRANSFER PRICING AND ACCOUNTING STANDARDS

The Investor shall scrupulously comply with such obligations as may arise under internationally agreed guidelines or standards relating to-

(i)   transfer pricing;

(ii)   uniform transparent accounting, including guidelines and standards on the above matters as evolved from time to time by the UNCTAD or the OECD.

EXPLANATORY NOTE:

(i)   An obligation should be imposed on Investors-

   (a)   not to resort to unfair transfer pricing; and

   (b)   to maintain uniform transfer accountancy standards.

(ii)   It may be mentioned that-

   (a)   the OECD is itself working on transfer price; and

   (b)   the UNCTAD is working on international accounting standards and reporting methods.

(iii)   Provisions to check unfair transfer pricing should prove useful to check unfair methods adopted to transfer profits or overload costs on inter-unit transfer of-

   (a)   technology;

   (b)   raw materials;

   (c)   intermediates; or

   (d)   finished goods.

(iv)   Uniformity in accounting methods would help to check tax evasion and unfair payment of dividends to share holders.

1.K ENVIRONMENTAL PROTECTION

Each Investor shall comply with the guidelines as to Environment Protection, as set out in the Appendix to these Articles.

EXPLANATORY NOTE: The justification for the above is obvious.4

PRUDENTIAL MEASURES

1.1 Notwithstanding any other provisions of the Agreement, a Contracting Party shall not be prevented from taking prudential measures with respect to financial services, including measures for the protection of investors, depositors, policy holders or persons to whom a fiduciary duty is owed by an enterprise providing financial services, or to ensure the integrity and stability of its financial system.

1.2 Where such measures do not conform with the provisions of the Agreement, they shall not be used as a means of avoiding the Contracting Party's commitments or obligations under the Agreement.

TRANSPARENCY

2.1 Each Contracting Party shall promptly publish, or otherwise make publicly available, its laws, regulations, procedures and administrative rulings and judicial decisions of general application as well as international agreements which may affect the operation of the Agreement. Where a Contracting Party establishes policies which are not expressed in laws or regulations or by other means listed in this paragraph but which may affect the operation of the Agreement, that Contracting Party shall promptly publish them or otherwise make them publicly available.

2.2 Each Contracting party shall promptly respond to specific questions and provide, upon request, information to other Contracting Parties on matters referred to in Article 2.1.

2.3 Nothing in this Agreement shall prevent a Contracting Party from requiring an investor of another Contracting Party, or its investment, to provide routine information concerning that investment solely for information or statistical purposes. No Contracting Party shall be required to furnish or allow access to information concerning particular investors or investments, the disclosure of which would impede law enforcement or would be contrary to its laws, policies, or practices, protecting confidentiality.

SPECIAL TOPICS

KEY PERSONNEL

A TEMPORARY ENTRY AND STAY

A Contracting Party, shall, <u>subject to its laws applicable from time to time relating to the entry and sojourn of non citizens</u>, permit natural persons of other Contracting party and personnel employed by legal entities (or other investors who are not natural persons) of other Contracting Parties to enter and remain in the territory for the purpose of engaging in activities, connected with investments.

EXPLANATORY NOTE:

<u>TEMPORARY ENTRY</u>

A particular country be compelled to impose restrictions on entry etc. not only for reasons of public health etc. but also for other reasons.

Examples are:

- Excessive under-employment;
- Over population;
- Regional economic imbalance, etc.

Hence, the draft suggested above.5

EMPLOYMENT REQUIREMENTS

A Contracting Party shall permit investors of another Contracting Party and their investments to employ any natural person of the investor's or the investment's choice regardless of nationality and citizenship, provided that such person is holding a valid permit of <u>sejour</u> and work delivered by the competent authorities of the former Contracting Party and that the employment concerned conforms to the terms, conditions and time limits of the permission granted to such person. (Based on ECT, Article 11 (2)).

IV. PERFORMANCE REQUIREMENTS

PARAGRAPH 1

Subject to the provisions of paragraphs 2 to 7, no Contracting party may impose, force or maintain any of the following requirements, or enforce any commitment or undertaking, in connection with the establishment, acquisition, expansion, management, operation, or conduct of an investment of <u>an investor of a Contracting Party or of a non-Contracting party</u> in its territory:

(a)   to export a given level or percentage of goods or services;

(b)   to achieve a given level or percentage of domestic content;

(c)   to purchase, use or accord a preference to goods produced or services provided in its territory, or to purchase goods or services from persons in its territory;

(d)   to relate any way the volume or value of imports to the volume or value of exports or to the amount of foreign exchange inflows associated with such investment;

(e)   to restrict sales of goods or services in its territory that such investment produces or provides, by relating such sales in any way to the volume or value of its exports or foreign exchange earnings;6

(f)   to transfer technology, a production process or other proprietary knowledge to a natural or legal person in its territory except when the requirement is imposed or the commitment or undertaking is enforced by a court, administrative tribunal or competition authority to remedy an alleged violation of competition laws or to act in a manner not inconsistent with other provisions of the Agreement;

(g)   to locate its headquarters for a specific region or the world market in that Contracting Party;

(h)   to supply one or more of the goods that it produces or the services that it provides to a specific region or world market exclusively from the territory of that Contracting party;

(i)   to achieve a given level or value of production, investment, manufacturing, sales, employment, research and development in its territory;

(j)   to hire a given level or type of local personnel;

(k)   to establish a joint venture; or

(l)   to achieve a minimum level of local equity participation.

PARAGRAPH 2

A measure that requires an investment to use a technology to meet generally applicable health, safety or environmental requirements shall not be construed to be inconsistent with paragraph 1 (f).

PARAGRAPH 3

Paragraph 1 (F) (g) (h) (i) (j) (k) (1) do not apply if the requirements described in one or more of these provisions are conditions for the receipt or continued receipt of an advantage in connection with the establishment, acquisition, expansion, management or operation, or conduct of an investment of an investor (of a Contracting Party or a non-Contracting Party, in its territory), and in particular, if the requirements and the advantage are subject to a contractual obligation between the investor or investment on the one side and the host state or its sub-federal entities on the other.

PARAGRAPH 4

Nothing in paragraph 3 shall be construed to prevent a Contracting Party from conditioning the receipt or continued receipt of an advantage, in connection with an investment in its territory of an investor of a Contracting Party or of a non-Contracting Party, on compliance with a requirement to locate production, provide a service, train or employ workers, construct or expand particular facilities, or carry out research and development, in its territory.

PARAGRAPH 5

Provided that such measures are not applied in an arbitrary or unjustifiable manner, or do not constitute a disguised on international trade or investment, nothing in paragraph 1 (b) or (c) or 3 (b) or (c) shall be construed to prevent any Contracting Party from adopting or maintaining measures, including environmental measures:

(a)   necessary to secure compliance with laws and regulations that are not inconsistent with the provisions of this Agreement;

(b)   necessary to protect human, animal or plant life or health; or

(c)   necessary for the conservation of living or non-living exhaustible natural resources.

PARAGRAPH 6

The provisions of:

(a)   Paragraphs 1 (b), (c), (f) and (i), and 3(b) and (c) do not apply to qualification requirements for goods or services with respect to export promotion and foreign aid programmes.

(b)   Paragraphs (1)(b), (c), (f) and (i), and 3(b) and (c) do not apply to procurement by a Contracting Party or a state enterprise; and

(c)   Paragraphs (3)(b) and (c) do not apply to requirements imposed by an importing Party relating to the content of goods necessary to qualify for preferential quotas.

(d)   Paragraph (1) does not apply to requirements imposed by a Contracting Party as a part of privatisation operations.

PARAGRAPH 7

Notwithstanding anything contained in paragraph 1, a Contracting Party shall be free to adopt a measure otherwise prohibited by that paragraph for compelling social or economic reasons.7

EXPLANATORY NOTE:

PERFORMANCE REQUIREMENTS

In the draft, under the head "Performance Requirements", certain obligations have been sought to be imposed on the Contracting States. Broadly speaking, paragraphs 1 and 3 impose the substantive obligations, while paragraphs 2,4,5 and 6 permit certain relaxations thereof.

Paragraph 1 contains 12 clauses-(a) to (1), these clauses prohibit a Contracting Party from imposing, enforcing or maintaining requirements (or even enforcing any commitment or undertaking) in connection with an investor in its territory failing under any of the 12 clauses. It is not possible here to reproduce, or even to summarise, their content. But, it is sufficient to state that they prohibit the Contracting States from imposing requirements relating to export, production local purchase, volume of imports, sales, transfer of technology, location of headquarters, supply of goods, achieving a given level of production, etc. hiring local personnel, establishing joint venture or achieving a minimum level of local equity participation.

Several points need elaboration.

(i)   harsh set of obligations would become difficult to accept for many countries. Hence some relaxation has to be provided for.

(ii)   Benefiting the national economy through the processes and products of an industry promoted through foreign investment is one of the objects of inviting such investors. This object will be almost totally defeated by a sweeping provision.

(iii)   In particular, a prohibition, in toto, of any stipulations intended to encourage export would mean putting an end to the legitimate desire of learning foreign exchange- desire which is understandable, with an adverse balance of payments position.

(iv)   Again, a prohibition against requiring a foreign investor to transfer its specialised technology to local citizens would, in effect, mean that the level of technology in the host country would remain stagnant for all times to come. If the host country extends certain benefits, it should, in its turn, be allowed to derive benefits also.

V. PRIVATISATION

PARAGRAPH 1 NATIONAL TREATMENT AND MOST FAVOURED NATION TREATMENT

Each Contracting Party shall accord treatment as defined in Paragraph XX (National Treatment, MFN Treatment) in case of a privatisation-

(a)   both as regards the initial privatisation; and

(b)   as regards subsequent transactions involving a privatised assets between investors or investments.

PARAGRAPH 2

Nothing in this agreement shall be construed as requiring any Contracting Party to privatise.

PARAGRAPH 3 TRANSPARANCY

For the purpose of this Article each Contracting Party shall promptly publish the essential features and procedures for privatisation.

PARAGRAPH 4 PRIVATISATION DEFINED

Privatisation means a partial or complete sale or other mode of transfer of the function of the Government or the ownership or control of assets of Government-owned enterprises or Government controlled enterprises-

(a)   from a Government in a Contracting State or from a corporation, authority or entity owned or controlled by the Government in a Contracting State;

(b)   to an investor or investment not owned or controlled by a Contracting Party or by Government or by a corporation, authority or entity owned or controlled by Government in the Contracting Party.

VI. MONOPOLIES/STATE ENTERPRISES

A. MONOPOLIES

1.   Nothing in this Agreement shall be construed to prevent a Contracting Party from maintaining, designating or eliminating a monopoly.

2.   Each Contracting Party shall endeavour to accord non-discriminatory treatment when designating a monopoly.

3.   Each Contracting Party shall ensure that any monopoly that its national or sub-national governments maintains or designates or any privately-owned monopoly that it designates and any government monopoly that it maintains or designates:

   (a)   acts in a manner that is not inconsistent with the Contracting Party's obligations under this Agreement wherever such a monopoly exercises any regulatory, administrative or other governmental authority that the Contracting Party has delegated to it in connection with the purchase or sale of the monopoly good or service or <u>any other matter</u>.8

   (b)   provides non-discriminatory treatment to investors of another Contracting Party and their investments in its sale of the monopoly good or service in the relevant market;

   (c)   provides non-discriminatory treatment to investors of another Contracting Party and their investments in its purchase of the monopoly good or service in the relevant market. This paragraph does not apply to procurement by governmental agencies of goods or services for government purposes and not with a view to commercial resale or with a view to use in the production of goods or services for commercial sale;

(d)   does not use its monopoly position, in a non-monopolised market in its territory, to engage, either directly or indirectly, including through its dealing with its parent company, its subsidiary or other enterprise with common ownership, in anti-competitive practices that might adversely affect an investment by an investor of another Contracting Party, including through the discriminatory provision of the monopoly good or service, cross-subsidisation or predatory conduct.

(e)   except to comply with any terms of its designation that are not inconsistent with subparagraph (b), (c) or (d), acts solely in accordance with commercial considerations in its purchase or sale of the monopoly good or service in the relevant market, including with regard to price, quality, availability, marketability, transportation and other terms and conditions of purchase or sale.

Nothing in Article A shall be construed to prevent a monopoly from charging different prices in different geographic markets, where such differences are based on normal commercial considerations, such as taking account of supply and demand conditions in those markets.

4.   In case of a demonopolisation which has the effect of extending the obligations under the Agreement to a new area, the principle of standstill does not intend to prevent any Contracting Party from lodging any reservation to the Agreement for this new area.

5.   Each Contracting Party shall notify to the Parties group any existing monopoly within (60) days after the entry into force of the Agreement and any newly created monopoly within (6) days after its creation.

6.   Neither investors of another Contracting Party nor their investments may have recourse to investor-state arbitration for any matter arising out of paragraph 3(b), (c), (d) or (e) of this Article.

B. STATE ENTERPRISES

1.   Each Contracting Party shall ensure that any state enterprise that it maintains or establishes acts in a manner that is not inconsistent with the Contracting Party's obligations under this Agreement wherever such enterprise exercises any regulatory, administrative or other governmental authority that the Contracting Party has delegated to it.

2.   Each Contracting party shall ensure that any state enterprise that it maintains or establishes accords non-discriminatory treatment in the sale, in the Contracting Party's territory, of its goods or services to investors of another Contracting Party and their investment.

3.   Neither investors of another Contracting Party nor their investments may have recourse to investor-state arbitration for any matter arising out of paragraph 2 of this Article.

C. DEFINITIONS RELATED TO MONOPOLIES AND STATE ENTERPRISES

1. "Delegation" means a legislative grant, and a government order directive or other act transferring to the monopoly or state enterprise, or authorising the exercise by the monopoly or state enterprise of, governmental authority.

2. "Designate" means to establish, designate or authorise, or to expand the scope of a monopoly to cover an additional good or service, after the date of entry into force of this agreement.

3. "Monopoly" means an entity, including a consortium or government agency, that in any relevant market in the territory of a Contracting Party is designated as the sole provider or purchaser of a good or service, but does not include an entity that has been granted an exclusive intellectual property right solely by reason of such grant or "Monopoly" means any person, public and private, designated by a national or local government authority as the sole supplier or buyer of a good or service in a given market in the territory of a Contracting Party.

4. "Relevant market" means the geographical and commercial market for a good or service.

5. "Non-discriminatory treatment" means the better of national treatment and most favoured nation treatment, as set out in the relevant provisions of this Agreement.

6. "State enterprises" means, an enterprise owned, or controlled through ownership interest, by a Contracting Party.

C—EXCEPTIONS FOR CERTAIN STATES

The provisions contained under "A." Monopolies" and "B. State Enterprises" above, shall not bind Contracting Parties, where their statutory provisions conflict with aforesaid provisions.

EXPLANATORY NOTE:

In countries, where, there is extensive statutory regulation of business, it may be necessary to examine the implications of the obligations so undertaken, regarding investment so that there is no conflict between the statutory framework and the obligations under the multinational agreements on investments.

Hence, the need for the matter under "C—EXCEPTIONS FOR CERTAIN STATES", suggested in this draft.

ARTICLE

1. The Contracting Parties confirm that Article XX (on National Treatment and MFN) applies to the granting of investment incentives.

2. The Contracting Parties acknowledge that, in certain circumstances, even if applied on a non-discriminatory basis, investment incentives may have distorting effects on the flow of capital and investment decisions. Any Contracting Party which considers that its investors or their investments are adversely affected by an investment incentive adopted by another Contracting Party and having a distorting effect, may request consultations with that Contracting Party. The former Contracting Party may also bring the incentive before the Parties Group for its consideration.

3. In order to further avoid and minimise such distorting effects and to avoid undue competition between Contracting Parties in order to attract or retain investments, the Contracting Parties shall enter into negotiations with a view to finalising further arrangements [within three years] after the signature of this Agreement. These negotiations shall recognise the role of investment incentives with regard to the aims of policies, such as regional, structural, social, environmental or R&D policies of the Contracting Parties, and other work of a similar nature undertaken in other fora. These negotiations shall in particular, address the issues of positive discrimination, transparency, standstill and rollback.

4. For the purpose of this Article, an "investment incentive" means:

The grant of a specific nature arising from public expenditure, being any expenditure in connection with the establishment, acquisition, expansion, management, operation or conduct of a investment of a Contracting Party or a non-Contracting Party in its territory.

VII. CORPORATE ENTERPRISES: SENIOR MANAGERS

No Contracting Party may require that an enterprise in the territory of that Party, which is an investment of an investor of another Contracting Party, shall appoint, to senior managerial positions in that enterprise, individuals of any particular nationality. An exception to this obligation shall, however, be permissible where such a requirement, is considered necessary, having regard to the following considerations:

(a) the technical or financial or other participation in the enterprise, contributed by the Contracting Party, or by any Corporation, authority or agency owned or controlled by the Government in the Contracting State; or

(b) some compelling, economic or political interest of the Contracting Party.

EXPLANATORY NOTE:

The draft is self-explanatory.

VIII. APPLICABLE LAW

1. Except as otherwise provided in this Agreement, all investments shall be governed by the laws in force in the territory of the Contracting Party in which such investments are made.

2. Notwithstanding paragraph 1 of this Article, nothing in this Agreement precludes the host Contracting Party from taking action for the protection of its essential security interests or in circumstances of extreme emergency in accordance with its laws normally and reasonably applied on a non-discriminatory basis.

EXPLANATORY NOTE:
The above provision, could become useful in certain situations. (compare Article 12, Government of India model text).

IX. INVESTMENT PROTECTION: GENERAL TREATMENT

1.1. (a)   Each Contracting Party shall accord, to investments (in its territory) of investors of another Contracting State, fair and equitable treatment and full and constant protection and security, <u>including such treatment, protection and security</u> in respect of the operation, management, maintenance, use, enjoyment or disposal of such investment.

(b)   In no such case shall a Contracting Party accord, to such investments, treatment or <u>protection</u> that is less favourable than that required by <u>customary</u> international law.

EXPLANATORY NOTE:

The draft is self-explanatory.

EXPROPRIATION AND COMPENSATION

2.1 A Contracting Party shall not expropriate or nationalise directly or indirectly an investment in its territory of an investor of another Contracting Party or take any measure or measures having equivalent effect (hereinafter referred to as "expropriation"") except :

(a)   for a purpose which is in the public interest;

(b)   on a non-discriminatory basis;

(c)   in accordance with due process of law; and

(d)   accompanied by payment of prompt, adequate and effective compensation in accordance with Articles 2.2 to 2.5 below.

2.2 Compensation shall be paid without delay.

2.3 Compensation shall be equivalent to the fair market value of the expropriated investment immediately before the expropriation occurred. The fair market value shall not reflect any change in value occurring because the expropriation had become publicly known earlier.

2.4 Compensation shall be fully realisable and freely transferable.

2.5 Compensation shall include interest at a commercial rate established on a market basis for the currency of payment from the date of expropriation until the date of actual payment.

2.6 Due process of law includes, in particular, the right of an investor of a Contracting Party which claims to be affected by expropriation by another Contracting Party to prompt review of its case, including the valuation of its investment and the payment of compensation in accordance with the provisions of this article, by a judicial authority or another competent and independent authority of the latter Contracting Party.

2.7 <u>For the purpose of deciding whether expropriation by a Contracting Party is for a purpose which is in the public interest within the meaning of clause (a) of Article 2, it shall be permissible</u> to use the following as persuasive (though not binding) material, namely:

(a)   statutory precedents in the Contracting Party (in whose territory the investment is situated), providing for expropriation of any property, undertaking or assets;

(b)   judicial decisions relevant to the concept of public purpose or analogical concepts in the context of expropriation of any property, undertaking or assets."

EXPLANATORY NOTE:

2. EXPROPRIATION AND COMPENSATION

Paragraph 2.1 to 2.6 deal with expropriation and compensation. The main emphasis is on compensation or expropriation or nationalisation of investments. The most important article is Article 2.1, which provides that expropriation must be:

(a)   for a purpose which is in the public interest;

(b)   on a non-discriminatory basis;

(c)   in accordance with due process of law; and

(d)   accompanied by prompt, adequate and effective compensation.

The meaning of "due process of law" (required under Article 2.1) is spelt out in paragraph 2.6.

The concept of "public purpose", is generally regarded as an essential ingredient of the validity of acquisition of property by the Government. In India, this is, for example, an essential requirement for acquiring land under the Land Acquisition Act, 1894. In fact, (leaving aside enactments of the land), from the wider perspective of constitutional law also, it is implicit that acquisition of the property of a citizen by the State can be ordered only for a public purpose. In India also, though Article 31 of the Constitution was deleted by a later amendment, the requirement of public purpose for acquisition of property still continues according to general thinking on the subject.

Further, it needs to be mentioned that in India, case law as to "public purpose" (in the context of acquisition of land etc.) is highly rich in its content and fairly prolific in its volume and variety. A number of nice points which could not be conveniently incorporated in the statutory language have been settled by the case law. It seems desirable to provide, in the draft agreement under consideration, that such law shall have persuasive value for interpreting an agreement like the MAI Agreement. It may also be mentioned that in practice, law officers who have to advise the Government or a Government corporation in connection with an acquisition, or who have to draft or scrutinise proposed legislation involving acquisition of property, usually study and follow the Indian case law on the subject.

It is proper that the benefit of the extensive case law on the subject should not be lost and that such case law should be regarded as relevant, for the purpose of interpreting the MAI Agreement also.

Accordingly, it is suggested that, Article 2.7 should be incorporated as proposed in this draft.

3. PROTECTION FROM STRIFE

3.1 An investor of a Contracting Party which has suffered losses relating to its investment in the territory of an another Contracting Party due to war or other armed conflict, state of emergency, revolution, insurrection, civil disturbance, or any other similar event in the territory of the latter Contracting Party, shall be accorded by the latter Contracting Party, as regards restitution, indemnification, compensation or any other settlement, treatment no less favourable than that which it accords to its own investors or to investors of any third State, whichever is most favourable to the investor.

3.2 Notwithstanding Article 3.1, an investor of a Contracting Party which, in any of the situations referred to in that paragraph, suffers a loss in the territory of another Contracting Party resulting from:

(a)   requisitioning of its investment or part thereof by the latter's forces or authorities, or

(b)   destruction of its investment or part thereof by the latter's forces or authorities, which was not required by the necessity of the situation, shall be accorded by the latter Contracting Party restitution or compensation which in either case shall be prompt, adequate and effective and, with respect to compensation, shall be in accordance with Articles 2.1 to 2.5.

4. TRANSFERS

4.1 Each Contracting Party shall ensure that all payments relating to an investment, in its territory, of an investor of another Contracting Party may be freely transferred into and out of its territory without delay. Such transfer shall include, in particular, though not exclusively:

(a)   the initial capital and additional amounts to maintain or increase an investment;

(b)   returns;

(c)   payments made under a contract, including a loan agreement;

(d)   proceeds from the sale or liquidation of all or any part of an investment;

(e)   payments of compensation under Articles 2 and 3;

(f)   payments arising out of the settlement of a dispute;

(g)   earnings and other remuneration of personnel engaged from abroad in connection with an investment.

4.2 Each Contracting Party shall further ensure that such transfers may be made in a freely convertible currency. [Freely convertible currency which is widely traded in international foreign exchange markets and widely used in international transactions.] or [Freely convertible currency means a currency which is, in fact, widely used to make payments for international transactions and is widely traded in the principal exchange markets].

4.3 Each Contracting Party shall also further ensure that such transfers may be made at the market rate of exchange prevailing on the date of transfer.

4.4 In the absence of a market for foreign exchange, the rate to be used shall be the most recent exchange rate for conversion of currencies into Special Drawing Rights.

4.5 Notwithstanding Article 4.1 (b) above, a Contracting Party may restrict the transfer of a return in kind in circumstances where the Contracting Party is permitted under the GATT 1994 to restrict or prohibit the exportation or the sale for export of the product constituting the return in kind. Nevertheless, a Contracting Party shall ensure that transfers of returns in kind may be effected as authorised or specified in an investment agreement, investment authorisation, or other written agreement between the Contracting Party and an investor or investment of another Contracting Party.

4.6 Notwithstanding Articles 4.1 to 4.5, a Contracting Party may require reports of transfers of currency or other monetary instruments and ensure the satisfaction of judgements in civil, administrative and criminal proceedings through the equitable, non-discriminatory, and good faith application of its laws and regulations. Such requirements shall not unreasonably impair or derogate from the free and undelayed transfer ensured by this Agreement.

5. SUBROGATION

5.1 If a Contracting Party or its designated agency makes a payment under a indemnity, guarantee or contract of insurance given in respect of an investment of an investor in the territory of another Contracting Party, the latter Contracting Party shall recognise the assignment of any right or claim of such investor to the former Contracting Party or its designated agency and the right of the former Contracting Party or its designated agency to exercise, by virtue of subrogation, any such right and claim to the same extent as its predecessor in title.

5.2 A Contracting Party shall not assert as a defence, counterclaim, right of set-off or for any other reason, that indemnification or other compensation for all part of the alleged damages has been received or will be received pursuant to an indemnity, guarantee or insurance contract.

6. PROTECTING EXISTING INVESTMENTS

This Agreement shall apply to investments made prior to its entry into force for the Contracting Parties concerned and would be consistent with the legislation of the Contracting Party in whose territory it was made as well as investments made thereafter. This Agreement shall not apply to claim arising out of events which occurred, or to claims which had been settled, prior to its entry into force. Or this Agreement shall apply to investments existing at the time of entry into force as well as to those established or acquired thereafter.

7. PROTECTING INVESTOR RIGHTS FROM OTHER AGREEMENTS

Substantive Approach-Inclusive Respect Clause

Each Contracting Party shall observe any obligation it has entered into with regard to a specific investment of a national of another Contracting Party.

Procedural Approach-Limited Scope Dispute Settlement Clause

An investor of another Contracting Party may submit to arbitration in accordance any investment dispute arising under the provisions of this Agreement or concerning any obligation which the Contracting Party has entered into with regard to a specific investment of the investor through:

(a)   an investment authorisation granted by its competent authorities specifically to the investor or investment, or

(b)   a written investment agreement or contract granting rights with respect to natural resources or other assets or economic activities controlled by the national authorities, and on which the investor has relied in establishing, acquiring, or significantly expanding an investment.

X. DISPUTE SETTLEMENT: STATE-STATE PROCEDURES

A. GENERAL PROVISIONS

1.   The rules and procedures set out in Articles A-C shall apply to the avoidance of conflicts and the resolution of disputes between Contracting Parties regarding the interpretation or application of the Agreement, unless the disputing parties agree to apply other rules or procedures. However, the disputing Parties may not depart from any obligation regarding notification of the Parties Group and the right of Parties to present views, under Article B, paragraphs [1.a and 3.c], and Article C, paragraphs 1.a, 1c, and 4.e.

2.   Contracting Parties and other participants in proceedings shall protect any confidential or proprietary information which may be revealed in course of proceedings under Articles B and C and which is designated as such by the Party providing the information. Contracting Parties and other participants in the proceedings may not reveal such information without written authorisation from the Party which provided it.

B. CONSULTATION, CONCILIATION AND MEDIATION

1. CONSULTATION

(a)   One or more Contracting Parties may request any other Contracting Party to enter into consultations regarding any dispute about the interpretation or application of the Agreement.9

The request shall be submitted in writing and shall provide sufficient information to understand the basis for the request, including identification of the measures at issue. The requesting Party shall promptly enter into consultations. The requesting Contracting Party [may][shall]notify the Parties Group of the request for consultation.

(b)   A Contracting Party may not initiate arbitration against another Contracting Party under Article C of this Agreement, unless the former Contracting Party has requested consultation and has afforded that other Contracting Party a consultation period of no less than 60 days after the date of the receipt of the request.

2. MULTILATERAL CONSULTATIONS

(a)   In the event that consultations under paragraph 1 of this Article, have failed to resolve the dispute within 50 days after the date of receipt of the request for those consultations, [either Contracting Party in dispute] [the Contracting Parties in dispute, by Agreement] may request the Parties Group to consider the matter.

(b)   Such request shall be submitted in writing and shall give the reason for it, including identification of the measures at issue, and shall indicate the legal basis for the complaint.

(c)   The Parties Group may only adopt clarifications on issues of law and on the provisions of the agreement that have been raised by [one on the Parties in dispute, in accordance with

Article [Article which will allow the Parties Group to adopt clarifications in accordance with a procedure to be defined]. The Parties Group shall conclude its deliberations within [60] days after the date of receipt of the request.

(d)   In the event that a dispute is submitted to the Parties Group, none of the Contracting Parties shall submit the case to the arbitral tribunal before the expiration of the period delay mentioned in the paragraph C.

3. MEDIATION OR CONCILIATION

If the Parties are unable to reach a mutually satisfactory resolution of a matter through consultations, they may have recourse to good offices, including those of the Parties Group, or to mediation or conciliation under such rules and procedures as they may agree.

4. CONFIDENTIALITY OF PROCEEDINGS, NOTIFICATION OF RESULTS

(a)   Proceedings involving consultations, mediation or conciliation shall be confidential.

(b)   No Contracting Party may, in any binding legal proceedings, invoke or rely upon any statement made or position taken by another Contracting Party in consultations, conciliation or mediation proceedings initiated under this Agreement.

(c)   The Parties to consultations, mediation, or conciliation under this Agreement shall inform the Parties Group of any mutually agreed solution.

ARBITRATION

1. SCOPE AND INITIATION OF PROCEEDINGS

(a)   Any dispute between Contracting Parties concerning [the interpretation or application of] this Agreement shall, at the request of any Contracting Party that is a Party to the dispute and has complied with the consultations requirements of Article B, be submitted to an arbitral tribunal for binding decision. A request, identifying the matters in dispute, shall be delivered to the other Party through diplomatic channels, [unless a Contracting Party has designated another channel for notification and so notified the Depositary10 and a copy of the request shall be delivered to the Parties Group.

(b)   A Contracting Party may not initiate proceedings under this Article for a dispute which its investor has submitted, or consented to submit, to arbitration under Article D, unless the other Contracting Party has failed to abide by and comply with the award rendered in that dispute.

2. FORMATION OF THE TRIBUNAL

(a)   Within 30 days after receipt of a request for arbitration, each Party or, in the event there is more than one requesting Party, each side to the dispute shall appoint one member of that tribunal. Within 30 days after their appointment, the two members shall, in consultation with the Parties in dispute, select a national of a third State who will be Chairman of the tribunal. At the option of any Party or side, two additional members may be appointed, one by each Party or side.

(b)   If the necessary appointments have not been made within the periods specified in subparagraph (a) above, either Party or side to the dispute may, in the absence of any other agreement, invite the Secretary General of the Centre of the Settlement of Investment Disputes to make the necessary appointments. The Secretary General shall do so, as far as possible, in consultations with the Parties and within thirty days after receipt of the request.

(c)   Parties and the [Secretary General] [Parties Group Secretariat] should consider appointment, to the tribunal, of members of a roster of highly qualified individuals, willing and able to serve on arbitral tribunals under this Agreement, nominated by the Contracting Parties. If arbitration of a dispute requires special expertise on the tribunal, rather than solely through expert advice under the rules governing the arbitration, the appointments of individuals possessing expertise not found on the roster should be considered. Each Contracting Party should nominate up to (four) members of the tribunal roster. Nominations are valid for the renewable terms of five years.

(d)   Any vacancies which may arise in a tribunal shall be filled by the procedure by which the original appointment has been made.

(e)   Members of a particular arbitral tribunal shall be independent and impartial.

3. JOINDER/CONSOLIDATION 11

(a)   Contracting Parties in dispute with the same Contracting Party over the same matter should act together, as far as practicable, for purposes of dispute settlement under this Article. Where more than one Contracting Party requests the submission to an arbitral tribunal of a dispute with the same Contracting Party relating to the same measure, the disputes shall, if feasible, be considered by a single arbitral tribunal.

(b)   To the extent feasible, if more than one arbitral tribunal is formed, the same persons shall be appointed as members of both and the time tables of the proceedings shall be harmonised.

4. THIRD PARTIES

Any Contracting Party wishing to do so shall be given an opportunity to present its views to the arbitral tribunal on the issues in dispute. The tribunal shall establish the deadlines for such submissions in light of the schedule of the proceedings and shall notify such deadlines, at least thirty days in advance thereof, to the Parties Group.

5. PROCEEDINGS AND AWARDS

(a)   The arbitral tribunal shall decide disputes in accordance with this Agreement, or interpreted and applied in accordance with the applicable rules of international law.

(b)   The tribunal may, at the request of a Party, recommend provisional measures which either Party should take to avoid serious prejudice to the other pending its final award.

(c)   The tribunal shall render an award, setting out its findings of law and fact and its decision on the question whether the relevant measures are inconsistent with the agreement together with its reasons therefor, and may, at the request of a Party, award the following forms of relief :

(i)   a declaration that a measure of a Party is incompatible or a Party has failed to comply with its obligations under this Agreement;

(ii)   a recommendation that a Party should bring its measures into conformity with the Agreement:

(iii)   pecuniary compensation; and

(iv)   any other form of relief to which the Party against whom the award is made consents, including restitution in kind.

(d)   The tribunal shall draft its award consistently with the requirement of confidentiality set out in Article A, paragraph 2 and the requirements of subparagraph (e), below. It shall issue its award in provisional form to the Parties to the dispute, as a general rule within [180] days after the date of formation of the tribunal. The Parties to the dispute may, within [15] [30] days thereafter, submit written comment upon any portion of it. The tribunal shall consider such submissions, may solicit additional written comments of the Parties, and shall issue its final award within [15] days after closure of the comment period.

(e)   The tribunal shall promptly transmit a copy of its final award to the Parties Group, as a publicly available document.

(f)   Tribunal awards shall be final and binding between the Parties to the dispute unless the Parties Group, otherwise decides within thirty days after receipt of a copy of the award].

(g)   Each Party shall pay the cost of its representation in the proceedings. The costs of the tribunal shall be paid for, equally by the Parties unless the tribunal directs that they be shared differently. Fees and expenses payable to tribunal members will be subject to schedules established by the Parties Group and in force at the time of the constitution of the tribunal.

6. DEFAULT RULES

The [UNCITRAL arbitration rules] shall apply to supplement provisions of these Articles. 12

7. ENFORCEMENT OF AWARDS

(a)   In the event of non-compliance with an award of an arbitral tribunal, the Contracting Party in whose favour it was issued may raise the matter in the Parties Group. The Parties Group shall endeavour to bring about compliance. It may, by consensus minus the defaulting Party, suspend the non-complying Party's right to participate in decisions of the Parties Group.

(b)   Possible exhaustive list of permitted countermeasures-no draft provided.

(c)   Possible procedural safeguards on resort to countermeasures-no draft provided.

XI. DISPUTE SETTLEMENT
INVESTOR-STATE AND STATE-INVESTOR PROCEDURES
DISPUTES BETWEEN AN INVESTOR AND A CONTRACTING PARTY

1. SCOPE AND STANDING

(a)   This article applies to disputes between a Contracting Party and an investor of another Contracting Party, concerning an alleged breach of an obligation of the former under this Agreement which causes, or is likely to cause loss or damage to the investor or- his investment.

(b)   It also applies to disputes between a Contracting Party and an investor of an another Contracting Party, concerning an alleged breach of any obligations of such investor under this Agreement or under legislation enacted by the first mentioned Contracting Party, on a subject matter covered by this Agreement, which causes or is likely to cause loss or damage to the interests of the first mentioned Contracting Party. 13 14

2. MEANS OF SETTLEMENT

Such a dispute should, if possible, be settled by negotiation or consultation. If it is not so settled, the Claimant may choose to submit it for resolution:

(a)   to the Competent Courts or administrative tribunals of a Contracting Party to the dispute [or of the investor, as the case may be];

(b)   in accordance with any applicable previously agreed dispute settlement procedure; or

(c)   by arbitration in accordance with this Article, under:

    (i)   the Convention on the Settlement of Investment Disputes between States and Nationals of other States (the "ICSID Convention"), if the ICSID Convention is applicable;

    (ii)   the Additional Facility Rules of the Centre of Settlement of Investment Disputes ("ICSID Additional Facility"), if the ICSID Additional Facility is applicable;

    (iii)   the Arbitration Rules of the United Nations Commission on International Trade Law (UNCITRAL), [if neither the ICSID Convention nor the ICSID Additional Facility is applicable]15 [Provided that the venue of arbitration under paragraph 2 (c) shall be in the Contracting State in every case]. 16

By submitting a dispute to arbitration in accordance with this Article under paragraph 2 (c), the investor consents to the application of all provisions of this Article, 17

3. CONTRACTING PARTY CONSENT

(a)   Subject only to paragraph 3 (b), each Contracting Party hereby gives its unconditional consent to the submission of a dispute to international arbitration in accordance with the provisions of this Article.

(b)   A Contracting Party may, by notifying the Depository upon deposit of its instrument of ratification or accession, provide that its consent given under paragraph 3 (a) applies only on the condition that the investor and the investment waive the right to initiate any other dispute settlement procedure with respect to the same dispute and withdraw from any such procedure in progress before its conclusion. A Contracting Party may, at any time, reduce the scope of that limitation by notifying the Depositary.

4. TIME PERIODS AND NOTIFICATION

A claimant may submit a dispute for resolution, pursuant to paragraph 2(c) of this Article, after (ninety) days following the date on which notice of intent to do so was received by the opposite party, but no later than (six) years from 18 the date the claimant first acquired (or should have acquired) knowledge of the events which give rise to the dispute. Notice of intent, a copy of which shall be delivered to the Parties Group, shall specify:

(a)   the name and address of the claimant;

(b)   the name and address, if any, of the investment;

(c)   the provisions of this Agreement alleged to have been breached and any other relevant provisions;

(d)   the issues and the factual basis for the claim; and

(e)   the relief sought, including the approximate amount of any damages claimed.

5. WRITTEN AGREEMENT OF THE PARTIES

The consent given by the Contracting Party in subparagraph 3 (a), together with either the written submission of the dispute to resolution by the investor pursuant to subparagraph 2 (c) or the investor's advance written consent to such submission, shall constitute the written consent and the written agreement, of the Parties to the dispute, to its submission for settlement for the purposes of Chapter II of the ICSID Convention, the ICSID Additional Facility Rules, Article 1 of the UNCITRAL Arbitration Rules and Article II of the United Nations Convention on the Recognition and Enforcement of Foreign Arbitral Awards (the "New York Convention").

6. APPOINTMENTS TO ARBITRAL TRIBUNALS

(a)   Unless the Parties to the dispute otherwise agree, the arbitral tribunal shall comprise three arbitrators, one appointed by each of the disputing Parties and the third, who shall be the presiding arbitrator, appointed by agreement of the disputing Parties.

(b)   If a tribunal has not been constituted within 90 days after the date that a claim is submitted to arbitration, the arbitrator or arbitrators not yet appointed shall, on the request of either disputing party, be appointed by the appointing authority. For arbitration under paragraph 2, subparagraphs C(i), C(ii), and C(iii), and paragraph 8, the appointing authority shall be the Secretary General of ICSID.

(c)   The parties to a dispute submitted to arbitration under this article and the appointing authority should consider the appointment of:

(i)   members of the roster maintained by the Contracting parties pursuant to Article C, paragraph 2 (c), and

(ii)   individuals possessing expertise not found on the roster, if arbitration of a dispute requires special expertise on the Tribunal, rather than solely through expert advice under the rules governing the arbitration.

(d)   The appointing authority shall, as far as possible, carry out its function in consultation with the Parties to the dispute.

(e)   In order to facilitate the appointment of arbitrators of the Parties' nationality on three member ICSID Tribunals under Article 39 of the ICSID Convention and Article 7 of Schedule C of the ICSID Additional Facility Rules, and without prejudice to each party's right independently to select an individual for appointment as arbitrator or to object to an arbitrator on ground other than nationality:

(i)   the disputing Contracting Party agrees to the appointment of each individual member of a tribunal under paragraph 2 (c)(i) or (ii) of this Article; and

(ii)   a disputing investor may initiate or continue a proceeding under paragraph 2 (c)(i) or (ii) only on condition that the investor agrees in writing to the appointment of each individual member of the tribunal. [19]

7. STANDING OF THE INVESTMENT

An enterprise which is constituted or organised under the law of a Contracting party but which, from the time of the events giving rise to the dispute until its submission for resolution under paragraph 2 (c), was an investment of an investor of another Contracting Party, shall not, for the purposes of disputes concerning that investment, be considered "an investor of another Contracting Party" under this Article or "a national of another Contracting Party State" for purposes of Article 25 (2)(b) of the ICSID Convention.[20]

8. INDEMNIFICATION

A disputing party shall not:

(a)   as a defence, counter claim or right of setoff, or

(b)   in any other manner assert that indemnification or other compensation for all or part of the alleged damages has been received or will be received by the claimant, pursuant to a contract of indemnity, guarantee or insurance.

9. THIRD PARTY RIGHTS

The arbitral tribunal (on the request of a Contracting Party, which is not a party to the dispute) give to that party (after hearing the parties on such request) an opportunity to present its views on the legal issues in dispute.

10. APPLICABLE LAW

An arbitral tribunal established under this Article shall decide the issue in dispute in accordance with this Agreement, interpreted and applied in accordance with:

(i)   the law agreed upon by the parties; or

(ii)   absent such agreement, the law of the Contracting Party (including its rules on the conflict of laws) and such rules of law as may be applicable.21

11. INTERIM MEASURES OF RELIEF

(a)   An arbitral tribunal established under this Article may (order or)22 recommend an interim measure of protection to preserve the rights of disputing party or to ensure that the Tribunal's Jurisdiction is made fully effective, including an order to preserve evidence in the possession of control of a disputing Party. A Tribunal may recommend the non-application of the measure alleged to constitute the breach of obligation subject to the dispute.

(b)   The seeking, by a party to a dispute submitted to arbitration under this Article, of interim relief not involving the payment of damages, from judicial or administrative tribunals, for the preservation of its rights and interest pending resolution of the dispute, is not deemed a submission of the dispute for resolution for the purposes of a Contracting Party's limitation of consent under paragraph 3 (b) and is permissible in arbitration under any of the provisions of paragraph 2 (c).

12. FINAL AWARDS AND RELIEF TO BE GRANTED BY THE AWARD

(a)   An arbitration award may provide the following forms of relief:

     (i)   a declaration of the legal rights and obligations of the parties;

     (ii)   compensatory monetary damages, which shall include interest from the time-(of the award) (the loss or damage was incurred) until time of payment;

     (iii)   restitution in kind in appropriate cases, provided that the party against whom it is awarded may pay monetary damages in lieu thereof where restitution is not practicable; and

     (iv)   with the agreement of the parties to the dispute, any other form of relief. 23

(b)   An arbitration award shall be final and binding between the parties to the dispute and shall be carried out without delay by the Party against whom it is issued, subject to its post-award rights. 24

(c)   The award shall be drafted consistently with the requirements of paragraph 14 and shall be a publicly available document. A copy of the award shall be delivered to the Parties Group by the Secretary General of ICSID, for an award under the ICSID Convention or the Rules of the ICSID Additional Facility; and by the tribunal for an award under the UNCITRAL Rules.

13.A. MODIFICATION OF RULES

Parties to the dispute have the freedom to agree on modifications of the rules of procedure contained in this Article, paragraphs 9, 10, and 12. 25

13.B PRELIMINARY OBJECTIONS

(i)   Any objection by a disputing Party to the jurisdiction of the Tribunal or to the admissibility of the application, or other objection the decision upon which is requested before any further proceedings on the merits, shall be made in writing within 15 days after the appointment of the Tribunal.

(ii)   Upon receipt by the Tribunal of a preliminary objection, the proceedings on the merits shall be suspended.

(iii)   After hearing the Parties, the Tribunal shall give its decision, by which it shall either uphold the objection or reject it. The decision should ordinarily be given within 60 days after the date on which the objection was made.26

14. CONFIDENTIAL AND PROPRIETARY INFORMATION

Parties and other participants in proceedings shall protect any confidential or proprietary information which may be revealed in the course of the proceedings and which is designated as such by the party providing the information. They shall not reveal such information without written authorisation from the Party which provided it (except where such revelation is compelled by the applicable law)

15. PLACE OF ARBITRATION AND ENFORCEABILITY OF AWARDS

(a)   Any arbitration under this Article shall be held in a State that is party to the New York Convention;

(b)   Claims submitted to arbitration under this Article shall be considered to arise out of a commercial relationship or transaction for the purposes of Article 1 of the New York Convention;

(c)   Each Contracting Party shall recognise an award rendered pursuant to this Agreement as binding and shall enforce the pecuniary obligations imposed by that award, as if it were a final judgement of its courts.27

(d)   Paragraph 15(a) shall be subject to the right conferred on the Contracting State by paragraph 2, proviso. 28

16. TRIBUNAL MEMBER FEES

Fees and expenses payable to a member of an arbitral tribunal established under these Articles will be subject to schedules established by the Parties Group and in force at the time of the constitution of the tribunal.

17. COLLECTION OF STATES

For the purposes of paragraph 1 (b) of this Article, the expression "Contracting State" shall include more than one Contracting State so as to entitle any Contracting State to claim damages in accordance with that paragraph.29

18. CO-OPERATION

It shall be the duty of every Contracting Party, even if it is not a party to the dispute, to render all possible assistance, so as to make implementation of the provisions of this Article effective to the maximum extent possible.30

19. CLASS ACTIONS

Nothing in this Article shall be construed as excluding, restricting or modifying the right of any group of persons in a Contracting State to bring appropriate proceedings (including a class action) for any conduct for which such proceedings are available under the applicable law.

EXPLANATORY NOTE:

In view of recent trends in certain countries regarding class actions, it is considered desirable to have specific provisions on the subject.

20. EFFECT OF NON-COMPLIANCE

Without prejudice to the provisions of paragraph 13 above, non-compliance by a party with an award shall be deemed to constitute an independent breach of this agreement.

EXPLANATORY NOTE:

The provision is self-explanatory.

VI. EXCEPTIONS

GENERAL EXCEPTIONS

1. This Article shall not apply to Articles-(on expropriation and compensation and protection from strife).

2. Nothing in this Agreement shall be construed:

   (a) to prevent any Contracting Party from taking any action [which it considers] necessary for the protection of its essential security interests [including those]:

      (i) taken in time of war, [or] armed conflict, [or other emergency in international relations];

      (ii) relating to the implementation of national policies or international agreements respecting the non-proliferation [*inter alia*] of nuclear weapons or other nuclear explosive devices;

(iii)   relating to the production of arms and ammunition.

(b)   to require any Contracting Party to furnish or allow access to any information the disclosure of which [it considers] [would be] contrary to its essential security interests or to the maintenance of public order.31

(c)   to prevent any Contracting Party from taking any action in pursuance of its obligations under the United Nations Charter for the maintenance of international peace and security.

3.   Nothing in this Agreement shall be construed to prevent any Contracting Party from taking any action necessary for the maintenance of public order.

4.   Paragraphs 2 and 3 may not be invoked by a Contracting Party as a means to evade its obligations under this Agreement.

5.   Actions taken pursuant to this Article shall be notified to the Parties Group in accordance with Article of this Agreement.

EXPLANATORY NOTE:

GENERAL EXCEPTIONS

It is thought that besides security, "public order" should also be mentioned here because there is need to allow a special provision where the information demanded is such that its disclosure may impair public order without impairing security of the nation as a whole.

6.   If a Contracting Party (the "requesting Party") has reason to believe that actions taken by another Contracting Party (the "other Party" are not in conformity with [Article] [paragraphs -], it may request consultations with that other Party. That other arty shall promptly enter into consultations with the requesting Party and shall provide information to the requesting Party regarding the actions taken and the reasons therefor.

XII. RELATIONSHIP TO OTHER AGREEMENTS: NON-DEROGATION

If the provisions of the Constitution or laws of a Contracting Party or the obligations of a Contracting Party under an international agreement or customary international law, entitle the investors of other Contracting Parties or their investments to a treatment more favourable than that provided for by the present agreement, then nothing in this agreement shall be construed to derogate from such entitlement to the extent that it is more favourable than the present agreement.

XIII. IMPLEMENTATION AND OPERATION

THE PREPARATORY GROUP 32

1.   There shall be a Preparatory Group comprised of the Signatories to Agreement.

2.   The Preparatory Group shall:

     (a)   prepare for entry into force of the Agreement and the establishment of the Parties Group;

     (b)   conduct discussions with non-signatory to the final Act;

     (c)   conduct negotiations with interested non-signatories to the Final Act and make decisions on their eligibility to become a Contracting Party; and

     (d) 33

3.   The Preparatory Group shall elect a Chairperson, who shall serve in a personal capacity. Meetings shall be held at intervals to be determined by the Preparatory Group. The Preparatory Group shall establish its rules and procedures.

4.   Subject to paragraph 5, the Preparatory Group shall make decisions by consensus. Such decisions may include to adopt a different voting rule for a particular question or category of questions. A signatory may abstain and express a differing view without barring consensus.

5.   However, where a decision cannot be reached by consensus, the decision shall be made by a majority comprising two-thirds of the Signatories.

THE PARTIES GROUP

1.   There shall be Parties Group comprised of the Contracting Parties.

2.   The Parties Group shall facilitate the operation of this Agreement. To this end, it shall:

     (a)   carry out the functions assigned to it under this Agreement;34

     (b)   at the request of a Contracting Party, clarify the interpretation or application of this Agreement;

     (c)   consider any matter that may affect the operation of this Agreement; and

     (d)   take such other actions as it deems necessary to fulfil its mandate.

3.   In carrying out the functions specified in paragraph 2, the Parties Group may consult government and non-governmental organisations or persons.

4.   The Parties Group shall elect a Chair, who shall serve in a personal capacity. Meetings shall be held at intervals to be determined by the Parties Group. The Parties Group shall establish its rules and procedures.

5.   Subject to paragraph 6, the Parties Group shall make decisions by consensus. Such decisions may include a decision to adopt a different voting rule for a particular question or category of questions. A Contracting Party may abstain and express a differing view without barring consensus.

6.   However, where a decision cannot be reached by consensus:

(a)   decisions on budgetary matters shall be made by a two-thirds majority of Contracting Parties whose assessed contributions represent, in combination, at least two-thirds of the total assessed contributions specified therein; and

(b)   decisions on accession and other matters shall be made by a [two-thirds] majority of the Contracting Parties.35

7.   The Parties Group shall be assisted by a Secretariat.

8.   Parties Group and Secretariat costs shall be borne by the Contracting Parties as approved and apportioned by the Parties Group.36

APPENDIX I: ENVIRONMENTAL PROTECTION 37

1. Environmental Impact Analysis

The foreign investor shall provide an Environmental Impact Analysis of the proposed project, including:

(a)   a list of all raw materials, intermediates, products, and wastes (with flow diagram);

(b)   a list of all occupational health and safety standards and environmental standards (wastewater effluent releases, atmospheric emission rates for all air pollutants, detailed description and rate of generation of solid wastes or other wastes to be disposed of on land or by incineration);

(c)   a plan for control of all occupational health and safety hazards in plant operation, storage and transport of potentially hazardous raw materials, products and wastes;

(d)   a copy of corporation guidelines of the foreign investor for conducting environmental and occupational health and safety impact analysis for new projects ;

(e)   the manufacturer's safety data sheets on all substances involved.

2. Plant Performance

The foreign investor shall provide complete information on locations, ages and performance of existing plants and plants closed within the past 5 years in which the foreign investor has partial or full ownership, where similar processes and products are used, including:

(a)   a list of all applicable occupational health and safety standards and environmental standards, including both legal requirements (standards, laws, regulations) and corporate voluntary standards and practices for the control of occupational and environmental hazards of all kinds;

(b)   description of all cases of permanent and/or total disability sustained or allegedly sustained by workers, including worker's compensation claims;

(c)   explanation of all fines, penalties, citations, violations, regulatory agreements and civil damage claims involving environmental and occupational health and safety matters as well as hazards from or harm attributed to the marketing and transport of the products of such enterprise;

(d)   description of the foreign investor's percentage of ownership and technology involvement in each plant location and similar information for other equity partners and providers of technology.

(e)   names and addresses of governmental authorities who regulate or oversee environmental and occupational health and safety for each plant location;

(f)   explanation of cases where any plant's environmental impact has been the subject of controversy within the local community or with regulatory authorities, including description of practices criticised and how criticism was resolved in such cases;

(g)   copies, with summary, of all corporate occupational health and safety and environmental audits and inspection reports for each location, including such audits and reports by consultants;

(h)   copies of safety reports, reports of hazards assessment, and risk analysis reports carried out with similar technology by the foreign investor and its consultants;

(i)   copies of toxic release forms that have been submitted to government bodies (e.g. within the past 5 tears, for all plant locations);

(j)   any information considered relevant by the foreign investor.

3. Corporate policy

The foreign investor shall submit a statement of corporate policy on health, safety and environmental performance of world wide operations. This must include the corporate policy on laws, regulations, standards, guidelines and practices for new industrial projects and production facilities. The foreign investor shall explain how it is implemented by describing the staff responsible for carrying out this policy, its authority and responsibilities, and its position in the foreign investor corporate structure. Such description will also include the name, address and telephone number of senior corporate management officials in charge of this staff function. The foreign investor shall state whether it follows the same standards world wide for worker and environmental protection in all new projects, and if not, explain why not.

4. Access to facility

The foreign investor shall agree to provide the host country with immediate access to the proposed industrial facility at any time during its operation to conduct inspections, monitor exposure of workers to hazards, and sample for pollution releases.

5. Training

The foreign investor shall agree to fully train all employees exposed to potential occupational hazards, including potential health effects of all exposures and the most effective control measure.

6. Equipment

(a)   The foreign investor shall agree to provide the host country with equipment for analysing work place exposure and generation of pollution, for the life time of the proposed project.

(b)   The equipment shall include (but shall not be necessarily limited to) maintenance of all limits specified in paragraph 1 b) of this Appendix.

(c)   The foreign investor shall agree that the proposed project will pay to the Government of the host country the cost for all medical and exposure monitoring during the lifetime of the proposed project.

7. Compensation

The foreign investor shall agree that the proposed project will fully compensate any person whose health, earning capacity or property is harmed as a result of the occupational hazard and environments of the project, as determined by the Government of the developing country.

8. Marketing safeguards

The foreign investor shall follow marketing safeguards that are as restrictive as the safeguards which it applies anywhere in the world, so as to ensure that workers and members of the public are not harmed as a result of the use of its product.

9. Supervising risk to health or environment

If, at any time after the application for approval of the proposed project is submitted to the host country, the foreign investor becomes aware of a substantial risk of injury to health or to the environment which is likely to arise from a substance which the foreign investor manufactures or sells in the host country, being a risk not known and disclosed at the time of the aforesaid application, then the foreign investor shall agree to immediately notify the environmental protection agency of the Government of the host country, of such risk.

10. Officials

The foreign investor shall provide to the Government of the host country full information regarding:

(a)   the names;

(b)   designations;

(c)   addresses; and

(d)   phone and fax numbers,

of its senior corporate officials who are charged for the time being with the implementation of policies relating to the environment, occupational health, occupational safety, including (but not necessarily limited to), the following:

(i)   plant design and operations;

(ii)   corporate inspections and reviews of plant performance; and

(iii)   product stewardship.

EXPLANATORY NOTE:

(i)   It is desirable to ensure that a developing country should be able to require foreign investors to submit certain information in connection with the investor' application to build industrial projects or to conduct mining operations. Principal objects of such requirement will be to protect the environment, safety and health and to ensure high standards of performance.

(ii)   Connected with this aspect is the need to ensure that the host country Government will be provided with the equipment needed to protect against worker' exposure to hazards of health and safety beyond the permissible limits and further to ensure that the release of toxic substances does not exceed permissible limits.

(iii)   This would also involve, (where relevant), information about past experience of the foreign investor and other connected matters.

(iv)   Finally, leading global corporations have issued their own policy statements on health, safety and environment during recent years and announced that they will meet these requirements world wide. It is convenient to incorporate appropriate obligations on all these matters in the Investment Agreement. The Companies now say that they meet the same high standards world wide that they are required to observe in their own home country. It is considered desirable to have a detailed provision on the subject.

Endnotes:

1. See explanatory note below.

2. See explanatory note below.

3. In paragraph (iv) of the definition of "investment", the words referring to rights associated with land have been included to make the provision comprehensive.

4. See Appendix I-Environmental Protection.

5. Government of India, Model Text, Article 11.

6. In paragraph (under Performance Requirements) the opening words "subject to the provisions of paragraphs 2 to 7" have been used to bring out the fact that the mandate in paragraph 1 is, in some respects, modified by later paragraphs.

7. See explanatory note below.

8. In paragraph 3 (a) the words "or on any other matter" have been used in order to cover other functions.

9. The scope of consultations should be no broader than the arbitration and this paragraph should utilise whatever language is ultimately adopted in Article C, paragraph 1. A.

10. Diplomatic channels are the normal channel for notice of State-State disputes. See e.g. Article 2, paragraph 1 of the PCA Optional Rules for Arbitration Disputes between Two States.

11. This proposal is based on the WTO approach. An alternative is found in the investor-state consolidation provision in Article D, paragraph 8, which is NAFTA based.

12. Another option is that of rules of ICSID.

13. Paragraph is considered necessary to enable the Contracting State to claim damages against an investor.

14. As to Collection of States, see paragraph 17, infra.

15. Since only ICSID and ICSID Additional Facility are designed for arbitration between a State and a private party, the UNICTRAL option should be available only if the former are not. The ICC option is not considered convenient for developing countries.

16. The proviso regarding venue is considered necessary in view of financial considerations involved in conducting or defending litigation or arbitration outside the country.

17. This provision, though not strictly necessary could be useful to avoid controversies Provision for multiple claims consolidation is not considered desirable.

18. The period of 6 years appears reasonable.

19. This paragraph, based on NAFTA Article 1125, is intended to assure that a three member panel may include a national of the parties to the dispute, without requiring that each member of the panel be, in fact, chosen by agreement.

20. It is not considered proper to bring the host country to international arbitration at the instance of an organisation constituted under legislation of host country.

21. Compare Article 42, ICSID,

22. ICSID Arbitral Rules contemplate "recommended' interim measures only. UNICTRAL Rules provide for interim measures without characterising them as recommendations. ICC Rules do not provide expressly for interim measure. Proposed provision would theoretically give all arbitral tribunals the same right to order certain interim relief.

23. This final elastic sub-paragraph may provide a means for the parties to work out an award of relief, tailored to the circumstances of the case, which will have legally binding force. It will cover injunction, primitive damages or withdrawal of offending measure.

24. The post-award rights include Section 5 of the ICSID Convention on Interpretation, Revision and Annulment, and the rights of a Party regarding enforcement of awards in national courts.

25. Freedom to the Parties to modify the rules appears to be desirable (paragraph 13. A). Only certain rules mentioned in paragraph 13. A as proposed here will be subject.

26. Paragraph 13, B is intended to incorporate a procedure for preliminary objections.

27. The last sentence would serve to counter potential loopholes under the New York Convention, e.g. it would preclude a Contracting Party from denying enforcement based on limitations in its acceptance *of* the New York Convention, or on a claim that the subject matter was incapable of settlement by arbitration or that enforcement of the award would be contrary to its public policy.

28. The overriding effect given by proposed paragraph 15 (d) to the choice conferred by paragraph 2, proviso-is necessary for obvious reasons. Paragraph 2, proviso (as proposed) deals with venue.

29. Paragraph 17 appears to be needed, for certain cases.

30 As per suggested paragraph 18, an obligation of co-operation may be needed in some cases.

31. See explanatory note below.

32. The Preparatory Group would be contained in the Final Act.

33. This and any subsequent sub-paragraphs would be necessary, only if there is business that remains unfinished at the conclusion of the negotiations that the negotiators consider should be completed by the Preparatory Group; the further sub-paragraphs would itemise the clean-up tasks to be undertaken by the Preparatory Group.

34. The sub-paragraph 2 (a) refers to any operational functions and any future work as may be specified elsewhere.

35. Further work needs to be done on paragraph 6. This work would include consideration of whether we should draw a line between substantive and procedural questions. If all decisions were required to be made by consensus, paragraph 6 would be deleted.

36. Further work is required on paragraphs 7 and 8, if it is decided that the agreement itself should contain provisions on the initial budgetary principles and formula and on the structure and functions of a Secretariat.

37. See explanatory note below.

447

*   *   *

37. See explanatory note below.

TOWARDS A CITIZENS' MAI: AN ALTERNATIVE APPROACH TO DEVELOPING A GLOBAL INVESTMENT TREATY BASED ON CITIZENS' RIGHTS AND DEMOCRATIC CONTROL[*]
[excerpts]

(COUNCIL OF CANADIANS)

Towards a Citizens' MAI: An Alternative Approach to Developing a Global Investment Treaty Based on Citizens' Rights and Democratic Control was prepared by the Polaris Institute for the Council of Canadians in 1998 as a working instrument designed to assist citizens in developing an alternative MAI. Inputs were made by various individuals and institutions from Canada, India, Malaysia, Mexico, United Kingdom and United States. It contains a set of propositions with the aim that citizen activists in each country could study them, modify them if necessary, and develop a negotiating agenda. Thus, the proposed texts were seen as part of an ongoing process of developing consensus amongst civil society groups regarding an alternative approach to global investment rules.

---

1. OPERATING PRINCIPLES

1. Citizens' Rights: There are several categories of citizen rights and freedoms which are recognized and enshrined in the Universal Declaration and related Covenants and Declarations. They include: *Labour Rights* such as the right to employment, fair wages, and basic labour standards like health and safety, freedom to organize unions and collective bargaining; *Social Rights* such as quality health care, public education, social assistance, unemployment insurance, retirement pensions and special services to meet the needs of women, children, seniors and people with disabilities; *Environmental Rights* such as the preservation of the natural resources, species and bio-diversity of the planet for future generations through measures designed prevent the destruction of the air, waters, forests, fish, wildlife, and non-renewable resources; *Cultural Rights* such as the preservation and enhancement of peoples' distinct identity, language, values, customs and heritage. Any global set of investment rules should be designed to strengthen rather than to undermine these basic citizen rights.

2. State Obligations: As outlined in the UN Charter on the Economic Rights and Duties of States, governments are obligated to intervene in the market when necessary to ensure that economic development meets standards designed to enhance these basic citizens' rights. To do so, states have the right to maintain control over their fiscal and monetary policies as well as to

---

[*] *Source:* The Council of Canadians (CoC) (1998). "The Multilateral Agreement on Investment (MAI). Towards a Citizens' MAI: An Alternative Approach to Developing a Global Investment Treaty Based on Citizens' Rights and Democratic Control", A discussion paper prepared by the Polaris Institute, Working Instruments (Canada: Council of Canadians), mimeo.; available on the Internet (http://www.canadians.org/citizensmai.html). [Note added by the editor.]

enact laws, policies and programs designed to regulate the economy in the public interest. In particular, states have the right and responsibility to protect (a) strategic areas of their economies [eg. finance, energy, communications] by establishing public enterprises and (b) sensitive areas known as the 'commons' [eg. environment, culture, health care] through government-run public services. In this way, governments are able to fulfil their social obligations by ensuring that the capital raised through taxes for public revenues is used to serve the basic rights and needs of citizens. By doing so, however, states must also ensure that their public enterprises and public services are operated in an efficient manner.

3. Corporate Responsibilities: In the global economy, foreign based corporations do have the right to invest their capital and expect a reasonable return on their investment. And when their assets are expropriated for a public purpose, they can expect to be given fair compensation in exchange. But, in doing so, foreign based corporations have certain social obligations to maintain. First, they must ensure that their investment is designed to serve the public interest, primarily the basic rights of citizens, by meeting performance requirements such as labour and environmental standards. Second, they must recognize the right and responsibilities of states to protect, preserve or enhance strategic areas of their economies and the commons. Third, they must contribute to public revenues by paying their fair share of taxes so that a portion of this capital can be used to serve the 'commons' through social programs, environmental projects, cultural initiatives and a variety of public services. Any global body of investment rules must be designed in such a way as to bind corporations to the fulfillment of these basic social obligations.

The application of these operating principles will likely vary from country to country and region to region. Differences exist in the nature, role and capacities of the state around the world today. Small, less developed nations, for example, are often much more vulnerable than larger states when it comes to dealing with the power wielded by transnational corporations. What's more, the fact that the nation state is also caught in a dynamic tension between localism and globalism is also sparking demands for a re-invention of the state. As a result, there are bound to be diverse approaches to economic, social, environmental and cultural priorities for development. This pluralism needs to be recognized along with the various asymmetries of power between nation states when it comes to developing an alternative, citizens'- based MAI.

This is why these three operating principles regarding the social obligations of capital are proposed as the cornerstones for developing a Citizens' MAI. In applying them, it should be kept in mind that the second two are meant to be subordinate to the first, namely, the basic democratic rights and freedoms of citizens. This, in turn, points to the *political rights* of citizens in democratic societies to participate in decisions affecting their lives. In developing an alternative MAI, it is crucial that processes be devised for effective citizen participation and democratic control. When it comes to fulfilling the social obligations of capital, citizens must have the means for holding both corporations and governments accountable. Before taking up this task [see section 3 on Process], we need to turn our attention to what could be some of the main components of a Citizens' MAI based on these operating principles.

2. COMPONENTS

The following is a draft outline of some of the main components of a Citizens' MAI based on the operating principles discussed in Part 1.

Guiding Principles:

* Investment by foreign based corporations is welcome provided that it adheres to regulations designed to enhance the economic, social and environmental rights of citizens.

* The stored social value of capital provides a basis for making distinctions between foreign and domestic investment.

* Regulations on investment must be democratically determined by governments in consultation with their people.

* International agreements must take into account the asymmetries of power and different levels of development that exist between countries.

* Agreements must also respect the diversity of political jurisdictions [eg. states, provinces, municipalities, aboriginal governments] that exist within some countries.

* In the case of conflicts, internationally recognized citizens' rights [eg. Universal Declaration of Human Rights and its Covenants] take precedence over the rights of corporations or investors.

Regulatory Objectives:

* To enable governments to implement national economic policies[eg. including fiscal and monetary] along with social, environmental and cultural policies appropriate to each country.

* To ensure that corporations fulfill their social obligations by meeting economic, social and environmental standards and priorities.

* To provide a clear set of rules that will serve to stimulate rather than to stifle economic initiative and dynamism.

* To encourage productive forms of investment that will increase links between the local and the national economy and screen out investments that make no contribution to development priorities.

* To allow for development strategies that involve exclusive public ownership in strategic sectors, exclusive national ownership in other key sectors, along with those sectors where a mix of national and foreign participation would be complementary.

* To curb volatile, short-term, speculative forms of investment that lead to rapid capital outflows and cause economic collapse.

Non-Discrimination:

* The concept on "National Treatment" would be redefined in such a way as to reflect the operating principle regarding the social obligations of capital.

* Based on the principle of the stored social value of capital, governments could apply different rules for domestic and foreign investment.

* All foreign based corporations can be required to meet basic performance standards [see below] in order to fulfill their social obligations.

* The principle of non discrimination would apply among all foreign based corporations provided that they adequately meet their social obligations.

Performance Standards:

To ensure that corporations fulfill their social obligations, states may impose performance requirements such as the following:

+ *Job Creation*: require a certain percentage of domestic content or of local input as part of the investment; provide employment opportunities for their citizens and immigrants; balance imports and exports; transfer and make use of appropriate technology to create and maintain jobs.

+ *Labour Standards*: respect labour standards that are at least as high, but never lower, than those set by the International Labour Organization conventions On trade union freedom, collective bargaining, child labour and forced labour, as well as minimum wage, health and safety laws of countries.

+ *Environmental Safeguards*: adhere to standards and targets that are at least as high, but never lower, than international treaties like the Montreal protocol on ozone depletion or the Kyoto agreements on greenhouse emissions; plus regulations or restrictions pertaining to toxic waste disposal, clear-cut logging, food safety, and quotas on fishing or the export of non-renewable energy.

+ *Sustainable Communities*: require local permission for the exploitation of natural resources, such as fish or forestry products, for purposes of ecological conservation; give adequate notice to local communities of intent to shut down or move operations; plus provide adequate compensation to the local community, including payment for any environmental clean-up required.

+ *Social Security*: contribute to the social wage plans of workers such as pensions, health and unemployment insurance benefits; pay fair share of taxes to ensure that there are sufficient public revenues for education, health care, and social services, as well as various cultural support programs provided by government.

Investment Incentives:

In order to stimulate corporations to fulfil these and related social obligations, governments may make use of a variety of policy tools including:
* subsidies, grants or loans to both domestic and foreign based corporations;

* procurement practices [i.e. purchasing goods and services from companies that adequately adhere to performance standards];

* various kinds of tax incentives as well as limits on the annual remittance of profits [for those foreign-based corporations that fail to adhere to their social obligations].

Public Enterprises:

Governments also have a responsibility to use tax revenues for protecting the *commons* by making public investments such as:

+exercising public ownership over key sectors of the economy that affect all citizen [eg. electricity, communications, transport etc.]

+establishing social programs and public services to ensure delivery of adequate education, health care, and social services;

+protecting cultural heritage by supporting local artists and entertainers, legislating content rules, and by maintaining public broadcasting systems;

+safeguarding ecologically sensitive areas through national parks and preserves.

It is the responsibility of the state to ensure that these public enterprises are operated on a sound and efficient basis. Corporate takeovers of social programs or public services without majority citizen consent should be firmly resisted by governments. Decisions to privatize a public enterprise should be made with citizen participation. In selling a public asset, priority should be put on seeking options for community ownership.

Expropriation Measures:

* Expropriation of corporate assets to serve vital public purposes or community needs shall be permitted. In turn, fair compensation shall be paid to those corporations which have had their assets expropriated.

* Compensation shall be determined by national law with due regard to the value of the initial investment; the valuation of the properties for tax purposes and the amount of wealth taken out out of the country during the period of investment. Investors would have the right of appeal to national courts when they consider the compensation to be inadequate; appeal to international tribunals may only occur after all national procedures have been exhausted.

Financial Transactions:

* All governments have a right to maintain responsibility for fiscal and monetary policy in their countries by using policy tools to regulate the inflows and outflows of capital.

* To limit the current trends toward volatile, short term speculative forms of investment [hot money], governments could require that foreign investment be used for productive purposes rather than speculation;
* To avoid the destabilizing effects of fly-by-night portfolio investments, corporations could be required to deposit a percentage of their investment in local banks for a specified minimum period.

* To slow down currency speculation, a tax on foreign exchange transactions [eg. the Tobin Tax] could be instituted [preferably by several countries acting in concert].

Dispute Settlement:

+ In addition to the right of corporations and governments [both national and sub-national] to sue each other for violations of this investment agreement, citizen groups would have the right to sue both corporations and governments for breach of their social obligations under these investment rules.

+ Disputes filed by citizen groups would be heard by national courts which have the power to invoke injunctions as well as award monetary compensation for damages; international tribunals could provide subsequent avenues for appeal;

+ All proceedings, either through national courts or international tribunals, shall be fully transparent and open to public observation.

+ All proceedings, either through national courts or international tribunals, shall be fully transparent and open to public observation.

+ National and international funds should be established by governments to provide certain groups [eg. native communities, environmental and women's groups] with intervenor funding for these legal proceedings.

*   *   *

CORE STANDARDS*
[excerpts]

(WORLD DEVELOPMENT MOVEMENT)

The World Development Movement (WDM) prepared the Core Standards in February 1999, in the belief that transnational corporations should be regulated to ensure that they abide by basic standards in all their operations and that their subsidiaries and subcontractors also comply. The WDM further believed that such standards would give the business community a stable, accepted international framework for their operations, and would enable countries and their people to maximize the benefits and minimize the costs of transnational corporations' operations. Under each of these proposed standards the WDM has listed the existing international agreements from which the standard was derived. The Core Standards are not exhaustive but, rather, were presented as the basis for further debate.

Basic human rights

Multinational companies should respect the right of everyone to life and liberty; no-one should be subjected to torture, cruel treatment or arbitrary arrest. Companies should promote basic human rights, ensuring they are universally and effectively observed. Companies must ensure any security forces working for them abide by basic standards.

The Universal Declaration of Human Rights: Articles 3 and 5 and Preamble. The UN Code of Conduct for Law Enforcement Officials.

Working conditions

Multinational companies should uphold the rights of workers to form and join trades unions and bargain collectively and to a safe working environment. Multinational companies must not use child or forced labour.

ILO Conventions 29, 87, 98, 155, 105 and 138.

Multinational companies should offer the best possible wages, benefits and conditions, and when applicable, no less favourable than those offered by other comparable firms.

ILO Tripartite Declaration 34, 33

---

* *Source*: World Development Movement (WDM) (1999). "Core Standards", *in* "Making Investment Work for People", Consultation paper, People Before Profits Campaign, February 1999, Annex (London: World Development Movement), mimeo. [Note added by the editor.]

Multinational companies should maintain the highest health and safety standards, bearing in mind their experience within the whole company, including knowledge of special hazards. They should inform representatives of the workers and the government about health and safety standards they observe in other countries.

ILO Tripartite Declaration 37

Equality

Multinational companies should uphold the right of women and men have to equal pay. Companies should not discriminate in employment on the grounds of sex, race, beliefs or origin.

ILO Conventions 100 and 111.

Consumer protection

Multinational companies should uphold the right of Consumer to: accurate marketing and information on products, safe goods, instructions on their proper use and information on all risks.

UN Guidelines for Consumer Protection; WHO Codes on breast milk substitutes and on promoting pharmaceuticals, FAO convention on pesticides, Food standards of Codex Alimentarius.

The environment

Multinational companies have responsibilities to undertake environmental impact assessments, to prevent and clean up pollution and meet their responsibilities on climate change, biodiversity, the sea, and ozone-depleting substances. Prior informed consent is needed for the export of toxic waste or banned pesticides.

Rio Declaration, Agenda 21, Conventions on Climate Change, Biodiversity and the Law of the Sea, the Basle agreement, the Montreal Protocol, the Rotterdam Convention.

Local communities

Multinational companies should uphold indigenous people's rights to control their own development. They should respect their rights over lands, the environment and natural and mineral resources. Companies should act to compensate people relocated with their consent and ensure effective protection at work.

ILO Convention 169 on Indigenous and Tribal Peoples 7,14, 15, 16, 20.

Business practices

Multinational companies should not abuse market power or limit competition, such as through price fixing, predatory take-overs or collusive deals, and should provide the authorities with all necessary information.

UNCTAD Rules for the Control of Restrictive Business Practices (D 1-4).

Sovereignty and development strategies

Multinational companies should respect every state's right to choose its own economic system and to regulate foreign investment and the activities of transnational corporations within its jurisdiction.

UN Charter of Economic Rights and Duties of States, Articles 1 & 2.

Multinational companies should take account of countries' policy objectives including development and social priorities. They should pay due regard to using technologies which generate employment and consider giving contracts to national companies, using local materials and promoting local processing.

ILO Tripartite Declaration of Principles concerning Enterprises and Social Policy 10, 19, 20.

*   *   *

RULES AND RECOMMENDATIONS ON EXTORTION AND BRIBERY IN INTERNATIONAL BUSINESS TRANSACTIONS (1999 REVISED VERSION)*
[excerpts]

(INTERNATIONAL CHAMBER OF COMMERCE)

The International Chamber of Commerce (ICC) first published its Recommendations to Combat Extortion and Bribery in Business Transactions in November 1977 (see *volume III* of this *Compendium*). On 26 March 1996, the Executive Board of ICC adopted the Rules of Conduct to Combat Extortion and Bribery. In February 1999 the ICC published an updated version of the 1996 Rules of Conduct. They were accompanied by a Corporate Practices Manual to provide practical guidance for company managers. The Manual aims at facilitating compliance with the OECD Convention on Combating Bribery of Foreign Public Officials in International Business Transactions. The Manual is not included in this volume.

PART I - RECOMMENDATIONS TO GOVERNMENTS AND INTERNATIONAL ORGANIZATIONS

Recommendations for international cooperation

Basic criminal statutes of virtually all countries clearly prohibit extortion and bribery. In the interest of developing consistent standards of criminal legislation in this field, each government should review its statutes to ensure that they effectively prohibit, in conformity with its jurisdictional and other basic legal principles, all aspects of both the giving and the taking of bribes including promises and solicitation of bribes. Where no such legislation exists, the governments concerned should introduce it; in those countries where extortion and bribery are already clearly prohibited, the relevant legislation should be perfected.

Each government should take concrete and meaningful steps to enforce vigorously its legislation in this area. ICC also notes with approval that the OECD has urged governments to re-examine their legislation against extortion and bribery; action relating to the tax deductibility of bribes is of particular urgency. The WTO should involve itself with these issues to support the OECD in the implementation of its Convention and Recommendation.

NATIONAL MEASURES

In order to deal with the problem of extortion and bribery, governments should, in conformity with their jurisdictional and other basic legal principles, take the following measures, if they have not already done so.

---

* *Source*: International Chamber of Commerce (1999). "Extortion and Bribery in International Business Transactions (1999 Revised Version)"; available on the Internet (http://www.iccwbo.org/home/statements_rules/rules/1999/briberydoc99.asp). [Note added by the editor.]

Preventive measures

- **Disclosure procedures**

For the sake of transparency, procedures should be established providing for periodic reports to an authorized government body of measures taken to supervise government officials involved directly or indirectly in commercial transactions. Such reports should be open to public scrutiny.

For enterprises engaged in transactions with any government or with any enterprise owned or controlled by government, disclosure procedures should provide for access, upon specific request, by the appropriate government authorities to information as to agents dealing directly with public bodies or officials in connection with any particular transaction, and as to the payments to which such agents are entitled.

Governments should ensure the confidentiality of any such information received from enterprises and safeguard the trade secrets incorporated therein.

- **Economic regulations**

When laying down any economic regulations or legislation, governments should, as far as possible, minimize the use of systems under which the carrying out of business requires the issuance of individual authorizations, permits, etc. Experience shows that such systems offer scope for extortion and bribery. This is because decisions involving the issue of permits or authorizations are frequently taken in ways which make it almost impossible to ensure effective control and supervision. Where individual permits and authorizations remain in place, governments should take appropriate measures to prevent their abuse.

- **Transactions with governments and international organizations**

Such transactions should be subject to special safeguards to minimize the opportunities for their being influenced by extortion and bribery. The system for awarding government contracts might include disclosure, to an appropriate government entity independent of the one directly concerned in the transaction, as well as increased public disclosure, whenever feasible, of the criteria and conclusions upon which the award is based. ICC supports the growing practice of making government contracts dependent on undertakings to refrain from bribery, and recommends that such contracts should include appropriate provisions to ensure compliance with international, national or enterprise codes against extortion and bribery.

- **Political contributions**

Undisclosed political contributions can be a source of abuse. Governments should regulate the conditions under which political contributions can be made. Where payments by enterprises to political parties, political committees or individual politicians are permitted by the applicable legislation, governments should enact legislation which ensures that such payments are publicly recorded by the payors and accounted for by the recipients.

Enforcement measures

Governments, in conformity with their jurisdictional and other basic legal principles, should ensure:

i)   that adequate mechanisms exist for surveillance and investigation, and

ii)   that those who offer, demand, solicit or receive bribes in violation of their laws are subject to prosecution with appropriate penalties.

Governments should periodically publish statistical or other information in respect of such prosecutions.

Auditing

Governments, if they have not already done so, should enact appropriate legislation providing for auditing by independent professional auditors of the accounts of economically significant enterprises.

INTERNATIONAL COOPERATION AND JUDICAL ASSISTANCE

Implementation of the OECD Convention and Recommendation

ICC believes that the OECD Convention and Recommendation on Bribery in International Business Transactions provide a useful framework for government action. All governments, including non-OECD governments, should promptly take action to adhere to the Convention and implement the steps set forth in the Recommendation.

Cooperation in law enforcement

Governments should agree, under appropriate provisions for confidentiality, and in conformity with the OECD Convention, to exchange through law enforcement agencies relevant and material information for the purpose of criminal investigation and prosecution of cases of extortion and bribery. They should also continue to cooperate bilaterally on matters involving extortion and bribery, on the basis of treaties providing for assistance in judicial and penal prosecution matters.

Role of international financial institutions

International financial institutions, e.g., the World Bank, the European Bank for Reconstruction and Development, should aim to make a significant contribution to the reduction of extortion and bribery in international business transactions. They should take all reasonable steps to ensure that corrupt practices do not occur in connection with projects which they are financing. Similarly, in negotiating cooperation agreements with non-member countries, whether countries with economies in transition or developing nations, the governing or coordinating bodies of the European Union, NAFTA, ASEAN and other regional institutions, should seek to satisfy themselves that appropriate legislation and administrative machinery to combat extortion and bribery exists in the countries concerned.

PART II - RULES OF CONDUCT TO COMBAT EXTORTION AND BRIBERY

INTRODUCTION

These Rules of Conduct are intended as a method of self-regulation by international business, and they should also be supported by governments. Their voluntary acceptance by business enterprises will not only promote high standards of integrity in business transactions, whether between enterprises and public bodies or between enterprises themselves, but will also form a valuable defensive protection to those enterprises which are subjected to attempts at extortion.

These Rules of Conduct are of a general nature constituting what is considered good commercial practice in the matters to which they relate but are without direct legal effect. They do not derogate from applicable local laws, and since national legal systems are by no means uniform, they must be read mutatis mutandis subject to such systems.

The business community objects to all forms of extortion and bribery. It is recognized, however, that under current conditions in some parts of the world, an effective programme against extortion and bribery may have to be implemented in stages. The highest priority should be directed to ending large-scale extortion and bribery involving politicians and senior officials. These represent the greatest threat to democratic institutions and cause the gravest economic distortions. Small payments to low-level officials to expedite routine approvals are not condoned. However, they represent a lesser problem. When extortion and bribery at the top levels is curbed, government leaders can be expected to take steps to clean up petty corruption.

BASIC PRINCIPLE

All enterprises should conform to the relevant laws and regulations of the countries in which they are established and in which they operate, and should observe both the letter and the spirit of these Rules of Conduct.

For the purposes of these Rules of Conduct, the term "enterprise" refers to any person or entity engaged in business, whether or not organized for profit, including any entity controlled by a State or a territorial subdivision thereof; it includes, where the context so indicates, a parent or a subsidiary.

BASIC RULES

Article 1. Extortion

No one may, directly or indirectly, demand or accept a bribe.

Article 2. Bribery and "Kickbacks"

a) No enterprise may, directly or indirectly, offer or give a bribe and any demands for such a bribe must be rejected.

b) Enterprises should not (i) kick back any portion of a contract payment to employees of the other contracting party, or (ii) utilize other techniques, such as subcontracts, purchase orders or consulting agreements, to channel payments to government officials, to employees of the other contracting party, their relatives or business associates.

Article 3. Agents

Enterprises should take measures reasonably within their power to ensure:

a) that any payment made to any agent represents no more than an appropriate remuneration for legitimate services rendered by such agent;

b) that no part of any such payment is passed on by the agent as a bribe or otherwise in contravention of these Rules of Conduct; and

c) that they maintain a record of the names and terms of employment of all agents who are retained by them in connection with transactions with public bodies or State enterprises. This record should be available for inspection by auditors and, upon specific request, by appropriate, duly authorized governmental authorities under conditions of confidentiality.

Article 4. Financial Recording and Auditing

a) All financial transactions must be properly and fairly recorded in appropriate books of account available for inspection by boards of directors, if applicable, or a corresponding body, as well as auditors.

b) There must be no "off the books" or secret accounts, nor may any documents be issued which do not properly and fairly record the transactions to which they relate.

c) Enterprises should take all necessary measures to establish independent systems of auditing in order to bring to light any transactions which contravene the present Rules of Conduct. Appropriate corrective action must then be taken.

Article 5. Responsibilities of Enterprises

The board of directors or other body with ultimate responsibility for the enterprise should:

a) take reasonable steps, including the establishment and maintenance of proper systems of control aimed at preventing any payments being made by or on behalf of the enterprise which contravene these Rules of Conduct;

b) periodically review compliance with these Rules of Conduct and establish procedures for obtaining appropriate reports for the purposes of such review; and

c) take appropriate action against any director or employee contravening these Rules of Conduct.

Article 6. Political Contributions

Contributions to political parties or committees or to individual politicians may only be made in accordance with the applicable law, and all requirements for public disclosure of such contributions shall be fully complied with. All such contributions must be reported to senior corporate management.

Article 7. Company Codes

These Rules of Conduct being of a general nature, enterprises should, where appropriate, draw up their own codes consistent with the ICC Rules and apply them to the particular circumstances in which their business is carried out. Such codes may usefully include examples and should enjoin employees or agents who find themselves subjected to any form of extortion or bribery immediately to report the same to senior corporate management. Companies should develop clear policies, guidelines, and training programmes for implementing and enforcing the provisions of their codes.

PART III - ICC FOLLOW-UP AND PROMOTION OF THE RULES

To promote the widest possible use of the Rules set forth in Part II and to stimulate cooperation between governments and world business, ICC is establishing a Standing Committee on Extortion and Bribery. The Chairman of that body shall be nominated by the President of the ICC and the Secretary General shall be responsible for ensuring, in conjunction with ICC National Committees, that members of the Committee are representative of both developed and developing countries and that businessmen are adequately represented in the membership.

Among its primary tasks, the Standing Committee shall:

1. Urge ICC National Committees promptly to take all appropriate measures to ensure that enterprises and business organizations in their country - whether multi-disciplinary or sectoral - give strong support to these Rules of Conduct. In particular, international business groups shall be encouraged to ensure that their subsidiaries endorse the Rules, or other corporate rules having similar effect, and publicize them in their local environment;

2. Collect through National Committees a wide range of company codes of conduct on ethical issues, including extortion and bribery, and serve as an information clearing house for businesses seeking to develop their own codes and requiring advice on the problems involved;

3. Promote the organization, both by ICC International Headquarters and by National Committees, of seminars designed to stimulate interest in, and discussion of, the Rules among the business community;

4. Encourage National Committees to impress upon their governments the need to include, from the initial stages, the business community - through its representative organizations - in discussions aimed at enacting or strengthening legislation against extortion and bribery;

5. Ensure liaison with the OECD, the WTO and other international organizations to provide the ICC point of view concerning progress at the international level in combating extortion and bribery;

6. Conduct a study within two years on the most appropriate policies and procedures practiced by top management of companies to minimize risks of exposure to extortion of, and bribery by, personnel dealing with sensitive issues (participation in public tenders, privatizations, etc.);

7. Issue at least every two years a report to ICC's Executive Board and Council on results achieved concerning worldwide recognition of the Rules of Conduct and of progress otherwise made by business in combating extortion and bribery. Decisions concerning the dissemination of the Report shall rest with the Executive Board and the Council;

8. Review these Rules in the light of experience and recommend amendments, as necessary, to the Executive Board and the Council.

*   *   *

MODEL CLAUSES FOR USE IN CONTRACTS INVOLVING TRANSBORDER DATA FLOWS[*]
[excerpts]

(INTERNATIONAL CHAMBER OF COMMERCE)

The Model Clauses for Use in Contracts Involving Transborder Data Flows were prepared by the Working Party on Privacy and Data Protection of the Commission on Telecommunications and Information Technologies of the International Chamber of Commerce. The Model Clauses were first published in 1998 and a revised version was published in 1999, which is the version reproduced in this volume. They were intended to assist those who wish to transfer personal data from countries that regulate export of personal data to countries that do not provide protection for personal data that the source country finds adequate.

Introduction

Parties wishing to incorporate the Clauses into their contracts may do so by inserting the following sentence into their written agreements:

"The parties hereto agree that the ICC Model Clauses For Use In Contracts Involving Transborder Data Flows, Publication No.___ (1999), are hereby incorporated by reference in this agreement as if fully set out herein."

Model clauses for use in contracts involving transborder data flows

Definitions

For the purposes of these clauses (the "Clauses"), the following terms shall have the following meanings:

"The Authority" means the relevant data protection authority in the territory in which the Data Exporter is established;

"Data Controller" means a natural or legal person, public authority, agency or any other body which, alone or jointly with others, determines the purposes and means of the processing of personal data;

"Data Exporter" shall mean the party identified elsewhere in this contract which transfers such personal data to a the country where the Data Importer is situated;

---

[*] *Source*: International Chamber of Commerce (1999). "Model Clauses for Use in Contracts Involving Transborder Data Flows" (Paris: ICC), mimeo. [Note added by the editor.]

"*Data Importer*" shall mean the party to this contract as identified elsewhere herein in this contract which receives personal data from the Data Exporter for processing in accordance with the terms of this contract;

"*Data Processor*" means a natural or legal person, public authority, agency or any other body which processes data on behalf of the Data Controller;

"*Data Subject*" is a natural person who can be identified, directly or indirectly, in particular by reference to an identification number or to one or more factors specific to his physical, physiological, mental, economic, cultural or social identity;

"*Inspection Authorities*" means an auditor or inspection authority selected by the Data Exporter as described in Clause 4(g);

"*Personal Data*" or "*personal data*" shall mean any information relating to an identified or identifiable natural person and the personal data the subject of these Clauses is described in [Schedule [ ]] [Appendix][ ] [Annex][ ] to this contract (Note: complete as applicable);

"*Processing*" or "*processing*" shall mean any operation or set of operations which is performed upon personal data, whether or not by automatic means, such as collection, recording, organisation, storage, adaptation or alteration, retrieval, consultation, use, disclosure by transmission, dissemination or otherwise making available, alignment or combination, blocking, erasure or destruction and "**process**" shall have the appropriate corresponding meaning;

"*Sensitive Data*" means personal data revealing racial or ethnic origin, political opinions, religious or philosophical beliefs, trade-union membership, and the processing of data concerning health or sex life.

1.   Warranties of the Data Exporter

The Data Exporter warrants that:

a)   The Personal Data to be exported have been collected and processed in accordance with notice, consent or other requirements of all relevant laws of the country in which the Data Exporter is established;

b)   Where applicable, it is registered with the Authority and, where required, has provided notice that it exports personal data and/or has received any licence or consent necessary to do so lawfully in the country in which it is established; and

c)   Its processing of the personal data, as notified by the Data Exporter to the Data Importer, will not violate any current law or regulation of the country where the Data Exporter is established.

2. Undertakings of the Data Exporter and Disputes with Data Subjects or Data Protection Authorities

a)   The Data Exporter will take such actions as are necessary to ensure it has fulfilled, and will continue to fulfil the warranties set out in Clause 1.

b)   The Data Exporter will promptly respond to enquiries from the Authority about the use of the relevant personal data by the Data Exporter and, to the extent reasonably possible, by the Data Importer and to any Data Subject's enquiry concerning use of his or her personal data, (including whether the same has been exported by it) and provide the enquirer with the name of the Data Importer and the individual responsible at the Data Importer who will be informed of the enquiry and who has been designated and properly notified by the Data Importer to respond to inquiries from its national authorities.

c)   The Data Exporter confirms that it will supply a copy of the current laws in relation to data protection applicable in the country where the Data Exporter is established to the Data Importer prior to any processing of the exported personal data taking place. It also undertakes to notify the Data Importer as soon as possible of any changes to the said applicable laws.

d)   In the event of a dispute between the Data Exporter or the Data Importer on the one hand and a Data Subject or the Authority on the other hand concerning the Data Importer's processing of personal data, which dispute is not amicably resolved, the Data Exporter agrees to use reasonable efforts to defend the lawfulness of the Data Importer's processing of the Data Subject's personal data through available means of dispute resolution between Data Controllers and Data Subjects, or between Data Controllers and the Authority, as applicable, provided for in the country where the Data Exporter is established. The Data Importer agrees to abide by the decision of the Authority (or other authority or tribunal having jurisdiction of the dispute) with respect to such processing as finally affirmed by the judicial authority to which appeal of such decision may be made, as if it were party to the proceedings, and to provide reasonable assistance to the Data Exporter in defending such claims. The Data Importer hereby authorises the Data Exporter to settle any such dispute without recourse to completion of all such dispute resolution formalities pursuant to advice of counsel reasonably acceptable to the Data Exporter that such settlement is warranted and reasonable in the circumstances. The Data Importer shall execute and deliver to the Data Exporter any further documents or instruments necessary under the laws of any relevant jurisdiction to give effect to the foregoing.

e)   The Data Exporter shall notify to Data Importer, prior to export of any personal data to the Data Importer, the purposes notified to the Data Subject for the use of such data.

3.   Warranties of the Data Importer

The Data Importer warrants that it has:

a)   full legal authority in the country where the personal data will be processed to receive, store and process such data, to use it for the purpose(s) for which it has been collected by the Data Exporter, as set out herein, and to give warranties and fulfil the undertakings set out in this Clause 4;

b)   in place appropriate technical and organisational measures against accidental or unlawful destruction or accidental loss, alteration, unauthorised disclosure or access and adequate security programs and procedures to ensure that unauthorised persons will not have access to the data processing equipment used to process the exported personal data, that any persons it authorises to have access to the personal data will respect and maintain the confidentiality and security of the personal data, and that the measures and procedures that it used will be sufficient to comply with the requirements of the law referred to in Clause 2(c) above; and

c)   security programs and procedures under '(b) above, which reflect the level of damage that might be suffered by the Data Subject as a result of unauthorised access and disclosure and which are specifically designed to address the nature of Sensitive Data, where necessary, and any harm that might result to the Data Subject from their processing.

4.   Undertakings of the Data Importer

The Data Importer undertakes to:

a)   take such actions as are necessary to ensure it has fulfilled, and will continue to fulfil, the warranties set out in Clause 3;

b)   process the personal data in accordance with the laws applicable to a Data Controller in the country in which the Data Exporter is established;

c)   provide the Data Subject with the same rights of access, correction, blocking, suppression or deletion available to such individual in the country in which the Data Exporter is established

d)   not use the personal data in a way incompatible with the purposes for which first collected and notified to it under 2(e) above, or as may otherwise be authorised by the Authority or the laws or any relevant regulatory body in the country in which the Data Exporter is established;

e)   process the personal data solely for its own use [and, where the Data Importer is a Data Processor, only on the instructions of the Data Exporter] and not disclose or transfer the personal data to a third party or a third country without the prior written consent of the Data Exporter, and such consent will not be given unless the Data Exporter is satisfied with all the terms of such disclosure or transfer and that the personal data will receive an adequate level of security after such disclosure or transfer;

f)   appoint, properly train, and identify to the Data Exporter and to the Authority, an individual within its organisation authorised to respond to enquiries from the Authority, the Data Exporter or a Data Subject concerning its processing of his or her personal data. The Data Importer will deal with all enquiries relating to the personal data promptly, including those from the Data Exporter and the Authority, and in any event within any time frame stipulated by applicable laws in the country in which the Data Exporter is established;

g)   submit its data processing facilities, data files and documentation needed for processing to auditing and/or certification by the Data Exporter (or other duly qualified independent auditors or inspection authorities selected by the Data Exporter for that purpose and not reasonably objected to by the Data Importer) to ascertain compliance with the warranties and undertakings in these Clauses upon the request of the Data Exporter with reasonable notice and during business hours;

h)   comply with any changes in applicable laws notified to it by the Data Exporter. In the event it is unable to do so, it shall forthwith notify the Data Exporter, and the Data Exporter shall be entitled to terminate this contract, unless the parties have agreed or forthwith agree to take such steps as shall enable Data Importer to so comply; and

i)   notify the Data Exporter of any provisions in its local law, or of any changes in that law, which do or could affect the Data Importer's ability to perform its obligations under these Clauses.

5.   Dispute Resolution. Disputes between Data Importer and Data Exporter

In the event of a dispute between the Data Importer and the Data Exporter concerning any alleged breach of any provision of these Clauses, such dispute shall be finally settled under the Rules of Arbitration of the International Chamber of Commerce by one or more arbitrators appointed in accordance with the said rules[*]. The place of arbitration shall be [   ]. The number of arbitrators shall be [   ].

6.   Indemnities

Subject to Clause 2(d), the Data Exporter and the Data Importer will indemnify each other and hold each other harmless from any cost, charge, damages, expense or loss resulting from its breach of any of the provisions of these Clauses.

7.   Termination

In the event that:

a)   the Data Importer gives notice to the Data Exporter under Clause 4(h) above;

b)   the Data Importer is in breach of any warranties or undertakings given by it under these Clauses;

c)   the Authority or other tribunal or court in the country in which the Data Exporter is established rules that there has been a breach of any relevant laws in that jurisdiction by virtue of the Data Importer's or the Data Exporter's processing of the personal data; or

d)   a petition is presented for the administration or winding up of the Data Importer, which petition is not dismissed within the applicable period for such dismissal under applicable law; a winding up order is made; a receiver is appointed over any of its assets; a company voluntary arrangement is commenced by it, or any equivalent event in any jurisdiction occurs

then the Data Exporter, without prejudice to any other rights which it may have against the Data Importer, shall be entitled to terminate these Clauses forthwith.

---

[*]Note: parties may wish to choose another form of institutional arbitration. Also, parties are advised that in cases in which the amount in dispute is lower than 50 000 US$, ICC and other forms of institutional arbitration may not be the appropriate mechanism. In such cases, parties would ordinarily choose a form of ad hoc arbitration. Advice on the right dispute settlement method can be obtained from the secretariat of the ICC International Court of Arbitration or local alternative dispute settlement/arbitration centres.

In the event of termination of these Clauses, the Data Importer must return all personal data and all copies of the personal data subject to these Clauses to the Data Exporter forthwith or, at the Data Exporter's choice, will destroy all copies of the same and certify to the Data Exporter that it has done so, unless the Data Importer is prevented by its national law or local regulator from destroying or returning all or part of such data, in which event the data will be kept confidential and will not be processed for any purpose. The Data Importer irrevocably agrees with the Data Exporter that, if so requested by the Data Exporter or the Authority, it will allow the Data Exporter or its Inspection Authorities access to its establishment to verify that this has been done or will allow access for this purpose by any duly authorised representative of the Data Exporter.

8.   Governing Law

These Clauses shall be governed by the laws of the country in which the Data Exporter is established.

DATA IMPORTER   DATA EXPORTER

(Provide appropriate identification of parties, such as registered addresses, authorized signatories, jurisdiction of incorporation, or other information necessary to validate the contract as binding.)

APPENDIX I

Additional clauses to be incorporated in certain instances.

1.   Sensitive Data.

a)   If Sensitive Data is to be the subject of processing hereunder, the Data Exporter and the Data Importer shall take such additional measures as may be necessary to protect the security of such Sensitive Data and to comply with any specific provisions of the law of the country of establishment of the Data Exporter that apply to Sensitive Data held by a Data Controller.

b)   Where required under the law of the country of establishment of the Data Exporter, the Data Exporter shall obtain the consent from Data Subjects to process any Sensitive Data and to transfer Sensitive Data to the Data Importer.

2.   Data used for Marketing Purposes.

The Data Exporter warrants that the data transferred hereunder has been processed in order to indicate or to eliminate any Data Subjects who have opted out of use of their Personal Data for marketing purposes generally, or marketing by any particular medium, by communication with the Data Exporter. The Data Importer further agrees to exclude any additional Data Subjects from such processing after receiving notification from a Data Subject or the Data Exporter of such Data Subject's opting out of such use.

3. Automated decisions.

a) For purposes hereof "Automated Decision" shall mean a decision by the Data Exporter or the Data Importer which produces legal effects concerning a Data Subject or significantly affects a Data Subject and which is based solely on automated processing of data intended to evaluate certain personal aspects relating to him, such as his performance at work, creditworthiness, reliability, conduct, etc.

b) Neither the Data Importer nor the Data Exporter shall make any Automated Decisions concerning Data Subjects, except where:

   (i) such decisions are made by the Data Importer or the Data Exporter in entering into or performing a contract with the Data Subject, and

   (ii) the Data Subject is given an opportunity to discuss the results of a relevant Automated Decision with a representative of the party making such decision or otherwise to make representations to that party, or

   (iii) where otherwise provided by law.

*   *   *

Selected UNCTAD publications on
transnational corporations and foreign direct investment

A. Individual studies

World Investment Report 1999: Foreign Direct Investment and the Challenge of Development. 578 p. Sales No. E.99.II.D.3. $45.

World Investment Report 1999: Foreign Direct Investment and the Challenge of Development. An Overview. 86 p. Free of charge.

Foreign Direct Invesment in Africa: Performance and Potential. 89 p. UNCTAD/ITE/IIT/Misc. 15.

The Financial Crisis in Asia and Foreign Direct Investment: An Assessment. 101 p. Sales No. GV.E.98.0.29. $20.

World Investment Report 1998: Trends and Determinants. 430 p. Sales No. E.98.II.D.5. $45.

World Investment Report 1998: Trends and Determinants. An Overview. 67 p. Free of charge.

Bilateral Investment Treaties in the mid-1990s. 314 p. Sales No. E.98.II.D.8. $46.

Handbook on Foreign Direct Investment by Small and Medium-sized Enterprises: Lessons from Asia. 200 p. Sales No. E.98.II.D.4. $48.

Handbook on Foreign Direct Investment by Small and Medium-sized Enterprises: Lessons from Asia. Executive Summary and Report on the Kunming Conference. 74 p. Free of charge.

International Investment towards the Year 2002. 166 p. Sales No. GV.E.98.0.15. $29. (Joint publication with Invest in France Mission and Arthur Andersen, in collaboration with DATAR.)

World Investment Report 1997: Transnational Corporations, Market Structure and Competition Policy. 420 p. Sales No. E.97.II.D.10. $45.

World Investment Report 1997: Transnational Corporations, Market Structure and Competition Policy. An Overview. 70 p. Free of charge.

International Investment towards the Year 2001. 81 p. Sales No. GV.E.97.0.5. $35. (Joint publication with Invest in France Mission and Arthur Andersen, in collaboration with DATAR.)

World Investment Directory. Vol. VI: West Asia 1996. 192 p. Sales No. E.97.II.A.2. $35.

World Investment Directory. Vol. V: Africa 1996. 508 p. Sales No. E.97.II.A.1. $75.

Sharing Asia's Dynamism: Asian Direct Investment in the European Union. 192 p. Sales No. E.97.II.D.1. $26.

Transnational Corporations and World Development. 656 p. ISBN 0-415-08560-8 (hardback), 0-415-08561-6 (paperback). £65 (hardback), £20.00 (paperback). (Published by International Thomson Business Press on behalf of UNCTAD.)

Companies without Borders: Transnational Corporations in the 1990s. 224 p. ISBN 0-415-12526-X. £47.50. (Published by International Thomson Business Press on behalf of UNCTAD.)

The New Globalism and Developing Countries. 336 p. ISBN 92-808-0944-X. $25. (Published by United Nations University Press.)

Investing in Asia's Dynamism: European Union Direct Investment in Asia. 124 p. ISBN 92-827-7675-1. ECU 14. (Joint publication with the European Commission.)

World Investment Report 1996: Investment, Trade and International Policy Arrangements. 332 p. Sales No. E.96.II.A.14. $45.

World Investment Report 1996: Investment, Trade and International Policy Arrangements. An Overview. 51 p. Free of charge.

International Investment Instruments: A Compendium. Vol. I. 371 p. Sales No. E.96.II.A.9; Vol. II. 577 p. Sales No. E.96.II.A.10; Vol. III. 389 p. Sales No. E.96.II.A.11; the 3-volume set, Sales No. E.96.II.A.12. $125.

World Investment Report 1995: Transnational Corporations and Competitiveness. 491 p. Sales No. E.95.II.A.9. $45.

World Investment Report 1995: Transnational Corporations and Competitiveness. An Overview. 51 p. Free of charge.

Accounting for Sustainable Forestry Management. A Case Study. 46 p. Sales No. E.94.II.A.17. $22.

Small and Medium-sized Transnational Corporations. Executive Summary and Report of the Osaka Conference. 60 p. Free of charge.

World Investment Report 1994: Transnational Corporations, Employment and the Workplace. 482 p. Sales No. E.94.II.A.14. $45.

World Investment Report 1994: Transnational Corporations, Employment and the Workplace. An Executive Summary. 34 p. Free of charge.

Liberalizing International Transactions in Services: A Handbook. 182 p. Sales No. E.94.II.A.11. $45. (Joint publication with the World Bank.)

World Investment Directory. Vol. IV: Latin America and the Caribbean. 478 p. Sales No. E.94.II.A.10. $65.

Conclusions on Accounting and Reporting by Transnational Corporations. 47 p. Sales No. E.94.II.A.9. $25.

Accounting, Valuation and Privatization. 190 p. Sales No. E.94.II.A.3. $25.

Environmental Management in Transnational Corporations: Report on the Benchmark Corporate Environment Survey. 278 p. Sales No. E.94.II.A.2. $29.95.

Management Consulting: A Survey of the Industry and Its Largest Firms. 100 p. Sales No. E.93.II.A.17. $25.

Transnational Corporations: A Selective Bibliography, 1991-1992. 736 p. Sales No. E.93.II.A.16. $75. (English/French.)

Small and Medium-sized Transnational Corporations: Role, Impact and Policy Implications. 242 p. Sales No. E.93.II.A.15. $35.

World Investment Report 1993: Transnational Corporations and Integrated International Production. 290 p. Sales No. E.93.II.A.14. $45.

World Investment Report 1993: Transnational Corporations and Integrated International Production. An Executive Summary. 31 p. ST/CTC/159. Free of charge.

Foreign Investment and Trade Linkages in Developing Countries. 108 p. Sales No. E.93.II.A.12. $18.

World Investment Directory 1992. Vol. III: Developed Countries. 532 p. Sales No. E.93.II.A.9. $75.

Transnational Corporations from Developing Countries: Impact on Their Home Countries. 116 p. Sales No. E.93.II.A.8. $15.

Debt-Equity Swaps and Development. 150 p. Sales No. E.93.II.A.7. $35.

From the Common Market to EC 92: Regional Economic Integration in the European Community and Transnational Corporations. 134 p. Sales No. E.93.II.A.2. $25.

World Investment Directory 1992. Vol. II: Central and Eastern Europe. 432 p. Sales No. E.93.II.A.1. $65. (Joint publication with the United Nations Economic Commission for Europe.)

The East-West Business Directory 1991/1992. 570p. Sales No. E.92.II.A.20. $65.

World Investment Report 1992: Transnational Corporations as Engines of Growth: An Executive Summary. 30p. Sales No.E.92.II.A.24. Free of charge.

World Investment Report 1992: Transnational Corporations as Engines of Growth. 356p. Sales No.E.92.II.A.19. $45.

World Investment Directory 1992. Vol. I: Asia and the Pacific. 356 p. Sales No. E.92.II.A.11. $65.

Climate Change and Transnational Corporations: Analysis and Trends. 110p. Sales No. E.92.II.A.7. $16.50.

Foreign Direct Investment and Transfer of Technology in India. 150 p. Sales No. E.92.II.A.3. $20.

The Determinants of Foreign Direct Investment: A Survey of the Evidence. 84p. Sales No. E.92.II.A.2. $12.50.

The Impact of Trade-Related Investment Measures on Trade and Development: Theory, Evidence and Policy Implications. 108 p. Sales No. E.91.II.A.19. $17.50. (Joint publication with the United Nations Centre on Transnational Corporations.)

Transnational Corporations and Industrial Hazards Disclosure. 98 p. Sales No. E.91.II.A.18. $17.50.

Transnational Business Information: A Manual of Needs and Sources. 216 p. Sales No. E.91.II.A.13. $45.

World Investment Report 1991: The Triad in Foreign Direct Investment. 108p. Sales No.E.91.II.A.12. $25.

B. IIA Issues Paper Series

Lessons from the MAI. UNCTAD Series on issues in international investment agreements. 56p. Sales No. E.99.II.D.26. $12.

National Treatment. UNCTAD Series on issues in international investment agreements. 104p. Sales No. E.99.II.D.16. $12.

Fair and Equitable Treatment. UNCTAD Series on issues in international investment agreements. 64p. Sales No. E.99.II.D.15. $12.

Investment-Related Trade Measures. UNCTAD Series on issues in international investment agreements. 64p. Sales No. E.99.II.D.12. $12.

Most-Favoured-Nation Treatment. UNCTAD Series on issues in international investment agreements. 72p. Sales No. E.99.II.D.11. $12.

Admission and Establishment. UNCTAD Series on issues in international investment agreements. 72p. Sales No. E.99.II.D.10. $12.

Scope and Definition. UNCTAD Series on issues in international investment agreements. 96p. Sales No. E.99.II.D.9. $12.

Transfer Pricing. UNCTAD Series on issues in international investment agreements. 72p. Sales No. E.99.II.D.8. $12.

Foreign Direct Investment and Development. UNCTAD Series on issues in international investment agreements. 88p. Sales No. E.98.II.D.15. $12.

C. Serial publications

Current Studies, Series A

No. 30. *Incentives and Foreign Direct Investment.* 98 p. Sales No. E.96.II.A.6. $30. (English/French.)

No. 29. *Foreign Direct Investment, Trade, Aid and Migration.* 100 p. Sales No. E.96.II.A.8. $25. (Joint publication with the International Organization for Migration.)

No. 28. *Foreign Direct Investment in Africa.* 119 p. Sales No. E.95.II.A.6. $20.

No. 27. *Tradability of Banking Services: Impact and Implications.* 195 p. Sales No. E.94.II.A.12. $50.

No. 26. *Explaining and Forecasting Regional Flows of Foreign Direct Investment.* 58 p. Sales No. E.94.II.A.5. $25.

No. 25. *International Tradability in Insurance Services.* 54 p. Sales No. E.93.II.A.11. $20.

No. 24. *Intellectual Property Rights and Foreign Direct Investment.* 108 p. Sales No. E.93.II.A.10. $20.

No. 23. *The Transnationalization of Service Industries: An Empirical Analysis of the Determinants of Foreign Direct Investment by Transnational Service Corporations.* 62 p. Sales No. E.93.II.A.3. $15.

No. 22. *Transnational Banks and the External Indebtedness of Developing Countries: Impact of Regulatory Changes.* 48 p. Sales No. E.92.II.A.10. $12.

No. 20. *Foreign Direct Investment, Debt and Home Country Policies.* 50 p. Sales No. E.90.II.A.16. $12.

No. 19. *New Issues in the Uruguay Round of Multilateral Trade Negotiations.* 52 p. Sales No. E.90.II.A.15. $12.50.

No. 18. *Foreign Direct Investment and Industrial Restructuring in Mexico.* 114 p. Sales No. E.92.II.A.9. $12.

No. 17. *Government Policies and Foreign Direct Investment.* 68 p. Sales No. E.91.II.A.20. $12.50.

The United Nations Library on Transnational Corporations
(Published by Routledge on behalf of the United Nations.)

Set A (Boxed set of 4 volumes. ISBN 0-415-08554-3. £350):
Volume One: *The Theory of Transnational Corporations*. 464 p.
Volume Two: *Transnational Corporations: A Historical Perspective*. 464 p.
Volume Three: *Transnational Corporations and Economic Development*. 448 p.
Volume Four: *Transnational Corporations and Business Strategy*. 416 p.

Set B (Boxed set of 4 volumes. ISBN 0-415-08555-1. £350):
Volume Five: *International Financial Management*. 400 p.
Volume Six: *Organization of Transnational Corporations*. 400 p.
Volume Seven: *Governments and Transnational Corporations*. 352 p.
Volume Eight: *Transnational Corporations and International Trade and Payments*. 320 p.

Set C (Boxed set of 4 volumes. ISBN 0-415-08556-X. £350):
Volume Nine: *Transnational Corporations and Regional Economic Integration*. 331 p.
Volume Ten: *Transnational Corporations and the Exploitation of Natural Resources*. 397 p.
Volume Eleven: *Transnational Corporations and Industrialization*. 425 p.
Volume Twelve: *Transnational Corporations in Services*. 437 p.

Set D (Boxed set of 4 volumes. ISBN 0-415-08557-8. £350):
Volume Thirteen: *Cooperative Forms of Transnational Corporation Activity*. 419 p.
Volume Fourteen: *Transnational Corporations: Transfer Pricing and Taxation*. 330 p.
Volume Fifteen: *Transnational Corporations: Market Structure and Industrial Performance*. 383 p.
Volume Sixteen: *Transnational Corporations and Human Resources*. 429 p.

Set E (Boxed set of 4 volumes. ISBN 0-415-08558-6. £350):
Volume Seventeen: *Transnational Corporations and Innovatory Activities*. 447 p.
Volume Eighteen: *Transnational Corporations and Technology Transfer to Developing Countries*. 486 p.
Volume Nineteen: *Transnational Corporations and National Law*. 322 p.
Volume Twenty: *Transnational Corporations: The International Legal Framework*. 545 p.

D. Journals

Transnational Corporations (formerly *The CTC Reporter*).

Published three times a year. Annual subscription price: $45; individual issues $20.

ProInvest, a quarterly newsletter, available free of charge.

United Nations publications may be obtained from bookstores and distributors throughout the world. Please consult your bookstore or write to:

United Nations Publications

Sales Section   OR   Sales Section
Room DC2-0853   United Nations Office at Geneva
United Nations Secretariat   Palais des Nations
New York, NY 10017   CH-1211 Geneva 10
U.S.A.   Switzerland
Tel: (1-212) 963-8302 or (800) 253-9646   Tel: (41-22) 917-1234
Fax: (1-212) 963-3489   Fax: (41-22) 917-0123
E-mail: publications@un.org   E-mail: unpubli@unorg.ch

All prices are quoted in United States dollars.

For further information on the work of the Division on Investment, Technology and Enterprise Development, UNCTAD, please address inquiries to:

United Nations Conference on Trade and Development
Division on Investment, Technology and Enterprise Development
Palais des Nations, Room E-9123
CH-1211 Geneva 10
Switzerland
Telephone: (41-22) 907-5707
Telefax: (41-22) 907-0194
E-mail: medarde.almario@unctad.org

QUESTIONNAIRE

International Investment Instruments: A Compendium

Sales No. E.20.II.D.

In order to improve the quality and relevance of the work of the UNCTAD Division on Investment, Technology and Enterprise Development, it would be useful to receive the views of readers on this publication. It would therefore be greatly appreciated if you could complete the following questionnaire and return it to:

Readership Survey
UNCTAD Division on Investment, Technology and Enterprise Development
United Nations Office in Geneva
Palais des Nations
Room E-9123
CH-1211 Geneva 10
Switzerland
Fax: 41-22-907-0194

1. Name and address of respondent (optional):

_____

_____

2. Which of the following best describes your area of work?

Government	○	Public enterprise	○
Private enterprise	○	Academic or research institution	○
International organization	○	Media	○
Not-for-profit organization	○	Other (specify) _____	

3. In which country do you work? _____

4. What is your assessment of the contents of this publication?

Excellent	○	Adequate	○
Good	○	Poor	○

5. How useful is this publication to your work?

Very useful ○   Of some use ○   Irrelevant ○

6. Please indicate the three things you liked best about this publication:

_____

_____

_____

7. Please indicate the three things you liked least about this publication:

_____

_____

_____

8. Are you a regular recipient of *Transnational Corporations* (formerly *The CTC Reporter*), UNCTAD-DITE's tri-annual refereed journal?

Yes   o   No   o

If not, please check here if you would like to receive
a sample copy sent to the name and address you have
given above   o

* * *